The Bop Apocalypse

The Bop Apocalypse

The Religious Visions of
Kerouac,
Ginsberg,
and
Burroughs

University of Illinois Press

Urbana and Chicago

Library of Congress Cataloging-in-Publication Data
Lardas, John, 1971–
The bop apocalypse : the religious visions of Kerouac, Ginsberg,
and Burroughs / John Lardas.
p.   cm.
Includes bibliographical references and index.
ISBN 0-252-02599-7 (alk. paper)
1. American literature—20th century—History and criticism.
2. Beat generation.
3. Religious fiction, American—History and criticism.
4. Religious poetry, American—History and criticism.
5. Religion and literature—History—20th century.
6. Apocalyptic literature—History and criticism.
7. Spengler, Oswald, 1880–1936—Influence.
8. Burroughs, William S., 1914– —Religion.
9. Kerouac, Jack, 1922–1969—Religion.
10. Ginsberg, Allen, 1926– —Religion.
11. Visions in literature.
I. Title.
PS228.B6L37   2000
810.9'382—dc21   00-008649

C 5 4 3 2 1

For my mother, Diane Lardas

A morphology of religious history, therefore, is a task that the Faustian spirit alone could ever formulate, and one that it is only now, at this present stage of its development, fit to deal with. The problem is enunciated, and we must dare the effort of getting completely away from our own convictions and seeing before us everything indifferently as equally alien. And how hard it is! He who undertakes the task must possess the strength not merely to imagine himself in an illusory detachment from the truths of his world-understanding—illusory even to one for whom truths are just a set of concepts and methods—but actually to penetrate his own system physiognomically to its very last cells. And even then is it possible, in a single language, which structurally and spiritually carries the whole metaphysical content of its own Culture, to capture transmissible ideas of the truths of other-tongued men?

—Oswald Spengler

You can never figure out where anything begins. You can never figure it out, anything, where it begins.

—Don DeLillo

contents

Acknowledgments
xi

Introduction:
The Tradition of Subversion
The Elementary Forms of Beat Religious Life • Scratching the
Religious Surface • From Beat to Beatnik and Back • Religion and
Dissent • Apocalypse • Demythology
1

1. "America, When Will Your Cowboys Read Spengler?":
Anxiety and Influence in Postwar America
Oswald Spengler: Provocateur • Confidence Men and American
Jeremiahs • Spenglerian Jeremiads • Spenglerian Vernacular:
Kerouac's The Town and the City • Conclusion: From Spirit to Ethic
33

2. Sex, Drugs, and Theology: The Spenglerian Strain of Piety
Violence and the New Vision • Body and Time: The Holy Contours
of Life • Democratic Vistas • The Wolfeans and the Black Priest •
Fellaheen Role Models • Conclusion
79

3. "No Time for Poetry but Exactly What Is":
The Utopia of Beat Language
New Criticism and the American Scene • The Unspeakable
Visions of the Individual • Freedom within Salvation • Spiritual
Intercourse • Conclusion
131

4. "Storming the Reality Studios": Beat Remythologies
Mexican Pastorals and Fellaheen Ambulances • The
Fundamental Life • The Police-Poet • A Vertical Metaphysical
Study • "Putting His Queer Shoulder to the Wheel" • Conclusion
173

Conclusion:
The Seduction of Tradition
Pull My Daisy • Scientologist, Buddhist, Psychedelic • Burroughs,
Scientology, and "American Policy" • Kerouac, Buddhism, and
The Climax of German Thought • Ginsberg, LSD-25, and Spengler's
Ghost • Demythology
221

Notes
259

Works Cited
295

Index
311

acknowledgments

The Bop Apocalpyse grew out of my graduate studies at Miami University (Ohio). During this time, the writings of Jack Kerouac, Allen Ginsberg, and William Burroughs guided me away from a legal career and toward the study of religion. For that I am grateful.

In addition to those literary provocations, I have also encountered guidance in the form of colleagues and advisors. I would like to thank my friends at Princeton University, Miami University, and the University of California at Santa Barbara. I can think of no better educational experience—a journey.

Throughout this project, I have received insight and editorial advice from a number of sources. Those who read and commented on various aspects of this book never failed to enrich my knowledge of religion, literature, and history. Conversation partners included: Peter Williams, Alan Miller, Keith Tuma, Daniel Belgrad, Elizabeth Wilson, Catherine Albanese, Giles Gunn, Richard Hecht, Phillip Hammond, Ninian Smart, Douglas Brinkley, John Tytell, Michael Davidson, Robert Ellwood, Tom Price, Dean Moyar, Jeff Ruff, Tomas Matza, and Chip Callahan.

Special thanks goes out to John Sampas, the special collections staff at Stanford University, my editor Elizabeth Dulany, and the anonymous reader at the University of Illinois Press whose sage advice in the early stages of this book was much appreciated.

So many individuals helped frame my thinking on this project. Inevitably, most will go unnamed. Some indirect influences included: John Baumann, Anna Bigelow, Lisle Dalton, John Fagan, Nicole Heller, Martin Kaplan, Sarah Karesh, LeRoy Kim, Eugene Lowe, Kathryn McClymond, Matt Miller, Kerry Mitchell, Mark Moyar, Ellen Posman, Phil Ramos, Wade Clark Roof, Elijah Siegler, Rob Svets, Seiji Tszuki, Wendy Wiseman, Michelle Zimney, Pnin, and Galeani.

While I was writing this book, Elizabeth Kleine was the inspiration for my best ideas. Not only did she encourage me at every step, reading draft after draft, listening patiently to my musings on Beat minutia, but she also provoked at every step. For that I am grateful.

Finally, I would like to thank my mother, Diane Lardas, to whom this book is dedicated. Along with Dorothy Flay and Fern Baughman, she has been my most valued teacher.

Introduction

The Tradition of Subversion

Previous page, banner for "Beat Culture and the New America: 1950–1965,"
Walker Art Center, Minneapolis.

We are symbols and inhabit symbols; workmen, work, and tools, words and things, birth and death, all are emblems; but we sympathize with the symbols, and being infatuated with the economical use of things, we do not know that they are thoughts. The poet, by an ulterior intellectual perception, gives them a power which makes their old use forgotten, and puts eyes and a tongue into every dumb and inanimate object. He perceives the independence of the thought on the symbol, the stability of the thought, the accidency and fugacity of the symbol. . . . So the poet turns the world to glass, and shows us all things in their right series and procession.

—**Ralph Waldo Emerson, "The Poet"**

On August 6, 1945, a month after the detonation of the first atomic bomb in the New Mexico desert, "Little Boy" fell from the skies above Hiroshima. Because of the secrecy of the Manhattan Project, there had been little, if any, reflection in the public domain about the moral and political ramifications of deploying such weapons. As a character remarks in *Underworld* (1997), Don DeLillo's secret history of the cold war, "We all tried to think about war but I'm not sure we knew how to do this. The Poets wrote long poems with dirty words and that's as close as we came, actually, to a thoughtful response. Because they had brought something into the world that out-imagined the mind."[1]

Indeed, poets, politicians, and priests, as well as the most ordinary of Americans, ran for cover, attempting to shield themselves from the fallout of the unspeakable. In January 1951 Harry Truman created the Federal Civil Defense Administration, whose tasks included the preparation of school children for atomic attack ("duck and cover!") and the regular testing of air-raid sirens. During a period of unprecedented public trust, the government took the initiative in translating the unspeakable into terms everyone could understand:

WHAT YOU SHOULD DO IN CASE OF ATOMIC ATTACK
Keep calm.
If there is no time, get to a shelter at once.
If no underground shelter is close, get into the ground floor of a near-by building or even stand in a doorway if nothing better is available. . .
Get into the core of your building and under a desk or table if there isn't time to get to the basement.[2]

Such flights, whether toward the safety of backyard bomb shelters or to the "core of your building," were not merely retreats from the bomb's deathly radiance. On the contrary, they were acts of immersion—imaginative confrontations with a world enveloped by the shadow of apocalypse and suffused with the absurd rhetoric of civil defense.

They were, in short, affirmations of a world elsewhere, religious responses to a crisis of ultimate proportions. In the aftermath of World War II, the horrific and long-term consequences of the atomic age slowly set in, the death camps and Nazi atrocities came to light, and Americans looked to themselves as architects who would build a more perfect future in light of the deprivations of the past. The American Century was at hand and the promise of metamorphosis in sight. As the optative mood gathered momentum, the period was also a time of reassessment, particularly in the redefinition of moral responsibility after a nadir in human history. Church attendance among postwar Americans began to increase rapidly and would continue to do so throughout the 1950s. The burgeoning religious zeal seemed to converge with growing U.S. geopolitical influence and cold war paranoia. While might made right in foreign affairs, so, too, did the proper accouterments of faith hold sway in the domestic sphere. Indeed, the overlap of morality and politics climaxed in the mid–1950s when Congress voted to mark the most potent of American symbols, the almighty dollar and its host of coins and denominations, with a public declaration of faith: "In God We Trust."

Between the descent of the bomb and the steady increase in religious affiliation, William S. Burroughs, Jack Kerouac, and Allen Ginsberg came together at a subcultural crossroads: the intersection of Times Square addicts and petty criminals, Greenwich Village bohemia, and Columbia University intellectual circles. Despite their different backgrounds, Burroughs, Kerouac, and Ginsberg became very close very quickly. Soon after they met in 1944 they were sharing an apartment in New York City and had become, in Kerouac's words, a "libertine circle." Even after the dissolution of the libertine circle in 1946 they kept abreast of each other's progress and whereabouts—Burroughs in Mexico and later, Tangier; Kerouac criss-crossing America; and Ginsberg in the San Francisco literary scene. Even as the physical distance between them increased, however, the intimacy and intensity of their exchanges did not. Their collaborative season had endowed each writer with a common understanding of the world and their place within it, a foundation that remained solid and secure, continually generating insights and ideas. Because the winding paths originated from the same place, their points of view remained complementary as their personal horizons expanded. As late as 1952, Ginsberg wrote to Kerouac about the continuing cross-pollination within their group: "[M]y phantasies and phrases have gotten so lovingly mixed up in yours . . . I hardly knows whose is which and who's used what."[3]

In the mid–1940s, before writing the obscenity-laden manifestos that would earn them fame, opprobrium, and the group label the "Beat Generation," Burroughs, Kerouac, and Ginsberg had begun a collaborative project of literary and spiritual development, what they termed the "new vision."[4] That accumulation of insights—borrowed, stolen, and invented out of the fabric of their everyday surroundings—became the context for their philosophical musings and the filter through which they experienced the world. As the writers worked through the new vision amid the swirling energy of New York City, their aesthetic philosophy came to life. It became a theology of experience—a coherent, integrated, and embodied set of ideas that invested their lives with the air of ultimacy. The "new vision," then, was a platform for both belief and action, a religious sensibility that not only referred to each writer's personal understanding of the world but also to the world they yearned to glimpse. Together, the Beats set out on a journey toward utopia, their destination being an ever-elusive America of absolute freedom.

In doing so, they were part of a growing segment of the population that came to reject the intertwining cultural strands of boosterism, consumerism, and faith and the contradictory rhetoric of containment, solitude, and purity that bound these strands together. For in addition to the threat posed by communist infiltration, there also existed directives for what you should not do in case of atomic attack:

Don't telephone . . .
Don't eat or drink in a contaminated area.
Don't use metal goods in a contaminated zone . . .
Don't try to drive your car.
Don't get excited or excite others.[5]

Such matter-of-fact presentations of the end of the world necessitated alternative conceptions of self and country; new ways to live; and, in the Beats' case, a new conception of artists writing to, for, and about an America they could feel and imaginatively grasp but not fully inhabit.

Together in the 1940s, long before any interest in Buddhism, Scientology, or psychedelic drugs, Kerouac, Burroughs, and Ginsberg spoke of their world in religious terms. Even before writing their most critically acclaimed (and derided) works—Kerouac's "road" novels from 1950 to 1956, Ginsberg's *Howl and Other Poems* from 1952 to 1956, and Burroughs's *Naked Lunch* from 1953 to 1959—they behaved in accordance with a variety of religious assumptions. Although it may seem counterintuitive that a literary group would be considered religious and yet not adhere to traditional religious structures but glorify spontaneity, drugs, jazz, and sexual ecstasy, it was in their very opposition to the values and virtues of mainstream religiosity that they affirmed an alternative faith. In Kerouac's first published novel, *The Town and the City* (1950), the poet Leon Levinsky (Ginsberg) likens jazz to "an orgy . . . in which everyone will explode and become one." When someone asks, "Music does all that?," Levinsky replies, "Yes. I've felt that. It creates a frantic, almost daisy-chain rapport similar to marijuana, you see!"[6] "That" alludes to the Beats' shared reality, a sacred world they hoped to create that would be fundamentally different from the society in which they found themselves.[7]

The Beats did not put forth a coherent religious system of creeds and doctrines. On the contrary, their religiosity was embedded in how they lived and wrote. They adhered to a metaphysical religion, studying intently the happenings of the world in hopes of gaining insight into the human condition as well as the cosmos. Having seen avenues of transcendence in the particulars of everyday existence, Ginsberg wrote in 1950, "Reality is a question / of realizing how real / the world is already." Similarly, Kerouac noted that through "the brownlit windows of Sixth Avenue semi-flophouses . . . a piece of litter in the gutter . . . [and] a beat gray coupe . . . I know the city, and the universe." Burroughs's cosmic musings often assumed a more ominous tone: He once warned Ginsberg that the low-level radiation produced during atomic testing was dangerous not for the physical threat it posed but as an invisible agent of mind control.[8] Whether sanguine or paranoid, the Beats' understanding of their world was nothing less than extra-ordinary. Like many postwar Americans, they did not so much secularize the sacred as sacralize the secular, turning everyday existence into a drama of ultimate consequences.

The Elementary Forms of Beat Religious Life

In order to develop a critical vocabulary for discussing the religiosity of the ordinary and the ordinariness of religion, Charles H. Long has called for a broad understanding of religious experience. In order to capture "those moments of being and imagination which the human is graced to repeat and embody," I have adopted Long's understanding of religious meaning that "pushes beyond all the specific modern modes and paradigms, whether of language, logic, or writing, to the fullness and poverty of being which is designated by the term sacred."[9]

As an inherently contradictory phenomenon, the sacred refers to those moments that defy easy categorization, those events that out-imagine the mind. Despite all attempts at interpretive closure, their meaning remains inexhaustible. At its most fundamental level, religion is the human response to such moments and events. The most visible form that religion takes is institutional; the most visible function is conservative; the most visible currency is existential solace. As a mode of being, however, religion does not necessarily maintain the traditions, values, and comfort of the status quo. Nor should religion be considered solely in terms of denominational affiliation, church attendance, or parish activity. As I will argue throughout this volume, religion can be, and most often is, a profoundly destabilizing force. It is the quintessential act of improvisation, akin to a Charlie Parker solo and characterized by the expressive use of dissonance and a "profundity of ideas, individual tone, the ability to phrase subtly and swing constantly, [with] complete technical control."[10]

Religion can be positively destabilizing, carving out an alternative space that challenges the legitimacy of the majority culture by the very process of existing alongside of it. Anthropologist Clifford Geertz notes that ideas of the sacred extend well beyond "their specifically metaphysical contexts to provide a framework of general ideas in terms of which a wide range of experience—intellectual, emotional, moral—can be given meaningful form."[11] In that regard, Burroughs, Kerouac, and Ginsberg each possessed a constructive religious imagination, coordinating experiences, ideas, and gestures into a coherent perspective by which to enchant the world and live within it. The Beats' experiences were given extraordinary depth through their personal beliefs, which did not merely interpret reality but shaped it as well. They began to live according to a discernible, albeit loose, ethical structure. Their actions—sexual openness, drug use, criminality, traveling, and madness—were not simply transgressions of the period's social and moral codes but physical enactments of a religious representation of the world. Although never living "well-ordered, stabilized-within-the-photo lives," as Kerouac suggested, there was a method to their "raggedy madness and riot."[12]

To assess the content or even glimpse the constructive logic of Beat religiosity is a delicate task, but one made easier if the forms and functions of religion are clearly understood. In the Beats' case, the content of their religion was embodied not only in their behavior but also in the images and metaphors they used to characterize reality.[13] What they wrote about, how they wrote, and what they wrote about how they wrote all illuminate a shared orientation from which each man approached the world, lived in the world, and looked back on the world. The burden of their art was to create a religious world in which ordinary decisions and actions would continually broach questions of existential and cosmic gravitas. "Go back, go back to the old legend," wrote Ginsberg. "The Soul remembers and is true: / What has been most and least imagined, / No other, there is nothing new."[14]

As the foremost technique of centering and regulating existence, religion is, and always has been, work. Religion is composed of those acts of dedication on the part of the imagination to bring body and belief into some kind of meaningful alignment. Given the fact that such alignment is more often glimpsed than achieved, one's religious orientation is always under construction, always in process. In continually acting out what they believed (and believing in what they had just discovered), the Beats held religious views but were not held by them. In weaving a religious world alongside those of the majority the Beats produced a space for living that was convincing, meaningful, and "uniquely realistic."[15]

In addition to being a method of controlled subversion, religion can also be a means of unpredictable discovery, a way out method of de(con)struction for those seeking the way out. As opposed to religion being merely the ground for social or prophetic vision, religion is at its most powerful when it is deforming that which already exists—religion primarily as negative performance rather than invention; the genius for forgetting combined with the genius for memorialization. This dimension of religion is most often related to ecstatic experiences—those unsettling moments when the potential for self or social transformation arises. It is during such experiences that the world (and self) becomes undone, its vulnerabilities, illusions, and deceptions seen for what they are. It is precisely when pure experience propels vision through and beyond the fog of symbols that the boundaries between the visible and invisible, the mundane and the ultimate, the profane and the sacred, the inside and out, must be redrawn. "So-called solid reality is only crystallized dream," Burroughs wrote to Ginsberg shortly before completing *Naked Lunch.* "It can be undreamed. There is nothing stronger than dream, because dreams are forms of THE LAW."[16]

As tangible dream-scape, the religious world of the Beats was adversarial precisely because it depended upon the vital and volatile "law" of experience. Given its capacity to destabilize, religion cannot be reduced to yet another garden variety ideology. Ideology accounts neither for inchoate desires nor fears; nor does it recognize their subtle expressions. Ideology sets limits on conversation about what is real and what is possible. Religion, however, searches for those limits, testing them against both the materials of the everyday and the workings of experience. The breadth and depth of a religious world (to be dreamed and re-dreamed) is evidenced by the fact that it touches upon social, economic, and political realities, binding them together in a loose, albeit necessary, relationship that encompasses them from within. It also penetrates to the core of the individual life and hinges upon the most profound and mysterious questions humans can ask about themselves, other human beings, the world around them, and the invisible universe.

In order to even ask, let alone answer, such questions, symbols and metaphors are continually employed—words borrowed from everyday speech but stretched to their signifying capacity (or, in Kenneth Burke's apt phrase, "used with thoroughness"). Because religious experience does not possess its own descriptive language, it must speak indirectly—an endless but not necessarily hopeless process. Such indirect yet thoroughgoing speech is the tissue, blood, and bones of life—tangible words that lead to imaginary worlds. Take, for instance, Kerouac's experience of "sudden gut joy" when "the visions of great words in rhythmic order all in one giant archangel book go roaring through my brain, so I lie in the dark also seeing also hearing the jargon of the future worlds—damajehe eleout ekeke dhdkdk dldoud, —— —d, ekeoeu dhdhdkehgyt . . . poor examples because of mechanical needs of typing, of the flow of river sounds, words, dark, leading to the future and attesting to the madness, hollowness, ring and roar of my mind which blessed or unblessed is where trees sing." Regardless of whether Kerouac's words actually refer to some transcendental referent is beside the point. It is in his very attempt to catch up to his "archangel" that remains a fruitful subject of inquiry—the process of symbolization and the accomplishments of a word-mongering body and mind.[17]

Any analysis of faith commitments demands sensitivity to the symbol-making capacity of those who hold and profess them, a capacity that often defies analogies to the rationally thinking self. Returning to Charles Long for insight into this problem, one must first enter into the emotional responses and dreams of historical actors, accepting them on their own terms in order to translate them faithfully into the present.[18] Because religion embodies excess—a mode of being that refers excessively to reality—it cannot be represented without recourse to the aesthetic realm. Anthropologist Michael Taussig has spoken of the "representational pathos" that characterizes religion as the fundamental challenge for those wishing to explain it.[19] Because religion is primarily the work of the imagination—both positive and negative—and the vehicle by which people come to understand their world and live within it, those who study religion must be attentive to the variety of ways in which meanings and symbols of ultimacy are generated. With regard to the Beats, we must continually struggle to describe this imaginative faculty at work; how existing worlds are repossessed and made new; and, conversely, how worlds elsewhere are brought to bear on ones existing in the here and now.

The goal, then, is to appreciate the Beats' "raggedy madness" on its own terms and inhabit the gap between their experience in society and their representation of it. Like the improvisatory bebop musicians playing in, around, and through the traditional chord progressions, syncopations, and melodies, the Beats were not content to play the same old tune. During processes of symbolic transformation, Burroughs, Kerouac, and Ginsberg each dreamed of a self and an America that were radically different from what they were presented with. Both imaginaries referred to an extraordinary reality, the invisible metaphysical workings of the cosmos as each man perceived them. Subsequently, both the individual and his culture were invested—through relentless production of secular words—with the energy of the sacred.

In attempting to appreciate how, in Ginsberg's phrase, "existence itself was God," the Beats relied on experience in the world but looked to outside sources—metaphorical ciphers—to explain that experience to themselves and others.[20] What influenced them has been well documented and includes a long list of mythologized attendants to the Beat sensibility—the apocalyptic musings of Oswald Spengler; bebop musicians such as Charlie Parker, Lester Young, and Dizzy Gillespie; the psychology of Wilhelm Reich; the semantic theories of Alfred Korzybski; literary figures such as Ralph Waldo Emerson, Henry David Thoreau, Herman Melville, Mark Twain, William Blake, Arthur Rimbaud, and Jonathan Swift; and the hipsters, hoboes, and dropouts from whom the Beats derived aesthetic insight and street credibility.

Under the rubric of the "new vision," the Beats collected these pieces of cultural debris and wove them together in deliberate productions of the real. But too often such names become a laundry list of inspiration, sloppily invoked to explain this or that literary reference, public pronouncement, or lifestyle choice. As I will argue, this bricolage was an ethos that not only confirmed the Beats' intellectual and emotional experiences as reasonable but also endowed them with a sacred tenor. Such a "religious perspective," as defined by Geertz, is a particular mode of construing the world that "moves beyond the realities of everyday life to wider ones which correct and complete them, and its defining concern is not action upon those wider realities but acceptance of them, faith in them."[21] But what holds the Beats' influences together? What religious patterns become discernible from this shifting constellation of spurs and provocations?

The mosaic of idioms that informed the new vision as well as the "wider" reality to which it referred are the keys to understanding the religious dimensions of the Beats' collaborative project. In this volume, I contend that both take on vivid clarity when one considers the influence of the German historian Oswald Spengler upon the Beats' *opera* and lifestyles. Their exploration of ordinary and extraordinary realities, their lives and their literature, and their thinking about America were profoundly influenced by his two-volume work of philosophy and metahistory, *The Decline of the West* (English trans. 1926, 1928). This work stands as one of the most over-the-top works of modernist synthesis, unyielding in its reduction of the whole of existence—past, present, and future—into the language of German romanticism. During World War I, Spengler put forth the notion that the West, like all previous "Civilizations," was destined to collapse, but a new "Culture" would inevitably emerge to continue the organic cycle of history.[22] As Spengler wrote on the opening page of *Decline*, "The decline of the West, which at first sight may appear, like the corresponding decline of Classical Culture, a phenomenon limited in time and space, we now perceive to be a philosophical problem that, when comprehended in all its gravity, includes within itself every great question of Being."[23]

Although the Beats had drunk deeply from the well of American mythos, particularly the ideas of a New Jerusalem and an errand into the wilderness, they interpreted these cultural myths according to a Spenglerian blueprint. Spengler's philosophy of cultural cycles enabled the Beats to see themselves at both the end and the beginning of an era. They adopted a cosmic view of history and became infused with an apocalyptic sense of urgency. They were in tune with the "world beat," in Kerouac's words, "the sounds you expect to hear on the last day of the world and the Second Coming."[24]

Although many of the intellectual sources and poetic roots of the Beats' early work have been explored in great depth, Spengler's considerable influence has been largely undervalued. Many interpreters have made the connection between the Beats and their reading of *The Decline of the West* in the mid–1940s, but no one has made much of it.[25] Too often Spengler is invoked simply to demonstrate that the Beats were deeply dissatisfied with the present state of affairs. That assessment, while true enough, remains empty if not taken up and pursued. Writing "for the benefit of serious readers who are seeking a glimpse at life and not a definition," Spengler's prophecies compounded the Beats' already strong sense of cultural pessimism. More important, the prophecies invested their lives and literature with religious urgency.[26]

Spengler also provided a religious vocabulary laden with existential gravity, romantic flourish, and mystical inferences. Although his language is vague, it is poetically inspiring in the sense that it is open, readily interpreted, and easily read into. And that is exactly what the Beats did as their new vision moved from an oppositional aesthetic to a coherent theology of experience. As Spengler declared, his agenda was two-tiered: "Thus our theme, which originally comprised only the limited problem of present-day civilization, broadens itself into a new philosophy—*the* philosophy of the future, so far as the metaphysically-exhausted soil of the West can bear such. . . . And it reviews once again the forms and movements of the world in their depths and final significance, but this time in according to an entirely different ordering which groups them, not in an ensemble picture inclusive of everything known, but in a picture of life."[27] Spengler's metaphysical pronouncements channeled the Beats' artistic passions and desire for experience into a cosmic framework that made sense of their everyday lives but, at the same time, allowed them eventually to move beyond their inheritance. For even though Spengler's ideas were omnipresent, circulating in and around the Beat circle in the 1940s and 1950s, they were never omnipotent. Consequently, they built around and through Spengler, using his metaphysical allusions to diagnose a crisis of cultural and personal dimensions as well as fashion a mode of being that would address this crisis.

Spengler's importance to the Beats' early collaboration recalls how the Swedish mystic Emanuel Swedenborg influenced the religious sensibility of Ralph Waldo Emerson. Like Spengler, Swedenborg spoke with the authority of a visionary who had uncovered the secrets of the cosmos. His method of exegesis and three-tiered cosmology gained currency among the elite core of Transcendentalists, but it was their unappointed leader, Emerson, who most clearly articulated Swedenborg's principles even as he made them his own. Emerson's spirituality, cultural criticism, and vision of a "new, yet unapproachable" America were heavily influenced by his reading of Swedenborg. In fact, when *Nature* was anonymously published in 1836, many readers assumed it to be propaganda from the Swedenborgian Church even though Swedenborg's name was mentioned only once.[28] In 1854 Emerson identified his source of religious inspiration and boldly declared, "The age is Swedenborg's." As Swedenborg was for Emerson, so Spengler was for the Beats— the poet extraordinaire and "translator of nature into thought."[29]

To study the Beats in light of Spengler's intellectual project makes good interpretive sense. It helps in both contextualizing the swirl of influences within their world and delineating similarities and differences among Burroughs, Kerouac, and Ginsberg. As Ginsberg explained before his death in 1997, the Beats' shared reading of "Spengler on the decline of the West, the fall of Empires" impressed an apocalyptic mentality upon each of them. Consequently, their lives and literature focused on the future as well as the perceived corruption of the present. "At the time," Ginsberg recalled, "this was being called the American Century and the central character [was] an advertising logo called the Man Of Distinction, which is a guy dressed in English Oxford grays with a brushed mustache, like the CIA or something, drinking whiskey. This [was] the opposite of what we took for our ideal."[30]

This volume explores the Spenglerian nexus that bound the Beats together through the 1940s and into the 1950s. Although Burroughs, Kerouac, and Ginsberg each performed a distinctive riff upon a set of common themes, asking how and why each man responded to Spengler's narrative of decline sheds light on their religious imaginations—in process and at work. As a religious biography of the Beats from the mid–1940s to the late 1950s, this study is neither a testament to a stable faith nor a point-by-point outline of certain beliefs and practices they espoused at one time or another. Instead, it is a reconstruction of how certain beliefs and practices came into being through their imaginative faculties. The process of assimilating Spenglerian historiography and metaphysics, drug experiences, Reichian psychology, the experiences and consequences of their sexual transgressions, Rimbaud's notion of phantasmagoria, criminality, Korzybski's General Semantics, the trope of madness, American mythos, traveling in and around the United States, and bebop rhythms unfolded as a series of fluid interactions and continuing integration. Like the continual transitions in scale and melody of a smooth yet frenzied Charlie Parker composition, Beat religiosity was an ever-evolving, ever-expanding complex of ideas, experiences, idioms, and insights. Instead of focusing on the most visible expressions of Beat religiosity in the late 1950s—Burroughs's dabbling in Scientology, Kerouac's turn toward Buddhism, and Ginsberg's embrace of psychedelica—I contend that religion was already the lingua franca of their collaborations, a currency stamped with a declaration of Spenglerian faith.

Scratching the Religious Surface

Although much can be made of the fact that the Beats were close friends, lived together for a time in New York City, and continually wrote to each other as well as about each other, their commonalties go still deeper than their association in the popular imagination. The most satisfying account of this shared depth remains John Tytell's *Naked Angels: The Lives and Literature of the Beat Generation* (1976), the first comprehensive study to take Kerouac, Ginsberg, and Burroughs seriously, on their own terms, as a coherent literary group. Without delving into Spengler's influence on the Beats, Tytell wrote that "the mutuality among these men developed . . . as a result of a mythic outlook on their own lives and interactions."[31] This "mythic outlook," as well as what Tytell referred to as the Beats' "visionary sensibility" and "romantic militancy," are the main concerns of *The Bop Apocalypse*. Although Tytell was certainly sympathetic to the category of religion, he intended to paint neither an exhaustive portrait of the Beats' religious sensibility nor its manifestation in their lives and literature. Tytell, to his credit, legitimized the Beats, forcefully arguing for their inclusion into the canon of American literature. In many ways, this book is an interpretive extension of Tytell's pioneering work, an attempt to make religious sense of the Beats' "aesthetic and intellectual discoveries" and their "sweeping discontent with American 'virtues' of progress and power."[32]

Despite Tytell's work, assessments of the Beats have too often focused on the sensational realities—innovative literary techniques, brutally honest narratives, sex, drugs, criminality, and madness—without exploring the internal logic that connected these narrative threads. Analyses that do not seek to connect literary practice with social practice with personal biography in a direct yet discriminating manner only "scratch the Beat surface," to use Michael McClure's phrase.[33] They ignore the processual dimensions of the Beats' imaginations: how and why they discussed certain material, how some ideas informed others, and, finally, how ideas, in turn, were heavily nuanced by past events or present experiences. Although accurately recreating every detail and exhaustively tracing the path of each snapping synapse is a hopeless task, to ask the same questions the Beats asked in the same language they used goes much further in understanding and assessing their world. The burden of this study is not to recover how the Beats translated the world confronting them but to see that world as they did. Once these symbolic lenses and metaphorical filters have been attentively reconstructed, the possibility of seeing clearly their concerns, evaluations, and wishes presents itself anew. In my attempt to take the Beats at face value, religion emerges as the most pressing interpretive category.

It is ironic yet telling that the Beats neatly reflected the mainstream religious demographics of postwar America. Burroughs was a Protestant from the suburbs of St. Louis, Missouri; Kerouac, a Catholic raised in the mill town of Lowell, Massachusetts; and Ginsberg, a Jew brought up in a left-wing political atmosphere in Paterson, New Jersey. As their careers progressed, only Kerouac consciously retained any allegiance to his childhood faith, whereas Burroughs and Ginsberg remained ambivalent if not openly hostile to organized religions. Although it would be myopic to place them within a context that emphasized their Judeo-Christian heritages, one must be aware how the religious language of their youth was translated into the aesthetic language of their adulthood, rife with metaphysical subtleties gleaned from Spengler, Reich, Korzybski, romanticism, jazz, and drug highs. In other words, we need to be aware of those strands of imagination that connect with a previously held faith, not to label a particular idea or action "Catholic" or "Jewish" but to discern how it became transfigured in the process of recall and contextualization. Conversely, we must also recognize that the Beats' adoption of Spengler et al. was a complex affair, neither divorced from past perspectives nor present interests. Religion is a process and not an indelible insignia. It is a faculty of the imagination—an interplay of ordinary thoughts, ideas, and gestures that transcend, by virtue of their extraordinary referents, the ideological and behavioral material of one's world.

In the history of discussing and interpreting the Beats, the category of religion has been given much lip but very little service. Many have adopted the rather provincial attitude first expressed in 1957 by Michael Rumaker, that the Beats and religion do not mix. Rumaker wrongly insisted that the Beats only confused the boundaries between art and religion. "You cannot have religion and art," he declared, "art does not concern itself with systems of religion—or systems of any kind."[34]

What Rumaker and other critics have failed to discern is the extent to which the private imagination—volatile, discordant, and unsystematic—was brought to bear in Beat literature. They ignore the way in which Beat works were verbal strategies employed amid the contestations of meaning in the complex cultural field of postwar America. Fleeting appearances of religion in later studies have referred to Eastern spirituality, focused on the "latent" Catholicism of Kerouac and the Jewish roots of Ginsberg's prophetic laments, or denounced altogether the religious content of their work as "intellectual sentimentality."[35] The only contemporary critic who has taken seriously their "thundering onslaught upon God, Eternity, the cosmos" has been Stephen Prothero, who places the Beats within the purview of American religious historians.[36] Due to its brevity, however, Prothero's argument is limited to insightful yet undigested assertions about the religious character of Kerouac, Burroughs, and Ginsberg as well as other writers who later became associated with them. Prothero's historical jump-cuts and broad strokes span twenty-five years and include discussions of the poet Gregory Corso, who met Ginsberg in 1950, and Lawrence Ferlinghetti, a San Francisco poet and publisher who met Ginsberg in 1954. While laying the groundwork for future interpretations, Prothero treats religion as a theoretical category that can be applied to the Beat phenomenon and not as a lived reality for those writers who toiled in obscurity until the mid-1950s.

Not surprisingly, John Clellon Holmes's "This Is the Beat Generation"

(1952), the first attempt to interpret Kerouac and Ginsberg as well as Burroughs in absentia, was centered on religion and their "perfect craving to believe." Holmes, who had become close friends with Kerouac in 1948 as a late addition to the Beat inner circle, wrote of the group's agenda as "a desperate craving for belief" in order to counter the "spiritual" crisis of contemporary America: "[The Beat Generation's] ability to keep its eyes open, and yet avoid cynicism; its ever-increasing conviction that the problem of modern life is essentially a spiritual problem; and the capacity for sudden wisdom which people who live hard and go far, possess, are assets and bear watching."[37] Living "hard" referred not to the bohemian excesses of the Beats so much as the intensity that each brought to the task at hand—to counter and assuage the "[spiritual] problem of modern life." Holmes's recognition of the Beats' religious character was so on the mark that Burroughs, upon reading it, wrote to Ginsberg in his matter-of-fact style: "I saw Holmes's article. OK in an obvious way."[38]

In this study, I hope to recover the religious language of the Beats—the idiom of "craving to believe." If one apprehends their religious world on its own terms, the Beats are no longer the property of sociologists or the mute objects of literary criticism. Such reclamation, however, requires an extraordinary sensitivity to the Beats' collective fluency in the rhetoric or religion between 1944 and the mid–1950s. As Ginsberg wrote in "Howl," "Highs! Epiphanies! Despairs! Ten years' animal screams. . . . New loves! Mad Generation! down on the rocks of Time! Real holy laughter in the river! They saw it all! the wild eyes! the holy yells!"[39] During that decade the Beats inhabited a world they had created by themselves for themselves. Consequently, this study approaches them through the symbolic language they shared and used to approach the unspeakable. I have tried to recreate a sense of how the Beats lived as normal human beings trying to make sense of the events around them. As artists, they proved to be extraordinarily sensitive to questions of ultimacy and the human condition. Their religious world was continually on display in journals, letters, and their art. My task is to be sensitive to the subtle ways in which that world was created symbolically and resist the temptation to interpret the symbolic material either literally or separately from the actual circumstances of their lives.

From Beat to Beatnik and Back

Kerouac, Ginsberg, and Burroughs have been subject to a voluminous array of interpretations, critical studies, biographies, unabashed celebrations, knee-jerk condemnations and satire, and, more recently, eulogies and nostalgic retrospectives.[40] They have become, for better or worse, revolutionary commodities to be purchased or discarded by the public at-large. The subtlety and gravity of their collaboration has too often been overlooked, given the social phenomenon of the "Beat Generation" in the late 1950s as well as the appearance, soon after, of Kerouac's essays in the glossy pages of *Esquire* and *Playboy*. Despite the sustained media frenzy during those years, one of the most insightful accounts of Beat literature was John P. Sisk's "The Beatniks and Tradition" (1959). Although Sisk did not discuss religion in particular, his article appeared in *Commonweal*, a weekly journal edited by Catholic laypeople. Sisk placed the Beats within the "subversive tradition of American literature." Most important, he took seriously their cultural criticism as well as their adherence to "traditionally sacred American patterns of thought and action."[41]

As Sisk's account implies, the Beats worked within a subversive tradition and harbored a utopian desire to construct an alternative mode of community that would serve as a transformative catalyst for the rest of American society. As a constructive religious practice, they were concerned with both personal salvation and the spiritual health of the nation. Their critique of America occurred first on the individual level, identifying as well as addressing a cultural crisis within themselves. Consequently, their intense focus on inner fulfillment reflected a belief that personal reorientation to the cosmos would precipitate change on the social level.

Although the severity of the Beats' criticism of an American present often overshadowed their affirmations of an American future, these writers were part of a long tradition of American religious dissent. The strains of antinomianism that most closely parallel the Beats are the traditions of Walt Whitman and the Transcendentalists, those who claimed religious authority based not on institutions but on a personal, experiential appeal to reality. It is not surprising, then, that the Beats would identify with Whitman's "democratic vistas" and the self-reliant ethos of Emerson and Henry David Thoreau while celebrating their individualism and personal experience within the confines of a small but select group. Although the Transcendentalists sprang from the ranks of the Unitarian church, the Beats neither wrote nor acted within an institutionalized religious tradition. They invented their own and in doing so represent a profound instance of the religious imagination at work. For the Beats, as with both Whitman and the Transcendentalists, personal and cultural salvation were intimately bound together. Personal transformation undergirded attempts to instigate a cultural transformation within America, for societal renewal could only follow through the cultivation of self—the "home-cosmographies" of which Thoreau once spoke.[42]

In the mid-nineteenth century, Emerson, Thoreau, Theodore Parker, and Margaret Fuller, among others, were ridiculed as "Transcendentalists," religious mystics accused of having their heads in the clouds. Similarly, because of their close association during the 1940s and 1950s, Burroughs, Kerouac, and Ginsberg have garnered the group label of "Beat," a self-descriptive adjective that Kerouac first applied to the entire generation of postwar youth. During the media deluge of the late 1950s, however, "Beat" lost its religious connotation—beat down but capable of overcoming oppression through spiritual development. Initially, media alarms over "violence and criminality" fueled reactionary literary assessments, a frenzy that produced dismissive and often paranoid accounts of the new "bohemian" scene. The Beats met with an onslaught of vituperative attacks from the dominant institutions they had called into question. *San Francisco Chronicle* columnist Herb Caen added the suffix *nik* to the word *Beat*, making a connection with the recently launched Russian satellite *Sputnik*. *Life* magazine also exhibited the period's binary categorization by associating them with things un-American and subversive: "talkers, loafers, passive little con men, lonely eccentrics, mom-haters, cop-haters, exhibitionists with abused smiles and second mortgages on a bongo-drum—writers who cannot write."[43]

Because of the Beats' antiestablishment tendencies, by the middle of the decade many critics had positioned them as a literary manifestation of the cult of "juvenile delinquency." Even among sympathetic voices such as the novelist Norman Mailer and the elder statesman of the San Francisco bohemian scene Kenneth Rexroth, the Beats represented a reactionary nihilism and, in Rexroth's phrase, practiced the art of "disengagement."[44] "Nothing but lame sociological bullshit," a resentful Ginsberg wrote in 1958 of critics' wholly inadequate understanding of the religious dimension of their literature—a paradigm that had equated their stylistic innovations with middle-class rebellion.[45]

Ginsberg's vitriol was directed at *Partisan Review* contributor Norman Podhoretz, who earlier in 1958 had labeled the Beats "know-nothing bohemians" and portrayed them as a nihilistic threat to political activism and social commitment, literary equivalents to Jim Stacks from *Rebel without a Cause*. Podhoretz characterized Beat "style" as "hostile to civilization; it worships primitivism, instinct, energy, 'blood.' To the extent that it has intellectual interests at all, they run to mystical doctrines, irrationalist philosophies and left-wing Reichianism. The only art the new bohemians have any use for is jazz and of expressing contempt for coherent, rational discourse which being a product of the mind, is in their view a form of death."[46] In fact, the Beats did "worship" the qualities of "primitivism, instinct, energy, 'blood,'" but not as forms of antisocial nihilism. On the contrary, their descriptions of both a new American frontier and the heroes who would occupy it were filled with the imagery of the interconnectedness and vitality of nature. Their style, or rather their apparent lack of style, betrayed a frontier desire for that which lay beyond language. Consequently, their praise of such feral restlessness and intuitiveness was both an expression of profound dissatisfaction with middle-class respectability and a protest for the emergence of a *terra nuova*.

As the "Beat Generation" became a popular fad after publication of *Howl and Other Poems* in 1956, *On the Road* in 1957, and *Naked Lunch* in 1959, "beat" came to mean anything that opposed the values and mores of middle-class Americans. Films such as *The Beat Generation* (1959) and *The Beatniks* (1960) as well a number of exploitative books depicted Beats as everything from junkies and delinquents to serial rapists and killers. A 1959 *Life* magazine article memorable for an alliterative and prolix title—"The Only Rebellion Around: But the Shabby Beats Bungle the Job in Arguing, Sulking, and Bad Poetry"—became the standard interpretation. The accompanying studio photograph featured two paid models "sulking" around their "Beat" apartment. Captioned "The Well-Equipped Pad," the photograph identified twenty-two "essentials of uncomfortable living," including "1. Beat chick in black . . . 5. marijuana for smoking . . . 7. paperback library of Beat classics . . . 11. bearded Beat wearing sandals, chinos, and turtle-necked sweater and studying a record by the late saxophonist Charlie Parker . . . 13. empty beer cans . . . 14. ill-tended plant . . . 22. Beat baby, who has gone to sleep on the floor after playing with beer cans."[47] Such parodies went a long way in defining "Beat" as a fashion of youth—a temporary Oedipal revolt—and a phase that would soon pass with maturity. The term *Beat* is still degraded and contested, referring alternately to a pre-hippie youth movement and to almost any artist who had antiestablishment credentials and lived in or around New York City or San Francisco during the late 1950s.

The tendency to view the Beats in terms of binary oppositions—self versus society, hip versus square, and rebellion versus the maintenance of the status quo—is still an underlying assumption in many interpretations. For the most part, both celebrations and contentious dismissals of the Beats have chosen not to engage the messy, ambiguous, and at times contradictory thicket of their cultural position. More dexterous interpreters have reduced the oppositional categories into one—that of ideology. For example, Sacvan Bercovitch comments that "the social protest poems of the Beats" were hollow and inevitably silent screams against the dominant culture. "In every case," Bercovitch writes, "the defiant act that might have posed fundamental social alternatives became instead a fundamental force against social change." In Bercovitch's opinion, the Beats were wholly subsumed by what he calls elsewhere "the American ideology."[48] Instead of sensationalizing the Beats as rebels without a cause, Bercovitch depicts them as cranks without a viable social message. Writers as diverse as cultural historian Greil Marcus and conservative pundit George F. Will have also pointed out that the Beats were active participants in their own commodification and celebrity.[49]

Either/or assessments fail to discern the complexity of the Beats' cultural position as well as the subtlety of their cultural criticism. They were neither social anarchists nor corporate sell-outs, "beatniks trying to make it rich" as Donovan sang in "Season of the Witch," his disillusioned take on the end game of bohemian protest. For the first ten years of their friendship the Beats worked in relative obscurity, away from any factories of the culture industry. That is not to gainsay their oppositional status but to interrogate what exactly their oppositional character entailed. As Ginsberg wrote of this critical failure in 1957, "People keep seeing destruction or rebellion . . . but that is [a] very minor element, actually; it only seems to be so to people who have accepted standard American values as permanent. What we are saying is that these values are not really standard or permanent, and we are in a sense I think ahead of the times—though not too far ahead. . . . That's just what we as a 'group' have been trying to do."[50]

The Beats anticipated a new America but not by much, for the idea of America is always in process, the reality of which is always elusive. In developing a religious apparatus to deal with this changing world, the Beats were following, as well as revealing, larger trends in postwar society. As opposed to many accounts of the Beats, this study looks at them in light of this ordinariness. Although they lived extraordinary lives and produced extraordinary literature, the fundamental way in which they inhabited the world was unremarkable and similar to that of many Americans in the postwar years. In other words, their stylized rebel status begins to fade as they take on the strange hue of familiarity. They become threatening only when they become recognizable. Indeed, "Anonymity in the world of men," as Kerouac wrote in 1952, "is better than fame in heaven."[51]

The first task of this study is to restore the word *Beat* as a term for critical and descriptive use by digging below the layers of media hype, parody, and scholarly reduction. Despite its excessive usage and attribution to those not associated with its coinage, the term *Beat* is still quite useful if one looks to the collaborative context from which it originated. Burroughs, Kerouac, and Ginsberg, in fact, did share a great deal beyond mere dissatisfaction. What bound them together in common cause was their distinctive brand of religious dissent, in Prothero's words a "protest for" change rather than a "revolt against" established institutions.[52] The Beats' relationship with the dominant culture was characterized by unqualified dissent as well as ambiguity. They repossessed dominant trends. And in the very act of engaging the mythic terrain of American exceptionalism, the Beats paralleled the actions of those from a variety of fields, including other artists and musicians, religious adherents, labor leaders, and Supreme Court justices—all who not only questioned the world but also acted upon such impulses.

Religion and Dissent

Any history of the Beats must be put into a religious context given that the cultural climate in which they lived and worked was publicly defined in religious terms. Such religious beliefs, emotions, and political rhetoric fell under the rubric of what has been termed public or civil religion, a set of national symbols and commemorations that sacralized the American political experiment. What Americans thought about their country, and themselves as members of it, was the most tangible expression of a theological structure that went much deeper than political slogans or the white marble facade of monuments. When the cultural metaphysics of exceptionalism were momentarily thrown into question by the initial murmurs of cold war and atomic paranoia, hope and anxiety became alternate expressions of the same national faith. To be an American was either to be part of God's covenantal plan or subject to divine judgment. Either way, the divinity shone upon each American and his or her country. After the war, public religion was the connective tissue that bound the mainline faiths together in common cause. In the wake of unprecedented economic boom and anxiety over "Godless" communism, religious affiliation became ever more prominent in the domestic sphere as religion in general became more visible in popular culture as well as a common topic in public debates. Never before had so many Americans belonged to, attended, or associated themselves with religious institutions. The heightened popularity of Billy Graham's evangelical crusades, Fulton Sheen's television series *Life Is Worth Living*, and Norman Vincent Peale's self-help spirituality contributed to and reflected a postwar "turn to religion."[53] Contemporary observers used terms like *religious revival* and *theological renaissance* to describe the sudden insurgencies of patriotism and faith.[54] In hindsight, such terms were not altogether inappropriate. Although William McLoughlin's claim of this trend being "nothing short of a Great Awakening" may be somewhat hyperbolic, Americans did reorient themselves in relation to the new social facts of conspicuous consumption and mushroom clouds.

Such reorientations often possessed a patriotic subtext; they were rarely unreflective submissions to the authority of nationalist ideals. On the contrary, they were volatile, creative affairs. Even in the mainline traditions, church members were not all of a piece, nor did they all turn to religion in order to become more American. Religion both provided a way to conform to dominant ideological trends and provided the means to resist them. Unlike the stereotypical, consensus-ridden 1950s, the postwar period was actually rife with critical vigor of a religious nature—from the burgeoning civil rights movement and mandarin assessments of conformity, flying-saucer enthusiasts, the spirituality boom, and the example of Trappist monk Thomas Merton to various avant-garde pockets in New York, San Francisco, and Black Mountain, North Carolina.[55] America, as it had always been, was a matter of perspective—a contest of competing imaginations. Postwar America was not made up only of its members, the land they traversed, the infrastructure they built, or the technologies they invented. Above all, it was composed of the different ideas they had of the nation.[56]

The perception of self in relation to country went a long way in determining how one viewed the past, the hopes and fears one possessed in the present, and the actions one would take in the future. That is the role that "America" assumed in the imagination of its eponymous people and invested the idea of America with religious import. During a period of rapid economic change and burgeoning anxiety, the very idea of America became a battleground where various conceptions of nation were defended and performed. The scramble by politicians and corporate liberals to refashion the myth of American exceptionalism for an angst-ridden population was moderately successful given the new forms of mass communication. Even while public religion operated through the media to ensure social cohesion, due to the mass proliferation of radios and televisions after the war the message of triumphalism became much louder if not always more consistent.

In 1955 Will Herberg made a bold claim that continues to hold sway even in academic circles, albeit in a sublimated form. He argued in *Protestant, Catholic, Jew* that the American religious landscape had become desiccated because its dominant religious forms had converged into a seamless political ideology, what Herberg called "the American way of life."[57] Herberg ignored the volatile nature of religious belief and practice in the 1950s by focusing on religion from a political perspective. Consequently, he saw religion merely as a support system for American politics, implicitly denying the possibility of religious discourse to critique the status quo or offer viable social alternatives.

Although Herberg did not follow his argument to its logical conclusions, others have carried the torch for this binary form of consensus history. For example, Sydney Ahlstrom has described the 1960s as the end of the "Great Puritan epoch in American history." Although attuned to the religious pluralism of the past, he is still taken aback by events of the 1960s that "have so radically changed the American situation." Implicit in the arguments of Ahlstrom or those of Sacvan Bercovitch are denials of religious innovation or creativity and the relegation of all such attempts to the dustbin of historical anomaly. The notion of religious identity as a process, as work, is obscured when too much emphasis is placed on the radical newness of a "postprotestant era" or the ubiquity and potency of an "American ideology." Conservative forces have been at work throughout American history, but to privilege them at the expense of attending to the details of dissent obscures more than it illuminates.[58]

Such consensus accounts of American religious history tend to simplify and truncate the role religion plays in cultural life, assigning it the conservative functions of maintaining the status quo and containing dissent within a bipolar historical structure. The assertion that some sort of violent rupture or reaction occurred in the 1960s, a paradigm shift as it were, assumes the existence of a seamless paradigm of American religion—the same assumption Herberg made in *Protestant, Catholic, Jew.* That is not the case. After the war, there were many narratives of American religion, just as there had been many narratives before the war—competing yet interwoven beliefs and practices. Within this cultural palimpsest, religious orientations were sometimes related, sometimes antagonistic, but all were examples of religion within the United States.

To understand the 1950s within the context of American religious history is to focus on its radicalism, that is, to go back to the roots and trace its gradual evolution into the 1960s, tilling the ground of its multiple flowerings. That has been done, to a certain extent, by Robert Ellwood in *The Fifties Spiritual Marketplace* (1997). Ellwood categorizes the Beat Generation phenomenon as part of an "underground" religious economy. Although not dealing with Burroughs, Kerouac, and Ginsberg on their own terms, his identification of the social phenomena that followed in their wake as an important aspect in the story of American religion is right on the mark. To his credit, he discusses events, persons, and groups that American religious historians have traditionally ignored. In dealing with the Beats, however, Ellwood's sociological approach tends to emphasize the ideas of a wide range of people over the actions of a few, poetry over the life behind it.[59]

The Bop Apocalypse takes issue with the wrenching story often told by religious historians and sociologists—that the American religious landscape changed dramatically during the 1960s with the profusion of new religious movements and spiritual styles. Such an assumption prevents one from accessing the continuities between the apparently placid 1940s and 1950s and the sociological tumult of the 1960s, between the Apollonian "American way of life" and its Dionysian counterpart, "Turn on, tune in, drop out." Although the Beats' did not single-handedly generate the evolution of American religion at mid-century, their example reminds religious historians that much religious activity occurs outside institutions and does not initially appear to be religion. This book presents a case study, albeit from a peculiar angle, of the changes that affected the postwar religious landscape. The Beats are not representative of the whole of American religion, but neither are they prurient detritus to be cast aside. They are one representation of the dynamic nature of religion and of the dynamism often overlooked in the study of religion during this period.[60] As a consideration of the large-scale changes that were to occur in America, this volume is a challenge to certain assumptions held by sociologists and historians of postwar America and engages what Ninian Smart, a scholar of religion, has called "religion on the ground."

Apocalypse

Tending this ground, the first thing one notices about postwar American culture is its profound ambiguity. Even as the waves of postwar celebration and self-congratulation continued to pound America's public shore, a severe undertow of pessimism and alarm existed. Such feelings were not necessarily a dialectical backlash, however, but rather a periodic eruption of America's apocalyptic imagination. As Douglas Robinson notes, the very idea of America in history is apocalyptic. Since the historicizing of Reformation millennialism on American soil, America has been conceived as both the end of one age and the beginning of the new. It has become an undefinable promise to be carried forward, a way of envisioning the present in terms of what has already been revealed once upon a time. The technical meaning of *apocalypsis* implies a negative performance: *apo,* meaning "from" or "away," and *kalupto,* meaning "to conceal" or "cover over." Although the technical meaning is to "uncover" or "to reveal," it carries with it a particular sense of uncovering or revealing. Unlike, say, millenarian thinking *apocalypsis* is fundamentally a hermeneutical revelation—a way of seeing and interpreting the world. Given this precise definition of *apocalypsis,* Spengler's *Decline of the West* was an apocalyptic revelation for Kerouac, Ginsberg, and Burroughs— neglected and misunderstood in its own time but taken up by them in the mid–1940s. They, in turn, assumed the role of religious critics who would make the revelation clear to the postwar generation.[61]

As the Beats read Spengler's prophecies of decline apocalyptically, they were already working within an apocalyptic climate—a period fraught with conflicting impulses and cross-currents of emotion. It was a time of woeful contemplation over what the twentieth century had wrought as well as a period of unabashed optimism in what the future would bring. As the economy soared, there was both celebration and discontent. In 1951 Kerouac expressed that double-edged emotional state while speaking into one of the first commercial models of the tape recorder. Even as he was taking full advantage of a consumer electronics revolution, he was also recoiling from its social consequences. "The density of the tragedy in America is confusing and immense in volume" he lamented but quickly countered with an assertion of childlike joy: "Everybody is important and interesting."[62] Such impulses may seem contradictory in nature, but they were, in fact, expressions of a larger cultural confusion. Although Americans may have been unsure of which side they came down on, they were fully prepared to accommodate themselves to an apocalyptic reality. Because they believed themselves to be living at the end of an era as well as at the beginning, what concerned them most was what to leave behind and what to take with them. Burroughs, Kerouac, and Ginsberg were confronted with the same decisions as they forged ahead in search of the unspeakable, mysterious America. Even as they sloughed off "stagnant orthodoxies," they were looking ahead toward new traditions.

Given the ever-present seams in the canopy of public religion, Burroughs, Kerouac, and Ginsberg each found room to express his own alternative vision of America, visions that were apocalyptic in the sense of that word already realized.[63] Their dissatisfaction was due, in large part, to their impression that American triumphalism was not only empty rhetoric but also socially irresponsible and self-destructive. At the same time, however, they actively participated in these cultural fashions, displaying an ardent religious faith in the promise of America. Consequently, the Beats' interest in America as geographical space was surpassed only by their singular focus on America as idea—highly abstract yet infinitely malleable and both an object of derision and the source of redemptive hope. Through a symbolic revisioning, the Beats created a world inside a world—their own private America. Its foundation resembled that of the majority culture—relying as it did on mythic paradigms of individualism and democracy, possessing a pragmatic emphasis on the authority of experience and sounding a certain tone of apocalyptic celebration of America's millennial promise.

For the Beats, however, America was substantively different from the nation celebrated in other areas of the public sphere.[64] It was a more open terrain, a masculinized frontier no longer tied down by institutions and the claims they made on each citizen. It was a place where radical transformation was still possible. For example, Burroughs believed that all was not well with America's "hygienic facade," for institutional strictures had become internalized. He wrote of his fellow Americans as having a "special horror of giving up control, of letting things happen in their own way without interference." To make his metaphysical point in physical terms, Burroughs added, "They would like to jump down into their stomachs and digest the food and shovel the shit out."[65]

Evident in Burroughs's wry satire is a more general belief that motivated much of the Beats' early cultural musings: America had lost touch with its organic roots. According to the Beats' reading of Spengler, America had become uprooted and entangled in the web of European "Civilization." The Beats' appropriations of *Decline* were not black and white usurpations but complex affairs involving selectivity and at times strong misreadings. They gained insight and inspiration from Spengler instead of strictly adhering to the letter of his theories.

Even as the Beats supplemented Spengler's ideas with other idioms, his historical schema remained their basis for repossessing the founding myths of America. First, they used a Spenglerian viewpoint to identify an essentially religious crisis: America's inability to escape the orbit of a decaying Western civilization. Second, in selectively reading Spengler they saw themselves as either defenders of the future promise of America (Kerouac and Ginsberg) or as soldiers in the final battle to defeat the forces of personal enslavement unleashed by the Enlightenment (Burroughs). In both readings, each Beat positioned himself in relation to a future, post-apocalyptic America. Third and most important, the Beats viewed the situation as both a cultural and individual crisis. Their Spenglerian belief in the correspondence between internal spirituality and the transcendent laws that governed the workings of the cosmos invested their individual quests for salvific knowledge with political resonance. Notions of individualism and human freedom became intimately tied to notions of social transformation.[66]

As rumors of the apocalypse circulated after World War II, Hermann Hagedorn's *The Bomb That Fell on America* (1946) was published in Santa Barbara, California. A cross between religious testimonial and epic poem, the book consists of three movements that question the morality of Harry Truman's decision the previous year to deploy the atomic bomb in the Pacific. At the time, the "modern psalm" received glowing reviews from journalists and critics alike. It begins: "A bomb fell on Hiroshima / It wasn't much in size, as bombs go, it wasn't much in weight . . . / God be with that in them which no bomb can reach!" Hagedorn woodenly laments the sins of America as he juxtaposes the voices of himself, the Lord, and "the conscience of America." Declaring that "the old worlds have lost their meaning," Hagedorn assumes the role of prophet, albeit in banal and understated terms:

This is the beginning of international order.
This is the end of western civilization.
This is the dawn of the greatest era in history.
This is the world's all-time high in headaches.[67]

Despite a certain melody in these lines, Hagedorn's verse exemplified the apocalyptic confusion of postwar Americans' thinking. The neo-orthodox theologian Reinhold Niebuhr gushingly praised Hagedorn's work as "full of the profoundest moral and religious insights." Lewis Mumford, a historian, spoke of Hagedorn as the prophet of the new atomic age: "No one has expressed better our moral guilt as a people and our latent moral convictions, through the action of which, please God, we may repair the grievous damage we have wrought."[68]

Despite such earnest comments, *The Bomb That Fell on America* is of little critical merit save for its striking resemblance to the attitude and style the Beats espoused during the same period. In "Two Sonnets" (1948), for example, Ginsberg first sees a new age dawning. "I witness Heaven in unholy time," he writes. But when he converses with the "Angels in the air," he delivers a much more dire forecast. "But all the streets are burning everywhere," he soon realizes, "Woe unto thee Manhattan, woe to thee."[69] Despite their differences, both *The Bomb That Fell on America* and Ginsberg's early verse reflect the history of rhetorical apocalypticism—from Michael Wigglesworth and Jonathan Edwards to Billy Sunday and Billy Graham and all the would-be Jeremiahs in between.

⌐┘

From 1660 to 1690, amid struggles over land ownership, natural disasters, and the perception of moral deterioration among second- and third-generation Puritans, the jeremiad became a common sermonic and literary form in Puritan New England. As such, it was both a political sermon delivered by Puritan clergy and a ritual response to a perceived weakening of social cohesion. The jeremiad had three parts. First, it affirmed the original covenant and put forth a communal ideal; second, it castigated the present as a declension from that ideal; and, finally, it called for a renewal of both purpose and zeal so that a lethargic people could return to their original sense of mission. Numerous sermons of the period exhibit this pattern, from Increase Mather's "Day of Trouble Is Near" (1674) to Samuel Hooker's "Righteousness Rained from Heaven" (1677).

Perhaps the most famous jeremiadic plea is Samuel Danforth's "A Brief Recognition of New England's Errand into the Wilderness" (1671): "Such as have sometimes left their pleasant cities and habitations to enjoy the pure worship of God in the wilderness are apt in time to abate and cool in their affectation thereunto; but then the Lord calls upon them seriously and thoroughly to examine themselves, what it was that drew them into the wilderness, and to consider that it was not the expectation of ludicrous levity nor of courtly pomp and delicacy but of the free and clear dispensation of the Gospel and kingdom of God."[70] On one hand, the jeremiad contains a centripetal force, shaming and calling a wayward flock back into the fold. On the other hand, there is also a centrifugal force, reassuring the people of the legitimacy of their divine status and thereby implicitly sanctioning further transgression. As a rhetorical device used by the Puritan clergy, the jeremiad embodied a paradox: It was a forward-looking strategy in the present designed to precipitate a return to the past.

The nature of this return has generated as much discussion about the relationship between literature and religion as it has insight into the sociopsychological context of the early Puritan settlements. Because the Puritan jeremiad participated in both the world of ideas and the realm of everyday experience, it has become an interpretive focus by which to study literature and social practice. With the seminal work of Perry Miller and the later work of Sacvan Bercovitch, what began its life in the "new" world as a rhetorical formula used by Puritan clergy has become a point of entry into a highly contested debate over the social meaning of literary texts. American Jeremiahs were very much a part of the dominant social order yet simultaneously critical of it. That insight provides a point of entry in assessing the Beats' brand of cultural criticism.[71] In working within the jeremiadic tradition, their relationship with the majority culture was highly antagonistic yet strangely intimate. The tone of Beat literature oscillated between reproach and celebration, self-imposed alienation and the desire to assume representative status.

In adapting the jeremiadic form to their own literary purposes, the Beats participated in a tradition of religiously based cultural criticism. Central to an understanding of their criticism and subsequent construction of a world inside a world is the notion of liminality. Victor Turner describes liminal time as one for discovery, innovation, challenge, and interrogation within a ritual setting. In studying the transformative potential of ritual, he extended the notion of liminality as a metaphor beyond ritual to other domains of "expressive cultural action." His ideas are grounded in the work of Arnold van Gennep, who first identified the phase of freedom and disorder that occurs in initiation rituals as a "liminal" period. Turner not only developed the notion of liminality in regard to rites of passage but also used that idea to analyze cultural production and change. While Turner describes such anti-structural phases as usually affirming and strengthening the existing social order, he also views such environments as containing "the potentiality for cultural innovation as well as the means for effecting structural transformations within a relatively stable sociocultural system."[72]

The Beats employed a "liminal strategy" in their lives and literature. The notion of liminality, that is, the capacity to transcend received cultural input and step outside the normal structures of life, is an integral part of the creative imagination. As a critical strategy for the Beats, the process of deep play was one of delineation, of probing the boundaries of human behavior and the sharp edges of social facts, not in order to break through but to push outward. The goal of such criticism was both to decenter the status quo and force it to reposition itself. What is at stake in this discussion is not merely an account of the relationship between religiosity and literary practice but, more important, the assessment of Beat literature as both products of and reflections upon mid-century American culture. It is essential that religion, conceived as both a coherent set of beliefs and a strategic practice, not be neglected in favor of either formalist or ideological methods of literary criticism. By considering religion as a rich source of imagination and creativity, it becomes much more than an ideology; it becomes a disruptive force that operates in and through experience itself.

The Beats did not impose ready-made metaphors simply upon reality but first tested their metaphors in the real world. They did not interrogate American values and mores by calling attention to the contradictions between a secular present and a sacred past, but, more important, they pointed out the contradictions between common understandings of the world and their experiences within it. Particularly in their more mature work of the 1950s, they engaged in sustained criticism of American culture and wrote about social trends, concerning themselves mainly with the ontological and cosmic significance of such trends. Their specific critiques of the dominant ideology were contained within a broader concern for the narratives, traditions, and epistemological theories that informed and molded America's most resonant meanings. Furthermore, the Beats' mythification of social outcasts such as the Denver muse Neal Cassady and the Times Square hustler Herbert Huncke reflected their desire to challenge the dominant ideological climate and participate in an alternative social reality. Their literature celebrated those who were socially inferior and transposed an aversion to dominant social structures into spiritual insights. For example, in *On the Road,* Kerouac wrote of the fictionalized Cassady, Dean Moriarty, as having "blossomed into a weird flower," a symbol of both a new consciousness and concomitant American culture. "Whooee," yells Moriarty, barreling down the highway toward a mysterious connection: "'Here we go!' And he hunched over the wheel and gunned her; he was back in his element, everybody could see that. We were all delighted, we all realized we were leaving confusion and nonsense behind and performing our one and noble function of the time, *move.* And we moved! . . . and Dean and I sat in the front seat and had the warmest talk about the goodness and joy of life."[73]

Driving into the future, Moriarty embodies an affirmation of faith in a redeemed America. In a direct allusion to Spengler's reference to emerging cultures as "sublimated life-essences, [which] grow with the same superb aimlessness as the flowers of the field," Kerouac wrote, "Holy flowers floating in the air, we're all these tired faces in the dawn of Jazz America."[74] Like the first European settlers, the Beats and their heroes defined the meaning of America as a space of Edenic innocence and a container of spiritual wisdom. Using contemporary forms, they followed the mythological lines set down centuries earlier. The Beats did not reiterate old ideas and values, they transformed them. They *made* them new. As artists in the age of mechanical reproduction, their religious imagination served as a ghost in the machine. They produced an art and an idea of "America" that were intimately familiar but wholly unrecognizable.

Demythology

In attempting to make the Beats recognizable, this volume is divided into four sections. Chapter 1 contextualizes the Beats within postwar America. It demonstrates how Spengler's cosmological frame formed the basis of the Beats' jeremiadic reading of America amid a cultural climate surfeited with Jeremiahs. Chapter 2 explores how the Beats pieced together a theology of experience using Spengler as both matrix and connective tissue. It catches them in the religious act, as it were, of world-making and bodily transformation. Extending the theological underpinnings of Beat religiosity, chapter 3 recovers how their lived religion became incorporated into the way they wrote. In that sense, the act of composition was tantamount to a ritual renewal of both self and culture, confirming their religious world with each letter written and with each typewriter key depressed. Chapter 4 revisits the major works that Kerouac, Ginsberg, and Burroughs produced in the 1950s in terms of critical content and argues that they engaged America on moral grounds through the discourse of public religion. Kerouac's *On the Road* and *Visions of Cody,* Ginsberg's *Howl and Other Poems,* and Burroughs's *Naked Lunch* all emanated from the religious world they had constructed during the previous decade. Consequently, their more mature works must be contextualized within the jeremiadic tradition of American literary and religious history. In conclusion, I identify the trajectories of each writer as their season of collaboration waned and argue that the religious imaginations of Burroughs, Kerouac, and Ginsberg remained quite active as each pursued a different path—Scientology, Buddhism, and LSD, respectively—through Spengler's America. When all is said and done, I hope to have given historical and religious depth to one of the most influential literary friendships of the twentieth century.

ᒥᒧ

Historians are supposedly the arch-investigators of time. Their focus, however, is inevitably on space, for it is only by way of the open meanings of texts and objects that historians can move beyond a grounded analysis of texts and objects into a discussion of change and ephemerality. When the meaning of a document has been secured, bound in a complex web of historical meaning, its mystery has been forever reduced. This mystery is what Hayden White means by the "historical sublime," referring to the open-endedness of the past and the lived experience of historical actors, a reality saturated with possibilities.[75] Even if one rejects truth with a capital T, one does not necessarily have to discard its lower-case relative. Historians are compelled to adopt a pragmatic temper, in William James's words "the open air and possibilities of nature, as against dogma, artificiality, and the pretense of finality in truth."[76] As a history of the Beats' early collaborations, *The Bop Apocalypse* is an attempt to acknowledge the claims that the past continually makes on the present. The living reality of the Beats' world will forever remain a realm of mystery and indeterminacy, a sphere that resists futile attempts to essentialize and categorize. Although we can never go back to the beginning, we can begin to make sense of it. Through dialogue, through language, and through prolonged engagement, we return to the present with something to say.

For the most part, the story of the Beats, even when told by historians above the media fray, has been subsumed under the often rigid imperatives of popular history. The narrative has taken on a mythic hue. The relevance and resonance of the Beats have been sacrificed to our need to have a story that is appealing and satisfies our prurient desires and need for narrative

closure. The story of the Beats describes shaking walls or ineffectively bang-
ing heads against those walls, both descriptions telling us what we think we
already know. Ironically, the Beats have become victims of the same American myths they attempted to repossess at mid-century. They now fit neatly
into the categories of either rebel agitator or media sensation, taking their
place on the dusty shelf beside Elvis, Brando, Camus, and Dean. But as usu-
al, the story is much more complicated. The subtlety of their hopes and fears
has been lost as they have become sensationalized. They have become pre-
packaged celebrity caricatures: Kerouac and the open road, Ginsberg and his
"om" chants in 1968 Chicago, and Burroughs, the celebrated heroin addict
and "grand old man of American freakdom."[77] In such roles, the Beats become either heroes or cranks, never Americans running up against barriers,
making sense of the world, and finding their place within it.[78] On the contrary, the Beats confronted "the poor hidden brick of America," in Kerouac's
words, "the actual place . . . you must go if you must bang your head to bang
it at all, the center of the grief and . . . the center of the ecstasy."[79] Such is the
place to practice the tradition of subversion, a tentative repossession of something never possessed in the first place.

chapter

1

INTER.

wn of Megalopolitan
ilization. Extinction
piritual creative force.
e itself becomes prob-
atical. Ethical-prac-
l tendencies of an
ligious and unmeta-
sical cosmopolitan-
.)

OF SCIENCE, UTILITY

Communistic, atheistic, Epi-
curean sects of Abbassid
times. "Brethren of Sin-
cerity"

XI. ETHICAL-SOCIAL IDEALS OF LIFE. EPOCH OF "UNMATHEMATICAL PHILOSOPHY."
SKEPSIS

Tendencies in Buddha's time	Hellenism	Movements in Islam	Schopenhauer, Nietzsche
	Epicurus (d. 270)		Socialism, Anarchism
	Zeno (d. 265)		Hebbel, Wagner, Ibsen

XII. INNER COMPLETION OF THE MATHEMATICAL FORM-WORLD. THE CONCLUDING
THOUGHT

(lost)	Euclid, Apollonius (about 300)	Alchwarizmi (800)	Gauss (d. 1855)
	Archimedes (about 250)	Ibn Kurra (850)	Cauchy (d. 1857)
		Alkarchi, Albíruni (10th Century)	Riemann (d. 1866)

XIII. DEGRADATION OF ABSTRACT THINKING INTO PROFESSIONAL LECTURE-ROOM
PHILOSOPHY. COMPENDIUM LITERATURE

| The "Six Classical Systems" |

XIV.

| Indian Buddhism |

"America, When Will Your Cowboys Read Spengler?"

Anxiety and Influence in Postwar America

Previous page, from table 1, "'Contemporary' Spiritual Epochs," in Oswald Spengler, *Form and Actuality*, volume 1 of *The Decline of the West*.

The essence of every culture is religion, so—and *consequently*—
the essence of every civilization is irreligion.
  —**Oswald Spengler,** *Form and Actuality*

Therefore, I prophesy the fall of America.
  —**Allen Ginsberg, "Death to Van Gogh's Ear"**

On March 18, 1956, five months after his first reading of "Howl" at the Six
Gallery in San Francisco, Allen Ginsberg took center stage at the Berkeley
Town Hall. The Beat phenomenon was still in the early stages of its media-
induced unfolding, and, true to form, Ginsberg was taking full advantage of
the spotlight. The persona he used to attract as well as to shield himself from
the glare was part trickster silliness, part preacherly indignation. Alternating between the two, he hoped to communicate his message while not becoming pigeonholed by supporters as a literary rapscallion or reduced by his
critics to an enfant terrible.

By the time of the Berkeley performance, Ginsberg had become slightly
annoyed by his notoriety and the "hip static" surrounding his public appearances. In response, he introduced his poem "America" to an audience perhaps less interested in the critical content of Ginsberg's poetry than in his
avant-garde status and ribald presentations. Among both friends and drunk-
en revelers Ginsberg quietly and with an air of sincerity prefaced his new work
with a few words: "An unfinished poem which I'll finish sooner or later, but
I'd like to read the . . . uh . . . first half of now."[1] That almost inaudible line
framed as well as explained the censure that ensued. On one level, the line
rebuked the fashionable voyeurism of the "underground" scene. More important, however, given the interrogatory blitzkrieg that followed in "America," the line challenged the audience to complete the poem with the poet
and answer the barrage of questions he was about to unleash. It was a call

for introspection and an open invitation to join him in the renewal of the American community. Just as the poem was unfinished and unrefined, so, too, were the poet, the audience, and the America Ginsberg was about to invoke.

In "America," Ginsberg zealously and somewhat recklessly discovered an undiscoverable country, an idea and place that remains forever a homestead of the imagination. After his twelve-year collaboration with Burroughs and Kerouac, Ginsberg's youthful habit of conflating the personal and political became an overt strategy. His performance that evening in Berkeley was both a distillation and dissemination—a projected incarnation of more than a decade's worth of shared experiences. Ginsberg's tone was self-righteous: "America how can I write my holy litany in your silly mood?" His medium was the religious rhetoric of the jeremiad, an art form used to bring the sins of the nation to bear on the individual conscience of each audience member. Assuming the poetic mantle, Ginsberg veiled his anger and condemnation in a comic dialogue between himself and America. In the first line, he acknowledged the depth of his critique and the personal toll it had taken: "America I've given you all and now I'm nothing."

After its opening, "America" becomes a sardonic political rant, mocking everyone and everything in its path, including the poet. It is filled with humor and self-deprecation, the same antagonistic style Lenny Bruce would soon adopt at Ann's 440 Club in North Beach. But in the rest of the poem Ginsberg chose to downplay its critical edge and revel in the absurdity of his rhetoric: "America when will you take off your clothes? . . . When will you be worthy of your million Christs? . . . When will you send your eggs to India? I'm sick of your insane demands. . . . When will your technicians get drunk and abolish money? . . . When can I go into the supermarket and buy what I need with my good looks?" Although Ginsberg did not literally suggest that these situations would could come to pass, he used comedy to make the ridiculous seem possible and the present state of affairs seem ridiculous. Reprimands paraded as questions. Vitriol was masked by humor.

As he assumed a prophetic mantle, Ginsberg's poem juxtaposed the present state of affairs with a timeless ideal of America. He saw his task as revealing how other Americans were desecrating their beliefs and values by not living up to their sacred inheritance. To mobilize that potential, that inalienable right of progressive perfectibility, he evoked a mythic past of America. Unlike the traditions drawn upon by Old Testament prophets and their New World counterparts the Puritan clergy, however, the past to which Ginsberg referred was based on memories rather than biblical creeds: "America I feel sentimental about the Wobblies . . . you should have seen me reading

Marx!" Such reminiscence was no mere agitprop, for the poet did not demand imitation of any political paradigm. Instead, he demanded that the unful-filled American promise be collectively realized. The ideal America, as he conceived it, was a matter of perception, the pursuit of utopia in the present. "After all America," Ginsberg reminds, "it is you and I who are perfect not the next world." As Kerouac and Burroughs often did in their work, Gins-berg cloaked his appeal in contradictions and invoked an unobtainable ide-al in the name of cultural reform. Unlike the Puritan jeremiads, however, he did not characterize this ideal as "a City upon a Hill" nor as the shining light of Christendom.

To what allegory, then, did the Beats' ideal correspond?

In "America," Ginsberg proposed that hope for a collective future lay in a willingness to pose questions that had no ready answers. The very struggle to answer them, it seemed, would bring about an exceptional America. Ac-cording to Ginsberg on that particular evening, the place to begin this struggle was Oswald Spengler's *The Decline of the West*. Pleading "America, when will your cowboys read Spengler?" (the buried and forgotten retort that does not appear in the written draft), Ginsberg illumined the gravity and subtlety of Beat cultural criticism as well as the common ideological framework that each had worked through individually by 1956. Like much of the Beats' early work, the line challenged cold war stereotypes of American identity concerning both secular and sacred politics. On one hand, Ginsberg questioned the hyper-masculine, solitary, and unemotional cowboy hero of John Wayne westerns and its geopolitical counterpart, the cold warrior. On the other hand, and more important, he condemned Americans for failing to take responsi-bility for their country's providential mission.

Spengler's historiography and metaphysical schemes cover the Beat oeu-vre with a transparent sheen, invisible but ever-present. From the beginning of the Beats' friendship, *Decline of the West* was a central topic of conversa-tion. In those spring months of 1944, New York City before the carnage of D-Day, *Decline* had already become a shared point of reference, the center around which the Beats framed literary discussions and formulated deeply felt religious questions. Whether "expounding Spengler" in their journals or referring to "Spenglerian degeneration" in their letters, the Beats regularly, albeit quietly, invoked him throughout the 1940s and 1950s.[2] Burroughs, who had presented *Decline* to both Ginsberg and Kerouac during their first meet-ing, gave Kerouac his two-volume copy, enjoining, "EEE di fy your mind, my boy, with the grand actuality of Fact."[3]

Kerouac, already familiar with Spengler, spent the next decade working through his ideas as they related to art and life. While attending the New

School for Social Research, for example, in 1949 Kerouac wrote a paper surveying the various schools of philosophy throughout history and concluded, like Spengler, that no philosophy, religion, or morality outlasted the particular cultural environment that produced it.[4] Likewise, an early draft of "Howl" eulogized those "who investigated the FBI by reading Spenglerian newspapers on Peyotl."[5] But references do not tell the whole story of the Beats' reading of *Decline*. Spengler's grand vision of historical cycles struck a chord in their collective imagination. His book was audacious even by the heady standards of modernism—a summation of all of world history and a user's guide for the apolcalypse. The first volume ends with three fold-out tables charting a different trajectory of decline—spiritual, cultural, and political—across time and space. Spengler's flowery, often obscure language became a mystery to be deciphered, a code that once cracked would reveal the secret meaning of their experience or, more specifically, their experience as distinctly American.

The Beats' search for the sacred meaning of America reflected their contemporary environment as a low hum of anxiety murmured across the American cultural landscape. Nowhere was that more evident than in the discourse of religion and its language of myth, symbol, and allegory. In the decade following the Allied victory, church attendance and religious affiliation grew at an unprecedented rate, and critical debate over the significance of the increase reached a fevered pitch in intellectual circles as well as popular culture. During an era that witnessed the obliteration of Hiroshima and Nagasaki, as well as the Nuremberg trials, a neo-orthodox revival, the beginning of the cold war, and the Korean conflict as well as congressional investigations into un-American activities, the postwar "turn to religion" took place within a heightened atmosphere of crisis, conspiracy, and conformity.

Such concerns no doubt helped fuel a large-scale return to the pews, but more important and somewhat ironically they were often manifested in critical evaluations of America's spiritual and moral health. Despite unprecedented material wealth, dire assessments abounded below the triumphalist surface. In *The Hero with a Thousand Faces* (1949), Joseph Campbell urged each American to tap the Gilgamesh inside in order to resist a world dominated by business ethics, uncritical patriotism, "ineffectual" religious organizations, and their "monkey-holiness." Irving Howe, in a *Partisan Review* symposium entitled "Religion and the Intellectuals" (1950), denounced the "religious turn" as "part of a historical moment of sickness." In *The Organization Man* (1956), William Whyte chronicled the decline of the Protestant ethic and the "pursuit of individual salvation through hard work, thrift, and competitive struggle." In its place, Whyte discerned a more ominous situation—the abdication of individual responsibility and the "worship of the organization" in all of its bureaucratic glory. Recycling the oratory of the Puritan jeremiads, critics from a variety of ideological corners perceived a declining state of affairs and called for the recovery of an uncorrupted mode of existence.[6]

As the fault lines of this tension took shape in the 1940s, Ginsberg, Burroughs, and Kerouac quickly found in Spengler the terms and categories to participate in the drama. In many respects Spengler's narrative of cultural decline resonated with the dueling attitudes of anxiety and hope that permeated postwar America. Drawing continually upon Spengler's condemnation of the West, the Beats skillfully employed the rhetoric of probation. With an apocalyptic certainty wielded most stridently in youth, each writer called the whole of American history into question and suggested that America's political and technological accomplishments were corruptions of its "authentic" spiritual identity. Resembling the Jeremiahs of the second- and third-generation Puritans as well as those of the postwar years, the Beats were committed to America's sacred past but critical of its secular present. An unwavering faith in the promise of America, a promise Ginsberg, Burroughs, and Kerouac would come to define somewhat differently, enabled each to apply and tweak Spengler's narrative of decline to the point that it became a guide to the nation's cultural redemption. The terms of salvation that each found in *Decline* were oddly similar to those offered by the Calvinist God of absence and wrath.

In *Decline*, Spengler built his entire thesis around the Protestant notions of predestination and providential history, intellectual columns supporting both the German theological tradition from Luther to Hegel and American cultural identity from the time of William Bradford and John Winthrop. Like all these men of faith, Spengler believed the movement of history was guided by spiritual principles. He rejected, however, Luther's (and the Puritans') Christian millennialism as well as Hegel's vision of human rationality marching triumphantly toward absolute truth. For Spengler, history was neither a process of God's will nor dialectical thought but one of life. All human communities follow the same organic pattern of birth, growth, decay, and death.[7] He described that process of decline as a movement from the "springtime of Culture" to the "winter of Civilization," giving pseudo-scientific justification to the Culture-Civilization opposition that German mandarins often employed. In Spengler's poetic description, "The Civilization is the inevitable destiny of the Culture. . . . Civilizations are the most external and artificial states of which a species of developed humanity is capable. They are a conclusion, the thing become succeeding the thing-becoming, death following life, rigidity following expansion, intellectual age and the stone-built, petrifying world city following mother-earth. . . . They are an end, irrevocable, yet by inward necessity reached again and again."[8] All of history could thus be understood as a manifestation of this basic principle of entropy. History may be predestined, Spengler seemed to say, but the divine law of life could be inferred from the historical record available to all.

Spengler analyzed the life-cycles, or seasons, of the cultures he saw as paradigmatic examples of his metahistorical thesis: Greek, Roman, Indian, Arabian, and Mayan. But it was contemporary European civilization and its ideological expressions that drew most of his attention. Before the "last spiritual crisis that will involve all Europe and America," Spengler wrote, "'The Decline of the West' comprises nothing less than the problem of *Civilization.*" Such an understanding derived from his belief that the West, like all previous world civilizations, had reached the final stages of its life-cycle.[9] The world was always moving inevitably toward apocalypse. Consequently, Spengler's work contained an implicit message of hope, specifically that once the present crisis had passed, a new Culture would appear. In other words, the promise of new beginnings could be realized only after the decline of the West.

By way of Spengler, the Beats looked to both the American past and present for clues to their own spiritual predicament. They found existential comfort in Spengler's explication of universal laws that determined not only the ways of humanity but also the cycles of history and the intricate workings of the cosmos. The magical appeal of Spengler's argument lay in his conclusion that the most vexing questions about the human and the divine could be derived from historiography.

Under Spengler's influence, the Beats' literary pronouncements cast a shadow of judgment upon their fellow Americans even as the Beats' attitude betrayed an underlying hope. In retaining the jeremiadic formula and its internal tensions and ambiguities, Ginsberg, Burroughs, and Kerouac remained stereotypically American—paradoxical and mysterious yet predictable in their choices of material and tools used to construct their world and live within it. The mythic realm they engaged and drew upon was popularly referred to as the "American way of life," a set of beliefs and practices based on the soaring postwar economy as it produced a level of material abundance and patriotism unequaled in American history.

It was an "exceptional" time. Millions of citizens acquired new homes in the suburbs, purchased new cars, and spent freely on leisure activities. Everything, it seemed, was getting bigger, brighter, and faster and was full of wonder and expectation. The rising tide of confidence generated by the materials of the everyday—transistor radios, Frigidaires, and air-conditioning—soon overflowed into the less tangible world of religious faith. The symbols and metaphors the Beats extracted from Spengler's narrative of decline were consistent with this rhetoric of redemption and renewal. Indeed, they read *Decline* in light of typically American concerns: individualism, democracy, and a pastoral vision of self and country set apart from the corrupting influences of the European aristocracy. But even as they read Spengler in terms of America, they read America in terms of Spengler. By doing so they generated a radically different version of American exceptionalism from that espoused by presidents and pundits alike.

The Beats' group unity was premised on a shared Spenglerian opposition to both the established institutions of American society and the cultural conditions those institutions legitimized and enforced.[10] The Beats undermined the most common justifications for America's exceptional status. They replaced the material discourses of technological gadgetry, corporate liberalism, and nuclear proliferation with Spengler's emphases on the capacity of the human body, individual refinement, and the ways of the "Cultural" soul. The two languages, one of capital and one of spirit, were incompatible if not entirely contrary ways of describing the world, yet they did share one fundamental assumption. Neither espoused a "new" era so much as a continuation of an exceptionalist past. America was created differently and was historically privileged by its essential uniqueness. Consequently, the perspective from which the Beats should be evaluated is from within the myth of American exceptionalism. Their aversion to dominant markers of postwar American might was not outright rejection of the American way of life but a reconfiguration of its content.

In general terms, Ginsberg, Burroughs, and Kerouac were no different from the majority of postwar Americans in their attempt to come to grips with the horrors of war, the rapidly expanding economy, and the deceptively volatile cultural moment. The America that the Beats made together in the 1940s was not entirely derivative nor was it completely new. In certain ways it may have resembled the Main Street and Wall Street versions of America referred to in congressional caucuses and corporate boardrooms and dreamed up by Hollywood producers and hometown preachers. The Beats' America bore the stamp of their personalities as well as Spengler's. Indeed, the Prussian historian and philosopher became a spectral participant in their inner circle, and they internalized his categories to such an extent that they became unspoken assumptions—ideological seams binding them together in common cause.

Appropriating Spengler's framework involved interactions among psychological dispositions, personal choices, and cultural forces. That process was neither immediate nor static, for the Beats' reading of Spengler continued to evolve well into the late 1950s and moves from negation to affirmation. As the Beats borrowed from Spengler's reservoir of symbols and metaphors, they made them their own by finding a religious interpretation and explanation of their nation in his oracular style and mystical phrasing. Despite differences among them, each Beat approached America, via Spenglerian allegory, as a religious state of being, a mode of civic identity, a moral stance, and an idealistic faith in a utopian form of nationhood.

The burden of this chapter is to begin the recovery of Spengler's influence by putting the Beats' reading of his work into a larger context of postwar history, middle-class religious trends, and popular culture. The chapter concludes with a discussion of Kerouac's first published novel, *The Town and the City*, with an eye toward its Spenglerian subtext. In the final analysis, the Spenglerian ground that each man shared continued to generate insights, even as their individual styles diverged and their work became separate bands in the spectrum of the postwar avant-garde.

Oswald Spengler: Provocateur

Before turning to the Beats' appropriation and application of Spengler's ideas, it is important to understand what Spengler said and the impetus behind his intellectual creativity. His philosophy, forged in pre–World War I Germany, was an index of that volatile period and a response to the undulating waves of German nationalism. On the eve of World War I, Spengler intended *The Decline of the West* to be a much-needed rallying cry for other Germans. After completing the first draft in 1914, he continued to envision his work as part of the war effort, galvanizing the will and rallying the spirit of the German *volk*. He echoed the sentiments of cultural elitists going back to the eighteenth-century poet and philosopher Johann Gottfried von Herder (1744–1803), who asserted that each national group was unique in its customs, mores, virtues, arts, psyche, and worldview. Herder had popularized the notion of the "volk," a people unified not by political contracts or even a shared culture but the mystical bonds of blood. Integrating philosophical idealism and a rabid form of patriotism, *volkisch* thought was a constant presence in nineteenth-century Germany, from the political tracts of Johann Gottlieb Fichte and the music of Richard Wagner through the establishment of the German youth movement in 1896. The latter's recruitment campaigns were part of a neo-romantic revolt against the rising tide of modern industry. Their rhetoric of antimodernism appealed to those alienated members of the middle-class who were suspicious of Western democracy, feared the strictures of socialism, and yet harbored desires for a simple life of rural virtue.[11]

As the war turned decidedly against Germany, Spengler, like many other Germans, became even more enamored by the neo-romantic vision of his country united against Western oppressors. When *Form and Actuality,* the first volume of *Decline,* was finally published in April 1918, it reflected a mix of despair and renewed commitment to romantic nationalism. Spengler had tempered the triumphalism of the first draft, and consequently his work had taken on a more ambiguous tone. Despite the apparent absence of any grinding political axe, *Form and Actuality* was tremendously popular and went through forty-seven different editions in four years. Many Germans of a conservative bent welcomed the work as the master script of their nation's phoenixlike rise from the ashes of decadent Europe. Spengler later became a leading spokesperson in the revival of volkisch thought, a conservative movement that gained momentum in 1919 as middle-class Germans reacted against the Treaty of Versailles, economic reforms, and the democratic ethos of the Weimar Republic. The resentment still harbored against European and American enemies led many to translate military conflict into the language of metaphysical struggle—us versus them, or the inner, spiritual freedom of the German people versus the external freedom that Western liberalism offered. Spengler, it seemed, had provided the blueprint for Germany's victory in an on-going conflict.[12]

As the charge of Spengler's work spread through German academic and political channels, it catalyzed a number of reactions, both sympathetic and critical. Among a certain conservative elite, the book was understood as a full historical articulation of their culture's current predicament. The Spengler embraced by a younger generation of intellectuals such as Hans Freyer, Thomas Mann, and Ludwig Wittgenstein reinforced the popular notion that Western civilization was on the verge of total collapse but implied that Germany would emerge triumphant from this crisis. Others, both conservative and liberal, condemned Spengler's work as dubious, arbitrary, and unproven. Even those dedicated to volkisch extremism, such as the racialist Houston Stewart Chamberlain and the conservative revolutionary Arthur Moeller-Bruck, denounced Spengler's work as overly defeatist and derivative of the pessimism that had come to dominate the aesthetic and philosophical circles of Europe. Spengler became something of a cause célèbre, a fashionable prophet of either Germany's national resurgence or nihilism, often depending more on personality than one's political sympathies.[13]

Perspectives of World-History, the second volume of *Decline,* appeared in

May 1922 and was more overtly political than *Form and Actuality*. In it Spengler attacked the Weimar Republic directly and promoted a program of national socialism over and against what he perceived as a bankrupt form of commercial-minded, bourgeois liberalism.[14] Some previous admirers were put off by Spengler's incendiary politics; Mann later referred to him as "Nietzsche's clever ape."[15] Others also detected nihilism as the driving force behind Spengler, who self-consciously inherited the intellectual mantle of Friedrich Nietzsche and believed his program to be the real-world manifestation of the will to power. In light of a perceived feminization of culture by bourgeois morality, as well as increasing insecurity among intellectuals no longer supported by the state, Spengler insisted, "We do not need ideologues anymore, we need hardness, we need fearless skepticism, we need a class of socialist master men."[16]

Spengler did not heed his own command, for throughout the 1920s and early 1930s he continued to critique the democratizing changes instituted by the Weimar Republic. Remaining an ideologue, he struggled to make sense of dramatic increases in social instability and political ferment. Despite his own political impotency, Spengler had combined social critiques with a specific outline for the future, providing in the process a religious explanation for the increasingly dismal state of affairs within Germany. Writing in 1930, Walter Benjamin sensed the tragic implications of such etheral justifications. He condemned those, like Spengler, who "continued to celebrate the cult of war when there was no longer any enemy." As Benjamin's words attest, *Decline* became for many Germans a cultural theodicy.[17]

In addition to being politically motivated, Spengler's metahistory was also the product of theological contemplation. Amid a backdrop of intense theological activity in Germany, Spengler believed his to be *"the* philosophy of the future," one that revealed the meaning in history and the meaning of history.[18] In order to answer such profound questions, Spengler relied on a mystical vision that permitted him to see the contours of process in history. His chosen method of inquiry reflected the religious fashions within conservative ranks. Many of those attracted to volkisch thought held up the medieval German mystics Meister Eckhart and Heinrich Suso as exemplary models of Germanic religion—valorizations intended to oppose the faddish rediscoveries of eastern mysticism by the likes of Martin Buber and Rudolph Panwitz. This Germanic religion was also believed to trump the Judeo-Christian scriptures, bypassing as Eckhart and Suso had done, the corrupt institutions of the West in order to connect with the "God above God."[19]

Drawing from Eckhart as well as Hegel's idea that understanding the past enables self-understanding, Spengler believed the key to comprehension lies in an ability to merge with the oneness of infinite reality in the midst of change—"to see world-history as a picture of endless formations and transformations."[20] As one critic perceptively noted, Spengler "learned to view history as a shadow-play of appearances in which the tangible world of events and ideas could do no more than suggest, in fragmentary and partial form, the eternal spiritual architecture of the universe."[21] This mystical orientation was of the romantic variety. Working with the Nietzchean distinction between Dionysian and Apollinian existence, Spengler set aside reason and experiment in favor of "feeling, intuition, imaginative insight, and above all, symbolism." Despite the encompassing scope of *Decline*, however, he was no systematizer. "Men of theory," he disparagingly wrote, "commit a huge mistake in believing that their place is at the head and not in the train of great events."[22]

Because Spengler believed that all cultures were spiritual formations, he compared them in terms of ideal types and symbolic meanings rather than adhering strictly to empirical data. In other words, he strolled through the historical record as he would a museum. He insisted that intuiting organizational principles rather than reading the brochures would result in a more natural, and therefore more accurate, appraisal of the past. Spengler's "morphology of history" involved, quite literally, the study of cultural expressions, his perception of interrelationships that bound these expressions together, and the elucidation of the underlying unity that governed all cultures. The inspirations for Spengler's organic metaphor were the scientific theories of Johann Wolfgang von Goethe and his method of contemplating natural phenomena in their entirety. Assuming Goethe's position that dissection for dissection's sake obscured rather than illuminated objects, Spengler identified the unifying principle of each culture under study. He termed this essential quality the "prime symbol."[23] Accordingly, all the expressions and forms of a culture were branches of this prime symbol and were bound together in a wholly natural relationship. Spengler believed that by identifying this unifying principle he could foresee historical change in the West as derivative of that essential characteristic. Through a mystical engagement with history, he positioned himself as both a prophet and a proselytizer, foretelling the future in order to enlighten the masses.

Spengler did not differentiate between European and American nation states because they existed as extensions of the same prime symbol of the West. On the opening pages of *Form and Actuality*, he boldly declared, "In this book is attempted for the first time the venture of predetermining history, of following the still unraveled stages in the Destiny of a Culture, and specifically the only Culture of our time and our planet which is actually in the phase of fulfillment—the West-European-American."[24] He used the word

Faustian as a descriptive name for the symbolic unity of European-American civilization, in reference to the limitless ambition and destructive will to power of Goethe's Faust. Modern democratic, industrial society was a direct extension of the spirit that had produced Gothic cathedrals, the Protestant quest for salvific certainty, the imperialist character of European monarchies, and the Enlightenment emphases on individual rights and social contracts. "The Faustian instinct," Spengler wrote, "active, strong-willed, as vertical in tendency as its own Gothic cathedrals, as upstanding as its own 'ego habeo factum', looking into distance and Future, demands toleration—*that is, room, space*—for its proper activity, but only for that."[25] Consequently, all of the West—its religion, language, philosophies, mathematics, architecture, art forms, and even the craftsmanship and choice of building material—was no longer capable of real achievement, only an endless recycling of itself unto death.

In Goethe's retelling of the Faust myth, inspired in part by his meeting in 1770 with Herder, Faust is depicted as a professional scientist who has become bored with book learning. He is plagued by restlessness of spirit and yearns for the capacity to "extend myself to embrace all human selves."[26] Spengler interpreted Faust's search for experience, even at the expense of his mortal soul, as presaging "the whole future of Western Europe." According to Spengler, Faust, like the West, continued to strive beyond his present spiritual possessions despite the fact there was nothing left to possess. Spengler described the soul of the West as "an Ego lost in Infinity, an Ego that was all force, but a force negligibly weak in an infinity of greater forces, it was all will, but a will full of fear for its freedom."[27] Westerners, like Faust, had become imprisoned by their desire to achieve at any cost. According to Spengler, Faustian man "has become *the slave of his creation*. His number, and the arrangement of life as he lives it, have been driven by the machine on to a path where there is no standing still and no turning back. The peasant, the hand-worker, even the merchant, appear suddenly as inessential in comparison with the *three great figures that the Machine has bred and trained up in the cause of its development: the entrepreneur, the engineer, and the factory worker.*"[28]

Relying on a series of analogies, Spengler pictured the whole of Faustian existence—from capitalism to scientific inquiry and industry—as representing the basic tendency to reach out into pure, limitless space. Trapped within a mechanistic worldview where both science and philosophy were equally abstract and equally divorced from practical human concerns, communal relations in the West were no longer natural tendency but only political necessity. According to Spengler, the possessive individualism at the heart of the West had begun to turn against itself, and with tragic consequences.

Because literary flourish took precedent over coherent organization or even internal consistency, Spengler's sweeping argument was subject to various and competing interpretations. In Europe, such interpretive imbroglios were common among intellectuals debating the future of their continent and searching for a collective theodicy after the horrors of World War I. Provocation continued to follow provocation, even as Spengler's ideas made their way across the Atlantic to American political and literary circles. As it had in Europe, his work became a kind of Rosetta stone, a means of interpreting America's future in the context of world history. Although the guilt and responsibility that Europeans felt were inescapable realities, America's infrastructure had remained relatively unaffected by the war. Consequently, Spengler's argument resonated in America more on the ideological level, readily abstracted and open to interpretations not possible given the intellectual pessimism of Europe.

Charles Francis Atkison's English translations of both volumes of *The Decline of the West* (1926, 1928) did not receive much academic fanfare yet "admirably fitted the prevailing temper of a rather callow skepticism" of Americans.[29] Spengler's ideas circulated widely among American writers after World War I, becoming, in the words of Alfred Kazin, a reliable source of "aristocratic pessimism."[30] Even before their English translation, Spengler's ideas had been taken seriously in literary circles, particularly by modernist writers such as T. S. Eliot, Ezra Pound, and William Butler Yeats. Eliot's *The Waste Land* (1922) was replete with Spenglerian imagery, as was Yeats's "The Second Coming" (1921). Pound, who once called Western civilization "an old bitch gone in the teeth," was a dedicated student of Spengler's work, as was Joseph Campbell, who in 1932 wrote that "Spengler has become my major prophet."[31]

Even after the initial buzz surrounding the English translations of *Decline* subsided, modest sales continued throughout the 1930s. In the 1940s *Decline* enjoyed a brief critical revival in American historical circles, in part because of the publication and popularity of Arnold Toynbee's *A Study of History* (ten volumes by 1954) as well as such works as *Time and Western Man* (1927), Wyndham Lewis's critique of Spengler.

Notwithstanding the contextual divide, Americans greeted Spengler's work with both animus and enthusiasm. When Burroughs, Kerouac, and Ginsberg began their readings of *Decline* in the early 1940s they were not alone, nor were they even the first who found in Spengler a meaningful future for America in the tragedies and exploits of its history. On American soil, *Decline* often functioned as a crystal ball, mirroring the hopes and desires of those who looked upon it even as it justified and exacerbated their anxiety.

As Spengler's words filtered through America's Protestant unconscious, they began to resemble the vocabularies of Manifest Destiny, apocalypticism, prophetic history, and pastoral retreat. Regardless of who was reading, Spengler's harsh, dogmatic language did not waver; what was certain was that history would do exactly as he predicted.[32] Such confidence shone through Atkison's translation and was noticed by a number of Americans looking for a source of strength by which to achieve power in the world as well as over it. As was the case in Germany, provocation continued to follow provocation.

Confidence Men and American Jeremiahs

Before visiting the Beats' interpretation of Spengler, it is important to sketch the immediate cultural context in which their reading took place, the forces both visible and invisible that influenced how, why, and to what purpose the young writers read *Decline*. Although a new era may have been dawning in post–World War II America, the quality of that newness is elusive but palpable, even to contemporary observers. Economic and demographic numbers aside, the period was one of cultural transition from the muggy days of radio to the air-conditioned ones of television and from a world one could imagine making safe for democracy to one threatened by the turn of a key. On one hand, things felt and meant differently even as they sometimes looked the same. On the other hand, things could feel and mean the same despite changes in appearance. Such were the contradictions that permeated the idea of the American Century. And such were the conditions that generated the need for, and instability of, that peculiar existential currency, confidence.

In the 1940s, the idea of "America," as it had been throughout the twentieth century, was under radical reconstruction. At the beginning of the decade, the memory of the Great Depression and debates over New Deal reforms as well as isolationism were quickly eclipsed by graphic images of Pearl Harbor. Even after the Allied victory in 1945, cries for national unity continued unabated. In 1946 Republicans became the majority in both the Congress and the Senate. Anticommunism was on the rise, and a backlash against New Deal policies was gaining momentum. The centripetalism continued not out of a siege mentality but stemmed from Americans' desire to reenvision themselves as an emerging geopolitical superpower and the embodiment of everything that Europe and Russia were not. Although the ideological struggle occurred on the level of symbols and rhetoric, its consequences on the psychological and cultural levels were quite real.

The cold war began quietly with George Kennan's 1946 "long telegram" from Moscow about the ominous and inevitable expansion of the Soviet

Union into Eastern Europe. Policy recommendations of containment turned quickly into warnings of American vulnerability, warnings often bordering on paranoia. In 1947, two years before he became secretary of state, U.S. State Department official Dean Acheson warned Americans that they "must be on permanent alert" against the Russians.[33] That same year, the Central Intelligence Agency (CIA) was established, in part to protect America against the machinations of communists.

The tendency to demonize the Soviet Union and its state ideology quickly gained rhetorical momentum. As confidence games in the geopolitical sphere intensified, ordinary Americans participated in this peculiar national pastime of self-posturing and self-invention. Many Americans gained self-assurance through a form of identity inflation at the expense of the "other." From the most zealous of anticommunists to apolitical, suburban newlyweds, they were constructing identities for both self and country—often over and against an imagined foe, whether communists, homosexuals, juvenile delinquents, or even invaders from outer space. The American social body, it seemed, was under attack by contaminating forces. In order to alleviate that threat of corruption, Americans used the religious language of myth and symbol to forge personal religious worlds at a time when the stability and safety that such worlds promised were in high demand. As cold war anxieties became palpable and the stakes were raised, both foreign policies and domestic theodicies were on the table.

Amid contests and negotiations over the meaning of America, the Beats were not the only voices to confront the fatalistic legacy of Spengler or to distill through decontextualization his relevance. Some perceived Spengler as a foreign threat to American ideas of democracy and justice. In 1929 James T. Shotwell denounced Spengler as a European crank who had failed to recognize the utopian promise of science and technology for America's future.[34] Shotwell and other like-minded critics delimited their triumphalist politics precisely through opposition to the more fatalistic aspects of Spengler's thesis. Despite barbed denouncements, their reaction against Spengler was part of their understanding and continued invention of the American tradition. From an altogether different perspective, in the 1920s American communists such as Joseph Freeman interpreted Spengler's prophecy to mean that a great new civilization, following the example of Russia, would take the place of the bourgeois world of American capitalism.[35] Even for communist sympathizers, the promise of America was not to be denied.

What bound together most Americans who encountered Spengler, regardless of ideological persuasion, was an eagerness to enlist him in their own causes. In "American Communiqué" (1940), Edwin Franden Dakin defended and reinforced the nation's preeminence by extending "the Spengler point of view to a consideration of some of the problems immediately with us." These "problems" included concerns over how to reinvigorate the Ford and Chrysler corporations, how to better integrate "our great entrepreneurs . . . with the state," and how to relieve anxiety over Roosevelt's New Deal. In declaring that "America could doubtless endure indefinitely, if the Spengler readings are correct," Dakin confidently assured readers that America would continue to be led by "strong men in quite the same tradition" of America, who manipulated "Congress, the courts, the organs of publicity and opinion." Dakin's tone reflected the historical context in which consensus and celebration took precedence over critical dissension. He ignored the most critical and dire of Spengler's predictions, confidently stating, "With an eye to that future, it is possible to say that *The Decline of the West* could as well be called *On Our Way to World Empire and Peace.*"[36]

As the Beats read Spengler in the 1940s, the metanarratives of containment and the cold war provided a context in which popular religious interest merged with more overt economic and political concerns. On the level of public religion, the evangelical rhetoric of Henry Luce's *The American Century* (1941) had already reconfigured the myth of American exceptionalism on the geopolitical scale. Throughout the 1940s the *Time-Life* media mogul called upon Americans to renounce isolationism and "exert upon the world the full impact of our influence, for such purposes as we see fit and by such means as we see fit."[37]

In contrast to Dakin's enthusiastic appropriation of Spengler, Luce rejected Spengler's ideas altogether, ridiculing "European philosophers who prophesy the final collapse of Western Civilization." In a 1946 address to the graduating class of Duke Divinity School, Luce denounced anyone who voiced such "irresponsible pessimism" and flatly declared that "there is no compelling reason for being pessimistic about America." Ironically, Luce countered Spengler's neo-romanticism with a form of home-grown empiricism, arguing that hard evidence of America's decline was scant indeed. Under an empirical guise Luce detailed the "triumphs and achievements" of the United States as evidence of its geopolitical as well as its moral superiority.[38] In the mid–1940s the latter claim was carried out with much zeal (and funding) by foreign missions sponsored by the National Association of Evangelicals. Fundamentalist religious leaders such as Harold Ockenga told followers that "the evangelization of the world" would follow a "revival in America" of that old-time religion, which, incidentally, had come to resemble the foreign policy dictates of the nation.[39]

In spite of attempts, both political and overtly religious, to shore up the rough-hewn edges of the American Century, unabashed boosterism did not wholly reflect the cultural mood. On the contrary, the struggles Luce and others looked forward to with such bravado—the same conditions they understood as political, economic, and religious opportunities—others approached with a sense of unease. The deathly echoes of Hiroshima and Nagasaki as well as those of Auschwitz still reverberated. No matter how much America seemed to move forward economically, memories of human depravity and destructiveness were not easily forgotten. Fear, doubt, and dissatisfaction were not entirely extinguished, despite unprecedented abundance and a new emphasis on leisure. Even Luce once charged Americans with lacking an adequate amount of "moral capital" to ensure the continuing success of the American Century and called on them to renew the national "relevance" of Christian doctrine.[40] In the domestic sphere, the American way of life had become the antithesis of godless communism.

Such rhetoric of fear and probation was squarely within America's jeremiadic tradition. As politics overlapped with the public discourse of religion at the beginning of the cold war, these jeremiads emphasized military defense and heightened suspicion as means to cultural renewal. Ironically, the postwar "turn to religion" and reveille in the name of democracy and capitalism were premised on, and intensified by, an overwhelming perception of danger, both within the nation's borders and without. In addition to the House Un-American Activities Committee (HUAC), federally regulated programs such as the National Intelligence Authority (NIA) and the National Security Agency (NSA) espoused military might and bureaucratic corporatism as the way to ensure the country's supremacy on a geopolitical scale. These agencies, however, often undermined Americans' sense of security. In 1948, well before the McCarthy hearings, Attorney General Tom Clark declared that "those who do not believe in the ideology of the United States shall not be allowed to stay in the United States."[41] Attempting to reaffirm the Smith Act of 1940 outlawing any conspiracy to overthrow the U.S. government, Clark's message seemed an ominous parody of frontier justice. Such speeches reflected deep uncertainty in the political sphere and no doubt contributed to it on the domestic front.

Cold war debates over public security soon begot domestic paranoia. By the late 1940s, civil defense strategists were urging American women to prepare their households for nuclear fallout. School children were taught to huddle beneath their desks in case of nuclear attack, shield their eyes from the radioactive glare, and place their hands around their heads in order to keep their skulls intact. Backyard bomb shelters began to appear with increased regularity. By 1952, New York City had distributed, free of charge,

2,500,000 dogtags for postatomic, postmortem identification purposes.[42] The American Dream, it seemed, had come at a price. In order to relieve daily pressures, many Americans began to act out their resentment and moral uncertainty by any means necessary. In moments as diverse as the protests surrounding the executions of Julius and Ethel Rosenberg, the 1954 *Brown v. Board of Education of Topeka, Kansas* Supreme Court decision, or simply an ironic reading of a *Father Knows Best* episode, America became a vehicle of expression, a coded language through which people voiced not only their gravest fears over the loss of security but also their most utopian of desires about the future.

Just as public optimism was decidedly ambiguous, so, too, were the undercurrents of unease. Couched in terms of antimodernism, dispensational premillennialism, and the corruption of cultural tradition, the mythic reservoir of American exceptionalism lay beneath expressions of pessimism and doubt. Critiques of America's present inadequacy were inverted expressions of hope and belief in its millennial promise. From almost any perspective, it seemed, America embodied a progressive view of history. As both moral critiques and jingoistic reverie abounded, most often they occurred together, one hidden beneath the rhetorical surface of the other. In both cases, however, whether the rhetoric be triumphant or judgmental, America was the focal point where religious belief and cultural anxiety converged upon the myth of exceptionalism. Such were the contradictions of the American Century.

After the war, the exceptionalist myth had become a continually recycled advertisement for American selfhood. Rooted in Puritan belief that they were a covenanted people carrying out God's will on an "errand into the wilderness," this foundation of American cultural identity is structured upon the idea of an elect nation with a special religious privilege and set apart from the rest of the world. Historical examples include John Winthrop's promise of a "Citty upon a Hill"; the Deism of the Founders, who believed America would embody the Enlightenment ideals of the social contract; nineteenth-century Manifest Destiny and westward expansion; and the romantic era's belief (most vividly expressed by Walt Whitman) that the common person's intuition of an ideal life was uniquely American. This sense of a sacred mission, along with laments that it would go unfulfilled, have been recurring themes within American history.

Regardless of the period, American Jeremiahs often brought the exceptionalist myth into clearer focus, illuminating the tensions and contradictions of their America through the symbolic economy of religion. Some critiques were self-consciously prophetic after the war, predicting the end time as either divine judgment of America's sins or the beginning of heaven on earth.

Others were more academic and less sensational but nevertheless called for the renewal of American society by condemning it. Within this climate of uncertainty and ambivalence, the America being critically engaged was often a matter of perspective. Similarly, apocalyptic revelation was largely a function of what one sought and where one stood while conducting the search. The Beats employed a Spenglerian template for describing the present crisis and, like other American Jeremiahs, adopted a particularly American political template for redressing the situation. Participating in the jeremiadic culture of the postwar years, they did not so much secularize the sacred as sacralize the secular, turning postwar existence into a drama of ultimate consequences. A concert of jeremiads filled the public sphere, each resembling the other but speaking of and to a different America.

⌐⌐

Reflecting the public atmosphere of consensus and the private desires to conform, many jeremiads bore a close resemblance to conservative propaganda, political as well as religious. Nowhere was this more in evidence than in the fundamentalist revival of the 1940s and 1950s. Its message of premillennial dispensationalism was eagerly embraced by those who found spiritual comfort in getting the inside scoop on Armageddon. In his 1949 Los Angeles crusade, evangelist Billy Graham, whose national career was being partly funded by Luce as well as William Randolph Hearst, summarized this politicized faith. "If you would be a true patriot," Graham pleaded, "then become a Christian. If you would be a loyal American, then become a loyal Christian." Speaking from a platform wired for sound, he called for the restoration of "the Ten Commandments as the basis for our moral code" and threatened his audience, via God's wrath, with technological hellfire and brimstone: "Do you know the area that is marked out for the enemy's first atomic bomb?" Graham responded with a list that could have passed as an itinerary of Kerouac's journeys the previous summer. "New York! Secondly Chicago! And thirdly, the city of Los Angeles." Graham's fervor gave his conservative politics an eschatological weight: "There is no alternative. . . . The world is divided into two camps! On the one side we see Communism . . . [which] has declared war against God, against Christ, against the Bible, and against all religion! . . . Unless the Western world has an old-fashioned revival, we cannot last!"[43]

As was the case in most critical assessments of postwar America, underlying the rhetoric of apocalyptic condemnation was a fervent belief in the exceptional status of America in relation to Europe. According to Graham, who soon became known as "the machine gun of God," a new Reformation was underway, this time against the entire continent. Preaching to more than three hundred thousand potential converts during the seven-week crusade, Graham claimed, "I have been in Europe six times since the war and have seen devastated cities of Germany and the wreckage of war. I believe the only reason that America escaped the ravages and destruction of war was because God's people prayed. Many of these people believe that God can still use America to evangelize the world."[44] As in John Winthrop's "A Modell of Christian Charity," Graham viewed America as the sole and guiding light of Christendom in a sea of European decadence. But he continued to betray the schizophrenia at the heart of the jeremiadic message. Only a year later he predicted that "America has only three or four more years at the most and then it will be over and we will fall as Rome fell and Germany fell."[45]

In Catholic circles the closest equivalent to Graham's brand of revivalism was Msgr. Fulton J. Sheen, a media celebrity in his own right. Sheen, also a confidant of Luce, integrated militant anticommunism and the teachings of traditional Catholicism to forge a doctrinally lax yet strident message of religious nationalism. His popularity reflected a desire on the part of American Catholics to prove their patriotism and forge an identity outside the shadow of the Vatican. In addition to numerous books, Bishop Sheen's television program *Life Is Worth Living* first aired in 1952 and attracted more than twenty million viewers on 123 stations despite competing against Milton Berle and Frank Sinatra for ratings.[46] His vociferous critique of communism was less an allegiance to American capitalism than it was a rejection of the materialism and atheism central to Marxist doctrine. Although an articulate spokesperson for the Roman Catholic Church, Sheen appealed to a wide audience looking for spiritual guidance in an entertaining presentation of moral rectitude. Percolating beneath the media niceties, however, was a scathing critique of what he believed to be the moral bankruptcy of European philosophy. His critical disdain for Europe and its intellectual heritage resembled the Beats' reading of Spengler in both content and, surprisingly, metaphor. Sheen called for his own *Naked Lunch*—dismantling all ties between America and the alienating doctrines of Western philosophy. In this vein of cultural cleansing, he believed that Americans "want to be whole again. They are sick of being thrown into a Darwinian pot to boil as a beast, or into a Freudian stew to squirm as a libido, or thrust into the Marxian sandwich."[47]

Following World War II, middle-class Americans of Protestant, Catholic, and Jewish persuasions took comfort in their country's religious heritage. Indeed, it was a time of ecumenical uplift, and religion became a marker of American identity and social position. Others, however, particularly those associated with "New York Intellectuals," drew strength from critical analysis of this convergence of religion and patriotism. Disillusioned by the recent tragedies in Europe and committed to an anti-Stalinist, democratic socialist position, critics such as Lionel Trilling and, later, Daniel Bell were more than willing to inaugurate a post-ideological, post-religious age. Even Americans' attendance of church services in record numbers was seen as a betrayal of their country's sacred mission. The spring 1950 issue of *Partisan Review* was the most venomous critical discussion of this revival. Sidney Hook, John Dewey, Dwight MacDonald, and Irving Howe viewed the increased interest in both personal sin and "a power beyond ourselves" as a reaction against New Deal pragmatic liberalism. For these self-described "positivists," "naturalists," and "secular radicals," the new revival and abandonment of New Deal reforms and the tenets of social science represented "a failure of nerve."[48]

Summarizing the ambiguity of America's increasingly religious character was Will Herberg's *Protestant, Catholic, Jew* (1955). Despite Herberg's praise for ecumenicism, he condemned the American Dream of conspicuous consumption as lacking religious depth.[49] Arguing that the homogenization of religion had resulted in moral retreat and social complacency, Herberg wrote, "It is only too evident that the religious characteristic of America today is very often a religiousness without religion, a religiousness with almost any kind of content or none, a way of sociability or 'belonging' rather than a way of reorienting life to God." Speaking to the transformation of America's Judeo-Christian heritage, Herberg discerned a culture and "a religiousness without serious commitment, without real conviction, without genuine existential decision."[50] But even as Herberg condemned, he admired the unifying force of America's "faith in faith," placing in capital letters the new value system: American Way of Life. Although Herberg leveled trenchant criticism upon America's religious mettle, he still found reason to believe that the nation could overcome its present problems through shear force of character.

Similar in scope to Herberg's back-handed affirmation of American exceptionalism was David Riesman's cold war defense of autonomous individualism in *The Lonely Crowd* (1950). He, too, echoed the dominant myth of exceptionalism by arguing that Americans were the most developed of a new sort of people living in a new kind of society. Amid such progress, however, there still existed crisis on the individual level. Riesman's thesis had much in common with other radical critiques of American prosperity—from Marxian sociologists such as C. Wright Mills to evangelical pundits such as Graham—in its assertion that modern life was characterized by profound psychological hardship. Riesman, however, located the causes of the crisis not in the "workings of capitalist progress" or in moral failing but in the malady of "other-directedness." In a damning assessment of American cultural conformity, Riesman posited that "other-directed" persons responded neither to tradition nor to an internal set of values, but rather they internalized the actions and beliefs of the culture around them.[51]

For Marxist critics such as Mills, Herbert Marcuse, and Eric Fromm, "the uneasiness of our time" was not a problem of being conscious but of having become falsely conscious. Such assessments betrayed heightened suspicion of the totalitarian features of American mass culture. For example, the maverick sociologist Mills dwelled on the anomie caused by the "synthetic molding" of a new mass society and the complicity of religion in this process. In *White Collar* (1951), he accused the new culture of leisure of creating widespread apathy and a climate void of meaning: "The uneasiness of our time, is due to this root fact: in our politics and economy, in family life and religion—in practically every shape of our existence—the certainties of the eighteenth and nineteenth centuries have disintegrated or been destroyed and, at the same time, no new sanctions or justifications for the new routines we live, and must live, have taken hold. So there is no acceptance and there is no rejection, no sweeping hope and no rebellion." Mills posited that traditional religious practice had been co-opted by "a new universe of management and manipulation."[52]

Both institutionalized religion and its popular counterpart had not only been rendered impotent as means of self-discovery and community strength but were also being used as tools of political manipulation. In the same year that Mills's polemic was published, Kerouac showed similar suspicions toward this marriage of politics and religious faith. In what later became *Visions of Cody,* he wrote of a priest quoting from the pulpit: "MacArthur Old Soldier crap—mixing theological verities with today's headlines, blah, blah, I now go out tired, into my own thoughts and have no place to go but find my own road."[53]

Other public voices echoed similar concerns from within the religious establishment. For example, the neo-orthodox theologian Reinhold Niebuhr located psychological restlessness and anomie in the conflict within consciousness. He was more than aware of humanity's penchant for self-destruction in an age where technology reigned supreme. As early as 1932, in *Moral Man and Immoral Society,* Niebuhr had lamented the difficulty in establishing "a rational social force by which society achieves its cohesion."[54] In *The Nature and Destiny of Man* (1941–43) his disillusionment increased as he attacked the doctrine of historical progress. He pointed out the utter sinfulness of human nature and consequently laid the foundation for his later critique of the myth of American exceptionalism. A sense of urgency ran through his calls for moral and intellectual humility. The crisis would subside only once Americans realized the tragic sense of life and confronted their inadequacies head-on. His message was more prophetic than evangelical in that it was suffused with both moral condemnation and an eschatological sense of hope.

Niebuhr, a trenchant observer of the disjunction between optimistic beliefs in progress and recent political and technological transformations, gave voice to a prevailing cultural mood. Scientific eruptions in the form of Einstein's theory of relativity and Heisenberg's "unsharpness principle" (the principle of uncertainty) rendered the comforting logic of direct causality and absolute knowablity inapplicable. The psychological implication of these scientific discoveries was troublesome to say the least. No longer was there certainty in the relationship between matter and energy, body and mind. No longer could one confidently assume a direct relationship between cause and effect. No longer could one assume a logical relationship between thought and expression. Furthermore, the unthinkable brutality of Nazism and Italian Fascism seemed to legitimate the psychological theories of Freud and Jung, which stated that one could not rely on natural logic to rule society because humans were inherently flawed, unable to determine right from wrong or act upon rational choices. Such atrocities and discoveries exposed the limitations of rational thought and cast suspicion on the consensus model of inevitable American progress.

The theological temper of the nation was changing as the Beats began to read Spengler in the fall of 1944. In the 1930s and 1940s American neo-orthodoxy began to take shape around a core group of ideas and a vast array of thinkers. The clerical advice of such figures as Reinhold Niebuhr, despite its tenor of social realism, continued to resemble a Puritan election day sermon in its paradoxical character. The neo-orthodox message was learned, full of perfunctory condemnations, but looked through the present state of sin in order to reclaim a glorious heritage for the future. In *The Irony of American History* (1952), Niebuhr reflected on the discrepancy between historical reality and politically imagined American exceptionalism.[55] Detecting a pervading sense of anxiety, he was one of the first critics to discuss the incongruity between the ideal of America's self-image and the reality of the contemporary moment.[56] Niebuhr rejected the providential theory of empire and held to the notion that humans, inheritors of original sin, could not follow scientific rationalism to its successful ends. He hoped to expose the moral pretensions and political shallowness of American exceptionalism by aggressively attacking the pride endemic to the nation's self-conscious exceptionalist status. In doing so, however, he did not escape the grasp of the exceptionalist myth. Niebuhr's call for Americans to differentiate themselves morally from Europe by assuming responsibility in world affairs only re-hearsed that myth in a new key.[57]

Sober assessments of conflict between rhetoric and reality in American neo-orthodox circles were rooted in the same ideological ground from which *Decline* originated. Although Spengler's ideas of cultural despair did not di-rectly influence religious intellectuals in the United States, the spirit of the European crisis spread through a number of other channels, particularly work emerging from the theological renaissance then stirring on the Conti-nent. As one historian has noted, during the neo-orthodox revival in the Unit-ed States, "God once again seemed to be speaking German." Protestant theo-logians such as George Merz and Friedrich Garten in Germany and Karl Barth and Emil Brunner in Switzerland began writing social criticism in the 1920s, a genre later known as the "theology of crisis." Similar to Spengler's manifesto in some of its basic assumptions, these writers were intensely con-cerned with repudiating liberalism's faith in progress and optimistic view of the Kingdom of God.[58] As was the case with Spengler, the sense of crisis was reimagined in more indigenous terms when their writings were disseminat-ed in America.

Although diverse in their diagnoses, Billy Graham, Will Herberg, David Riesman, C. Wright Mills, and Reinhold Niebuhr as well as *Partisan Review* intellectuals all advocated a return to tradition, often a traditional religiosi-ty, in order to relieve a perceived crisis, whether communist threat, social complacency, other-directedness, bureaucracy, moral laxity, or political ap-athy. The Beats were not deaf to these cries of anxiety or to the calls for cul-tural renewal that reverberated through the American public sphere. Like other symbolic constructions of America and the jeremiads that supported them, the Beats' Spenglerian rhetoric had much in common with postwar religious imagination. All of these critical assessments of America contained the same ambiguity inherent in the jeremiadic form, caught between the push of secular history and the pull of its sacred counterpart. Subsequently, even as the Beats rejected the capitalistic, scientific, and militaristic terms central to the postwar version of the exceptionalist myth, they recalibrated that myth using Spenglerian categories. Eschewing even the intellectual and theologi-cal critiques in the realist vein that most resembled their own, the Beats grounded religious analysis of a perceived social crisis and its potential res-olution in a Spenglerian discourse of spirit and the volkisch notion of cos-mic nationalism. Like other Americans, they strove to make sense of the world and their place within it by negotiating the symbols of religious nationalism presented to them. As the Beats read Spengler they were also reading Amer-ica, looking to him for insights into the contemporary scene and looking to

America in order to validate Spengler's pronouncements. Burroughs, Kerouac, and Ginsberg were journeying through the mythic terrain of America, making it new and creating a religious world in their wake.

Spenglerian Jeremiads

As the Beats began to read Spengler, Burroughs's interests were often either the focus or point of departure for intense debates and bull sessions. Even as they exchanged ideas and traded insights—Kerouac's vast knowledge of American and European literary history and Ginsberg's interest in working-class politics—Burroughs expanded their moral and intellectual horizons with his reservoir of arcane facts and experiences. Kerouac later described him as a "great teacher in the night."[59] Guided by Burroughs, the Beats also began to experiment with drugs as well as writing styles. They began to explore their sexuality and the criminality of the Times Square underworld. Under Burroughs's tutelage they became intimately familiar with Spengler as well as with a number of other texts that did not so much complement Spengler's vision but were nevertheless read in a complementary fashion.[60]

With his interest in science and medicine, Burroughs was a natural systematizer who encouraged Kerouac and Ginsberg to synthesize their daily insights into coherent worldviews. Even as he disabused them of their more domesticated habits, he revealed an urbane world guided by an altogether different logic. Kerouac recalled that Burroughs had introduced him to the "finkish world" with a "terrible intelligence and style." Burroughs was also responsible for Ginsberg's "sense of Spenglerian history and disrespect for all laws."[61]

Burroughs was born into an upper-class St. Louis family in 1914. Despite a biography and family history that at times seemed a direct overlap with an American history textbook, Burroughs took pride in cultivating his outsider persona. His family's wealth stemmed from his paternal grandfather, the inventor of the adding machine and founder of the Burroughs Adding Machine Company. Although the business ran into financial trouble during the depression, the family remained wealthy enough to afford Burroughs a monthly stipend of $200 throughout the 1940s and 1950s. From childhood, Burroughs yearned to escape the pedestrian lifestyle and confining morality of St. Louis. Increasingly marginalized because of homosexuality as well as his eccentric interests in guns and gangsters, he was sent to a military school in New Mexico. The Los Alamos Ranch School, founded by one of Theodore Roosevelt's Rough Riders, infused Burroughs with a frontier survivalist spirit. He matriculated to Harvard in 1933 and graduated in 1936 with a degree in

American literature. After graduation, he traveled through Eastern Europe, drifting in and out of the homosexual subcultures of Germany and Vienna. He briefly enrolled in medical school in Vienna and upon his return to the United States took psychology courses at Columbia University. By 1942 he was working as an exterminator in Chicago. It was a deliberate attempt to live outside his social class and familiarize himself with the workings of the criminal underworld. From Chicago, Burroughs made his way back to New York City and an apartment at 69 Bedford Street in Greenwich Village.[62]

Spengler's mix of Manichaeanism and esoteric prose seemed to fit Burroughs's eccentric personality and gave him a language by which to compare his experiences of the Midwest, the cityscapes of New York and Chicago, and the climate of pre–World War II Europe. On one level, *Decline* clearly delineated the faults and fault lines of Western civilization. On the other, it contained underneath its simplistic Dionysian/Apollinian oppositions an obscure and complex philosophical framework. Burroughs used Spengler's insights as a basis for syncretic philosophical musings and a justification for unorthodox, even criminal, behavior. Through a peculiar mix of occultism and science he was attempting to create the enchanted world denied him in youth—a world of explicable mysteries and mysterious explanations. Indeed, it was a magical universe in which unseen forces were at play, and deception and illusion became the sole methods of truth-telling. Reflecting the irony of inversion that characterizes much of Burroughs's work, even as a petty criminal he continued to dress impeccably in a three-piece suit. In doing so he was not merely rejecting his WASP heritage but subverting it from the inside out. Burroughs literally wore his Protestant heritage on his sleeve, putting it on display and transforming it into a fashion statement. By turning the Enlightenment mode of rationality against itself, he hoped to expose that it was not an absolute but rather a reflection of the last stages of the historical cycle of the Faustian West.

When Ginsberg entered Burroughs's orbit in 1944 and the Beat "libertine circle," he, too, perceived himself as being on the fringes of American life. Ginsberg's mother, Naomi, was a member of the American Communist Party. She was also a diagnosed schizophrenic who had drifted in and out of mental hospitals during his youth. Ginsberg's father, Louis, taught high school and, more important, gave his son a healthy respect for the poetic vocation through the example of his own verse writing. Although Judaism was not an integral component of Ginsberg's upbringing, the utopianism of leftist politics took the place of childhood faith. Marxism pointed to a world devoid of class struggle and promised solutions to the global fissures caused by the free market. Reflecting that politicized ecumenism, he wrote to the *New*

York Times in 1942, "We are, or should be, building a world in which all nations will live together in amicable cooperation."[63]

As Ginsberg became increasingly cognizant of, and ill at ease with, his homosexuality, his awkwardness translated into righteous impatience with the moral rectitude and intellectual assumptions of the status quo. In 1943, just months before he met Burroughs and Kerouac, Ginsberg entered Columbia University, intending to study law or labor economics. He drifted away from the legal path and soon became interested in literature under the tutelage of Lionel Trilling and Mark Van Doren. Ginsberg disagreed with many of their refined academic perspectives, particularly their dismissal of his literary hero Walt Whitman as a serious poet. His political interests combined with his academic discontent led him down the road of the artistic avantgarde. Like Whitman, he came to believe that art should serve a social purpose. "The concomitant potential of all art is communication," he wrote in his college journal. "Art may communicate morality by open espousal of cause, or by enriching quality of expression, whatever the thought, which satisfies the sensitive and happy few or the great masses."[64] Such youthful musings made Ginsberg receptive to Burroughs's eclectic pragmatism and Spenglerian judgments against the current intellectual climate.

By the time Kerouac met Ginsberg and Burroughs at the beginning of 1944, the all-American image he had cultivated on the football field and carried with him to Columbia in 1940 had become somewhat tarnished. Born in Lowell, Massachusetts, in 1922, Kerouac was raised in a Franco-American Catholic family. Unlike most Catholic families in Lowell, Kerouac's parents encouraged him to pursue a college education. A star football player, he attended Horace Mann Prep, an elite Ivy League feeder school, and was recruited by Columbia. After quitting the Columbia football team, and college altogether, in 1942, Kerouac continued his education on the street. Kerouac avoided the draft by joining the National Maritime Union, subsequently serving on the *S.S. Dorchester* and the *S.S. George Weems*. In 1943 he attended navy boot camp in Newport, Rhode Island, where he was soon discharged for possessing an "indifferent character." With plans to "write noble words," he became even more open to new experiences while commuting back and forth between New York City and his parents' house on Long Island. His love for jazz deepened as he attended the performances of Charlie Parker, Dizzy Gillespie, and Count Basie's Big Swing Machine, which featured Lester Young on the saxophone.[65]

As Kerouac became more familiar with the urban lifestyle of New York, his skepticism about the Catholic Church increased. His intense nostalgia for the ideals and perfection of the past ranged from the romantic longings of his youth to the reactionary conservatism of his later years. As Kerouac had written shortly before meeting Ginsberg and Burroughs, the beautiful particulars of existence "sustain and make for life—without them, a man may never know that life is truly worthwhile (divested from the time-worn shibboleths and metaphysics, those superficial attempts to rationalize our stay on earth.) . . . For this reason, I am going to try to make these sadly-written beliefs comprehensible to the world, in a series of art-works."[66] Imbued with an immigrant Catholicism, Kerouac would spend his entire adult life oscillating between the promise of universal acceptance and the alienation he experienced due, in part, to his ethnic status.

Kerouac's "antitriumphalist immigrant mysticism," as James Terrance Fisher has termed it, reflected the legacy of French Catholics who immigrated to New England between 1860 and 1920.[67] In search of work in the textile mills, they brought a siege mentality toward outside efforts to assimilate them. As Richard Sorrel has noted, the immigrants viewed religion in terms of community survival:

> [They] carried the concept of a providential mission with them from French Canada: past and future, heritage and destiny, were linked together by a divine union of nationalism and Catholicism. They were the pure Catholic nationality which would expand the kingdom of God and expose the false material values of Protestantism. Religion thus became a way of life rather than just a part of life, as Catholicism became increasingly associated with nationalism in Quebec, and with conservative and even reactionary theological and social views.[68]

Despite his fluctuating attitude toward the Catholic Church, Kerouac's ethnic religiosity and penchant for nostalgia instilled a life-long desire that his writing contain an American catholicity in the radical, original sense of the word. Reminiscent of the concept of the "volk," Kerouac's ethnic heritage provided him with a sense that the soul of a community was unique and intimately connected to its natural surroundings.

In response to his disillusionment with the Catholic faith, Kerouac embarked on a course of study that he hoped would lead to a universal form of knowledge.[69] His focus shifted from Catholic symbolism to the cultural symbolism of America, his goal being the discovery of religious meaning underneath the rhetoric of politics. In January 1943 Kerouac wrote of his admiration for the novelist Thomas Wolfe and Wolfe's discovery of an American essence: "No one in America, notwithstanding, has ever said as much as Wolfe said . . . Wolfe wrote about the essential and everlasting America, not the V-for-Victory America."[70] Kerouac continually struggled with his own religious questions and looked for answers everywhere, from the public library to the street. In meeting Ginsberg and Burroughs, he found a group of friends with whom he could continue his inner theological debate and artistic pursuits.

Despite the differences among them, each writer was infused with both hope and discontent. Bonding over their mutual attraction to Spengler, they looked to the promise of the future while dwelling on the imperfection in the present. As the Beats began to form a creative nucleus, however, each used his personal history to color his individual reading of Spengler. Each was buoyed by youthful enthusiasm (in Burroughs's case, more of a sage curiosity) and the desire to create, be it the great American novel (Kerouac), an experiential base of knowledge (Burroughs), or poetry (Ginsberg). What they had in common was intense dissatisfaction with the present state of affairs. "I feel," Kerouac wrote in *Visions of Cody,* "as though everything used to be alright; and now everything is automatically—bad."[71] That critical demeanor, however, was complemented by an idealistic belief that the situation could be rectified through some sort of recovery, whether a universal religious ethic (Kerouac), enchanted world (Burroughs), or humanitarian politics (Ginsberg).

Given the severity of the Beats' unease and the depth of their idealism, Spengler's narrative of decline provided a framework within which to reconcile these contradictory attitudes. At one level, it allowed them to "read" America differently, seeing promise in what was discarded by the dominant culture while rebuking widely held ideas and values. At another level, Spengler's hierarchy of symbols—Culture versus Civilization, experience versus book learning, and the rootedness of the folk versus the artificiality of middle-class existence—provided a unique perspective from which to engage in a cultural conversation about the meaning of America and what it meant to be an American.

At still another level, Spengler's catalog of world history provided a base of knowledge from which to begin artistic and spiritual quests. As the Beats read *The Decline of the West,* they found not only a critical voice but also a useful vocabulary for aesthetic and cultural philosophies. Reading Spengler in jeremiadic terms, Burroughs, Kerouac, and Ginsberg created a common network of ideas that each would use to interpret postwar America. While *Decline* all but invited different interpretations, the Beats' jeremiadic reading was grounded in both the text and their daily lives. Emphasizing some passages over others, even ignoring passages that may have contradicted their intentions, the Beats remained faithful to themselves. They used *Decline* to confirm, supplement, and extend many of their inchoate attitudes and beliefs.

The Beats readily mapped *Decline* onto the tripartite formula of the jeremiad: a sacred promise followed first by declension and, finally, by a call for a renewal that would transform the present state of corruption. In its broadest terms, *Decline* was structured around the absolute laws of historical cycles (promise), a resigned condemnation of the present state of decline, and a call for redemption. Spengler summed up these three components in the opening pages and assured readers that the inevitable decline of the West contained promise of a new cultural cycle. "What are we to think of the individual," he asked, "who, standing before an exhausted quarry, would rather be told that a new vein will be struck to-morrow than be shown a rich and virgin clay-bed nearby? The lesson, I think, would be of benefit to the coming generations, as showing them what is possible—and therefore necessary." Despite such potential, concluded Spengler, corruption of the present was evident. After the optimistic prelude, he immediately struck a more petulant tone: "Hitherto an incredible total of intellect and power has been squandered in false directions. The West-European, however historically he may think and feel, is at a certain stage of life invariably uncertain of his own direction; he gropes and feels his way and, if lucky in environment, he loses it." After lamenting the grim state of personal and cultural waywardness, Spengler confirmed, even celebrated, the inevitable decline of the West. He confidently insisted that the promise of the new culture would be fulfilled by those who accepted the challenge put forth in his work: "And I can only hope that men of the new generation may be moved by this book to devote themselves to technics instead of lyrics, the sea instead of the paint brush, and politics instead of epistemology. Better they could not do."[72] Although Spengler believed that Western civilization had reached its final stages, he nonetheless held out hope that a new culture was on the horizon. He assured readers that the same macrocosmic laws that portended decay also foretold rebirth.

Spengler's premise that there were immutable laws of history, and that those who understood the nature of the laws were capable of prophecy, or at the very least were privileged, was of great appeal to the Beats. In Spengler, they found an epistemology in which to place their millennial hopes— an alternative religious vocabulary that replaced the scientific lexicon of empiricism and causality with that of intuition. The whole realm of culture, from the natural world to architecture, military battles, and even the seemingly random occurrences of everyday life, were reflections of the same principle of living things and could be studied and decoded for their ultimate significance. Spengler's cosmological frame of reference was one of correspondence, a model that assumes no radical break between knower and known, subject and object, or sacred and profane. He declared in no uncertain terms the existence of a universal spirit active in both history and the individual and also connecting the two. Because no barriers separated the universal from the human community, the macrocosmic from the microcosmic, the same universal laws governed each; structure and movement in one were replicated in the other. Catherine L. Albanese, a historian of religion, has described this ancient mode of understanding, in reference to the worldview of the Transcendentalists, as possessing "a sense of a law implicit in the scheme of things, a controlling providence, a natural or moral law that unfolded in the very order that the cosmos represented."[73] Accordingly, life as experienced by humans and the energy pulsating through the universe were mere reflections of each other.

In recognizing the overlap between macrocosmic universality and microcosmic particularity, the Beats looked to this world for answers to their most profound questions. By evaluating and taking note of the world around them, they hoped to gain insight into the cosmos and its logic. For Burroughs, a scientist of the occult, Spenglerian correspondence fulfilled a certain desire to see the affairs of the world as somehow predestined and therefore intelligible. Rejecting the Christian polarization of the human and supernatural realms into a conflict between good and evil, Burroughs inhabited a magical universe and understood the world in terms of invisible spiritual forces. For Ginsberg, the notion that the things of this world were reflections of the divine, and even tangible evidence of divine judgment, held out the possibility for mystical experience. As he wrote in "Metaphysics" (1949):

This is the one and only
firmament; therefore
it is the absolute world.
There is no other world.
The circle is complete.
I am living in Eternity.
The ways of this world
are the ways of Heaven.[74]

For Kerouac, Spenglerian correspondence provided an alternative language in which to express deep-seated mystical orientation. In Spengler's immutable cycles of history Kerouac found confirmation of a Catholic apocalypticism and the intellectual leverage by which to ground it cross-culturally. He already tended to view the world analogously—that is, he had inherited a worldview of correspondence that privileged continuity between this world and its sacred counterpart. For Kerouac, Spenglerian organicism was never divorced entirely from a Catholic perspective. The two worldviews were complementary in that each assumed that the world was made in the image of divine reality. As Kerouac wrote of his fictional hometown, "Living continues in Galloway like the seasons themselves. . . . through which life pulses processionally in moods and leaps and bounds, while the moods of the universe flank across the skies endlessly."[75]

As the Beats looked for an authority to substantiate their critical insights into culture, they found in Spenglerian correspondence a viable means for assessing America's relationship to the essence of life.[76] In addition to possessing Platonic sensibility, Spenglerian correspondence contained an element of organicism in its assumption that all life forms sprung from a primordial essence (the "protospirituality"). In language reminiscent of Goethe and Hegel, Spengler wrote, "A Culture is born in the moment when a great soul awakens out of the protospirituality of ever-childish humanity, and detaches itself, a form from the formless, abounded and mortal hinge from the boundless and enduring." During the life-cycle of a culture, this divine principle played a determinative role in history. Spengler saw the Hegelian promise of dialectic transformation being fulfilled in the last stages of the life-cycle. A culture dies and eventually returns to and merges with this universal spirit: "It blooms on the soil of an exactly-definable landscape, to which plant-wise it remains bound. It dies when the soul has actualized the full sum of its possibilities in the shape of peoples, languages, dogmas, arts, states, sciences, and reverts into the proto-soul."[77] Everything seen or interpreted was an offshoot of this universal, distinctive but reflecting a larger reality. The Beats' Spenglerian valence allowed them to see the most mundane events and activities as ways to interpret the spiritual vitality of the American people.

Promising to unveil the future in the present, Spengler's work fueled the Beats' apocalyptic sensibilities. In this regard, *Decline* provided a critical template by which to understand, in Spengler's words, "the last spiritual crisis that will involve all Europe and America."[78] But while Spengler lumped Europe and America together in the Faustian "mudheap," the Beats differentiated the two. Their critical rants were selective, criticizing what they perceived to be the Faustian elements of America and not America itself. Much of their apocalyptic rhetoric derived from a belief that America was trapped within the stultifying shadow cast by European Civilization. The subterfuges of Enlightenment rationality, social engineering, and the fashions of Continental philosophy had prevented the emergence of an *American* Culture. Kerouac wrote of the difference between Europe and America: "It's the difference between a culture of turmoil, resentment, and inter-human struggle and a culture of livelihood, purpose, land, and natural struggle." While Kerouac lamented that America had "lost contact" with itself and now was "disgruntled by natural phenomena," Ginsberg wrote of the insidious nature of Faustian influence, so infectious that he was having "dreams of the old civilization."[79]

The Beats' differentiation between America and its Faustian enemy involved a bit of interpretive license in their reading of *Decline*. As Spengler exhaustively described the exploits of Western civilization, he spoke of the precedent for mature Civilizations to become sterile, parasitically clinging to more youthful, developing cultures. He pointed out many examples of this process of contamination and defined it organically as the "tragedy of 'Pseudomorphosis,'" a situation arising when an emerging culture becomes deformed and "cheated of its maturity—like a young tree that is hindered and stunted in its growth by a fallen old giant of the forest." In the mineralogist's lexicon, pseudomorphosis describes volcanic crystals "whose inner structure contradicts their external shape." According to Spengler, such a corruption occurred when "an older alien Culture lies so massively over the land that a young Culture, born in this land, cannot gets its breath and fails not only to achieve pure and specific expression-forms, but even to develop fully its own self consciousness. All that wells up from the depths of the young soul is cast in the old molds, young feelings stiffen in senile works."[80] In what could pass for a peculiar version of William Carlos Williams's modernist nativism, Spengler described pseudomorphosis as a phenomenon that goes against the grain of indigenous progress. As the idea of pseudomorphosis entered their critical vocabulary, the Beats seemed to have internalized that notion when addressing the crisis of America.[81]

Although Spengler never cited the United States as an example of pseudomorphosis, it remained an attractive metaphor in an era in which there was a strong desire to differentiate and distance America from the perceived corruption of Europe. After the war, this sense of corruption, or dis-ease, manifested itself most vividly in the panic about communist subversion. Setting up boundaries around the purified notion of America reflected the rhetoric of containment that George Kennan would fully articulate in the "long telegram" from Moscow in 1946 and "The Sources of Soviet Conduct" (1947). The Beats' emphasis on corruption touched upon the two meanings of containment, as delineated by Andrew Ross: a threat from outside the social body and a threat from within.[82] Using Spengler's binary between Culture and Civilization, the Beats transposed the language of health and infection of the social body into a mythic language that spoke in terms of metaphysical ideals and ontological absolutes.[83]

Spengler's interpretive category of pseudomorphosis also enabled the Beats to revere the idea of America by attributing its problems to the external forces of Faustian civilization rather than any inherent flaw. By absolving America of responsibility for its decline, its sins could be overcome once the Faustian soul had been exorcised. In 1951, amid the celebration of the "great American drinking night," Kerouac unleashed a flurry of Caulfield-esque accusations: "Bunch of sweating phonies! Oh the sins of America!"[84] Ginsberg agonized over a nation left impotent by the inheritance of European civilization. "The stakes are too great," he later explained, "an America gone mad with materialism, a police-state America, a sexless and soulless America prepared to battle the world in defense of a false image of its Authority." Moreover, Ginsberg contrasted that corrupted state with the America of his romantic predecessors: "Not the wild and beautiful America of the comrades of Whitman, not the historic America of Blake and Thoreau where the spiritual independence of each individual was an America." He also boasted that "only those who have entered the world of the Spirit know what a vast laugh there is in the illusory appearance of worldly authority."[85]

Under the terms put forth by Spengler, the Beats were able to identify both the promise of America and the reasons behind its fall from grace. Spengler's emphases on propaganda, mass culture, and forms of political manipulation not only sharpened the Beats' critical skills but also increased their sensitivity to the "seepage of nerve-gas over the radio" and "the mustard gas of sinister intelligent editors" and other vestiges of Europe's tragic heritage on American soil.[86] Burroughs was also wary of European influence but did not share Kerouac and Ginsberg's romantic hope that America could be separated from the West. For Burroughs, America could not escape the Faustian stronghold. Using the imagery of sexual predation, he described the situation in terms of vast, masculinized power differential: "My cock is four and one-half inches and large cocks bring on my xenophobia . . . 'Western influence!' I shriek." In the same piece, Burroughs described America as a land of victims: "a great plain under the wings of vultures husk in the dry air."[87]

Within a cold war culture seemingly obsessed with fears of contamination—from UFO sightings to films such as *Invasion of the Body Snatchers* (1956)—it was Spengler's pseudomorphosis that gave Burroughs's notion of the virus a range of critical meanings. Burroughs viewed the corruption of the present—language, institutions, culture, and people—as resulting from Faustian infection. Although Alfred Korzybski's linguistic theories and Wilhelm Reich's psychology also influenced Burroughs's thinking on this matter, his description of the virus in *Naked Lunch* echoed Spengler's description of pseudomorphosis. In a scientific swagger, Burroughs declared, "It is thought that the virus is a degeneration from a more complex life form. It may at one time have been capable of independent life. Now it has fallen to the borderline between living and dead matter. It can exhibit living qualities only in a host, by using the life of another—the renunciation of life itself, a *falling* towards inorganic, inflexible machine, towards dead matter."[88] At the heart of Burroughs's magical universe, a world in which unseen forces were at play, was Spenglerian organicism and the metaphor of Faustian control.

In 1938 Burroughs had cowritten a short story, "Twilight's Last Gleamings," with his college friend Kells Elvins. In addition to being an ironic allusion to America's national anthem, the title was a pun on the German title of *The Decline of the West: Der Untergang des Abendlandes* ("twilight" or "sinking away" of the West). The story reveals Burroughs's long-held Spenglerian belief that an apocalypse was imminent. Given its adherence to the antiquated models of Europe, America, as it were, was going down with the ship. Loosely based on the *Titanic* disaster, Burroughs metaphorically depicted the sinking of the luxury liner *S.S. America* as a parable of the demise of civilization. As the ship sinks, an array of aristocrats scramble for lifeboats, displaying the greed, cowardice, and dissimulation Burroughs identified as the characteristics of a "civilized" American public. As the musicians play "The Star Spangled Banner," passengers desperately attempt to escape by stealing, pillaging, and abusing authority in their final moments. In one instance, the captain of the ship kills a woman for her wig and brassiere. According to Burroughs, he has become the quintessential American, donning a ridiculous disguise at the expense of others and, eventually, himself. While making his way to the lifeboat in disguise, the captain shoots a purser who is stealing money and jewels from the safe, seizes the valuables for himself, and makes his way to temporary safety, pushing aside women and children.[89]

Regardless of the logistics that would precipitate the end of civilization and inaugurate a purified culture, each Beat viewed America from a Spenglerian viewpoint. For them, his open-ended description of civilization bore ominous resemblance to the conditions of their contemporary America. Amid a postwar economic boom, a dramatic increase of science and technology, and vigorous critiques of these trends, the Beats were sensitive to Spengler's condemnation of material values. Their ranting, however, was not Marxist-inspired diatribe. Their subtle invocation of a Spenglerian worldview was directed more against the felt presence of science in everyday life than against the complacency of the bourgeois. Although most were aware of the practical dangers of "scientific worlds," the Beats viewed the dominance of scientific objectivity as desiccating the country's natural spiritual energy. At the end of the Faustian cycle, according to Spengler, objectivity was privileged at the expense of cultural growth. "The brain rules," he wrote, "because the soul abdicates."[90] As Doctor Benway, the excessively sane scientist in *Naked Lunch* and colonizer of human imagination, triumphantly declares, "The study of thinking machines teaches us more about the brain than we can learn by introspective methods. Western man is externalizing himself in the form of gadgets."[91]

Spengler's method of accumulating examples of Faustian decline at a rapid-fire pace inspired the Beats to make connections among spheres of culture, something not often accomplished outside sociology departments. They quickly and quite correctly discerned, for example, that technological advancement was yet another incarnation of the postwar spirit of Manifest Destiny. Either on-the-job training, the onslaught of patriotic propaganda, or the valorization of atomic scientists as model social reformers caused large sections of the population to experience the postwar techno-economic paradigm. In the telling phrase of Vannevar Bush, science was the new "endless frontier" for Americans to explore and celebrate. Bush, director of the Office of Scientific Research and Development, issued a report in 1945 that encapsulated much of the postwar rhetoric about the value and importance of science. "Advances in science," he wrote, "mean more jobs, higher wages, shorter hours, more abundant crops, more leisure for recreation, for study, for learning how to live without the deadening drudgery which has been the burden of the common man for ages past. . . . But to achieve these objectives . . . to maintain a position of world leadership—the flow of new scientific knowledge must be both continuous and substantial."[92] As a number of historians have since pointed out, the psychological consequence of such rhetoric was a sense of dehumanization and estrangement.[93] In the late 1940s Ginsberg spoke of the same disruption and the dismissal of subjectivity while he took jabs at Freudian analysis:

> I suddenly realized that my head
> is severed from my body;
> I realized it a few nights ago
> by myself,
> lying sleepless on the couch.[94]

In addition to technology, Spengler warned of the growing dominance of money, which would signal the abstraction of personal experience and the end of meaningful exchange between members of that society: "[Money] no longer merely serves for the understanding of economic intercourse, but *subjects* the exchange of goods to its own evolution. It values things, no longer as between each other, but *with reference to itself.*"[95] Adopting a Spenglerian vocabulary, Kerouac rhetorically asked, "What's happened to our society or our arrangement of living and trading with one another that without the feeling of righteousness you shrivel away like a pru—." Because he feels "so damned small and sick" he is unable to finish the sentence. In a journal entry in 1946 he had noted that "money is only a step in Faustian becoming."[96]

Spengler's ideas not only confirmed the Beats' critiques but also invested them with significance for America as well as themselves. In 1944 Ginsberg wrote a short prose story called "A Version of the Apocalypse," a piece Kerouac later included in *The Town and the City*. In the fragment, Ginsberg characterized New York City as falling victim to the death cloud enveloping contemporary America, a European storm disguised as the American dream of materialism: "the final scenes of disintegrative decay . . . all the children of the sad American paradise." Ginsberg prophesied the consequences of a false and repressive ideology that inhibited interpersonal communion, suppressed individual sentience, and would eventually collapse upon itself:

> In the end, everyone looks like a zombie, you realize that everyone is dead, locked up in the sad psychoses of themselves. It goes on all night, everyone milling around uncertainly among the ruins of bourgeois civilization, seeking each other, don't you see, but so stultified by their upbringings somehow, or by the disease of the age, that they can only stumble about and stare indignantly at each other. . . . All the neurosis and the restrictive morality and the scatological repressions and the suppressed aggressiveness has finally gained the upperhand on humanity—everyone is becoming a geek![97]

That vision reflected how the Beats interpreted the plight of America in terms of the destructive influence of civilization upon culture.

The Beats explained America's failure to claim its full spiritual inheritance in terms of Spenglerian myth. Accordingly, Faustian parasitism had prevented the expression of a natural America in and through the people. Ginsberg later used the term *karmic hangover* to explain the tragic situation, simultaneously referring to a rapacious invasion onto American soil by European civilization and Americans' failure to defend themselves. He celebrated a fellow Paterson native, William Carlos Williams, as the first poet to reckon with this legacy. Moreover, he described how repression and ambivalence had psychologically disabled many Americans, preventing them from confronting non-European roots and realizing their essential "Americaness." Ginsberg employed the cultural philosophy of his hometown mentor to triangulate a reading of Spengler's volkisch notion that the "power of the landscape" exerts a "secret force" upon a people, enabling them to cohere and prosper:[98]

> America never did belong to us. So that's why our forefathers were always looking up to English manners and English poetry. Williams finally comes along and has to confront that effect . . . recognizing how we took over the

actual land by force [getting] this neurosis of not wanting to see the land we had taken, not wanting to actually live here, but wanting to live in a mechanical dream world. With imports from England for thought, meter, poesy, music, philosophy, rather than having to feel the tragic fact that we're trespassers in our own bodies and our own land.[99]

According to Ginsberg, Americans were unable to live on the land as it had intended them to do. Racked by unconscious guilt, they refused to acknowledge any connection with the land. Although they may have conquered it, they never possessed it or became one with it. They never, in Spengler's words, experienced life in "a new manner" by "enter[ing] a culture-soul . . . so intimately as to absorb into one's self."[100]

Spenglerian Vernacular: Kerouac's *The Town and the City*

The exaggerated sound effects of Beat apocalypticism masked an earnest belief in the need for radical cultural renewal. Following the antimodernist path set down by American writers from Ralph Waldo Emerson to Henry Adams, the Beats carried on a long tradition of negating the conditions of their time in hopes of creating or returning to something purer and more natural than modern society. Among the Beats, Kerouac was the most ardent in this belief. In both literature and life he obsessed over America's (and inevitably his own) contradictions. Both, it seemed, were always caught between tradition and progress. After Kerouac's Catholic faith in the harmony between God and creation had filtered through Spengler's notion of correspondence, what remained was an overriding belief in the lack of cosmic harmony and religious meaning in the present. Kerouac's first published novel, *The Town and the City* (1950), represents his first major attempt to reconcile boyhood religion with adult intellect. While infused with allusions to the work of Herman Melville, Fyodor Dostoevsky, and Thomas Wolfe, *The Town and the City* nevertheless demonstrates the extent to which Spengler's ideas infiltrated the Beat inner circle, mixing with their beliefs, coloring their metaphors, and providing a referent for their celebrations and condemnations of America.

Although Burroughs had introduced Kerouac to a variety of arcane works in 1944, Kerouac was already acquainted with Spengler's description of the West's inevitable decline. After being introduced to *Decline* by his childhood friend Sebastian Sampas, Kerouac spent many evenings in Lowell, discussing the implications of Spengler's ideas.[101] In a 1943 letter, Sampas outlined the contemporary relevance of Spengler's philosophy by summarizing the spiritually destructive ego of Western man and proclaiming the moribund state of Faustian civilization. Moreover, he warned Kerouac of the consequences of following the ideals of this imposed model:

> In all of us, Jack, there is a great spirituality, that flowers in our youth and should bear fruit in our maturity. That it does not is [because] there is a dissonance between ideals and life, between Civilization and the "landscape" whence it was rooted. . . . There are no more worlds to conquer in the Western Civilization. It remains for the intellectuals of the Western World to rearrange, to comment, to imitate but not to create, to actualize the fullest possibilities of the All-soul. The form set too thickly—its earth roots are withered, the soul is dead.[102]

Sampas's Spenglerian distinction between "ideals and life," "Civilization and the 'landscape,'" left an indelible mark on Kerouac. So, too, did the admonition not to imitate but to create as nature did, relying on the fertility of one's own imagination.

After Sampas was killed in the Allied landing at Anzio, Kerouac was distraught and became prone to fits of melancholy. In late 1945, as his father lay dying at the family home, he began serious work on what would become *The Town and the City.* The title was not merely an allusion to Spengler's distinction between the vitality of folk traditions and the decadence of urban centers but a prolonged meditation on decay. Kerouac was attempting to harness the ruinous energies of loss to justify Sampas's death and alleviate his depression. "Surrounded by the decline of the West on all sides," *The Town and the City* was a work haunted by the ghost of Sampas and his Spenglerian prophecies.[103]

The style and tone of *The Town and the City* owed much to that of *Decline* as well as to Atkison's translation. A year after the novel was published, Kerouac remarked, "Charles Atkison, a singer in incomparable prose, the basis of modern prose his roughest outlines . . . the translator of Spengler's poem *Decline of the West.*"[104] The structure and content of Kerouac's early work was also thoroughly Spenglerian, from his extended Spenglerian musings on women and "feminine knowledge" to his habit of capitalizing the word *Spring* throughout.[105] It is of no surprise that the staid surface of *The Town and the City* covers a torrent of philosophical speculation. As Kerouac announced, it was to be a "huge novel explaining everything to everybody."[106] It does, in fact, explain Kerouac's Spenglerian-inflected Catholic ethos: a sensitivity to sin and the crisis of cosmic authority, the importance of ritual communities, and the unwavering hope in miraculous intervention. The themes of loss, sickness, and death predominate. But amid even this dark landscape Kerouac affirmed the possibility of transcendence and the need for a religious faith to counteract the chaos and disruption of the present moment.

In many respects, the characters in *The Town and the City* reflect the range of Kerouac's emotional spectrum. In the novel he traces the lives of the Martin family through one generation. Based loosely on Kerouac's own family, the action centers around two brothers, Peter and Francis, and Peter's friend, Alexander Panos. The two brothers may be seen to represent the two poles of Kerouac's personality as he mapped them onto the two ends of the Spenglerian cultural cycle. Peter is "goaded on by all the fantastic and fabulous triumphs that he sees possible in the world" and "filled with unspeakable premonitions of Spring." Francis, however, is incapable of such energy or enthusiasm. Peter's Faustian counterpart is always "moping and sulking," musing "with a feeling of aged understanding" on the "wild carelessness of a savage rhapsodic America in its shouting youthfulness."[107] In Francis one detects the guilt that would plague Kerouac throughout his life: being implicated in the ego-driven culture from which he recoiled.

The character of Alex Panos is based directly on Sebastian Sampas. In the role of the Spenglerian prophet, Panos mediates between the two poles of the novel, revealing the sins of the present and pointing to a salvific future. Just as Kerouac believed the present to be at the end of the Faustian cycle and at the beginning of the American, Panos embodied this paradox of being and becoming. The character was associated with the ambiguity of the "rainy night," a recurring symbol in Kerouac's oeuvre. When introducing Panos, he asked and answered his own question: "Who walks along the river listening to the rain? Alexander Panos—he walks the town at night in sheets of shrouded rain." Throughout the novel Kerouac employs the motif of the rainy night to represent natural entropy. The "decline" of the rain drops, however, also signifies a time of renewal when Americans can transcend hidebound perspectives and connect with each other and the laws that govern the universe. Consequently, Panos reveals the undeniable and inescapable ambiguity of life in all its "irony" and "mighty drama."[108] For Panos, there are no absolutes in life except for change and the inevitable sense of mystery. As he presciently remarks, no perspective can remain stable because reality is always in process: "We're on the threshold of a new age, and God knows what it's going to be—in any case, hugely important to mankind! And how is each one of us going to fare in the great convulsion of the times, what are we going to contribute individually?" But process also contains contradictions and inevitable suffering, as Panos is very much aware. "It's my whole life," he says, "sensing that conflict and being tortured by it."[109]

Everyone and everything in *The Town and the City* is conflicted, torn among different choices or paths to follow. Even the Sampas character is not immune to confusion. In a letter written right before his death, Panos intimates that even his perspective may be a tragic intellectual self-deception: "I wanted to suffer with the masses and be among them, humble and patient. But I have found since . . . I've been cheated, I've been cheated! I wish with all my might there is a God!"[110] Panos's fear is everyone's. Kerouac laments this loss of confidence, but in the end confirms that such tension is the stuff of life. For him, life must be lived and not incessantly thought about. The inevitable suffering of life must be continually affirmed, for only then does the continuing cycle of history not contradict itself. Progress and loss are but the same word in a Spenglerian universe. That insight not only conforms to a Catholic understanding of the universe but also prefigures Kerouac's later interest in Buddhism.

The Town and the City was very much a product of Kerouac's Catholic and Spenglerian sensibilities. It was a book of contrasts: between the town of Galloway and the city of New York, between the brothers Peter and Francis, between youth and old age, and between two different philosophical dispositions. The juxtapositions that Kerouac put forth, however, were different ends of Spengler's organic spectrum, for the differences were not oppositions but reflections of an infinite reality of "endless sources and unfathomable springs." As Kerouac notes on the opening page, even his hometown, like America, was ripe with contradictions:

> The little children of Galloway sit on the banks of the Merrimac and consider these facts and mysteries. In the wild echoing misty March night, little Mickey Martin kneels at his bedroom window and listens to the river's rush . . . and he ponders the wellsprings and sources of his own mysterious life.
>
> The grownups of Galloway are less concerned with riverside broodings. They work—in factories, in shops and stores and offices, and on the farms all around. The textile factories built in brick, primly towered, solid, are ranged along the river and the canals, and all night the industries hum and shuttle. This is Galloway, milltown in the middle of fields and forests.[111]

Although tensions were never entirely absent, Galloway was "rooted in earth in the ancient pulse of life and work and death."[112] Just as America was an Indian land for Kerouac, Galloway, too, represented an ancient purity under threat from the "factory stacks rising higher that the church steeples." Kerouac's love-hate relationship with the city, particularly the urban environs of New York, inflected his reading of *Decline*. According to Spengler, the city contained the future of the world, even as that world disintegrated: "In place of world, there is a *city, a point,* in which the whole life of broad regions is collecting while the rest dries up."[113]

In the end, *The Town and the City* was Kerouac's attempt to shore up the fragments of his young life within a Spenglerian perspective. He strove to see himself as Peter, a man of "the new generation," continually on the road of discovery. At the very end of the novel, Peter stands on the side of a highway, "alone in the rainy night." He is "on the road again, traveling the continent . . . going off to further and further years." Amid the chaos of the present, Peter remains sure-footed. He has learned the lesson taught to him by Alexander Panos. The Spenglerian prophet has given him strength in the howling wilderness: "When the railroad trains moaned, and river winds blew, bringing echoes through the vale, it was as if a wild hum of voices, the dear voices of everybody he had known, were crying: 'Peter, Peter! Where are you going, Peter?' And a big soft gust of rain came down." Peter's reaction is not to respond but to move forward. Just as the Beats continued the struggle to find and actually experience their literary voices, Peter "put up the collar of his jacket, and bowed his head, and hurried along."[114]

Conclusion: From Spirit to Ethic

Spengler put forth a convincing cosmology and provided a religious language of symbols and metaphors that Burroughs, Kerouac, and Ginsberg used to read America—and themselves in relation to it. Due, in part, to Spengler, the Beats shared, from the beginning of their friendship, a jeremiadic understanding of American history. In adopting Spengler's historiography, they not only identified the promise of America but also the reasons behind its failure to deliver on that promise. Their appraisal of the failings of the dominant culture, and the ranges of their behavior and literary output, were profoundly influenced by Spengler and *The Decline of the West.* The Beats were provoked by Spengler and, in turn, relied on him to guide their lives and imaginations. Such is the function of truly powerful religious literature—a translation written over translation, symbolic structure built upon symbolic structure, and provocation initiating provocation.

Spengler did not write a jeremiad, and certainly not one of the American variety, but the Beats read him as such. And as they read, they began to allegorize the world, reproducing it in terms of Spenglerian-tinged realities. This critical process of mythogenesis was not merely ideological but emotional and experiential as well. The Beats sought more to engage rather than merely to explain the symbolic meaning of America, more to repossess its meaning through experience than to analyze it. Consequently, the mythic structure of the jeremiad, as filtered through Spengler, became a critical as well as effective mode of knowledge. In light of their literary agendas and exaggerations, the Beats invented an America in which their desires and fears determined the contours of the real. It was an America shaped as much, if not more, by the energies of their imagination as by empirical facts, a religious world dominated and controlled by meanings, sacred symbols, and the promise of cosmic experience held out in their reading of *Decline*.

As the Beats read Spengler, they did not merely apply his critical apparatus but worked from as well as through his ideas and assumptions. They would often read between the lines of *Decline* and willingly ignore those aspects of Spengler that did not fit their immediate agenda. In selectively ignoring his skepticism regarding the merit of artistic forms and philosophy at the end of a cultural cycle, the Beats charged ahead and viewed their art and poetics as pragmatic, exploratory, and vehicles for personal as well as social change. The subtle differences in how Burroughs, Kerouac, and Ginsberg would apply Spengler to their daily lives stemmed from personal disposition as well as individual readings of his call to arms. When the Beats looked upon their country, Spengler's ideas gave them direction on their journey to discover for themselves "the music and the madness of the Spring night and the American spaces."[115]

Energized by Spengler's sweeping cosmology and notion of correspondence, the most mundane issues of everyday life and questions concerning ultimate reality became one and the same. In Spengler's description of the attributes and qualities that characterize a culture at its early stages, the Beats found an ethical ideal on which to model their lives. Before they were able to resolve the present crisis, the Beats first had to formulate a convincing theology from which to *experience* America. Buoyed by their ethical reading of Spengler, they distilled a basis of a lived philosophy. As ideas, insights, events, and people began to swirl around their inner circle, *Decline* became filter, an organizing principle, and the matrix within which they developed a theology of experience. Such issues are the focus of the next chapter.

chapter

2

TABLE II. ''CONTEMPORARY'' CULTURE EPOCHS

	EGYPTIAN	CLASSICAL	ARABIAN	WESTERN
RE-CULTURAL PERIOD.	CHAOS OF PRIMITIVE EXPRESSION FORMS. MYSTICAL SYMBOLISM AND NAÏVE IMITATION			
	Thinite Period (3400–3000)	Mycenean Age (1600–1700) Late-Egyptian (Minoan) Late-Babylonian (Asia Minor)	Persian-Seleucid Period (500–0) Late-Classical (Hellenistic) Late-Indian (Indo-Iranian)	Merovingian-Carolingian Era (500–900)
EXCITATION				
ULTURE.	LIFE–HISTORY OF A STYLE FORMATIVE OF THE ENTIRE INNER–BEING. FORM–LANGUAGE OF DEEPEST SYMBOLIC NECESSITY			
ARLY PERIOD ament and architec- as elementary ex- ion of the young H-feeling.) (The mitives ")	OLD KINGDOM (2900–2400)	DORIC (1100–500)		
	Dynasties IV–V. (1930–1625) Geometrical Temple style Pyramid temples Ranked plant-columns Rows of flat-relief Tomb statues			

Sex, Drugs, and Theology

The Spenglerian Strain of Piety

Previous page, from table 2, "'Contemporary' Culture Epochs," in Oswald Spengler, *Form and Actuality,* volume 1 of *The Decline of the West.*

Art is the highest task and the proper metaphysical activity of this
life.

—Friedrich Nietzsche

Oswald Spengler's constellation of ideas and images continued to influence
Kerouac, Burroughs, and Ginsberg throughout the 1940s and into the early
1950s. For the Beats, his work was not necessarily a strict code to which they
faithfully adhered but a reservoir of ideas, attitudes, and insights to which
they returned again and again for personal and artistic inspiration. *The Decline of the West* functioned as an esoteric text centering their spiritual quest.
And like a work of occult wisdom, it was specific enough to solidify an intellectual framework but sufficiently vague and abstract to allow the Beats a
large degree of creativity when applying Spengler's ideas to their art and daily
lives. Their injection of his metaphysics into everyday life is the focus of this
chapter.

As the Beats began to take themselves seriously as "men of the new generation," they began to *theologize around* Spengler's theory of correspondence. In other words, having assumed the existence of macrocosmic laws,
they began to interpret and order everyday reality according to their metaphysical implications. Such an enterprise was at once both practical and spec-
ulative, empirical as well as imaginative. Even as the Beats filtered experience
through a Spenglerian worldview, they were simultaneously molding, testing, and validating it. In doing so, this worldview framed their hopes and
troubles, guided their searches for ultimate meaning, and provided a description as well as an explanation for what they found.

The Beats' Spenglerian strain of piety was just that: a stance toward reality based on a conviction that there was a world beyond, a macrocosmic reality that nevertheless could be understood in the here and now. In November 1944, Kerouac gouged himself and transcribed in his own blood a

quotation from Friedrich Nietzsche: "Art is the highest task and the proper metaphysical activity of this life." Both words and action attest to the fact that Beat piety was a creative, deeply personal practice akin to art. As opposed to more austere notions of religious faith, Beat piety was an aggressive commitment to live close to those creative wellsprings of which Spengler spoke. As "the proper metaphysical activity," art transcended itself and became, in Kerouac's words, something more than "poems, stories, essays, aphorisms, journals, and nine unfinished novels." As Spengler had written, art could become a practice "(as Nietzsche somewhere remarks) before God as the supreme witness." According to Spengler, such art was an activity that "bridged" the "Microcosm" and "Macrocosm," a "wholly religious" devotion that "consists in an identity of inner activity between the soul and body 'here' and the world-around 'there' which, vibrating as one, becomes one."[1]

In this chapter, I will discuss the Spenglerian logic behind the Beats' desire to fortify their grip on reality, a process of bricolage that resulted in a syncretic, ordered accumulation of metaphysical idioms. Among others, the idioms included the visionary poetry of Arthur Rimbaud and William Butler Yeats, the "orgone" theories of Wilhelm Reich, the linguistic treatises of Alfred Korzybski, the nativist modernism of William Carlos Williams, the mystical imagery of William Blake, Nietzsche's existentialism, the improvised phrasing of bebop, and the dynamist philosophy of the new physics. For the Beats, the process of accumulating, organizing, and integrating various idioms into a coherent whole was an act of religious devotion. In making these insights cohere under Spengler's metaphysical frame, they rendered everyday reality no longer everyday. By making visible and tangible that which was not, they had negated the commonplace and replaced it with the magical.

As Kerouac's blood ritual confirms, what began as an ongoing literary and philosophical discussion, what the Beats called the "new vision," quickly developed into something much more encompassing. Given the dexterity of each writer's religious imagination, the shift from poetics (a particular way of understanding the world in terms of aesthetic principles) to style (a particular way of being in the world) was fluid. During their most intense period of religious work in the 1940s and early 1950s the Beats fine-tuned their perception of the world and developed unique ways of expressing themselves within it. In terms of motivation, the process was as much conscious as unconscious, planned as much as evolving naturally. The result was an ensemble of strategies that Pierre Bourdieu has called the "habitus." First and foremost, the habitus is a function of the imagination. It refers not to a set of fixed and finite rules but to the development of a "generative principle of regulated improvisations."[2] Assuming that human beings simultaneously constitute and are constituted by the world around them, the habitus is the dynamic intersection of the two: the interaction between social constraints and individual agency, between imposed structure and spontaneous action. As an interpretive category, the habitus points to the limits the Beats faced in their dissent from received cultural norms. More specifically, it illuminates exactly how they freely existed within a structured space of possibilities, borrowing from their environment while radically reconfiguring that which they borrowed. Although the Beats were far from systematic, they were pragmatic in coordinating their thoughts with deliberate action and then filtering these experiences back into their thoughts. Mind and body became extensions of one another by sharing the same ground of raw experience.

The Beats understood their collaborative efforts as a response to a crisis of both public and private proportions, what Ginsberg later referred to as the mass "suppression of contemplative individuality."[3] Even before the era of the House Un-American Activities Committee and Alger Hiss, the Beats perceived the rhetoric of American individualism as empty slogans concealing more sinister forces in the culture at large. Individualism, they believed, had become a code word for conformity bereft of any knowledge of "the secret rhythm of all things cosmic."[4] Furthermore, due to the parasitical invasion by Faustian Civilization, America had been corrupted, its populist democratic vision transformed into a rigid ideology supported by wartime propaganda, political posturing, and a media barrage of American triumphalism. The trumpeting of freedom and individual rights by various ideologues was soon reflected in the Marshall Plan, the attorney general's list of subversive organizations, repressive visa and passport laws, loyalty boards for all federal employees, and a propagandist zeal for American democracy. Both during and after World War II, that drive toward a standard definition of Americanism tended to suppress conflict and difference at the price of denying real social problems and diversity. Before meeting in 1944, each of the Beats had sensed these restrictive trends, but it was their collaboration outside the political arena, initially focused around questions of art and philosophy, that enabled them to channel their urgency into a coherent religiosity.

The Beats gazed excessively at a world elsewhere, in their case, a Culture of Spenglerian contours. Together, they fashioned a distinctive theological perspective from which to continue gazing, a response to contemporary events yet possessing historical lineage. During a perceived time of crisis, the desire for introspection is often accompanied by the validation of personal experience as the source of ultimate authority. Together they run like intertwining threads through the fabric of American religious history, from Anne Hutchison and the antinomian controversy to New Age spirituality. One particularly relevant example is that of Transcendentalist leader Ralph Waldo Emerson. Stressing intuition in favor of institutionalized structure and individual solutions over society's ills, Emerson wrote that all "attempts to protect and establish a Cultus with new rites and forms" were "vain," for "faith made its own forms." He proposed that the remedy for these dying forms was individual spirituality and faith, which would render the forms "plastic and new."[5]

Unfortunately, while historians have been quick to identify this desire in America's religious past, they too often ignore how it is consummated in the realm of everyday life.[6] On a similar note, although the category of "experience" goes hand in hand with any critical discussion of the Beats, there has to this point been no systematic explanation among literary critics about why they valued moments of ecstasy and joy, how they interpreted such experiences, and to what purpose they advocated them. The Beats' emphasis on "kicks" was not just upon "hipster" experiences of sexual ecstasy or altered consciousness but rather on the whole spectrum of experience—intellectual, sensual, emotional, and moral. As Kerouac described them, kicks could be considered everything from "goofing off," to "being lazy," to "listening to music that came under the heading of an emotional kick, or you were in love which was another kick, or you hated somebody and put his name in a little black book and *that* was a certain kind of kick—and so on, all of it divided into neat categories through which existence kicked along."[7]

The Beats responded to a perceived crisis of cultural authority by finding refuge in their experiences, a religious commitment nonetheless loyal to a world outside the self. In this chapter I will explore the articulation and practice of the new vision, specifically how it touches upon various elements of the Beats' habitus, or improvisational piety: its subtext of violence, its emphasis on the physical body as locus of spirituality, its concern with time and the rhythms of the universe, its communal character, and the subtle but profound differences in the way each writer conceived and practiced it.

Kerouac, Ginsberg, and Burroughs approached *Decline* from slightly different angles and conceived of Spengler's America in terms of their own personalities. Kerouac and Ginsberg, for the most part, concentrated on a nostalgic America, a paradise to be salvaged. Burroughs, however, conceived of America as wholly unapproachable, an ideal to be sought within the dystopian present and that would not be realized until after the decline of the West. That difference in perspective was reflected in how each man came to terms with his environment. But even as the Beats sought different versions of transformative experience, it was the common desire to collaborate in the work of nature, to assume the role of modern alchemist, that bound their new visions together.

Violence and the New Vision

In December 1943, as American involvement in World War II entered its third year, Columbia University junior Lucien Carr introduced his younger classmate, freshman Allen Ginsberg, to William S. Burroughs. A Harvard graduate, Burroughs, thirty at the time, was a formidable intellectual force. Since leaving Cambridge University in 1936, he had traveled extensively throughout Europe, enrolled in medical school in Vienna, returned to Harvard University in order to study Mayan civilization, and worked as an exterminator in Chicago. When Ginsberg met him he was unemployed, collecting a $200 monthly allowance from his parents and planning elaborate schemes, including a Brinks truck heist and the holdup of a Turkish bath.[8] The young and impressionable Ginsberg, still shy of his eighteenth birthday and planning to become a labor lawyer, was taken by Burroughs's intelligence and sophistication. Despite favorable first impressions of each other, he did not see Burroughs again until later that summer.

During this time Carr was also friends with Jack Kerouac, twenty-two and a former Columbia football player with whom he had been having intensive discussions about philosophy and the vocation of the artist. Together, Kerouac and Carr began to speak of a "new vision" and the simultaneous renewal of self, literature, and world. They borrowed the term *new vision* from William Butler Yeats's occult pronouncements in "A Vision" and Arthur Rimbaud's declaration in *Une Saison en Enfer* (A season in hell) that one should be "absolutely modern" in formulating a self or society based on "vigor and real tenderness."[9]

Both Kerouac and Carr understood Rimbaud as celebrating the heightened sensitivity of the artist and calling for mental acuity through experience in order to have access to the realm of the universal. They were attracted to Rimbaud's doctrine of the *voyant,* his theory that an artist's true vocation was that of visionary or seer. In his New York City apartment, Kerouac pinned a Rimbaud quote to the wall above his writing desk: "When shall we go, over there by the shores and mountains, to salute the birth of new work, the new wisdom, the flight of tyrants, and of demons, the end of superstition, to adore . . . the first ones! . . . Christmas on earth!"[10]

Underlying the new vision was the notion that artists could intuit the structures and rhythms of the cosmos and by doing so somehow manipulate the universe for the benefit of themselves and humanity. This "artistic morality," in Kerouac's words, was superior to "all this overlaid mental garbage of 'existentialism' and 'hipsterism' and 'bourgeois decadence.'" Kerouac, already familiar with Spengler, was convinced that these trendy avenues of expression were futile given that "the city intellectuals of the world were divorced from the folkbody blood of the land and were just rootless fools."[11]

As first conceived by Kerouac, the new vision complemented the worldview of correspondence put forth in *The Decline of the West.* Indeed, in the 1938 edition of "A Vision," Yeats spoke of having found a kindred spirit in Spengler, a coincidence not lost on Kerouac.[12] As Spengler became a driving force behind the development of the new vision, Kerouac and Carr speculated that the manipulation of reality could succeed precisely because this world and the transcendent cosmos were intimately connected, "rooted" as it were, in the same universal laws. These laws may have resembled recent discoveries made by quantum physicists but could not be reduced to scientific principles alone. They were to be detected intuitively on the extreme cusp of experience rather than through rational observation in the confines of a laboratory.

Informed of Carr and Kerouac's conversations, Ginsberg independently began writing in his journal about the new vision. In volkisch mode, he cited Carr's comment to him that "ideals are inextricably rooted in personality and character" and concluded that "ideals are an extension of the ego."[13] By the time Ginsberg introduced himself to Kerouac in the late spring of 1944, the young poet had already subscribed to an "artistic morality" of his own making. Meeting Kerouac would help give shape to Ginsberg's loose framework of ideas. The men were attracted to each other immediately, each finding in the other a complementary sense of artistic ambition, wonder, and idealism. Although Kerouac had met Burroughs earlier that February, one of the first things he and Ginsberg did together was pay Burroughs a "formal visit" at his apartment in Greenwich Village.[14]

In addition to introducing Ginsberg to Spengler and reviving Kerouac's interest in *Decline,* Burroughs offered further insights into Yeats as well as Franz Kafka, Rimbaud, Blake, Korzybski, Mayan codices, Louis-Ferdinand Celine, and shamanism. His worldly demeanor, eclectic collection of books, and eccentric nature catalyzed all involved. During this period of introductions, with Burroughs playing the initiating magus, the Beats' metaphysical worldview began to take shape. Burroughs, Kerouac, and Ginsberg, together in the West 115th Street apartment of Joan Vollmer Adams, worked through the confluence of intellectual streams and began to make sense of each other's contributions.

By integrating a variety of philosophical meditations and aesthetic insights, the Beats constructed a unique religious perspective. Due, in part, to Burroughs's pragmatic influence, together they possessed an internal logic and a distinctive pattern. As Ginsberg recalled, "Burroughs was primarily a master of gnostic curiosities and in his approach to the mind he had the same yankee practicality and inquisitiveness as his grandfather who had invented an adding machine."[15] While Burroughs's hyper-rationality counterbalanced the more mystical demeanors of Kerouac and Ginsberg, Spengler's hierarchy of symbols provided an orderly framework by which to organize various aesthetic theories and borrowed metaphysical idioms. Because *Decline* was both reference point and filter, the effect was synergistic. On one hand, Spengler's work galvanized the disparate components of the new vision, mobilized the Beats' collaborative efforts, and encased their intuitive insights and half-formed ideas within a comprehensive metaphysics and cosmology. On the other hand, the various idioms that the Beats "added up" complemented as well as buttressed Spengler's abstractions, giving them concrete form through the buildup of substantive images and detailed metaphors. Furthermore, despite its eclectic makeup, this metaphysical spirituality centered upon certain fundamental conceptions: that universal laws governed both the microcosm and the macrocosm; that both self and America were somehow misaligned, preventing them from fulfilling their spiritual potential; and that such disorder would be righted through renewed attention to personal experience, raw and unmediated. In early 1945 Ginsberg wrote a draft of the new vision based on his discussions with Kerouac. "The new vision," he wrote, "is in a sense the product of a strictly rational system," an allusion to the logic that motivated their eclectic assimilation of ideas.[16]

By working through the new vision, the Beats constructed a theology of experience in order to know what they felt and to feel what they knew. That religious mentality validated and valorized personal experience by interpreting even the most mundane of activities within a context of universal significance. In focusing so intently on the category of experience in all its manifestations, the Beats assumed distinct patterns of thought, expression, and behavior that imparted cosmic significance to their lives. They modeled their experiential ethic upon those around them, most notably the petty drug addicts, criminals, hipsters, and jazz musicians who inhabited the New York City underworld.

Ironically, the Beats looked outside themselves in order to give concrete form to experiences that manifested the secret of correspondence. The perseverance of the Times Square hustler Herbert Huncke, the kinetic exuberance of Neal Cassady, and the syncopated saxophone wails of Lester Young and Charlie Parker all demonstrated a particular mode of being in the world, more human, more alive than others. The Beats modeled their poetics and behavior on these figures, garnering insights into what exactly constituted the full range of personal experience and what kinds of experience would manifest the secret of correspondence.

What Burroughs, Kerouac, and Ginsberg shared was a foundational metaphysics, a privileging of experience above and beyond all forms of knowledge that each would continue to develop as their careers progressed and diverged. They each expressed the new vision somewhat differently because it bore the mark of individual concerns and religious pasts. Amid such personal idiosyncrasies, the new vision was solid ground that gave individual utterances consistency and collective force. Given the Beats' Spenglerian valence, the new vision was as much constructive theologizing as it was a response to perceived religious crisis. There was a method to their madness. The shared theological project greatly influenced the verbal and stylistic forms in which they communicated. More important, it reflected how they lived in the mundane world of food, drink, sleep, jazz clubs, skyscrapers, subways, and buses—always with an eye toward extraordinary powers, meanings, and values.[17]

<figure>⌐⌐</figure>

For all three, the new vision was derived from life in the streets, where criminal activity and drug use were pervasive. Violence, either directed outward or self-inflicted, was part of reality—ever-present in their lives, in what they read, and in the public sphere. It is no surprise that their descriptions of America and their psyches were laced with allusions to violation and debasement, often projected onto the plane of Spenglerian myth in which Civilizations, even as they self-destructed, breached the integrity of more innocent Cultural forms. They theologized these currents of violence and incorporated them into their religious perspective, placing both self and country on the defensive.

Given the Beats' prejudicial reading of Spengler, particularly his notion of "pseudomorphosis," the crisis in America also affected individual Americans. Because the Faustian spirit had imposed itself upon America and its people, the predicament was metaphorically envisioned in terms of an imposition—infiltration, invasion, infection, and what later became a central trope for Burroughs, a parasitical virus. Once commenting that the "middle-class U.S.A." is "one of the worst in Space-Time," Burroughs alluded to the "Spenglerian Cycle routine" as well as the Mayan concept that human behavior is intimately linked to the universe. In 1951 he wrote to Ginsberg about the resulting psychological savagery: *"Envy or resentment is only possible when you can not see your own space-time location.* Most of the people in America do not know where they really are so they envy someone else's deal" and not their own. Earlier, Burroughs had spoken of the consequences of this cosmic dislocation and warned Ginsberg of a brutalizing climate of ignorance and conformity in which persons had been given two contradictory messages. The situation had resulted in the "continual misrepresentation of one's personality," because the "corrupt government" had forcibly conditioned persons to maintain "a constant state of pretense and dissimulation."[18] Kerouac discerned a similar rupture in the American psyche. In a 1949 letter to Ginsberg, he confirmed Burroughs's assertion that America was in crisis because its value system was based on hypocrisy and self-deception: "As Bill says, the human race will become extinct if it doesn't stop doing what it doesn't want to do."[19]

As the new vision developed during the 1940s, Kerouac, Ginsberg, and Burroughs were on the defensive. They militantly opposed those personal norms set aside for white male breadwinners—domestic responsibility, corporate ladder-climbing, and celebratory patriotism—that they felt were dictated by the media and institutions of America. "[During] the first perceptions that we were separate from the official vision of history and reality," Ginsberg recalled, "we realized that there was a difference between the way we talked—Jack, Burroughs, and myself, as comrades among ourselves in order to get information and give each other our best stories." The difference, noticeable even on the mundane level of a democratic political rally, was that of new versus official, organicism versus parasitism, Culture versus Civilization, and America versus the West: "I remember Burroughs saying during one Presidential campaign, I think when Truman was running for President, that if an elephant had walked up in front of all those candidates in the middle of a speech and shat on the ground and walked away, the candidate would have ignored it. Consciousness wasn't present there on the occasion when they were talking, consciousness was an abstract, theoretical state. A theoretical nation, the actual nation was not there." The implication was that political discourse, supposedly of, by, and for the American people, had become so removed from day-to-day affairs that it could not take sensory experience into account, even Burroughs's hyperbolic representation of the natural world, a defecating elephant. According to Ginsberg, the minds of both politicians and the public had become clouded by a self-perpetuating fog of rhetoric: "So we realized that we were in the midst of a vast American hallucination, that a hallucinatory public consciousness was being constructed in the airwaves and television and radios and newspapers, even in literature."[20]

The "hallucinatory public consciousness" implied that the articulation and communication of those perceptions, those physical sentiments, that were unique to the individual had been either denied or truncated by the social and moral value systems of the majority. It also implied that the ignorance wrought by technology, industrialization, and urban centers was only a temporary setback. The usurpation of reality by theory could eventually be redressed by an aggressive imagination—the assumption of a soldierly form of intuition.

The metaphors of violence and militarism the Beats used to describe cultural and personal trials of identity reflected the general cultural climate during and after World War II. In addition to the military disasters of Pearl Harbor and Bataan with which the war began, there was also a violent tenor to affairs on the domestic front, notably the Japanese internment camps and the race riots in Detroit, Harlem, and Los Angeles.[21] Most significant, however, was the rhetoric of American exceptionalism, so pervasive during this period, that rested on the myth of the frontier and the notion that progress was achieved through violent conflict and conquest.

Understanding progress as militant action had become an integral part of American cultural memory and historically had been a central component of Americans' self-identification. The idea manifested itself most often in the form of the "savage war," what Richard Slotkin calls the "characteristic episode of each phase of westward expansion" and the "operative category of military doctrine."[22] American identity had been continually forged out of conflict with the other, negatively defined in terms of both military conquest and ideological opposition. So, too, were the Beats' conceptions of America and themselves. Amid an American culture pervaded by the violent tropes of war images, mushroom clouds, propaganda, and representations of combativeness in both the news media and Hollywood westerns, the Beats drew on the common mythic language of the period. In doing so, their new vision and its extension into behavior exhibited a propensity for violence, at times righteous and regenerative and at others wholly destructive.

Within the Beats' inner circle, the undercurrent of violence had first become evident in the late summer of 1944. As Burroughs, Kerouac, and Ginsberg were solidifying their friendship on the edges of the criminal underworld, their talk of merging art with life became a tragic reality. For some time, Lucien Carr had been amorously pursued by David Kammerer, a friend of Burroughs from St. Louis. Kammerer had been Carr's youth group leader in junior high school and had since continually followed him around the country, from St. Louis to Andover, to Bowdoin College, to the University of Chicago, and finally to Columbia University. Kammerer had abandoned his career as an English instructor in the process. For the most part, Carr did not seem to mind the attention. But as those in and around the Beat circle likened the circumstances to Verlaine's obsessive pursuit of Rimbaud, Carr became increasingly enraged and irrational over Kammerer's homosexual advances. Along with Kerouac, Carr had planned to join the Merchant Marines to escape Kammerer but instead remained at Columbia. The situation culminated on the morning of August 14, 1944, when Carr stabbed Kammerer twice in the heart with a Boy Scout knife and dumped his body in the Hudson River. Carr, in blood-stained clothes, then visited both Burroughs and Kerouac for emotional support and legal advice. Claiming self-defense, he was soon indicted for second-degree murder; Burroughs and Kerouac were also arrested for failing to notify the authorities. The *Daily News* reported that the two books Carr carried with him to the Tombs were Rimbaud's *A Season in Hell* and Yeats's *A Vision*.[23]

Although the results of the Carr-Kammerer episode were troubling— Carr was convicted of first-degree manslaughter and spent two years in Elmira Reformatory—the incident fueled creative collaboration among the Beats. That fall, Ginsberg began working on a novel based on the incident, but when he submitted the first chapter to his creative writing class he was ordered to stop working on "smutty" material.[24] Kerouac and Burroughs also began a work about the affair. They each wrote alternating chapters of a satirical detective story, *And the Hippos Were Boiled in Their Tanks,* that went unpublished during their lifetimes. After Carr was imprisoned, Kerouac urged Ginsberg to work with him in order for the "New Vision [to] blossom." "I find in you a kindred absorption with identity, dramatic meaning, classic unity, and immortality," Kerouac wrote, distancing himself and Ginsberg from the nihilism that had overtaken Lucien Carr's "post-human post-intelligence" concept of the new vision. "I prefer the new vision in terms of art," he continued. "I believe . . . that art is the potential ultimate. Out of the humankind materials of art, I tell myself, the new vision springs."[25]

The violent episode enforced and legitimated the Beats' desire to assume the roles of cultural seers by viewing the human condition in aesthetic terms. The outcome of the Carr-Kammerer relationship was seen as preordained, for as with Rimbaud and Verlaine, an unrequited homosexual attraction had resulted in violent retribution. Given the rampant homophobia within American culture at the time in addition to the Beats' macho disdain for effeminate, fawning homosexuals, the murder could be explained away, albeit uneasily. More ominously, however, the fact that Carr and Kammerer had somehow assumed fictional identities, donning the masks of Rimbaud and Verlaine, gave credence to the fact that Americans were somehow living a lie, not allowing for full disclosure of their natural selves. In the end, the tragic event of that summer brought the Beats closer and validated their Spenglerian paranoia as well as the proposition that art and life were cut from the same material.

⌐⌐

Among the Beats, Ginsberg most often equated the Faustian siege with a form of psychological warfare. The result was schizophrenia; on one side was the natural, personal, physical essence, and on the other was a socially conditioned product of the state. In his early poem "Paterson," the speaker has become neurotic after being trapped between natural instinct and middle-class respectability:

> What do I want in these rooms papered
> with visions of money?
> How much can I make by cutting my hair?
> If I put new heels on my shoes,
> bathe my body reeking of masturbation and
> sweat, layer upon layer of excrement
> dried in employment bureaus, magazine
> hallways, statistical cubical, factory stairways . . .
> what war I enter and for what prize![26]

As parental authority merges with advertising ideals to create an iron cage, the poet becomes a prisoner before the war has even begun. In addition to being psychologically victimized, he has been prevented from taking care of himself physically. Bodily fluids have become impeded and no longer flow outward but are forced back upon themselves. The poet's only choice is to conform by bathing, thereby erasing any trace of a physical self, or to be buried under "layer upon layer of excrement" as he waits in "magazine hallways." Indeed, Ginsberg viewed the climate of consensus in human—more specifically, physiological—terms, signaling the internalization of socially determined norms at the expense of a self-sustaining, organic communion between self and world.

"Paterson" is an example of how the Beats viewed psychological conditioning as a physical assault and violent usurpation of the senses. Evoking the opening line from "Howl," Ginsberg once described the postwar years as "a time when there was a definitive shrinkage of sensitization, of sensory experience, and a definite mechanical disorder of mentality that led to the cold war. . . . The desensitization had begun, the compartmentalization of the mind and heart, the cutting off of the head from the rest of the body, the robotization of mentality."[27] Kerouac could detect such neuroses through bodily stasis. "How clear the realization one's going mad," he wrote. "The mind has a silence, nothing happens in the physique, urine gathers in your loins, your ribs contract." Similarly, Burroughs once wrote Ginsberg about physiological crisis: "I have thought a great deal about Schizophrenia (S in the trade). Convinced that it is as much a disease of disturbed metabolism as diabetes. In my opinion psychological treatment is not only worthless but absolutely contraindicated, certainly while the disease process is in operation." Further emphasizing his disgust with a misguided psychoanalytic profession, he distinguishes between the "trade" spelling and his own: "Psyzophrenia."[28]

Such holistic formulations were in stark contrast to a central tenet of postwar thought. From economics and technology to the literary criticism of the New Critics and the reified tenets of Freudian psychoanalysis, there was an emphasis on objectively derived knowledge, an epistemological paradigm that often compartmentalized experience and accepted forms of knowledge. Such dualism dismissed subjective perceptions that were incongruent with previously defined standards of uniformity, consensus, and order. Adhering to a basic Spenglerian proposition, the Beats viewed the perpetuation of scientific objectivity as not only a crisis of society but also one felt on an individual level. As Spengler noted, the privileging of objectivity came at the expense of the subjectivity of the individual: "Scientific worlds are superficial worlds, practical, soulless, and purely extensive worlds. . . . Life is no longer to be lived as something self-evident—hardly a matter of consciousness, let alone choice—or to be accepted as God-willed destiny, but is to be treated as a problem, presented as the intellect sees it, judged by 'utilitarian' or 'rational' criteria. . . . The brain rules because the soul abdicates."[29]

Given their romantic proclivities, the Beats used art as a defense against a world seen as increasingly hostile to nonlinear, nonrational, and mystical thought processes. Reflecting Spengler's view of Enlightenment rationality, they understood the social ills of contemporary America as a turning away from personal intuition toward the abyss of "cold, abstract, reason." America's disconnection from its source was personal, resulting in the forced separation of reason from emotion, mind from body, and intellect from senses.

For Burroughs, this Spenglerian insight into the division between a "theoretical" and "actual nation" was given full articulation in the semantic theories of Count Alfred Korzybski. Burroughs had admired Korzybski's *Science and Sanity* (1933) since attending a series of lectures Korzybski had given at the Chicago Institute of General Semantics in 1939.[30] Through Korzybski by way of Burroughs, the Beats were able to link directly the consequences of Faustian imposition to both psychological and physiological debasement. Despite a few minor differences, Korzybski was "in full agreement with the great work of Spengler" and wrote in *Science and Sanity* that "*The Decline of the West* may be considered as a preliminary and preparatory survey of the great cultural spasms which have rocked mankind." Like Spengler, Korzybski thought that "a period of human development had ended" and that the contemporary crisis was one of "identification." The correspondence between word and the thing it names was now being taken too literally. Such naive verbal realism, frought with self-deception, failed to acknowledge the invisible reality of signification and the fact that truth was a product of willed discovery beyond the surface of language. Korzybski believed that neither the nervous system nor the mind functioned properly because persons in the West identified themselves as such, following the dictates of the social environment rather than those of will. The problem involved "deeply rooted 'principles' which are invariably false to facts and so our orientations based on them cannot lead to adjustment and sanity." Consequently, those in the West had been conditioned by language—in Korzybski's words, "infected" with a disease that "retards the development of sane human relations and prevents general sanity."[31] Burroughs constantly lectured Kerouac and Ginsberg about the practical consequences of Korzybski's insights, replicating his messianic tone about the need to reexamine their thought processes and the ways in which the media, the state, and the rhetoric of popular culture create divisions within the self.

The Beats countered the violence visited upon the mind by reclaiming lost ground, using the trope of madness not only to assert beleaguered solidarity but also to assume an offensive position against standards of psychological health. The group was familiar with prolonged psychological counseling. In 1940 Burroughs spent four weeks in Bellevue after cutting off the tip of the little finger on his left hand, à la Van Gogh, in a fit of jealous rage. In 1942, while attending navy boot camp, Kerouac had been diagnosed as having a "schizoid personality." After putting down his rifle and abandoning drill practice, he had walked to the naval library, where the military police found him, reading and taking notes, and arrested him. Similarly, Ginsberg, whose mother was a diagnosed schizophrenic, spent six months at the Columbia Presbyterian Psychiatric Institute in 1949.[32]

By the mid-twentieth century, diagnoses of psychiatric problems had become increasingly sophisticated for defining normative personalities and proposing methods for social adaptation.[33] Consequently, the definition of insanity became a culturally specific site of ideological contestation; the Beats used it to diagnose the nation's schizophrenic identity. On one level, they entered the debate by using the notion of madness as a strategy to question the "sanity" of the dominant social structure and reveal the cosmic situation of pseudomorphosis. On another level, they equated mad behavior as an index of authentic Americaness in that it symbolized liberation from the conditioning spell of Faustian Civilization.

Madness pointed to the split identity of America, the psychological consequences for the individual, and the ability to overcome them both. For example, in *On the Road*, Kerouac acknowledges the emancipatory qualities of such behavior, writing, "The only people for me are the mad ones, the ones who are mad to live, mad to talk, mad to be saved, desirous of everything at the same time . . . burn, burn, burn like fabulous yellow roman candles exploding like spiders across the stars and in the middle you see the blue centerlight pop and everybody goes 'Awww!'" In a veiled reference to Spengler, Kerouac then ridicules the lack of such verve in contemporary America, bitterly asking, "What did they call such young people in Goethe's Germany?"[34] In that sense, madness was a way to cast off Faustian influence and a means to reconnect to the universal macrocosm.

In a similar fashion Ginsberg exposed the debilitating nature of social norms and moral codes. Writing to Kerouac from the psychiatric ward, he flatly pronounced that "there are no intellectuals in madhouses," thus turning the accusations of insanity and illegitimacy against his accusers.[35] In poems such as "Howl," Ginsberg continued to affirm the vitality of those persecuted in asylums by turning schizophrenics into martyrs, transvaluing madness into a vehicle for social change. In that light, madness was something to be sought out not avoided. "Nobody cares when a man goes mad," Ginsberg wrote in "Refrain," "He is sorry, God is glad."[36] In "Bop Lyrics," he implied how communion with the divine was achieved when "smart went crazy": "I'm a pot and God's a potter," he wrote. "I'm so lucky to be nutty."[37]

The Beats' advocacy of madness as a social virtue is most evident in Kerouac's descriptions of Neal Cassady, whose psychiatric diagnosis labeled him "a sociopathic personality with schizophrenic and manic-depressive tendencies that could develop into psychosis."[38] His behavior was so completely different from accepted standards that Kerouac spoke of him as "absolutely mad in his movements; he seemed to be doing everything at the same time. It was a shaking of the head, up and down, sideways; jerky, vigorous hands; quick walking, sitting, crossing the legs, uncrossing, getting up, rubbing the hands, rubbing his fly, hitching his pants, looking up and saying 'Am,' and sudden slitting of the eyes to see everywhere; and all the time he was grabbing me by the ribs and talking, talking." For Kerouac, such madness had a regenerative quality, a mode of being that was primal in its desires and oblivious to the corrupted values of intellectual discourse. "Besides," he wrote, "all my New York friends were in the negative, nightmare position of putting down society and giving their tired bookish or political or psychoanalytical reasons, but Dean [Neal Cassady] just raced in society, eager for bread and love; he didn't care one way or the other, 'so long's I can get that lil ole gal with that lil sumpin down there tween her legs, boy,' and 'so long's we can *eat*, son, y'ear me? I'm *hungry*, I'm *starving*, let's *eat right now!*'"[39] Cassady's exuberance was a rudimentary form of sexuality interlaced with violent themes. It was an affirmative violence, however, a mode of being that not only resisted Faustian norms but also sought to destroy them in order to connect with the forces of nature.

The violence undergirding the Beats' new vision was both real and imagined, a product of their time as well a reaction against a perceived threat. It is no surprise that initial assessments of the Beats in the mid–1950s would focus on their "frantic defiance" and "anguished anathema hurling."[40] Their violent energy of the 1940s never entirely dissipated, although the ways in which Burroughs translated and channeled it differed significantly from Kerouac's and Ginsberg's methods. Burroughs continually drew on the violent energies within himself and his world, whereas Ginsberg and Kerouac, given their pacifistic demeanors, directed such undercurrents into more affirming directions. But even while their uses of violence as an oppositional force differed, they shared a fundamental assumption: If America and its people were under siege, the required response must be equally intense. Consequently, the violent terms in which they perceived the crisis were inevitably present in the solutions they proposed to it. Provocation followed provocation.

Body and Time: The Holy Contours of Life

By the late 1940s, the Beats had formulated a notion of individualism far different from the stereotyped renditions of postwar intellectual debates in which David Riesman's lonely crowd and William Whyte's organization man took center stage.[41] Motivated by a pervading sense of victimization, loss of personal autonomy, and fractured self-identity, the Beats began to formulate a new, holistic vision of the self. Given Spengler's valorization of those who could actually feel the "beat of cosmic cycles," the body and the experiences of the body became metaphors through which the Beats expressed a particular brand of individualism.[42] Because self and culture were intricately laced together in the cosmic scheme, such persons were to become both mediators and combatants, aligning their physical bodies and their culture with the macrocosm in order to cast off the yoke of Civilization. Consequently, human actions could have direct social repercussions. Spengler asserted that the "spirituality" of both the culture and the individual were intimately connected: "In the history of the culture as in that of individual existence," he wrote, "we are dealing with the actualization of the possible; it is the story of an inner spirituality becoming the *style of a world*."[43]

The Beats' religious individualism, then, was not an existentialist opposition of the self versus society but one of self in service of society. Its focus was on somatic connection rather than intellectual exposition, apprehension and physical communion rather than abstract representations. In other words, the new vision of self was a metaphysical platform, a sensuous spirituality that not only described this self and defined its role in the cosmic cycles but also set the terms for achieving it. Even with its Spenglerian tenor, the project was part of the American tradition of reinventing the self in terms that granted it a unique and privileged status whose realization and tangible expression were intimately connected to the fate of the nation. In Kerouac's words, the new vision would spur the Beats into action, to "seek identity in the midst of indistinguishable chaos and sprawling nameless reality."[44]

The Beats' attempt to practice this form of religious individualism became an aggressive search for a reference point outside of the self yet intimately related to it and from which to participate in the dynamic logic that guided the universe. Ginsberg later commented that the new vision was "a breakthrough onto a new consciousness which is not like the social consciousness inculcated by television or radio or newspapers or politics, its another animal mammal consciousness that's unified with the world—you know, . . . the compassionate consciousness of the mind and the heart that we share."[45]

For the Beats, this wider reality was the organic law of a Spenglerian macrocosm, the same law that governed the human community. In this manner, the new vision focused on the really real of the transcendent cosmos while simultaneously attempting to overcome experiential obstacles. Just as the disorder of mind and body had a cosmic source according to Spengler, the solution also involved an appeal to cosmic forces, the same forces pulsating through the physical self: "The *one* great pulse-beat operates through all the detached souls, filling, driving, checking, and often destroying—that is the deepest of all life's secrets, the secret that all religious mysteries and all great poems seek to penetrate, the secret whose tragedy stirred in Goethe . . . where the child has to die because, brought into existence out of the discordant cycles of the blood, it is the fruit of a cosmic sin."[46]

The alternation of this pulse, like the beat of a heart, sustained the cycle of cultural life. Just as it was the source of life, it was also the source of death when it flowed improperly. Like a heartbeat, vital energy pumped through the universe, from macrocosm to microcosm and back again, continually revitalizing a culture and its inhabitants. The notion of correspondence was metaphysical as well as physical, providing not only a theodicy for understanding personal suffering but also a framework explaining that all was not harmonious in the microcosms of self and America. In Kerouac's words, neither were any longer "rooted in earth in the ancient pulse of life and work and death."[47]

The Beats' sensuous individualism was complemented by their use of drugs, particularly Benzedrine and marijuana. Like William James a half-century earlier, they preferred a religious praxis that was not a "dull habit" but rather induced an "acute fever."[48] Drugs helped them experience a holistic and immediate sensitivity to the cosmos, even moments of synaesthesia whereby natural facts became social ones and previous conceptions of self were rendered fraudulent. By enhancing immediate sense perceptions, drugs also enabled the Beats to transcend the limits imposed by well-worn ideas, even those of space and time. As early as 1945, Kerouac confirmed that Benzedrine broached new levels of awareness and recovered aspects of his personality denied by conventional modes of thought: "Benny has made me see a lot. The process of intensifying awareness naturally leads to an overflow of old notions, and viola [sic], new material wells up like water following its proper level, and makes itself evident at the brim of consciousness. Brand new water!"[49] Seven years later, Kerouac described an experience in Mexico to Neal Cassady: "Eternity is the only thing on my mind permanently, and you are a part of it. One good thing about Mexico, you just get high and dig eternity everyday."[50] Ginsberg often likened his drug perceptions to a decentering of the rational mind. He wrote that purely "straight," respectable, middle-class perceptions were limited in scope when compared to moments of "eyes and ears full of marijuana, / eating the god Peyote on the floor of a mudhut."[51] For Burroughs, the process of drug withdrawal was a means to increased sensitivity. As he wrote in *Junky*, the body reaches a "condition of emergency" in which "sensations sharpen [and] the addict is aware of his visceral processes to an uncomfortable degree, peristalsis and secretion go unchecked."[52]

For the Beats, drug use did not so much reveal alternative realities as it allowed the formulation of alternative understandings of this one. Akin to what Emerson once called "self-cultivation," expanding individual consciousness via drugs had definite social and political implications. Like the

Transcendentalists before them, the Beats' social vision was an appeal to a new form of religiosity, free from the infringement of the dominant institutions and standards. As Emerson had asked, "Why should not we also enjoy an original relation to the universe? Why should not we have a poetry and philosophy of insight and not of tradition, and a religion by revelation to us, and not to the history of theirs?"[53]

Also like the Transcendentalists, the Beats attempted to reform the social realm through an appeal to fine-grained perceptions.[54] For example, in a 1949 letter, Kerouac commanded Ginsberg to "Roll your own," an allusion to the cultivation of individual consciousness through drugs and the need to revive atrophied modes of sense experience for the sake of humanity: "I decided someday to become a Thoreau of the Mountains. To live like Jesus and Thoreau . . . I'll wander the wild, wild mountains and wait for Judgment Day, but not for men . . . for society. . . . It is evil. It will fall. Jesus was right. Burroughs was right . . . I don't believe in this society, but I believe in man. . . . So, roll your own bones. I say. . . . All is well. Go, go; go roll your own bones. Bone-bone. Roll-bone your own go-bone, etc."[55]

Kerouac's playfulness and sexual innuendo puts a gloss on Thoreau's comment in *Walden:* "Every man is the builder of a temple, called his body, to the god he worships, after a style purely his own, nor can he get off by hammering marble instead. We are all sculptors and painters, and our material is our flesh and blood and bones." Moreover, Kerouac's emphasis on natural awareness is reminiscent of Emerson's notion of intuition as the "fountain and action of thought," which would see "old things pass away,— means, teachers, texts, temples fall."[56] The Transcendentalist emphasis on self-reliance as means to cultural renewal was consciously echoed by Kerouac. Like "Thoreau of the Mountains," he would "roll his bones" in order to return to a natural state of life, one dictated only by the laws of death and rebirth.

The Beats' cultivation of this "ancient heavenly connection" was redolent of the period's religious rhetoric and the popular currency of such works as Norman Vincent Peale's prayer-based trilogy *Guide to Confident Living* (1947), *The Power of Positive Thinking* (1952), and *Stay Alive All Your Life* (1957). Such popular sentiment celebrated prayer as a remedy for all personal problems and simultaneously denied that any of these problems derived from the period's social milieu.[57] The Beats, however, viewed moments of cosmic connection as precisely the way in which to make manifest the social origin of contradictory personal traits, inevitably leading to their diffusion. For them, drugs were an alternative to mass-marketed therapy from the likes of Peale and others. This form of therapy, however, was not aimed at suppression of anxiety but its resolution. The popularity of antianxiety drugs such as tranquilizers and Miltown after the war only masked personal problems by denying they existed. The Beats' conception of drugs, however, was antithetical to such popular rhetoric. For them, drugs were a vehicle for releasing blocked aspects of consciousness and restoring suppressed modes of awareness. By removing such mental limitations, they sought to create a communal base of shared experience, uncontaminated and unfiltered by social and psychological mechanisms of repression.

Using drugs and theorizing about them points to a somewhat paradoxical notion of community based on the tenets of individual freedom. In 1953 Burroughs traveled to the jungles of South America on a search for "the uncut kick that opens out instead of narrowing down like junk." After years of heroin addiction, his quest for a more "collective" experience reflected the increasing social engagement of his writing. In *Junky,* Burroughs confirmed his belief in the liberatory nature of a hallucinogenic vine, yage, the Indian name for *Bannisteria caapi,* a fast-growing vine used by South American medicine men. Burroughs described its communal and communicative qualities: "Yage is supposed to increase telepathic sensitivity. . . . What I look for in any relationship is contact on the non-verbal level of intuition and feeling, that is, telepathic contact."[58] As opposed to heroin, Burroughs believed that yage was a "group" drug that could facilitate mental telepathy and emotional empathy. Being under the influence of certain drugs such as marijuana, Benzedrine, and yage opened alternative lines of communication, enabling things to be expressed that could not be transmitted in any other way.

The paradoxical quality of the Beats' communal ideal was grounded in Spengler's abstract musings on the topic of group relations. Expanding on a number of his metaphysical pronouncements, they used the notion of cosmic flow to help create a new vision of the self within a communal context. Because the Beats discerned a suffocation of individual sentience, they tended to exaggerate the relevance and superiority of the subjective experience and its physiological (more specifically, sexual) dimensions. Sexual metaphors provided a language of liberation, at once violent yet exuberant and spontaneous. Spengler had emphasized the *"two cyclic organs of the cosmic existence, the blood-system and the sex-organ."* He spoke of the "whole body" as the "microcosmic" connection to the "cosmic beat." To establish that connection was a form of cosmic therapy, for it allowed persons to "reproduce themselves for the maintenance beyond themselves of the eternal cycle."[59] Spengler never detailed exactly how such renewal was to be accomplished. He did, however, write about it in such a way as to require the Beats to read their own experiences into his work, itself a process that revealed the religious agenda behind their collaboration. At first, they conflated psychology and physiology through Spengler and saw the workings of the mind and the body as interdependent. Later, the orgone theories in Wilhelm Reich's *The Function of the Orgasm* (1942) and *The Cancer Biopathy* (1948) supplemented their initial formulation.

Reich, an erstwhile Marxist and a former student of Sigmund Freud, had been expelled from the International Psychoanalytical Association in 1933 for insisting that the unconscious was purely biological and not psychological. Instead of focusing solely on the mind, Reich asserted that spontaneous sexual expression could free the body from social inhibitions, precipitating the reintegration of body and mind. Such reintegration would not only facilitate a recovery of a holistic self but also reestablish the connection between the individual and the material world.[60]

According to Reich's psychopolitical perspective, the orgasm held the key to the regulation of biological energy, allowing for a healthy reduction of physical tension and easing mental rigidity brought on by an authoritarian social order: "The central manifestation of life is expressed in the genital sexual function, to which life owes its existence and continuation. A society of human beings that has excluded the most essential manifestations of this function and made them unconscious is not capable of fully living rationally; indeed, everything it says appears distorted and pornographic. Only the mystics, far removed from scientific insight have preserved contact with the living process."[61] Reich hedged his theory of a physical unconscious with the concept of "orgone energy" (derived from the words *organism* and *orgasm*), specifically his assertion that the cosmos and all its parts were animated by a single, primordial cosmic energy. He claimed that "from the orgone ocean all being, physical as well as emotional, emerges Man . . . is, together with all living beings, a bit of especially varied and organized cosmic orgone energy."[62]

Burroughs introduced Kerouac and Ginsberg to Reich's unorthodox theories in 1947 after hearing about the Food and Drug Administration's investigation into Reich's Orgone Institute in Rangeley, Maine.[63] That same year, Burroughs suggested Reichian analysis to Ginsberg as an alternative to the life-denying effects of more popular forms of psychoanalysis: "As regards your psychiatric difficulties, I am not at all surprised. These jerks feel that anyone who is with it at all belongs in a nut house. What they want is . . . someone so scared and whipped down he would never venture to do anything that might disturb the analyst. I think you would do better with the Reichians who sound a good deal more hip."[64]

Burroughs's advice (and talk of conspiracy) echoed Reich's own rants against the personal and social "neuroses result[ing] from a stasis of sexual energy." By 1950 Burroughs had built his own "orgone accumulator," a narrow wooden box lined with sheet metal. The sheet metal was to trap orgone energy and create a force field that would then interact with the person sitting in the box. That same year, Burroughs wrote to Ginsberg again: "My experiments [have] convinced me that Reich's orgones are real and demonstrable. Yet so-called Scientists go around saying he is insane and refuse even to investigate his findings."[65]

Although the Beats did not subscribe to Reich's Marxist political agenda, they did borrow those ideas that resonated with their experience of and in the world, which was shaped by the Spenglerian ideals of flux and flow. In terms of a Spenglerian model of reality, the ubiquitous presence of orgone energy throughout the universe confirmed that both the macrocosm and microcosm were interactive and determined by the same flow of energy. "In spite of its infinite variety," suggested Reich, "nature is basically a unified whole. The unity and simplicity underlying nature is revealed when we work with orgone functions." Thus conceived, the sexual act became a way of connecting with the larger forces of the cosmos. Furthermore, when the rush of sexual fluids replicated the flow of the macrocosm, the sexual act could precipitate a religious form of knowledge.[66]

Reich believed that an unhealthy buildup of energy occurred when no outlets for sexual expression could be found and continually inveighed against the repressive "moralism" of the state. "We have outlawed the most important life function," he wrote. "We have stamped it sinful, even criminal, and denied it any social protection . . . we have lost our trust in the natural laws of life and now we are beginning to notice the consequences."[67] The result was a "biopathy," a cancerous disease resulting from "the disturbances of the biological pulsation." Echoing Korzybski's language of infectious disease, Reich viewed psychological and physical traumas in terms of cancer. "Cancer," he stated, "is the most significant somatic expression of the biophysiological effect of sexual stasis; schizophrenia is the most significant expression in the emotional realm."[68] Kerouac and Ginsberg did not take up that metaphor, but Burroughs did, writing in 1949 of "a cancer on the political body of this country which no longer belongs to its citizens."[69] In the following years he expanded the range of the metaphor, adorned it with the vocabulary of the street, and in *Naked Lunch* built his social theory of addiction around it.

Reich's diagnosis of physical disorder in the social body of the West and his call for "a revolution in thought and action . . . an achievement not of individuals but of society as a whole" found a sympathetic audience among the Beats.[70] Indeed, they inscribed Reich's opposition between orgasm and sexual stasis onto Spengler's cosmic frame of reference, humanizing it and making it flesh. The Beats, however, were concerned not only with moral repression of the body but also with the entire range of American beliefs— moral as well as political, scientific, economic, and religious. In other words, psychic disease did not have a single source but was characteristic of the last stage of civilization, in which repression of all creative life was commonplace, even inevitable. According to Spengler, it was during this stage that individuals relied on "systematic criticism" instead of "physiognomic tact," "causal Knowledge" instead of "Destiny-Experience," and "scientific methods" instead of "life experience."[71] The very air one breathed, it seemed, opposed the creative capacities of the individual, those traits that were, according to Ginsberg, Burroughs, and Kerouac, the "unique part of human sentience."[72]

In terms remarkably similar to Reich's, Spengler wrote about natural sentience under siege in the West and about the repression of "the organic logic of existence," a mystical state that brought one in touch with the "Destiny Idea."[73] His philosophy was based on the fundamental opposition between the "Destiny Idea" and the "Causality Principle," the former being the idea governing cultures in their prime and the latter being the determinative principle of the late stages of "Civilization." Vision, in Spengler's terms, became a whole-body experience of the cosmos. "The Destiny-idea demands life-experience and not scientific experience," he wrote, railing against the Enlightenment method of empiricism. He advocated "the power of seeing and not that of calculating, depth and not intellect" and declared in no uncertain terms, "There is an *organic logic,* an instinctive, dream-sure logic of all existence as opposed to the *logic of the inorganic,* the logic of understanding and of things understood—a logic of direction as against a logic of extension— and no systematist, no Aristotle or Kant, has known how to deal with it."[74] Urging readers to "live towards . . . the superabundant flow of things" so that one "feels that he himself is the meaning of what is to happen," Spengler described awareness of cosmic laws in terms of contemplation, intuition, and "physiognomic tact." "The words Time and Destiny," he wrote, "for anyone who uses them instinctively, touch life itself in its deepest depths—life as a whole, which is not to be separated from lived experience."[75] The Beats' mixture of Spenglerism and Reichian psychology resulted in an active metaphysical platform that intimately connected a sexualized self with America and positioned both in opposition to a restrictive Faustian environment.

The new vision was, in part, an articulation of an experiential ethic—a response to and extension of, by way of Reich and others, Spengler's sweeping pronouncements. It was simultaneously a pragmatic emphasis on personal experience as the source of universal truth and a means for regenerating the individual self and American culture. Spengler contrasted such a holistic approach to experience with the mechanistic science of the contemporary West, which he believed separated the individual from the world instead of promoting a physical alertness to cosmic flux. Claiming that "Nature-knowledge is a subtle kind of self-knowledge . . . [a] mirror of man," Spengler wrote that "the thinking man . . . is perplexed by movement; for the contemplative it is self-evident."[76]

Spengler also wrote of the futility of Faustian thought and its desire to make tangible what can only be felt privately: "The problem of motion touches, at once and immediately, the secrets of existence, which are alien to the waking-consciousness and yet inexorably press upon it. In posing motion as a problem we affirm our will to comprehend the incomprehensible, the when and wherefore, Destiny, blood, all that our intuitive processes touch in our depths. Born to see, we strive to set it before or eyes in the light, so that we may in the literal sense grasp it, assure ourselves of it as of something tangible." Hence, the new vision referred not only to how one perceived the world but also to how one gained such a cosmic perspective in everyday life. It was not an attempt to theorize "the cosmic as it appears in the macrocosm to the microcosm" but to feel it, seeking not the literal seeing of life but life itself.[77] "The difference," wrote Spengler, "is only in the eyes by which and through which this world is realized."[78]

From the outset, the Beats emphasized the human world but always in reference to Spengler's abstract formulations of the transcendental reality of the macrocosm. It was precisely this world that contained avenues to the divine. Reinforcing their immanental leanings was Spengler's description of Faustian Civilization's obsession with transcendence— people projecting themselves into space, faith in unending progress, retreat from the everyday, and refusal to acknowledge the laws of time and their physiological source. According to Spengler, Faustian Civilization was no longer in tune with the forces of destiny and the logic of time: "Culture-man lives inwards, Civilization-man outwards in space."[79]

Throughout *The Town and the City*, Kerouac employed the image of staring out into space to signal a Faustian disposition, most often with the character of Francis: "Francis had a habit of keeping to himself, reading, or just staring out the window of his bedroom," "staring into abysses," and "with a somewhat askance look out the window."[80] Similarly, in an early routine, "The Portuguese Mooch," Burroughs described an encounter with Antonio, a vulgar European, as "looking into space." Antonio is "a completely parasitic organism specialized to a point where he could not live without a host, a mutilated fragment of the human potential. His mere presence was an irritation. Phantom tendrils reached out from him, feeling for a point of weakness on which to fasten."[81]

In addition to Reich and Spengler, the new physics complemented the Beats' understanding of time. They, like many avant-garde artists after the war, applied the insights of quantum mechanics and processional ontology to social reality. In particular, the Beats gravitated toward insights that seemed to deny preordained absolutes and reveal a physical universe consisting of relative particles acting without evident controls. Such notions rejected the predictability of the Newtonian universe and the idea that particles in space existed independently of time, operating by way of a cause-and-effect model. In his poem "The Terms in Which I Think of Reality" (1950), Ginsberg articulated his view of a non-Newtonian universe in endless flux:

> Time is Eternity,
> ultimate and immovable;
> everyone's an angel.
>
> It's Heaven's mystery
> of changing perfection:
> absolutely eternity
>
> changes! Cars are always
> going down the street,
> lamps go off and on.
>
> It's a great flat plain;
> we can see everything
> on top of the table.
>
> Clams open on the table,
> lambs are eaten by worms
> on the plain. The motion
>
> of change is beautiful
> as well as form called
> in and out of being.[82]

The content as well as the disjointed syntax deny the Newtonian notion of atoms situated in absolute space and time and challenge the linear and chronological construction of time. The natural imagery of decay in the poem alludes to an organic entropy as well as to the natural, unmediated, cosmic awareness that comes with accepting cyclical history. As Spengler wrote, "The logic of time—is a fact of the deepest inward certainty, a fact which suffuses the whole of mythological religions and artistic thought and constitutes the essence and kernel of all history."[83]

Kerouac's early work was infused with overt references to Spengler's concept of historical time. Throughout *Doctor Sax* he distinguished between his childhood awareness of the "Sound of Time in the River" and the adult's following of "Clock Showing Bleak Time." A juxtaposition of the two modes of time runs throughout the novel. For example, Kerouac described the childhood game of "horseracing," using marbles to represent different horses running around a cardboard track, to depict the instinctive understanding of metaphysical realities: "Ceremony of racehorse-chipping, racehorse-*destinying*, things have to change in an organic picture of the world . . . horses had to go through processes of prime and decay like real horses." The natural sensibility that resulted was "something secretively wild and baleful in the glares of the child soul, the masturbatory surging triumph of the knowledge of reality."[84]

According to Spengler, an understanding of time and historical destiny could only be gained by orienting oneself to the natural rhythms of the lifecycle. In *On the Road,* Kerouac wrote often of such unmediated apprehension of the universe. Throughout the novel, the character Dean Moriarty constantly asserts "we know time!" in reference to his adherence to a Spenglerian metaphysics of time. The phrase becomes his mantra. Uttered during the most extreme states of frenetic joy achieved by Sal and Dean on their adventures, it encompasses both the mystery and meaning of life. Kerouac also referred to others, most often jazz musicians, as expressing such vision in that they also "knew time":

> Dean stood before him [Rollo Greb] with head bowed, repeating over and over again, "Yes . . . Yes . . . Yes." He took me into a corner. "That Rollo Greb is the greatest, most wonderful of all. That's what I'm trying to tell you— that's what I want to be. I want to be like him. He's never hung up, he goes every direction, he lets it all out, he knows time, he has nothing to do but rock back and forth. Man he's the end! You see, if you go like him all the time you'll finally get it."
> "Get what?"
> "IT! IT! I'll tell you—now no time, we have no time now."
> Dean rushed back to watch Rollo Greb some more.[85]

Kerouac's play on the word *time* expresses the fundamental difference between a Spenglerian interpretation of time and the chronological time of progressive history. Demonstrating that linear time is abstractly constructed into past, present, and future, Kerouac called for a dynamic, more organic understanding. Writing about "the restless exploring originality of the American jazz musician," he echoed Spengler's commandment to reject the Enlightenment's understanding of temporality as solely an "activity of the intellect" and to experience that "we ourselves are Time."[86]

By the early 1950s, the American public had been inundated with prescriptive messages of American progress, infallibility, and homogeneity, notions all underscored by a linear model of Manifest Destiny. In "America," Ginsberg condemned the push for consensus in the name of inevitable progress by subverting one of its most prominent mediums, *Time* magazine. In doing so the poet cleverly plays on Spengler's idea that "the *word* Time is a sort of charm to summon up that intensely personal something."[87] Through an elaborate pun, Ginsberg warned that superficial materialism had eroded Americans' internal awareness of time, and he ridiculed their acceptance of *Time* magazine:

> [America] I'm addressing you.
> Are you going to let your emotional life be run by Time Magazine?
> I'm obsessed by Time Magazine.
> I read it every week.
> Its cover stares at me every time I slink past the corner candy store.
> I read it in the basement of the Berkeley Public Library.

It appears that the speaker is buying into the materialistic and mediated ideal, but Ginsberg casts off the yoke of corporate liberal imperialism and its handmaiden, advertising. He asserts his oppositional personality through a subjective awareness of time rather than an objective reading of the magazine. Ginsberg rejects prevailing social codes of career advancement and reveals the psychological liberation of accepting Spengler's notion that "we ourselves are Time":

> It's always telling me about responsibility. Businessmen are serious. Movie
>   producers are serious. Everybody's serious but me.
> It occurs to me that I am America.
> I am talking to myself again.[88]

Ginsberg inverts the original meaning of time (conditioning and conformity) and transforms it into a self-referential symbol of cosmic awareness. He proposes that those reading "Time Magazine" look inward in order to experience time as a physiological reality instead of as a conceptual creation.[89]

Democratic Vistas

Such appreciation for "the laws of time" was a fundamental prerequisite for establishing an egalitarian base for group interaction. For Ginsberg and Kerouac in particular, the rhythmic interplay of jazz music was the quintessential expression of individual freedom within a group setting. The community exemplified on the jazz stage was a model to be emulated as Charlie Parker, Lester Young, Dave Brubeck, George Shearing, and other musicians took on representative American status. As the Ginsberg character (Levinsky) declares in *The Town and the City,* bebop is "a complete departure from the old European forms. It's a kind of wild Dionysian American music, pure emotion and frenzy that sends great vibrations through everyone. . . . It's just mad! . . . Almost like an orgy, don't you see, in which everyone will explode and become as one."[90] Accordingly, jazz musicians had the ability to "dig" their immediate situation as well as each other. In *Visions of Cody,* Cody explains the significance of recovering that awareness of self and other as found in jazz's "moment of rapport": "dig him, dig her, dig this place, dig these cats, this is all that's left, where else can you go Jack?" "It was absolutely true," Kerouac agrees.[91] Capable of improvising at will, jazz soloists complement other members of the band while pursuing their own flights of ecstasy. Ginsberg and Kerouac understood jazz, filtered through Spengler and Reich, as a communal yet utterly instinctual mode of existence. Even Burroughs acknowledged the intersubjective dimensions of jazz, querying Ginsberg in a letter, "Have you dug Brubeck, etc., new telepathic jazz."[92]

Spengler had written that music could be a cohesive group force, an "emancipation from the spell of the light-world and its facts. . . . For music is the only art whose means lie outside the light-world that has so long become coextensive with our total world, and music alone, therefore, can take us right out of this world, break up the steely tyranny of light, and let us fondly imagine that we are on the verge of reaching the soul's final secret."[93] Those words speak to Kerouac and Ginsberg's romantic proclivities to primitivize jazz musicians and view them as having mystical knowledge that rendered black communal forms more vibrant. Given Reich's insights, they considered the jazz ethos as a form of sexual expression, an attitude consisting of "*natural* sociality and sexuality, spontaneous enjoyment of work, [and] capacity for love."[94] In *On the Road,* Kerouac described such moments of expression in masturbatory terms. A white hipster sitting in on drums, for example, starts "the beat of a jump number, and he began stroking the snares with soft, goofy bop brushes, swaying his neck with that complacent Reichianalyzed ecstasy. . . . He smiled joyously into space and kept the beat."[95] Invoking Reich was in reference to "character armor" (or rather its dismantling), Reich's term for the defensive psychological and physiological traits acquired to protect oneself from social norms at the expense of uninhibited expression and engagement. Such defenses lead down the path of neurosis, for an individual "is not at ease 'within his own skin,' he is 'inhibited,' 'unable to realize himself,' 'hemmed in' as if by a wall; he 'lacks contact,' he feels 'tight enough to burst.' He strives with all his might 'towards the world,' but is 'tied down.'"[96]

Taking his cue from Reich's notion of character armor, Ginsberg viewed America's neurotic state as preventing any form of meaningful personal interaction. Attributing the nation's noncommunal atmosphere of fear and repression to "disbelief in that infinite self," he wrote, "I mean the whole cold war is the imposition of a vast mental barrier on everybody, a vast anti-natural psyche. A hardening, a shutting off of the perception of desire and tenderness which everybody knows . . . That desire built in. Blocked . . . [creating] a self-consciousness which is a substitute for communication with the outside. This consciousness pushed back into the self and thinking of how it will hold its face and eyes and hands in order to make a mask to hide the flow that is going on."[97]

That inability to connect with a universal human essence, what Ginsberg called a "depth perception of cosmos," had negated any and all potential for "the flow" of give-and-take conversation. Viewing obstacles to such "desire and tenderness" as tantamount to suppressing the natural American spirit, the Beats believed the public had been unable to confront its spiritual self despite the fact that people lived on the land. In a 1945 journal entry, Kerouac lamented the repression that resulted in the atomization of Americans: "We are all sealed in our own little melancholy atmospheres, like planets revolving around the sun, our common but distant desire."[98]

In Reich, the Beats found an apt metaphor to thematize communal desire. In Spengler, they found the reason behind its nonfulfillment: an emotional freeze because of America's fragmented "Cultural soul." Spengler asserted that a unified "Culture or spiritual community," unimpeded by foreign influence, depended on the "communicability of intuitions, sensations and thoughts from one to another—that is, the possibility of making intelligible what one has created in the style of one's own being, through expression-media such as language or art or religion, by means or word-sounds or formulae or signs."[99] In *On the Road*, Kerouac described those lacking such a natural awareness as needing "to worry and betray time with urgencies false and otherwise." Their adherence to a socially constructed model of time had rendered them "anxious and whiny" while "all the time *it* all flies by them."[100] In *Decline*, Spengler connected the "'it' and the 'we'" to those moments of cosmic harmony when "the microcosmic wall is obliterated." A feeling of *communitas* is evident when *"it* jostles and threatens, *it* pushes and pulls, *it* flees, swerves, and sways. In such cases," Spengler continued, no bridge is needed "to unite your sense of it with mine . . . limbs intertwine, feet rush, *one* cry comes from every mouth, *one* destiny overlies all. Out of a sum of little single words comes suddenly a complete whole."[101]

Such a kinetic description of community framed the Beats' appreciation of jazz ensembles. For example, later in *On the Road,* Dean Moriarty describes a jazz soloist's dislodging time as a recovery of the communal dimension of life, the collective counterpart to the pure subjectivity of "It": "Time stops. He's filling empty space with the substance of our lives, confessions of his belly button strain, remembrance of ideas, rehashes of old blowing. He has to blow across bridges and come back and do it with such infinite feeling soul-exploratory for the tune of the moment that everybody knows it's not the tune that counts but IT." A few moments later, Moriarty asks Sal (Kerouac) to "dig Denver together," affirming, *"We* know what IT is and *we* know TIME and *we* know everything is really FINE."[102]

Akin to their appreciation of jazz, openness to sexuality, particularly homosexuality, reflected their desire to identify themselves as an alternative community. Their celebration of sexuality was a conscious mutation of ex-isting moral codes, an extension that repudiated the status quo as well as produced a system of communication, form of expression, and means of group representation.[103] For the heterosexual majority of postwar Americans, sexual activity was a means of intimacy between husband and wife and a way shore up the base of the nuclear family. It was the yellow brick road that led straight to the American dream of suburban ranch houses, coffee klatches, and two-car garages. Although not a suitable topic for public discussion, sexuality was not a taboo subject if kept within the confines of suburban bedrooms. For the Beats in the 1940s and 1950s, however, sexuality was a constant topic of discussion, and that discussion was both critical strategy and a way to foster a sense of group intimacy not sanctioned by the domi-nant culture.[104] They continually sought emotional closeness in life and at-tempted to construct a community over and against "the military police bureaucracy state" that cultivated "a paranoia between men and a suspicion and fear of body contact and soul contact in order to keep people separate."[105]

In their celebration of both hetero- and homosexual experiences, the Beats attempted to recover a more egalitarian and democratic base of com-munity. They looked again to Reich in their opposition to a "sexless, soul-less" America.[106] His ideas of sex as an emotional-physiological transaction of mind-body complemented the already strong sense of the intersubjective dimensions of sex among the Beats. Ginsberg proposed that sexual intercourse as the "ultimate exchange of soul" could become the foundation of a religious-oriented community and recover the "ancient nature" of communal relations that had been "obliterated in modern culture." Similarly, for Dean Moriarty, "sex was the one and only holy and important thing in life."[107]

Echoing Walt Whitman's evocation in *Leaves of Grass* of queer comradeship as the grounds of American democracy ("The dependence of Liberty shall be lovers, / The continuance of Equality shall be comrades"), Ginsberg in particular depicted male sexuality as the most legitimate and most American basis for interpersonal relations, both straight and gay.[108] For example, in "Howl," he celebrates those

> who let themselves be fucked in the ass by saintly motorcyclists, and screamed
> with joy . . .
> who sweetened the snatches of a million girls trembling in the sunset . . .
> who went out whoring through Colorado in myriad stolen night cars.[109]

By equating "deviant" sexual behavior with transcendental communion, Ginsberg revealed the spiritual vitality of behavior not sanctioned by traditional mores. Similarly, Kerouac often broached the theme of friendship among males in order to call for the recovery of an inclusive American community that excluded women.[110] Ginsberg spoke of Kerouac's work as containing a "basic political prophetic value, not merely in discovering the body of the land . . . but as the presentation for the first time in a long time of unabashed emotion between fellow citizens."[111] In *Visions of Cody*, Kerouac grieved over the social consequences of repressing such natural feelings: "The sins of America are precisely that the streets . . . are empty where their houses are, there's no sense of neighborhood anymore . . . beyond this old honesty there can only be thieves. What is it now, that a well-dressed man who is a plumber in the Plumber's Union by day, and a beat-dressed man who is a retired barber meet on the street and think of each other wrong. . . . Looking at a man in the eye is now queer."[112] On one hand, Kerouac viewed the fear of contact stemming from homophobic hatred as the dishonest, that is repressive, nature of the dominant culture. On the other hand, he was revulsed by effeminate homosexuality, a stance consistent with his rejection of female authority and fear of being labeled a homosexual.[113]

Burroughs also advocated the intersubjective dimensions of sex while overturning common stereotypes associated with homosexuals. In much of his work, he incorporated homosexuality into the frontier myth, romanticizing the masculinity and courage of this new form of outlaw. As he wrote in *Naked Lunch,* "A *functioning* police state needs no police. Homosexuality does not occur to anyone as conceivable behavior. . . . Homosexuality is a *political* crime in a matriarchy." In such remarks, Burroughs revealed an even more misogynistic disposition than either Kerouac or Ginsberg. He was quick to make the "distinction between us strong, manly, noble types and the leaping, jumping, window dressing cocksucker."[114] In his assertion of the essential Americanness of homosexuality, Burroughs interrogated contemporary definitions that were limited to homophobic accusations of "un-Americanness" and normative imperatives of orthodox psychology. He rejected the question of whether homosexuality was a crime or an illness, claiming instead that it could be a liberating cultural practice.

The Beats' musings on sexuality were often reactions to the perceived threat of domestic containment, symbolized at mid-century by the "family man," cut off from the adventures of the road as well as himself. Furthermore, the Beats saw the postwar state of denial and refusal to acknowledge that homosexuality was a masculine pursuit as a social neurosis that had eroded American democracy and fomented the growth of the "machine state" of corporatism and manipulation. In their quest for rugged, entrepreneurial adventures, interpersonal experience, and support, they sought to reconnect to each other and manifest the secret of correspondence. It was religion in its most basic meaning—*re-ligare*—to reconnect or recreate a bond. As Ginsberg stated, "It's not merely a tolerance of love between men, it's a recognition of that as basic to democracy. As long as men are separate from each other and can't even touch each other, then how can they collaborate together in building a political structure? All they can do is build what we have here in America, which is this giant, robotic, criminally dominated city culture that actually not only exploits men but in which men exploit each other, exploit women and also exploit nature."[115]

Seeking a natural reconnection, the Beats were open to sexual experiences and celebrated them in their literature. In doing so, they sought to overturn the most familiar and familial ideological extensions of American triumphalism by exposing the socially destructive contradictions contained within them. Although their misogyny reflected larger trends within American society, the Beats rationalized their ways through recourse to the metaphysical.

The adventurous subtext of Beat sexuality was also reflected in a more literal rootlessness. Their well-known penchant for traveling, "beating one's way" as Kerouac often referred to it, not only symbolized their constant state of spiritual questing but were also rituals of perception by which they gained a new perspective on the values of the dominant culture. In *On the Road*, for example, Kerouac writes: "I had traveled eight thousand miles around the American continent and I was back in Times Square . . . seeing with my innocent road-eyes the absolute madness and fantastic hoorair of New York with its millions and millions hustling forever for a buck among themselves, the mad dream—grabbing, taking, giving, sighing, dying, just so they could be buried in those awful cemetery cities beyond Long Island City."[116] Purified by his journey across America, Kerouac encounters the greed and tragic blindness at the heart of the nation's economic prowess. While equating the American Dream with premature death, he can admire the "absolute madness" of the scene even while lamenting how that "hustling" energy is put to use.[117]

Although the dominant culture came to view Beat adventures "on the road" as mindless kicks, random travel enabled them to employ a liminal strategy to analyze traditional notions of community and articulate alternative paradigms. In that sense, traveling became a foundation and an oppositional matrix for their closed community.[118] To travel was a symbolic and literal flight from domestic responsibility as well as an assertion of male privilege. Although that may seem counterintuitive, Beat travels symbolically revealed the vacuity of "square" motivations by articulating a more authentic value system learned on the road—one that privileged the autonomy of the individual while simultaneously celebrating the deep camaraderie that traversed distance and time. Maintaining these communal ties, despite their individual sojourns, challenged the stable but often estranged relationships of nuclear, suburban American families.

It was through such emphasis on the communal ends of movement that Beats interrogated the increased travel of the dominant culture after the war. In particular, they questioned postwar desires to upgrade professional status and selfishly exploit the new prosperity. By questioning the motivations behind the American Dream, they showed that the ends did not justify the means. On the contrary, the Beats celebrated the richness of the journey rather than the material accumulation idealized in advertising and on television sitcoms. From a Spenglerian viewpoint, their apparent rootlessness was a form of cosmic rootedness. Because "Culture" and, consequently, America were both determined by the laws of time and not space, the Beats' cultural location was the whole of America rather than one specific place. In one sense, their attitude toward movement was reminiscent of a diasporic consciousness and maintained allegiance to a cosmic homeland despite their exile within Faustian "Civilization."

The Wolfeans and the Black Priest

As the Beats worked through the new vision, what resulted was a distinct theology, one that asked and answered the most fundamental questions about life through the category of experience. Although each Beat pursued the new vision, their personal demeanors influenced how each writer approached and applied this common fund of ideas. Despite holding core assumptions in common, each positioned himself somewhat differently in relation to Spengler's theory of correspondence and his metaphysical insights. Burroughs's application of the new vision was quite literal and pragmatic in intent, and those of Kerouac, and Ginsberg, even more so, were more mystical in orientation. The difference was not so much one of content but of attitude and temperament. Burroughs positioned himself within an America on the verge of total collapse, whereas Kerouac and Ginsberg believed they could somehow transcend present conditions and thereby halt the present cultural slide. All three men colored their personal readings of *Decline* to the extent that in it each found a framework that complemented their personal backgrounds.

As early as 1945 a self-conscious split occurred among the Beats. The predominantly heterosexual Kerouac and his friend Hal Chase were on the hopeful, pro-America side, and the homosexuals Ginsberg and Burroughs were on the more skeptical and "debaucherous" side. Referring to themselves as the "Wolfeans" (a reference to the pastoral fiction of Thomas Wolfe) and the "Black priests," respectively, the split hinged on whether America was seen as the source and location for a new Culture or whether it was to be swallowed by the decadence of Europe.

Ginsberg soon evolved into a Wolfean, becoming more optimistic about the future as the 1940s progressed. His turn-around was catalyzed by the introduction of Neal Cassady into the group in early 1947 and demonstrates that this boundary was permeable, hinging on personal disposition (both sexual and temperamental) rather than on unwavering ideological position. As Gerald Nicosia reports, "This distinction became a kind of inside joke" among the Beats but is nonetheless telling about how each understood themselves within a Spenglerian cosmic drama:

> They turned it into a drama, which they performed together. Wearing his father's straw hat, Jack played the wealthy but innocent "American in Paris." Bill wore a wig and a skirt as the "lesbian countess," who would bring Jack to the "well-groomed Hungarian," played by Allen. The Hungarian played upon guileless Wolfean Americans by selling them forged artistic masterworks, and the lesbian countess was his shill. Their apartment transformed into the Hungarian's "atelier," Allen would say, "Yes, young man, you

vant some culture, and I understand that you vant to buy some art vorks that I have brought from Hungary when I had to flee Hitler.[119]

Such humor reflects how their different orientations were not so much in opposition as they were complementary. Each writer was fundamentally concerned with his role in a cosmic struggle and his potential to effect its resolution. Their focus was squarely on America as it existed, for they believed they were living at a time of great personal and cultural crisis. Consequently, their lives were dedicated to America, whether defined by a romantic past or an indescribable future.

Such differences in orientation were reflected in how each Beat described his utopian vision of America and how each conceived of his physical role in creating it. For each, both ideals were defined in physical, even sensual, terms. It was not only subjectivity that was limited by Faustian conditioning but also the physical ability to interact with the environment and achieve a democratic collectivity. For Ginsberg after 1947, this idyllic America was prophesied in the erotic nativism of Walt Whitman's poetry, a voice he had admired since high school but whose influence deepened as his career progressed.[120] The romantic version of America came into being by those who lived not only in it but also with and through it. As Whitman wrote in *Democratic Vistas,* "We see our land, America, her literature, esthetics, &c., as, substantially, the getting in form, or effusement and statement, of deepest basic elements and loftiest final meetings, of history and man—and the portrayal, (under the eternal laws and conditions of beauty,) of our own physiognomy, the subjective tie and expression of objective, as from our own combination, continuation, and points of view." Kerouac, too, envisioned the America of Whitman (by way of Thomas Wolfe, whose prose style resembles that of both Spengler and Whitman)—an open, simple society of love and individual freedom: "The main thing being the average, the bodily, the concrete, the democratic, the popular, on which all the super-structures of the future are to permanently rest."[121]

Both Ginsberg and Kerouac envisioned an America in which physical connections with both other individuals and the cosmos were not only possible but also its defining quality. In that particular romantic mode, the individual is both outsider and insider, outlaw and representative, defying the accepted values of society yet at the same time bound to a collective ideal as mystically embodied in the land. The romantic proclivities of Ginsberg and Kerouac found a parallel in those of Spengler: the individual called upon to flee the "exhausted quarry" and the conformity of the age in order to discover "the rich and virgin clay-bed nearby," the source of a new culture.[122]

Similarly, Burroughs was also alarmed at the deadening of sensory experience but rather than look forward to the idyllic America of a romantic future he envisioned a provisional utopia. Subscribing to a more existential reading of America, his initial goal was to weather the Faustian storm. For him, individuals were capable of committing themselves to a purely subjective form of existence, thus removing themselves from their immediate environment and, in Korzybski's words, able to "look forward to full understanding of the next phase, get hold of this understanding, keep it under conscious and scientific control."[123] Such a commitment, however, signaled loyalty to a magical universe suffused with invisible forces and shared by only those who made the same commitment. The existential tenor was less Sartrean and more reminiscent of the Christian existentialism of Kierkegaard and the postwar neo-orthodox revival. Like the "crisis theology" of Karl Barth or Emil Brunner, Burroughs emphasized human connection with an unknowable other, in his case an untotalizable control system, a "leap of faith" that defied rational explanation.[124]

Regardless of each concluding that he lived in a time a great struggle, each Beat understood the Faustian siege in personal terms. Although each saw his own subjectivity as intimately bound up with larger cosmic forces, they diverged on how to express an "inmost spirituality" as well as what role such expression would play in the cosmic battle. Similarly, all three agreed that America and its people were suffering through a crisis of cosmic maladjustment, but they differed over the extent to which that crisis could be immediately overcome. Most significantly, they held different opinions about exactly what America (and which Americans) would emerge after the decline of the West. The differences hinged on an interpretation of Spengler's call for a "poet or a prophet . . . to enter the culture-soul . . . to make [it] part of one's life."[125] The writers differed over exactly what "culture-soul" they were to enter and, consequently, what elements of the current cultural climate they were to absorb and internalize.

Burroughs read Spengler literally, for not only did he see himself at the end of an age but he also took upon himself the same task Spengler was performing: "the last great task of Western philosophy . . . [to] foresee the way that destiny has chosen for" Western civilization.[126] For Burroughs, America had been so ravaged by the Faustian parasite that it could no longer be salvaged. Therefore, he looked to a post-Faustian America that would emerge after the infection had been isolated, contained, and eliminated. The current situation was hopeless. America, as it was currently conceived, was doomed to go down with the Faustian ship, a point he made in "Twilight's Last Gleamings" (1938): "S.O.S. . . . S.S. *America* . . . S.O.S. . . . S.S. Crapbox."[127] It was his task to march through the contemporary situation. Like the mythical Faust, Burroughs had a recklessness of spirit, disdainful yet acknowledging that this world was all there was. He confronted Faustian Civilization on its own terms in the hope of aiding in its dismantling and, eventually, seeing through it. In 1955 Kerouac acknowledged Burroughs's divergent perspective when he referred to him as the "last of the Faustian Men."[128]

Burroughs's project was in some ways masochistic, a Protestant-like form of liberation by means of reveling in original sin. He took upon himself the sins of cosmic misalignment, approaching the enemy directly and eradicating it through engagement. Experiences of the "cosmic beat" did not inevitably lead to immediate regeneration but imparted a critical knowledge of cosmic forces by which to continue the struggle. Again, like Faust, he confronted evil on its own terms. Consequently, Burroughs's goal was to absorb the decaying soul of Faustian Civilization and call attention to the dystopian present for the purpose of education and preparation. The America he absorbed was the viral America, the parasitical America, the one totally corrupted by European ways. His drug-addicted lifestyle, for example, reflected a personal mythology of internalizing evil to eventually overcome it. His battle with addiction also revealed his belief in a unique self, not yet fully corrupted, staving off the enemy, and waiting for a cure.

Kerouac and Ginsberg denied evil to a certain extent, however, and viewed it as an illusion of consciousness and history propagated through personal ignorance of Faustian infringement. Once that situation was recognized as a hallucination, right behavior and thought would follow. Theirs was a project of absorbing the positive energy of America, specifically the romantic and pastoral past covered by the cloud of death that hung over Europe after World War II. They viewed their task of absorption as a form of cultural recovery in order to act as conduits of a new yet still emerging America. Kerouac and Ginsberg tended toward a hopeful universalism in which the soul of contemporary America could be separated from the Faustian Civilization and salvaged on its own terms.

Fellaheen Role Models

The difference in perspective regarding Spengler's narrative of decline determined the trajectory each writer would follow as he developed the new vision within his own peculiar focus. As the Beats navigated the cultural demimonde of New York City, they read their encounters in terms of a Spenglerian allegory that invested them with an air of ultimacy. Although each Beat valued intuition as the key to religious revelation and privileged "everydayness" as a sacred realm that evoked the inner perception of truth, what constituted everydayness was a point of contention. Unlike the Transcendentalists, the external expanse of nature did not suggest the immanence of the Judeo-Christian God. On the contrary, it suggested an understanding of the universe that followed a Spenglerian metaphysical model of history and culture. Using the same general religious strategy as the Transcendentalists, the historical context of postwar America directed the Beats toward different metaphysical conclusions. Instead of looking to the brooks and streams of Concord or Thoreau's Walden Pond, they looked to the environs of Greenwich Village bohemia, the Times Square underworld, and the jazz clubs of Harlem. Just as they searched for an "other" America through an other mode of being, they inevitably looked to those persons deemed other as a promising location in which to search for alternative values to the Faustian status quo. For Kerouac and Ginsberg, these values would form the basis of an emergent American culture. For Burroughs, however, these values could be used to confront the Faustian oppressor. That fundamental difference in perspective determined not only who the Beats looked to for mystical insight but also the ways in which each put the new vision to use in their daily lives. What each determined as the other as well as how each sought to become transparent to the other colored their individual pursuits.

Ironically, the Beats sought to gain insight into themselves and the macrocosmic laws governing the universe by modeling their experiences on the actions and attitudes of others. Within the interpretive schema of *Decline of the West,* once Western civilization had reached its "final demise under the bright glare of cold, abstract reason," a timeless group would emerge, a reservoir of people who had remained outside the march toward Civilization. As Spengler noted, "The peasantry, 'everlasting' and historyless, was a people before the dawn of the Culture, and in very fundamental characters it continued to be the primitive people, surviving when the form of the nation passed away again." Spengler labeled these people "the fellaheen"—"the primitive blood . . . harboring in their stone masses" through which new cultures eventually sprung.[129] For each Beat, those despised and rejected people without status qualifications or socially desirable characteristics represented the essence of America.

Each writer looked to the "folkbody blood of the land," derelicts, criminals, and Harlem jazzmen, as precisely those who had been so psychologically and physiologically oppressed that they no longer subscribed to or followed the dominant modes of expression, communication, or representation. Hence, it was these men who embodied the term *beat,* beaten down by society but "beatific" following their natural impulses, their own "beat." According to the Beats, such persons exhibited an originality and creativity deemed lacking in mainstream society. Yet because the fellaheen were ever-present at both the births and deaths of cultures, Spengler described them with an ambiguity reflected in the different attitudes the Beats exhibited toward such entities. For Kerouac and Ginsberg, the vital culture they represented was simultaneously timeless and new, America before Columbus and after the decline of the West. According to Spengler, a burgeoning reality of "a new God-feeling. World Fear. World Longing . . . rural intuitive. Great creations of the newly awakened dream-heavy Soul. Super-personal unity and full-ness."[130] For Burroughs, however, those on the margins were wounded sur-vivors of a cosmic war, wiser for experience but nonetheless debased. Refer-ing to the fellaheen, Spengler wrote that "the primitive blood remains, alive, but robbed of its strongest and most promising elements," an allusion to their constant state of oppression.[131]

ᒋᒍ

In 1948 Kerouac described to John Clellon Holmes the experiential ethic of the hipster as both inspiration and clarification of the new vision. As Holmes recalled:

> One evening as he [Kerouac] described the way the younger hipsters of Times Square walked down the street—watchful, cat-like, inquisitive, close to the buildings, *in* the street but not *of* it—I interrupted him to say that I thought we all walked like that, but what was the peculiar quality of mind behind it? "It's a sort of furtiveness," he said. "Like we were a generation of furtives. You know, with an inner knowledge there's no use flaunting on that level, the level of the 'public,' a kind of beatness—I mean, being right down to it, to our-selves, because we all *really* know where we are—and a weariness with all the forms, all the conventions of the world."[132]

Kerouac had borrowed the term *beat* from the argot of the Times Square underworld to describe the disillusionment felt by his literary friends, attrib-uting their rejection to their superiority in an inferior world. Earlier, he had written that *On the Road* was "an imaginative survey of a new American generation known as the 'Hip' (The Knowing), with emphasis on their prob-lems in the mid-century fifties and their historical relationship with preceding generations. . . . This new generation has a conviction that it alone has known everything, or been 'hip' in the history of the world."[133]

For Kerouac, the term *beat* embodied the Spenglerian notion of media-tion between self and world. On one level, it transcended the natural world, reveling in the sacred details of nature and experiencing what Kierkegaard once termed the "sublime in the pedestrian."[134] On another, it meant being cheated or robbed, emotionally or physically exhausted. And, finally, it developed the connotation of "beatific" when filtered through Kerouac's Catholic sensibility: a rejected state with the potential for physical joy and spiritual redemption. As Kerouac once claimed, "I am not ashamed to wear the crucifix of my Lord. It is because I am Beat, that is, I believe in beatitude and that God so loved the world that he gave his only begotten son to it."[135] Because of the innocence and hardship stemming from nonparticipation in Civilization, Kerouac viewed the world of the fellaheen as full of inevitable suffering yet also endowed with avenues for personal transcendence.

In "The Origins of the Beat Generation" (1958), written at the height of his notoriety, Kerouac wrote of how the term *beat* had acquired a multileveled meaning: "Anyway, the hipsters, whose music was bop, they looked like criminals but they kept talking about the same things I liked, long outlines of personal experience and vision, nightlong confessions full of hope that had become illicit and repressed by War, stirrings, rumblings of a new soul (that same old human soul). And so Huncke appeared to us and said 'I'm beat' with radiant light shining out of his despairing eyes."[136]

Herbert Huncke, a well-known Time Square hustler, heroin addict, and petty thief, was perceived by Kerouac and Ginsberg as a liminal entity who embodied an alternative, more authentic, reality. When traveling in Mexico in 1952, for example, Kerouac wrote that the fellaheen Indians possessed many of the primitive qualities he admired in Huncke but lacked his hipster edge.[137] According to Ginsberg, Huncke "was to be found in 1945 passing on subways from Harlem to Broadway scoring for drugs, music, incense, lovers, Benzedrine Inhalers, second story furniture, coffee, all night vigils in 42nd street Horn & Hardart and Bickford Cafeterias, encountering curious & beautiful solitaries of New York dawn."[138] It was through figures such as Huncke, the beaten down, the "subterraneans," and "desolation angels," that "beat" came to represent both a personal and interpersonal awareness. It was a natural orientation that asserted "that same old human soul" over and against a climate that denied human sentience and interpersonal communication.

In Huncke, Ginsberg and Kerouac discerned the dormant potential of the fellaheen. Referring to the revolutionary promise embodied in such an individual, Ginsberg commented, "In his anonymity & holy Creephood in New York he was the sensitive vehicle for a veritable new consciousness which spread through him to others sensitized by their dislocations from History and thence to entire generations of a nation renewing itself for fear of Apocalyptic judgment."[139]

Despite his marginalization, Huncke was depicted as a "vehicle" of renewal, a positive force that outweighed and outshone any apocalyptic negativity or existential despair. With the rise of industrial capitalism, the commodification of everyday life, and the elimination of nature as a tangible force in the universe, only those outside the system of capitalistic social organization could offer an alternative model to the humanization of the environment and the subsequent dehumanization of the self. Huncke's acumen was of the street—that is, of the land—not the inflated knowledge of intellectual discourse. Kerouac and Ginsberg lamented the rejection of such characters as Huncke but viewed their suffering as redemptive. In other words, through the persecution of the fellaheen a new culture would eventually emerge. As Ginsberg explained, "So in the grand Karma of robotic Civilizations it may be that the humblest, most afflicted, most persecuted, most suffering lowly junkie hustling some change in the all-night movie is the initiate of a Glory transcending his Nation to its knees in tearful self-forgiveness."[140] Ginsberg's description of Huncke did not involve nihilistic visions of America and irreversible cosmic entropy but attributed transcendental significance to his suffering. In Beat literature, Huncke assumed the role of American martyr, innocent yet wise and to be pitied yet celebrated. For Kerouac and Ginsberg, Huncke was "a substitute for the sloppy improvisors of rebellion formerly known in literature variously as heroes, humanists, prometheans, or decadents."[141] For Burroughs, however, he represented the final remnant of the American frontier.

Ironically, Ginsberg's and Kerouac's optimistic view of social outcasts as sources of beatitude stemmed from a scenario of total destruction first brought to them by Burroughs in 1944.[142] Although both sides held a Spenglerian view of American society, they differed on the nature of the actual decline. Instead of ruminating on the nature of the new "Springtime Culture," Burroughs negotiated the winter terrain of contemporary America and negatively revealed a future utopia by detailing the dystopia of the present. Among the Beats, he was most closely associated with Huncke, living with him in the late 1940s and collaborating with him in various criminal enterprises. Burroughs immersed himself deeply in the underground world of crime and drugs and even became a petty criminal and dealer. Identification with Huncke was, in part, premised on an allegorical rendering of him as embodying the primitive adaptability of the fellaheen, the last spark of human freedom to be studied before the impending doom of Western civilization. Burroughs's fiction incessantly describes the purgatory of endless suffering and negation of human expression—"beat" in the sense of beaten down, oppressed, and dehumanized. Positioning the outcasts of society within an amoral, nihilistic, apocalyptic framework reflected a profoundly pessimistic reading of Spengler wherein cultural disintegration had to run its final course before a renewal could begin. For Burroughs, the fellaheen would survive, but the new cultural epoch would be centered around those who had internalized the essential qualities of the fellaheen, that is, Burroughs himself.

Reminiscent of the "outlaw Western" of the 1940s and the gangster film, its predecessor of the 1930s, Burroughs assumed the mythic role of a gunfighter. In the postwar years, those who assumed that outlaw identity became American heroes in popular culture. Burroughs cultivated a criminal identity as a sort of professional badge and a way to gain insight and empowerment through criminal expertise. Like the male heroes in the Dashiell Hammet and Raymond Chandler novels he enjoyed, outlaw heroes understood the world as essentially hostile. In that hard-boiled world, as Richard Slotkin explains, "human motives are rarely good, and outcomes depend not on right but on the proper deployment of might."[143]

The manipulation and employment of power were the only recourse in a world bent on self-destruction. Furthermore, power, for Burroughs, was not gender-neutral but reflected masculine aggression over and against the stereotypically passive ways of the feminine. For him, street violence was not without logic nor gender. Such an ethos was not random but a calculated response to oppressive conditions and a perceived feminization of American culture.[144] Burroughs viewed the criminal underworld as an exaggerated reflection of the bureaucratic hierarchy of the dominant culture, a location in which to gain insight and power over the forces of Faustian control. Criminality was a form of discipline. As Burroughs wrote to Ginsberg in 1948:

> "Crime" is simply behavior outlawed by a given culture. There is no connection between crime and ethics. I do not see a connection between lying and violation of the law. In fact, there is more lying in the course of a "regular job" most of which require a constant state of pretense and dissimulation . . . the line between legitimate and criminal activity has broken down since the war. Most everyone in business violates the law everyday. . . . I violate the law, but my present violations are condoned by a corrupt government.[145]

Similarly, Burroughs chose drug addiction as a way of life in order to replicate an exaggerated version of the Faustian soul. "Junk is a key," he noted, "a prototype of life. If anyone fully understood junk, he would have some of the secrets of life, the final answers."[146] As Huncke commented, Burroughs "became a drug addict principally as a result of research more than anything else."[147]

Constantly looking to procure his next fix, Burroughs immersed himself in the logic of addiction in order to gain knowledge as well as leverage over the forces of control. First introduced to morphine by Huncke, he believed this logic to be at the center of America's cultural situation, where material saturation was both norm and necessity due to the logic of its Faustian nature. The overwhelming need to acquire and obtain in order to create a sense of security can be traced to the founding covenants of America and a faith in never replicating but always exceeding the achievements of one's predecessors. Roland Delattre has written that such logic depends on "culturally defined expectations for more—more that is rarely experienced as sufficient—together with a haunting fear of inadequacy."[148] On one level, Burroughs welcomed the release from responsibility that came with dependence—a sense of liberation through submission to external forces of control. Such nihilistic activity reduced the self to bare components and destroyed society's constraints by the absorbtion into a reality that is wholly other. This masochistic attitude affirmed an overriding harmony between self and cosmos not clearly evident at the level of day-to-day experience.

Burroughs began writing *Junky* in 1950 while living in Mexico City. As a plotless autobiography revolving around the cycles of addiction and withdrawal, *Junky* recounts Burroughs's journeys into the drug subculture and his reasons for becoming addicted. All Americans, he implies, are junkies, unconsciously addicted to control systems: "You become a narcotics addict because you do not have any strong motivations in any other direction . . . you don't decide to be an addict, one morning you wake up sick and you're an addict."[149]

Burroughs was determined to learn from his addiction, or, more precisely, from the process of deconditioning. Addiction became the central metaphor of his fiction during the 1950s, as well as the matrix for his cultural criticism. As he went through the cycles of withdrawal, he theoretically was able to shed the "character armor" and social restraints that prevented the autonomy of the individual psyche.[150] That such mental freedom came at the price of physical debilitation revealed the contradiction of the American situation— the dualistic separation of mind from body that prevented alignment with the cosmos. By literally embodying this cultural crisis, Burroughs sought to learn from experience and discover how to overcome the forces of control that devour human identity. It was a scientific approach. "Junk is a cellular equation that teaches the user facts of general validity," he wrote. "I have learned a great deal from using junk: I have seen life measured out in eyedroppers of morphine solution. I experienced the agonizing deprivation of junk sickness, and the pleasure of relief when junk thirsty cells drink from the needle . . . I have learned the junk equation. Junk is not, like alcohol or weed, a means to increased enjoyment of life. Junk is not a kick. It is a way of life."[151]

Although Kerouac and Ginsberg often associated with the criminal element of New York City, they looked for critical insights from the other, more energetic sources than the haze of narcotics. For Kerouac, his Catholic roots continued to inflect his personal choices, particularly those he deemed worthy of fellaheen status. Following Spengler's model, Kerouac looked to those on the margins of Civilization and uncorrupted by Faustian decline, who naturally possessed positive mystical insight. Claiming "you got to legalize the fellaheen," Kerouac viewed social outcasts as the preeminent religious martyrs, integrating his boyhood Catholicism with a Spenglerian orientation in the hope of experiencing "the inexpressible softness of Biblical Day and Fellaheen Afternoon."[152]

Catholic universalism colored not only Kerouac's Spenglerian notion of the fellaheen but also internalized a mystical orientation that evolved throughout his life. Just as Spengler advocated a mystical knowledge in appreciating the contours of process and change in history, Kerouac actively sought mystical experiences to validate his belief in the universal accessibility of these laws. In a letter written before completing *On the Road,* for example, he described his goal of recovering the communal essence of human consciousness in order to precipitate "a great world religion."[153]

What remained after Kerouac's Catholic faith in the harmony between God and creation was filtered through Spengler was an overriding belief in the lack of cosmic harmony and connection. Amid a world disconnected from the universal laws of history, his analogical vision became even more exaggerated, and he began to seek relief in the found links between earth and heaven in everyday life. He began to recast the elaborate networks of intercession between worlds, binding Spengler's "macrocosm" and "microcosm" through a continued emphasis on mystical experience and preoccupation with saints. Kerouac's novels are replete with these saintly figures, including the various depictions of Neal Cassady and, later, Kerouac's brother Gerard, Gary Snyder, "desolation angels," and various bums, outcasts, and hobos—all "subterranean" saints and all associated with Spengler's notion of the fellaheen. Kerouac viewed these liminal entities not as socially resistant but as social alternatives to an increasingly technologized American culture.

Neal Cassady, however, most completely captured Kerouac's mythic imagination. Cassady, raised in Denver by an alcoholic father and a local legend for his delinquency and sexual exploits, met Ginsberg and Kerouac in early 1947. His entrance into the Beat social circle was catalytic. His good looks, charisma, and natural instincts pushed Kerouac and Ginsberg away from a more Burroughsian reading of the fellaheen. In Cassady, they found exactly what they had sought—someone whose infectious energy and passion complemented their vision of a post-Faustian world and vibrant American culture. For Kerouac, he was the quintessential American. For Ginsberg, too, Cassady was the fellaheen hero of the American West, a man who would trivialize abstract philosophical debates by means of his pure, unadulterated physical energy. According to Kerouac, Cassady's "intelligence was every bit as formal and shining and complete, without the tedious intellectualness. And his 'criminality' was not something that sulked and sneered; it was a wild yea-saying overburst of American joy; it was Western, the west wind, an ode from the Plains, something new, long prophesied, long a-coming (he only stole cars for joy rides)." Cassady was "mad with a completely physical realization of the origins of life-bliss," reflecting both the communal and instinctive qualities of the fellaheen.[154] More vibrant than Huncke, Cassady, the "primitive saint" of *On the Road* (Dean Moriarty) and *Visions of Cody* (Cody Pomeray), symbolized the rejuvenating rather than the exhausting qualities of the fellaheen.[155]

Both Kerouac and Ginsberg portrayed Cassady as a mythical man who had come to redeem a spiritually stagnant American culture. His personal history and natural talents were soon connected with Spengler's description of the essential fellah type, a "primeval man" characterized as a *"ranging animal, a being whose waking-consciousness restlessly feels its way through life, all microcosm, under no servitude of place or home, keen and anxious in its senses."*[156] In a 1943 letter to Kerouac, his childhood friend Sebastian Sampas invoked Spengler to predict that in America "a wind is rising" and that a "new soul is in conception" because art was no longer "lovingly created or experienced." Regretful that "people cease[d] to be concerned with its great symbolism," he urged Kerouac to discover this aesthetic tide, undoubtedly shaping how Kerouac would later perceive Cassady. "The land is pregnant," Sampas continued. "A primitive man, crude, raw, unfinished—superb—is shaping the heart of our land. He does not seek for 'other.' The meaning he knows is life. He and all his fellow-mankind are brothers in spirit. In him coarse, rough-hewn, lie all our hopes—his will be the civilization greater than all—all art will be an integral part of him."[157] As opposed to Huncke, Cassady exuded a life-affirming love of fellaheen instead of an air of enduring oppression and anticipation of gloom. Cassady was always moving forward, vital, youthful, ever in control.

For Kerouac and Ginsberg, Cassady's sexuality, kinetic energy, stress on human relationships, and emphasis on immediate experience represented the cosmic force that, according to Spengler, drove the evolution of primitive cultures. Throughout *On the Road,* Moriarty constantly refers to "it," an enigmatic term that describes the most inspired moments of interpersonal communication and awareness: "O man, I have to tell you, NOW, I have IT," shouts Dean. In a similar passage Kerouac writes, "As Dean and I both swayed to the rhythm and the IT of our final excited joy in talking and living."[158] "It" represents both intersubjective moments of intimacy and a heightened awareness of cosmic reality, both characteristics of Spengler's description of burgeoning cultures: "In all primitive existence the 'it,' the Cosmic, is at work with such immediacy of force that all microcosmic utterances, whether in myth, custom, technique, or ornament, obey only the pressures of the instant."[159]

⌐⌐

While each Beat attempted to grasp the indescribable "it" through drugs, sex, and various meditative practices, Ginsberg sought to induce heightened awareness to cosmic harmony as a matter of everyday concern. As the most mystical of the three, he was driven by a constant desire to locate ultimate meaning in the relationship between mind and body, microcosm and macrocosm, world known and world experienced. By 1948 Ginsberg was growing more and more disillusioned as a struggling artist and felt that the new vision, as he had conceived it, had not yet resonated with his experiences. Complaining to Cassady, he wrote that the new vision "had the ideas without the feelings" to bring to life the insights he had collected over the past few years.[160] Consequently, Ginsberg aggressively sought an experience that would make the new vision an emotional reality.

The turning point came in 1948 as Ginsberg sat in his apartment and studied the works of William Blake, William Butler Yeats, and St. John of the Cross, scanning them for clues to his emotional dilemma. While masturbating, he read Blake's "Ah Sunflower!" in bed and was suddenly overcome by the voice of the English metaphysical poet.[161] As he recalled years later, "It was like God had a human voice, with all the infinite tenderness and anciency and moral gravity of a living creator speaking to his son." Substituting the personal authority of Blake for Spengler's abstract macrocosm, the world became alive with the active presence of the cosmos: "So that I began noticing in every corner where I looked evidences of a living hand, even in the bricks, in the arrangement of each brick. Some hand placed them there—that some hand had placed the whole universe in front of me. That some hand had placed the sky. No that's exaggerating—not that some hand placed the sky but that the sky was the living blue hand itself. Or that God was in front of my eyes— existence itself was God." By orienting knowledge and feeling toward the material world, Ginsberg became aware of its richness and depth. Material objects pointed beyond themselves and to the greater whole: "What I was seeing was a visionary thing . . . and a sense of cosmic consciousness, vibrations, understanding awe, and wonder and surprise. And it was a sudden awakening into a totally deeper real universe than I'd been existing in . . . the total consciousness then, of the complete universe."[162]

Within the worldview of Spenglerian correspondence, the microcosm of subjective reality captured the power of the macrocosm, and it followed that each individual element in the world was charged with sacred authority. In adopting that stance toward reality, what was felt and what was perceived became indistinguishable. Any piece of the material world was seen to point beyond itself to a larger, more powerful reality and at the same time to contain the power and reality of the macrocosm.[163] Ginsberg's description of Blake's visitation reflects his increasingly optimistic take on Spengler. Commenting on how he later heard Blake reading "The Sick Rose" to him, Ginsberg describes Blake's voice as confirming the organic flux of reality "that applied to the whole universe, like hearing the doom of the whole universe, and at the same time the inevitable beauty of doom."[164]

Burroughs dismissed Ginsberg's mystical experiences as limited because Ginsberg did not transcend the "palpable objects" of reality and therefore did not understand their connectiveness and fluid interactions: "Why is it 'useless' and deceptive to look further'? What are you afraid of? Why all this insistence on confining your attention to 'non-supersensual reality,' to 'palpable objects'? Why this care to avoid any experience that goes beyond arbitrary boundaries (and boundaries set by others)?" For Burroughs, Ginsberg's mystical experience was an abdication of this world, a passive stance that reinforced enslaved status: "Mysticism is just a word. I am concerned with *facts* on all levels of experience."[165]

Burroughs's "factualist" criticism, however, betrayed his own brand of mysticism.[166] Although his experiential ethic discounted a wholly transcendent reality, it did so only to the extent that he believed experience to be so multilayered and inexhaustible that it contained within it all of reality. Assuming an existentialist pose, Burroughs viewed experience, in its radical multiplicity, as the only space shared by the human species. Writing to Ginsberg in 1950, he described his type of mysticism: "My own tendency is the opposite of identification with 'non-supersensual reality.' My personal experiments and experiences have convinced me that telepathy and precognition are solid demonstrable facts; facts that can be verified by anyone who will perform certain definite experiments."[167] Despite his pessimism, Burroughs's scientific tropes underscored a faith in exploration and the discovery of the magical world operating within this one, the one that lay behind the traffic of representation.

Conclusion

By the late 1940s the Beats found themselves on the outside of the postwar economic bubble, looking not in but glancing ever farther outward. Disillusioned with the self-conscious decadence of their close friends from New York, they viewed not only the contemporary literary trends and philosophical fashions but also the sociopolitical climate as preventing intimate connection with the universal laws of the cosmos. In response, they constructed a theology of experience from cultural materials that were available to them. They built in and around Spengler's hermetic yet often imaginatively powerful statements concerning the relationship between the macrocosm and microcosm. In yearning to experience a natural self amid the corruptions of the material world, the Beats found Spengler's comparison of the artistic struggle for self-expression with that of every Culture very appealing. "[Culture's] living existence," wrote Spengler, "is an inner passionate struggle to maintain the Idea against the powers of Chaos without. . . . It is not only the artist who struggles against the resistance of the material and the stifling of the idea within him. Every Culture stands in a deeply-symbolical, almost in a mystical, relation to the extended, the space, in which and through which it strives to actualize."[168] The Beats agreed wholeheartedly with the proposition that spiritual potential is fulfilled within individual life, thus participating in the development of both the immediate community and the Cultural soul. In late 1944, for example, having separated from his wife, Edie Parker, Kerouac dedicated himself fully to writing. His dedication was so intense that he would routinely burn pages of his work in order to demonstrate the value of the artistic discipline. Kerouac sacrificed himself to his writing, allowing his identity as an artist to subsume his entire being. Such sacrifice was motivated by the need to manifest a divine spark in order to connect to the larger forces of the cosmos. As he recalled, his existence was focused solely on a search for "self-ultimacy" through the creation of an "artistic morality": "I lighted a candle," Kerouac once wrote, "cut a little into my finger, dripped blood, and wrote 'The Blood of the Poet' on a little calling card, with ink, then the big word 'BLOOD' over it, and hung that upon the wall as reminder of my new calling. 'Blood' writ in blood."[169] In that morbid ritual the boundary between material reality and representation dissolved. Flesh became spirit. The microcosm became one with the greater macrocosm. Although Kerouac was unacquainted with Gnosticism until the following year, a Gnostic current ran through his intense dedication to craft that was distinctly Spenglerian.[170] "The artist's soul," Spengler writes, "like the soul of a Culture, is something potential that may actualize itself, something complete and perfect—in the language of an older philosophy, a microcosm."[171] In *The Town and the City,* Kerouac confirmed that belief in the existence of "a way, a proper manner, an order in all the disorder and sadness of the world—that alone must be God in men."[172]

Differences among them existed, yet the Beats' Spenglerian piety directly countered what they viewed as an overly deterministic cultural atmosphere that prevented engagement with the sacred reality binding all of life. They expressed these insights through their own work and in doing so attempted to articulate a qualitative, experiential dimension of life. It was precisely in the attempt, or desire, to shape the world in such a way as to be rendered meaningful that the Beats demonstrated religious imagination. "In those years at Columbia, we really did have something going," remembers Lucien Carr. "It was a rebellious group, I suppose, of which there are many on campuses, but it was one that really was dedicated to a 'New Vision.' It's practically impossible to define. Maybe it was a term we just sold ourselves. It was *trying* to look at the world in a new light, *trying* to look at the world in a way that gave it some meaning. *Trying* to find values . . . that were valid. And it was through literature that all this was supposed to be done."[173] In attempting to give the world "some meaning," the Beats inhabited a religious world of their own construction. Although it differed from the religious worlds of the mainline churches, it reflected many values of the majority culture, albeit in refracted forms.

The search for a felt experience of ultimacy independent of mediating forms has been a common impulse throughout American religious history. Reaction against authority has most often been premised on concerns for personal and spiritual well-being as well as the desire to dislodge dominant assumptions and traditional patterns of behavior. Peter Williams has noted that the manner by which such concerns are expressed reveals a great deal about the cultural matrix in which they are manifested.[174] In considering postwar American culture in terms of mythology, the Beats addressed issues of authority primarily through style, both metaphysical and physical, ideological and behavioral. Supplementing their artistic modus operandi were styles of belief and action based on the possibilities of the human spirit becoming coextensive with the sacred capacities of the cosmos. That religious style encompassed not only what they believed but also how they believed for the purpose of "not merely knowing the truth . . . but embodying it, living it, giving oneself unconditionally to it."[175] For the Beats, the truth was the basic law of the macrocosm as put forth by Spengler.

While the new vision began as an experiential approach to art, as the Beats totaled ideas, images, and metaphors, it developed into a more substantive and encompassing perspective. As their world and their view of it became increasingly complex, Beat poetics evolved into Beat style. Motivated by their desire for physical and social transformation, the Beats began to build around Spengler's historical schemata, and the new vision went from merely describing reality to engaging and interpreting it.

chapter

3

PRIMITIVE FOLK, TRIBES AND THEIR CHIEFS.
"POLITICS" AND NO "STATE"

Mycenean Age ("Agamemnon") 1600–1100	Shang Period (1700–1300)

ULTURE. NATIONAL GROUPS OF DEFINITE STYLE AND PARTICULAR WORLD–FEELING. "NATIONS." WORKING OF AN IMMANENT STATE–IDEA

I. EARLY PERIOD. *Organic articulation of political existence. The two prime classes (noble and priest). Feudal economics; purely agrarian values*

OLD KINGDOM (2900–2400)	DORIC PERIOD (1100–650)	EARLY CHOU PERIOD (1300–800)	GOTHIC PERIOD (900–1500)
Feudal conditions of IV Dynasty	The Homeric kingship	The central ruler (Wang) pressed hard by the feudal nobility	Roman-German Imperial period
Increasing power of feudatories and priesthoods	Rise of the nobility (Ithaca, Etruria, Sparta)		Crusading nobility
The Pharaoh as incarnation of Ra			Empire and Papacy
VI Dynasty. Break-up of the Kingdom into heritable principalities. VII and VIII Dynasties, interregnum	Aristocratic synoecism Dissolution of kinship into annual offices	934–904. I-Wang and the vassals	Territorial princes Renaissance towns. Lancaster and York
	Oligarchy	841. Interregnum	1254. Interregnum

II. LATE PERIOD. *Actualizing of the matured State-idea. Town versus countryside. Rise of Third Estate (Bourgeoisie). Victory of money over landed property*

			BAROQUE PERIOD (1500–1800)
			Dynastic family-power, and Fronde (Richelieu, Wallenstein, Cromwell) about 1630.

"No Time for Poetry but Exactly What Is"

The Utopia of Beat Language

Previous page, from table 3, "'Contemporary' Political Epochs," in Oswald Spengler, *Form and Actuality*, volume 1 of *The Decline of the West*.

For the experience of each new age requires a new confession, and the world seems always waiting for its poet.
  —Ralph Waldo Emerson, "The Poet"

There is only *personal* history, and consequently only *personal* politics.
  —Oswald Spengler, *Perspectives of World-History*

We know how to sacrifice our entire life every day. The Time of Assassins is here!
  —Arthur Rimbaud, "The Time of Assassins"

Intimately tied to the Beats' theology of experience was the desire to empower others with their new vision. They wanted the rest of society to notice and adopt a cosmic appreciation and attention to particularities "more instant and interesting, and always happening, and *everything always all right*."[1] According to Ginsberg's account, the Beats would often ride the New York City subway in the mid–1940s and, through a seemingly juvenile prank, prove to others the righteousness of their cause. While sitting together on the train, one of them would peer through a hole ripped in his newspaper, waiting for someone to notice him noticing them. "We were conscious of them," Ginsberg remembered, "and it was an opportunity for them to be conscious of us being conscious of them . . . to provoke some sort of human consciousness to bring eternity into the subway." Unfortunately, onlookers perceived the prank as an act of immaturity rather than an exhibition of serious concern regarding the state and fate of the nation.[2] Although the Beats encountered nothing but complacency on the subway, writing continued to hold the most promise for radical social action. They hoped that a revolutionary lan-

133

guage would emerge from their intelligence and determination, initiating, in Kerouac's words, a "gentle, invisible revolt in America."[3]

By the late 1940s, personal idiosyncrasies and various disruptions led to the dissolution of the Beats' "libertine circle" in New York City. The creative and spiritual depths they had mined together, however, remained fertile ground for individual pursuits. In 1946 Burroughs moved to Texas with his common-law wife Joan Vollmer Adams and with the help of Herbert Huncke began a small farming operation in New Waverly that centered on a marijuana crop. Soon he moved east to Louisiana and then quickly fled to Mexico City after being arrested for possession of narcotics and firearms in New Orleans. For Burroughs, the forces of control seemed to be always in pursuit. Kerouac, however, quietly drifted in and out of the New York scene as he completed final revisions on *The Town and the City*. Even before the volume was published he had become dismayed by its conventional style and lack of experiential vibrancy. After his father died in 1946, Kerouac began to travel across the country, first by himself to Denver and San Francisco and then, with Neal Cassady, to visit Burroughs in New Orleans among other destinations. On these cross-country excursions with Cassady, Kerouac began to write like he and Cassady lived—"no time for poetry but exactly what is."[4] During the same period, Ginsberg also visited Cassady in Denver, finished his bachelor's degree at Columbia University, and traveled to Dakar, Africa, on a freighter ship. In 1949 Ginsberg was arrested for harboring a cache of Huncke's stolen goods in his apartment. He then spent eight months at the Rockland State Mental Hospital in lieu of jail. There he met Carl Solomon, Dadaist rebel, master of dissociative logic, nephew of the publisher of Ace Books, and, eventually, the martyred hero of "Howl."

By the end of the frenzied decade, Burroughs, Kerouac, and Ginsberg had become interested in the professional side of the literary life and pursued channels for communicating with an audience beyond their immediate group of friends. In a publishing climate dominated by the academic standards of the New Criticism, they formed an ambiguous relationship with what they perceived to be the bureaucratization of the literary establishment. They were intimately familiar with the high-brow codes given their elite educations and considered them as the standard from which to dissent. Engaging the contemporary literary scene on its own terms, they began to concentrate specifically on poetics. Each man had begun to question the nature and function of literature, the principles that do or do not govern it, and its effects on writer and reader alike. In doing so they extended the assumptions of the New Critics to a breaking point, often sharing more with their imagined adversaries than they acknowledged.

In exploring the ethics of writing, Burroughs, Kerouac, and Ginsberg each brought similar religious concerns to their individual investigations. Through frequent visits and letters they continued to share provisional answers to the same set of questions generated earlier in the decade. Although they had always approached the world in terms of their art, they increasingly began to translate their most illuminating experiences back into their poetics. What began as a new vision of literature—and then a new vision of self—in America became indistinguishable from a new vision of the writer in America. Art had first merged with life, then life merged again with art.

From the beginning of the Beats' friendship, the communicatory dimensions of the new vision had been a subject of intense interest and discussion. Even before developing his spontaneous sketching technique, Kerouac had explained the nature of his visionary quest to Ginsberg: "Until I find a way to unleash the inner life in an art-method, nothing about me will be clear. . . . Last summer . . . I was searching for a new method in order to release what I had in me, and Lucien said from across the room, 'What about the new vision?' The fact was I had the vision . . . I think everyone has . . . what we lack is the method."[5] Ginsberg agreed wholeheartedly. When he, in turn, complained to Burroughs about his own struggle to find a style that would effectively communicate what he had to say, Burroughs sympathized and offered a solution: a quasi-scientific method of discovery through experimentation. "I am having trouble with my own writing," he commiserated, "I can well understand your difficulties in seeking suitable *form* for your poems. I have the same trouble, which led me to experiment with a *new language*."[6] In seeking a "way to unleash the inner life," style became an extension and more distilled facet of their message. So, too, did the physical actions behind the style. The Beats were attempting to develop a "metre-making argument" in which the finish of the verse as well as the act of composition were essential to the argument.[7]

In part because of Burroughs's encouragement, the Beats intended to discover a new means of perception and expression—or rather a new means of expression as perception. As Burroughs proudly declared to Ginsberg in 1948, "I have been a 'journalist' and an advertising man."[8] To the extent that the boundaries dissolved between subject and object, conscious and unconscious, and description and explanation, through their poetics they sought to achieve an uninterrupted, complete account of reality. By achieving that epistemological ideal, writing became a way to question as well as confirm their understanding of the world. It was the most privileged form of experience, a physical act on a par with sex, drug use, or any other "kicks." Most important, it was a regenerative act, heightening subjective awareness to the point of achieving an original orientation toward the cosmos.[9] The Beats sought an intimate knowledge of reality—in Georges Bataille's words, "a complete answer to a total question."[10]

How then did Beat poetics, via individual style, enter the realm of political engagement? How was the private act of writing conceived of as capable of engaging the social, let alone precipitating social change? Such questions are built upon an age-old paradox. In America, the tension between writer and community has often been resolved through the religious imagination, an Emersonian negotiation between the dissolution of self into nature and a self-imposed exile from the world. Emerson wrote that a poet is "isolated among his contemporaries by truth and by his art, but with this consolation in his pursuits, that they will draw all men sooner or later."[11] The Beats fully committed themselves to that precarious balancing act. As Kerouac complained to Cassady, what were writers supposed to do if society ignored them? What was to prevent a solipsistic retreat? "In the subway everybody was going home to rest," Kerouac lamented, "instead of gathering in the Final Church of Eternal Joy, and I felt bad to see it. I began dreaming of a monastery."[12]

Mixing his metaphors, Kerouac hinted that even in moments of retreat he saw his task as a writer as one of leading by example. The Beats, as a group, although conscious of the precipice along which the writer constantly walked, attempted to distance themselves from the edge and the slippery, declining ground. Their Spenglerian strain of piety prevented them from standing alone or remaining adrift in a narcissistic sea of social impotence. According to Spengler, politics "is the art of the possible."[13] Within a specific religious worldview, each writer assumed a radical political stance by positioning himself in relation to an imaginary community (America) and speaking to it, for it, and from it, all in the name of possibility.

As the Beats imagined America, they could not help but imagine themselves. Their attempt to write to, for, and from America was premised on the Spenglerian assumption of an organic relationship between the individual and society. They also believed that personal transformation was the first step toward the transformation of society.[14] As Ginsberg later reflected, the early Beat agenda, far from ignoring questions of politics, focused on the transmission of cultural values from the individual to the rest of society. Following a Spenglerian model of cultural growth and his dictum that there is "only *personal* politics," the first task was a correct alignment of personal experience: "The first necessity was to get back to Person, from public to person. Before determining a new public, you had to find out who you are, who is your person. Which meant finding out different modalities of consciousness, different modalities of sexuality, different approaches to basic identity, examination of the nature of consciousness itself."[15]

Despite the focus on the personal in Ginsberg's statement, Beat poetics were populist. As Kerouac once noted, by writing with absolute honesty about himself he sought to initiate "world-wide melling of minds."[16] Emphasizing the contiguous relationship between self and society, the Beats addressed contemporary social problems through various confessional writing strategies. As Spengler wrote of the "continual unburdening of the Ego" through "self-examination" and "confession," the Beats employed confessional modes not only to express a particular orientation toward the cosmos but also to establish the link.[17] Paradoxically, they consummated their metaphysical belief in an active self by conforming to the sacred laws of the universe as detailed by Spengler, or what Burroughs would intermittently call "facts." In doing so, they wanted their writing to correspond to "exactly what is"—an infinitely complex, invisible, yet nonetheless discernible reality. Their writing practice became a spiritual discipline in the Emersonian sense, a training ground from which both to think and act according to the law of nature as well a process of continual discovery of its infinite permutations. The potential outcome of that discipline was twofold: a mystical insight into the world at hand and a transformed social order informed and precipitated by self-examination.

The Beats proposed that by confronting the most intimate aspects of one's personality it was possible to not only release the self from the bonds of Faustian constraints but also catalyze the American soul. The confessional strategy became a way to speak openly about themselves, even to the point of narcissistic self-indulgence, while simultaneously addressing social issues. By way of their Spenglerian organicism and the nature of their language, the Beats began what eventually amounted to a moral engagement with their culture. For it was by first making the self, and, by extension, the concrete expressions of self, conform to the basic structures of reality that America would follow.

Like the Transcendentalists, each man's poetics reflected and expressed a particular brand of spirituality, a personal religious ground from which to pursue cultural reform. As opposed to a case of institutionalized religion, spirituality is a less-structured vehicle for personal discovery and articulation of sacred realities, what Catherine L. Albanese describes as a "system for making sense of the world and meeting its power."[18] Beat poetics reflected an embodied spirituality, a grounded mystical practice that encompassed the gestures of the physical body and, more importantly, made sense of the world in the world. Art, in these terms, was suffused with religious power. Through language, the world could be perceived as it really was and altered to accord with how it should be. Beat literature was end and means, abstract formulation as well as reification, belief system as well as ritual enactment. The particular idioms of Kerouac, Ginsberg, and Burroughs ordered their individual messages into certain patterns of expression that reflected a perspective from which the Beats engaged the world, in hopes of changing it.

This chapter will explore how the new vision became synonymous with the Beats' radical poetics, at once a spiritual practice and utopian politics. Essential to their renewal of self and society was the production of a new "culture language" by which to invest both self and America with verbal tangibility. Spengler's assertion that "nothing is more characteristic of a Culture than its inward relation to writing" enabled the Beats to understand their literary experiments as well as their ambitions in terms of social renewal.[19]

In the first section of this chapter, I will probe the Beats' assessment of a linguistic crisis and the way they read Spengler's pronouncements about language onto their contemporary literary scene. In the second section I explore their confessional strategies in the context of how they read Spengler and invested their poetics with social urgency. I then turn to the act of writing to account for the similarities among Burroughs, Kerouac, and Ginsberg in terms of different forms of mystical practice. To conclude, I will investigate the evangelical strain of Beat poetics, specifically how each writer conceived of his work as a strategy for altering the reader's concept of reality. For it was through their style—on the page and off—that the Beats aggressively challenged their audience to see things from a Spenglerian perspective.

New Criticism and the American Scene

According to the Beats, the crises of America and self had been initiated, in part, by a growing appetite for abstraction in expression and communication. They believed that language, the substance of reality, had been corrupted. Within the Beat circle, Burroughs trumpeted Korzybski's ideas, both on their own merits and in dialogue with Spengler.[20] Such overlap was not surprising given Korzybski's claim in *Science and Sanity* that his theories were an extension of Spengler's, a discovery of "semantic psychophysiological *mechanisms* of the events of which Spengler is giving us a very exceptional picture."[21]

Burroughs's lectures on semantics provided Kerouac and Ginsberg with healthy appreciation for the power of words, not only to create and liberate but also to subordinate and control. According to Burroughs's take on Korzybski, language had become an abstract mode of expression and communication due to pseudomorphosis and Faustian corruption. Furthermore, the increasingly abstract character of language in the West had neurological and physiological consequences. No longer was language an organic extension of the person or human experience but rather an artificial universe in which words were totally disassociated from their original context.[22]

Burroughs's critical stance toward language derived much from Korzybski and Spengler and focused on the printed word as a conditioning agent that controlled internal beliefs and external behavior. According to Burroughs, language had become unhinged from its human matrix, so sharp-edged and divisive as to cut like a razor. Words were no longer communicatory or even contextual but rather "weapons" of control used to inflict psychological and physical damage upon unknowing victims: "Words that cut like buzz saws. Words that vibrate the entrails to jelly. Cold strange words that fall like icy nets on the mind. Virus words that eat the brain to muttering shreds. Idiot tunes that stick in the throat round and round night and day."[23]

Burroughs set out to dismantle the epistemological and linguistic systems undergirding Western Civilization. His explorative deconstruction would culminate in *Naked Lunch,* his most radical assault on the literary code and the dominant social discourses, of which literature was but one. In addition to dealing with the unsavory subject matter of drug addiction and sadomasochistic sex rituals, Burroughs's "anti-narrative" had no beginning and no end. As a series of paratactic juxtapositions, *Naked Lunch* rejected the notion of progress and implied that the cause-and-effect model of reality was a pernicious deceit.

The use of pastiche and non-sequitur demonstrated that language did not always produce meaning but could challenge middle-class decorum by recoding itself continually: "Reading the paper. . . . Something about a triple murder in the rue de la Merde, Paris: 'An adjusting of scores.' . . . I keep slipping away. . . . 'The police have identified the author . . . Pepe El Culito . . . The Little Ass Hole, an affectionate diminutive.' Does it really say that? . . . I try to focus the words . . . they separate in meaningless mosaic."[24] Burroughs manipulated mass-culture argots, intellectual discourse, and the rhetoric of science to reveal that language perpetuated these illusions and blinded humans to the machinations of vast conspiracy. Language was a virus, emanating not from the human tongue but, as he would later theorize, from outer space.

Although Kerouac and Ginsberg were not as paranoid, they, too, understood the social ills of contemporary America as rooted in the abstraction of language from personal experience. Near the beginning of *On the Road,* Kerouac alludes to the divide between reason and human emotion when he describes Sal's attempt to sleep next to an electric fan, a "big bust of Goethe staring at [him]." That sculpture without a body is Faustian man, immovable, made concrete, possessing a reifying gaze, and determined to forge ahead using pure, "cold, abstract reason." Unable to sleep beside the statue, Sal is unable to tap into an emotional dream world because of the ominous symbol of America's life-threatening, Faustian disease: "I comfortably went to sleep," he remembers, "only to wake up in twenty minutes freezing to death. I put on a blanket and still I was cold."[25] In a similar vein, Ginsberg once noted, "[The] power of abstraction dooms us to lose touch with detail. And therefore the very roots of the trees are shriveling, withering, and the oceans are being polluted because we have reduced everything to a language which can be passed through machines."[26] That echoed Spengler's declaration that Faustian consciousness had been "cut-off by walls and artificialities from living nature and the land about it and under it, cognises nothing outside itself. It applies criticism to its imaginary world, which it has cleared of everyday sense experience."[27]

In addition to a generalized indictment of contemporary misuse of language, the Beats' vituperation was often a direct attack on contemporary literary standards and the critical apparatus that supported them. As is the case with many young artists, they desperately needed an esteemed model to write against. For them, particularly the politically savvy Ginsberg, the New Critics became straw men. By the late 1940s, New Criticism had become the standard mode of studying and teaching literature within universities. Adopting their name from John Crowe Ransom's *The New Criticism* (1941), the New Critics called for an interpretive approach that was "scientific" and viewed the assessment of literary works, in an exaggerated moment, as "technical act[s] of extreme difficulty."[28] Even though they made a sharp distinction between science and poetry, such rigid language was premised on ideals of precision and systemization. As Ransom wrote in his essay "Criticism, Inc.," "Criticism must become more scientific, or precise and systematic, and this means that it must be developed by the collective and sustained effort of learned persons—which means that its proper seat is in the universities."[29] The analysis discounted a poet's biography or intentions, the response to a poem, and the social utility of the poem. Instead, it asserted that a text should adhere to strict formal structures and maintain proper decorum in regard to subject matter. Any declaration of feeling or personal engagement with the text, including stylistic innovation, was viewed with critical scorn.

As intellectual refugees from the Ivy League, the Beats were intimately familiar with the New Criticism, whose advocates, in addition to the loose affiliation of Columbia University professors Lionel Trilling and Mark Van

Doren, included Ransom, Cleanth Brooks, Allen Tate, Robert Penn Warren, and W. K. Wimsatt.[30] The movement had grown out of a desire to professionalize literary criticism in the face of attacks from historical scholars who held that criticism was not a rigorous intellectual activity.[31] In their attempting to carve out a separate disciplinary sphere for literary study in the university curricula, much of the work the New Critics cited was "excessively difficult," to use Brooks's phrase, in order to justify a need for "specialists."[32]

The rhetoric of New Criticism was often excessive and, when interpreted by those less sympathetic to their literary politics, vulnerable to exaggeration. At the heart of the New Critical agenda was a democratizing impulse, its goal being to impart the techniques necessary to analyze a text independent of research scholars. For example, a series of analytical exercises in a widely used college textbook, Brooks's and Warren's *Understanding Poetry* (1938), could easily be interpreted as technocratic jargon, as was the case with the Beats' work. Indeed, they often ignored the cultural agenda behind the New Criticism, seeing it only in terms of professionalization and bureaucratic efficiency—a literary industrial complex. As Ginsberg declared, critics concerned only with definitions were oblivious to the fluid, holistic process of art. "Poetry has been attacked," he accused, "by an ignorant and frightened bunch of bores who don't understand *how it's made,* & the trouble with these creeps is they wouldn't know poetry if it came up and buggered them in broad daylight."[33]

The Beats' stylistic innovations, particularly the immediacy and physicality of their poetics, were simultaneously reactions against normative literary standards and logical extensions within their Spenglerian world. Kerouac and Ginsberg in particular understood New Criticism as excessively rigid and intolerant of the experimentalism that had energized early modernists. Like most perceived obstacles, such critical regulations were metaphorically associated with the artificial codes of Faustian Civilization.

Kerouac and Ginsberg had felt the sting of New Critical rejection from the English department of Columbia University. Even though the caviling from Professors Trilling and Van Doren was often accompanied by a modicum of encouragement, the Beats caricatured the formality of the New Criticism and incorporated it into their mythic understanding of the world. The institutionalization of that school of thought resonated ominously with Spengler's declaration that "in the course of this long evolution there comes about at the last the *detachment of speaking from speech. . . . The necessary concomitant of speech divorced from speaking is the notion of the school. . . . Finally, speech and truth exclude one another.*"[34] In *Visions of Cody,* Kerouac made a clever play on precisely that point while "cutting [on] Contemporary Civilization," Kerouac recalls his college days and employs a frenzied buildup of associations to counter "the school" in form, content, and even spelling: "I had nothing but disrespect for my perfessor," he wrote. "I did. Later on, when Mark Van Doren made me realize professors could be real interesting, I nevertheless spent most of my time dreaming on what he must be like in real reality instead of listening to what he was saying."[35]

Burroughs responded more provocatively to the situation where "speech and truth exclude one another" by violently assaulting the moral assumptions undergirding standards of literary decency and challenging their epistemological assumptions. In *Naked Lunch,* for example, he wrote, "Naked Mr. America, burning frantic with self-bone love, screams out: 'My asshole confounds the Louvre! I fart ambrosia and shit pure gold turds! My cock spurts soft diamonds in the morning sunlight!'"[36] On one level, such obscenity undercut the social pretensions of high-brow literature. On another level, the lewdness reconnected language to a more natural, visceral, and unadorned reality. Human waste, Burroughs implies, is an eternal verity. The artistic achievements of the West are not. On still another level, Burroughs meant for his scatological prose to disrupt stable (and socially determined) notions of truth. Not only does Mr. America's asshole "confound" the Louvre, but his most intimate representations—from his excrement to his speech—are also subject to otherness. They are not true in the sense of retaining an organic relationship with Mr. America. The secretions of body and mind are immediately made to conform to the symbolic life of language yet privileged as real and somehow beyond language. Becoming adorned, they begin to resemble that which they once "confounded." In an ironic form of self-critique, Burroughs claims that truth is not partially defined by what it is not but entirely constituted by that from which it stands apart. His words, once established on the page, are alienating—their rich experiential context reduced to the categories of their social environment. Burroughs's message is that the world is not as it seems and all definitions and descriptions of the material world are arbitrary, determined solely by categories of Faustian hegemony. The English language must be stripped bare before it can produce anything of value. It must also be reconnected to ostensible definitions in order to counter America's addiction to ideals. "Since Naked Lunch treats this health problem," Burroughs wrote, "it is necessarily brutal, obscene, disgusting."[37] He did not see his treatment as a recovery of an American idiom as much as a method of creating a clean slate on which to build anew. He associated his language with a Culture, however it was not the America of Kerouac and Ginsberg but one not yet imagined.

In addition to their reaction against conservative metrics and civilized morality, the Beats also viewed the formal structures of New Criticism as privileging European forms over and above distinctly American themes. The New Critics were, for the most part, Anglocentric in taste and skeptical of the idea of an indigenous American poetry. They were suspicious of literary nationalisms of all kinds, dismissing the sentimental musings of a poet such as Walt Whitman as the affectations of discredited romanticism.[38] Speaking to the perceived machinations behind New Critical methods, Ginsberg later charged them with a form of literary totalitarianism very much against the American grain: "I'm sick of the creeps bugging the scene, my scene, America's scene, we only live once, why put up with that grubby type of ambitious vanity. . . . And this is the product of the schools of the richest nation of the earth, this is the Intelligentsia that's supposed to run the world, inc. moon? It's a monster shambles."[39] The tirade recalls the more subdued modernist nativism of William Carlos Williams, who, like Ginsberg, rejected the idea of America as curator of an inherited European tradition and insisted on a literary style that was organically related to contemporary American speech patterns.[40]

As the ideas of Spengler, Korzybski, and Williams became intertwined and inextricable, the Beats, particularly Ginsberg, stood "solidly on terra firma admiring" an "American idiom." They preferred a vernacular mode of communication rather than "the national company full of Ionesque hallucinations of language."[41] In 1950 Ginsberg sent a letter to Williams to detail how he, too, was attempting to rediscover a forgotten American tongue buried under the European influences of Ezra Pound and T. S. Eliot, American expatriates and darlings of the New Critics. "Dear Doctor," he wrote, "I envision for myself some kind of new speech—different at least from what I have been writing down." During a peyote high in 1952 Ginsberg recorded his opinion of America's foreign and decadent language: "Language is very worn out. It is of necessity so abstract I have to find, among other things, a new word for the universe, I'm tired of the old ones, they mean too many things from other time & people." Literature had become disengaged from personal speech and reflected only the influence of European "thought, meter, poesy, music, [and] philosophy."[42]

Ironically, in their impassioned rejection of New Critical standards of objectivity and depersonalization, the Beats shared with their imagined foes a belief that language does not reflect the world but makes it according to its own logic. As Ransom noted, "True poetry . . . only wants to realize the world, to see it better." Like the New Critics, the Beats assumed that literature contained a unique form of knowledge. For Ransom it was a "democratic state," a reference to the heterogeneous elements at work in making a poem meaningful.[43] The Beats, however, differed radically in what that knowledge consisted of, its source, and how it was made manifest in literature. For them, the knowledge was experiential. It was derived from the physical body in the material world and tangibly present in the work itself. The stylistic innovations of Ginsberg, Kerouac, and Burroughs—recourse to the idioms of jazz and sex, a new orality with emphases on breath, spontaneity, verbal pastiche, and intimate testimonials—were alternative phrasings of a common theme: Spengler's call for a new "culture language" that would displace the Faustian modes of expression, description, and communication. His call in *Decline* ("men of the new generation may be moved by this book to devote themselves to techniques instead of lyrics") reverberated as each writer contemplated the nature and function of literature.[44] Each rejected outright the classic and straightforward "lyrical" form, with its underlying assumption of severe objectivity. Even Ginsberg's early imitations of classical verse distorted a stable authorial position and assumed complicity in the world. Instead of literature being the sole possession of the academy, Ginsberg, Burroughs, and Kerouac concluded that it should derive from life. In order to find a "new word for the universe," they sought to develop a writing technique that sustained the interdependence of subject and object within a world where everything was animate.

Nowhere is that search more evident than in the "Frisco: The Tape" section of *Visions of Cody*. In Kerouac's most radical experiment, he transcribed an audio tape of his conversations with Cassady as they joked, smoked marijuana, drank wine, spun jazz records, and ruminated on everything and anything that came into their heads. The scene is a whirlwind of vernacular energy. There are no moments of abstract philosophizing and there is nothing outside the conversational dynamic. There is only a shared intimacy between friends driven by a wild associative logic.

> Cody. (*laughing*) That's great . . . great shit. Now you're really talkin. (*Jack flutes*) All that tea has finally produced somethin
> Jack. It has, hey?
> Cody. Goddamn right. We'll have to get some more of that stuff
> Jack. You know what that sounds like though . . .
> Cody. What?
> Jack. It sounds like . . . the way that Dostoevsky started the, ah, *Underground, Notes From the Underground.*

The tape section is followed by the "Imitation of the Tape" in which Kerouac attempts to live up, as it were, to the previous section of chaotic vigor: "'Now up yonder in Saskahooty,' said Dead Eye Dick—no, I exaggerate, his name was Black Dan—'up yonder in Saskahoty,' said Dead Eye Dick Black Dan."[45]

One can only imagine Kerouac sitting at his desk, typewriter riveting like a machine gun as he attempts to replicate the energy and passion of the dialogues within himself. It was a violent, no-holds-barred struggle not to surpass, as W. T. Lhamon, Jr., has suggested, but to "imitate," to the point at which his art was no longer imaginary but "real unreality."[46] In such moments there was no time for poetry. Kerouac's example points to how the Beats reenvisioned the premises and functions of art even as they were reenvisioning life. As art and life contacted each other, each became something else. Both ceased to exist as they once were.

The Unspeakable Visions of the Individual

Although the Beats viewed themselves as spurning highbrow academic and intellectual scenes, they at the same time participated in the "triumph of the therapeutic," a cultural mood then fashionable among literary cognoscenti.[47] Philip Rieff's phrase for the pervasiveness of "post-communal" psychological practices at mid-century, although problematic, illuminated the diffusion of psychological language across a number of discourses after the war. As psychoanalytic principles gained currency in avant-garde circles, so, too, did the sociological trope of neurosis. The Beats embraced the trend and like other artists often spoke of their art, lives, and culture in terms of mental health, anxiety, suppression, and neuroses.[48] The magazine *Neurotica*, for example, nine issues of which were published between 1948 and 1951, contained the work of artists and intellectuals such as Kenneth Patchen and Marshall McLuhan. In a 1950 issue, an abbreviated version of Kerouac and Ginsberg's "Pull My Daisy" was first published as "Song: Fie My Fum." As Daniel Belgrad has noted, the editorial policy of *Neurotica*, as well as the Beats' "aesthetic of psychosis," linked psychoanalysis to social criticism. Each assumed that through a strategy of personal introspection one could disclose America's social neurosis.[49] The Beats' social psychology, however, was not merely an appropriation of avant-garde trends. Like most ideas they adopted, it had a Spenglerian aspect. Kerouac even went so far as to liken the "crazy" style of *Neurotica* to that of *Decline of the West*.[50]

The Beats equated social "neuroses" with the ideological contradictions of American society, but they understood those contradictions not clinically but mythically. They had come to view their country as increasingly divided between two realities: the parasitical infringement of late Civilization and the dormant values of the host. In "the neurotic nature of our times," Kerouac observed, most Americans were in a state of denial, ignoring both their Cultural heritage and the portents of decline in the present.[51]

Adopting the notion of individual as metonym for the social context, the Beats reasoned that if the land was possessed and invaded by the "spirit" of a foreign Civilization, in America's case, that of Western Europe, its native population would also be corrupted and unable to embrace fully their true spiritual selves. "You feel guilty of something, you feel unclean, almost diseased" shouts Irwin, the Ginsberg character in *The Town and the City*. "You have . . . feelings of spiritual geekishness—Don't you see, everybody feels like that now."[52] Despite their nation's cosmic dilemma, Americans were unwilling to face the uncertainty and risks that accompanied radical introspection, that is, the recovery of the American potential harbored within the individual. As Kerouac noted in *Doctor Sax,* just as Americans had lost contact with their identity amid "the gloom of the unaccomplished mudheap civilization," so, too, had America gotten "caught with its pants down from a source it long lost contact with."[53]

Given Spengler's idea of correspondence between microcosmic particularities and macrocosmic universals, an underlying assumption of Beat writing was that self-exploration was equivalent to a political struggle over the future of America. Although Beat poetics, unlike many popular models of the postwar years, notably Freud's and Jung's, was therapeutic in nature, the Beats did not assume an absolute opposition between human nature and the social order. Despite the strong influence of Wilhelm Reich and the intellectual fashions of Freudianism and existentialism, Beat literature entertained a more hospitable relationship between self and society.[54] Following Spengler's reasoning that the soul of the Culture and the soul of the individual were of the same source, the Beats' agenda was to revive what had been degraded in society by reviving what had been degraded in themselves. For those belonging to a specific Culture, such intimate elucidation would be grounded in the authority, that is the *geist* (spirit) of that culture.

According to Kerouac's and Ginsberg's reading of Spengler, it was through the recoveries of personal expression and communication that America would once again prosper. As Spengler wrote, "An inner change takes place in the language that makes it adequate for carrying the highest symbolic tasks of the ensuing cultural development."[55] Reflecting that sentiment in a letter to Neal Cassady, Kerouac confidently proclaimed in 1948 that an American literary revolution would instigate a cultural awakening: "Do you realize that a new literary age is beginning in America? . . . we young Americans are turning to a new evaluation of the individual: his 'position' itself, personal and psychic. Great new age. . . . The Prophets were right!"[56]

Kerouac's equation of cultural renewal with the recovery of individual position was understood in the romanticized terms of introspection and overcoming "emotional congestion, poor American folly, fear and self-horror."[57] Burroughs, however, grounded the authority of his declarations in a future America, not yet come to pass. Both trajectories emphasized the present state of crisis and the hope for radical transformation. The difference between them was that of recovery versus discovery. Kerouac and Ginsberg thought in terms of romantic renewal, whereas Burroughs viewed himself as an explorer of uncharted terrain.

In Beat poetics, despite differences between each writer the jeremiadic critique and subsequent affirmation of America became operative on the individual level in the form of confession. Their belief in a personal state of sin (neurosis) led to anxiety and self-doubt. Through the process of public confession, however, contrition became an affirmation of a future state of deliverance. "The unspeakable visions of the individual" became, in Kerouac's words, "the telling [of] the true story of the world in interior monolog." In Spenglerian terms, the "true story of the world" was the "highest symbolic task" for a self-consciously American writer. Kerouac's visions of self and America were unspeakable because they went beyond the merely discursive, originating as they did from the world of pure sensation.

As the highest symbolic task, confession was a two-tiered strategy. On one hand, a confession was a plea for forgiveness, a public disclosure of a long-held fault in order to gain or regain admission into an imagined community. On the other hand, a confession was self-assertive and a defiant declaration of personality against the status quo.[58] Both forms of disclosure carried utopian energy that opposed existing social conditions. The Beats' confessional strategy encompassed each declarative aspect (contrition and subversion), both solitary utterances in the name of community. The psychic loneliness implied by such an endeavor was offset, at least in part, by the immediate sense of community that the writers provided each other.

As literary artists, the Beats viewed the crisis of cultural guilt in terms of representation and communication. It was Burroughs who first reasoned that language had infected the American populace and corrupted social reality. According to Korzybski, his source, "[Language] enslaves us through the mechanism of semantic reactions and . . . the structure which a language inhabits, and impresses on us unconsciously, is automatically projected upon the world around us."[59] Given the dissimulating capacity of language, Burroughs believed it necessary to close the gap between appearance and reality, the signs of language (words) and the real power to which they refer.

Even as the Beats were painfully aware of the dangers and limitations of words, they looked to the medium of language as both the problem and the solution to cultural disconnection. Because Faustian linguistics were no longer grounded in experience, the Beats countered such abstraction with confessional language derived from the deep recesses of the self or, in Burroughs's case, the deep recesses of experience. Yet although he remained skeptical of the honesty of any linguistic expression, he still sought certainty in his writing—a confession not of the one true self but an honest assessment of the world. Kerouac, who had none of Burroughs's skepticism, instructed, "No fear or shame in the dignity of yr experience, language & knowledge." As Kerouac's Spenglerism developed along psychological lines, the essence of Culture became directly associated with unconscious modes of knowledge. Through his poetics, Kerouac sought to "purify [the] mind" in order to "write with 100% personal honesty both psychic and social."[60] In that sense, his ideal of spontaneous composition was a way of recovering the entire complex of personality in the name of America. By emphasizing unconscious modes of thought, Kerouac sought to become a conduit for the values of Culture.

Kerouac's celebration of confessional honesty derived from a deep sense of community and reverence for familial relationships and those moments when the self dissolves into reciprocity and the pedestrian becomes the sublime. For him, "the summation pinnacle possible in human relationships" was the cosmic stuff of everyday life from which a new America would spring. Such moments possessed "the same blind unconscious quality as the orgasm, everything is happening to all their souls—this is the GO. . . . four-way sex orgies, three-day conversations, uninterrupted transcontinental drives."[61]

A central focus of Kerouac's writing was an elaboration of an epistemological model of intersubjectivity in which reality emerged through a conversational dynamic rather than a hierarchical relationship between subject and object.[62] The emphasis on shared moments of ecstasy and honest dialogue in Beat literature revealed an alternative social reality. As the character of Carlo Marx (Ginsberg) expresses to Sal Paradise (Kerouac) in *On the Road*, it was a "new season [of] trying to communicate with absolute honesty and completeness everything in our minds." In a 1949 letter to Ginsberg, John Clellon Holmes had spoken of Kerouac's use of the confessional style as a mode of being: "I remember something that Kerouac said about characters in a novel that was bad: 'These people only talk. They're not real at all. He should have them running into each other's rooms, or raving through the streets, and all the dialogue should be *confession!*'"[63] Given Kerouac's populist sentiments, he was committed to the cultural possibilities of the grassroots conversation.[64]

Kerouac and Ginsberg viewed their art as a form of social therapy, for it was through individual confession that society would eventually be transformed. "[Personal] revelation is revolution." wrote Kerouac in a 1949 letter, showing preference for personal reform over direct political engagement.[65] In a similar fashion, Ginsberg subsumed the politics of writing under a theological paradigm. In "The Terms in Which I Think of Reality" (1950), he alluded to that psychology of correspondence:

Here we're overwhelmed
with such unpleasant detail
we dream again of Heaven.
For the world is a mountain
of shit: if it's going to
be moved at all, it's got
to be taken by handfuls.[66]

Despite the buildup of excrement, the potential for renewal exists only if one takes personal responsibility. In seeking to eradicate the unpleasantries he had encountered in himself, Ginsberg's use of the collective pronoun signified that he perceived himself as representative man, or, more specifically, as a representative neurotic in need of a cure. By confronting the crisis of America within themselves, he and Kerouac could initiate Cultural growth through exorcism (from the Greek *exōrkosis,* meaning to "out-oath") of that part of the self which had become civilized. Because the "authentic" self was "hid," in Kerouac words, "as so many things in America," their goal was to eradicate any layer of pretense by confronting the "unspeakable visions of the individual."[67]

Realizing and affirming a unified self were also forms of negation—shedding one's "character armor" for the sake of healing a separation.[68] For example, in a 1956 letter, Ginsberg proclaimed that through his poetic radicalism he was on one level rejecting the spirit of objectivity within the literary establishment and on another reconstructing a unified vision of the self. He proclaimed that he was constructing an alternative value system based on a rejection of Civilization and a discovery of American values, that is, individual values long suppressed by European epistemological models. In his poetry, he was "leaping out of a preconceived notion of social 'values' following my own heart's instincts, overturning any notion of propriety, moral 'value,' superficial 'maturity,' Trilling-esque sense of 'civilization,' and exposing my true feelings—of sympathy and identification with the rejected, mystical individual."[69] Casting a wide net, the poet blamed behavioral and ethical codes, socially constructed hierarchies and value systems, and even his former English professor at Columbia University, Lionel Trilling, for his own as well as America's fractured identity. Through the medium of language Ginsberg could identify and then expunge those elements of self that were not indigenous and had caused a schism within the self.

For Ginsberg, the way to heal the schism was through "compositional self-exploration," for such introspection promised to expose as well as eradicate the need for social norms.[70] For example, the lyrical bursts of "Howl" and Ginsberg's initial claim to its spontaneous composition suggest his desire to convey an authentic personal statement and a manifesto for America's liberation from the entrenched political, economic, and social categories of the United States. Like much of his poetry, "Howl" was grounded in the sense that Ginsberg had attempted to cleanse himself of all social facts before writing. Shortly after writing the original draft, he planned to attach a preface detailing the poem's mythic and prescriptive dimensions. Addressed to his "secret soul . . . my darkest deepest countryman," Ginsberg attempted to confess the part of himself and America that had been silenced, hidden, and repressed. He turned inward in order to reveal the liberating potential of the self and the "Dark America! toward whom I close my eyes for prophecy." The proem begins:

> I'll sing of America and Time,
> for as I lay in my bed alone one night
> I ruminated with my secret soul
>   in ancient rhetoric,
> "Inspire me tonight with a dreamlike poem
> foretelling in rapt naturalistic forms
> the fate of this country I hide in
> penniless and lovelorn waiting for the barren
> doom of my days:
>   Illuminate your tragic
> wisdom, my darkest deepest countryman,
> reveal in shorthand and symbolic images
> the paradigm of fortune for United States;
> witness the downfall and roar of daily life,
> in riches and despair amid great machinery."[71]

Central to the proem is the way Ginsberg differentiates America from the United States yet acknowledges that both existed simultaneously within his "secret soul." Moving from subjective hope toward objective despair, Ginsberg juxtaposes the timeless spirit of America, the basis of tradition, and its institutionalization in order to demonstrate how that process has also occurred on a personal plane. By alluding to his metonymic relationship with

America, he portrays both himself and the relationship as victims of social conditioning. Concerned with his "secret soul" and "this country I hide in," Ginsberg asserts that personal and cultural salvation depends on uncovering what has been prevented from being expressed in "naturalistic forms" and exorcising traits either learned or inculcated by the "trashy world" of Western Civilization.

As Ginsberg's proem attests, the Beats' search for authenticity had a darker, almost masochistic aspect. Even while they affirmed personal autonomy, their confessional practice seemed to indicate a loathing of that part of the self that had become "diseased." The desire to purge the individual soul for the sake of community was premised on violence, either against the compromised self or the compromised society. As Kerouac wrote in *On the Road*, "Every one of these things that I said was a knife at myself. Everything I had ever held against my brother was coming out: how ugly I was and what filth I was discovering in the depths of my own impure psychologies."[72]

As a confessional strategy, Kerouac's writing constituted an act of redemption. His compositional style translated a Catholic anthropology into Spenglerian terms. He believed that humans are made in the image of God, have fallen from that image, and must be redeemed in order to reflect the image of the creator, that is, to participate once again in the timeless moment of God's universal imagination. "Lord, I scribbled hymns to you" Kerouac wrote at one point in *Visions of Cody*. Later he described how God redeemed him through a violent onslaught. He had picked "up this midget New Testament Bible and in my huge-hearted state of high love I saw great words . . . and was so amazed with almost every sentence or that is line I saw that I felt *attacked* by words, overtaken by great blows of consciousness I should have absorbed a long time ago, realizations of Jesus I'd never dared before . . . including charmed and awed interpenetrations of the mystery of the Bible and especially of ancient Jewish need in rote." The Catholic metaphysics of his writing method, influenced by Spengler, precipitated a form of immanence in which Kerouac was "attacked" and overwhelmed by sacred messages. He had bared himself to the mercy of the universe. By steadfastly absorbing everything, he became absorbed, and pain became a form of mystical pleasure. Already running in a Buddhist direction, Kerouac's spontaneous sketching became a self-forgetful mode by which he emptied himself and remembered his identity as a participant in the universal macrocosm. "Everything belongs to me," he wrote, "because I am poor."[73]

The Beats' strategy of interpreting the problems of America as their own, even actively adopting them, is evidenced most clearly by Burroughs's heroin addiction. While composing and assembling *Naked Lunch*, he integrated his life as an addict with his writing practice. In a 1955 letter to Ginsberg, Burroughs first mentioned that "the only thing to do with junk sickness, like pain, is to plunge right in the middle of it." He then informed Ginsberg that "writing now causes me an almost unbearable pain. . . . Working on novel all day. It is terribly painful."[74] For Burroughs, writing became a process of withdrawal, a way out of addiction, and a means of confronting the enemy directly, that is, the "parasitic being" working against the self from the inside.[75] As with Kerouac and Ginsberg, Burroughs hoped to transform society by looking first to the personal plane—the "addict on the street." He, too, believed that personal revelation was revolution but in a more streetwise and less romantic sense than either Kerouac or Ginsberg. Instead of seeking to escape the dictates of the flesh, Burroughs sought to learn from them. Gaining sociological insight through the psychology of withdrawal, he wrote, "If you wish to alter or annihilate a pyramid of numbers in a serial relation, you alter or remove the bottom number. If we wish to annihilate the junk pyramid, we must start with the bottom of the pyramid: *the Addict in the Street, . . . The addict in the street who must have junk to live is the one irreplaceable factor in the junk equation.* When there are no more addicts to buy junk there will be no junk traffic." Burroughs sought social change by violent elimination of the "junk pyramid" on an individual level. As an addict, he voluntarily submitted to an exaggerated version of Faustian Civilization to learn how to escape its grasp. It was during drug withdrawal that his old subjectivity diminished as his sense impressions became sharpened. A new subjectivity emerged from under the "extremely painful" deluge of "facts," a "barrage of sensations external and visceral." Once "replacement of the junk-dependent cells" was accomplished, the forces of control would cease to find a point of entry into the human nervous system.[76]

Even more than Kerouac and Ginsberg, Burroughs understood the physical act of writing as a struggle between mastery and subjugation, a disciplining of the flesh in order to gain a foothold on the material world. In reference to the *Naked Lunch* manuscript, he confided in Ginsberg that "writing is more painful than anything I ever did. Parentheses pounce on me and tear me apart. I have no control over what I write, which is as it should be."[77] In the end, that masochistic strategy yielded a more authentic self that remained subject to personal, even self-destructive, desires but free of manipulation from the outside. Using a confessional strategy, "Honest Bill" sought to infiltrate the innermost depths of self in order to confront and exterminate that which was not organic. Declaring "I am not an entertainer" and claiming to be only a perfect "recording instrument," Burroughs blurred the boundary between subjectivity and objectivity, participant and observer, in order to destabilize each perspective. Bypassing the "cerebral event," he sought to get between and inhabit the space separating reality and self-consciousness before experience became appropriated in language. Through such anticipatory vision he hoped to see things as they were, with no "symbolic dressing." Like playing back a tape recording, he sought the "complete absence of nostalgia" to see which parts of self, and consequently America, were worth saving and which were not. As one character in *Naked Lunch* remarks, "There's always a space *between,* in popular songs and Grade B movies, giving away the basic American rottenness, spurting out like breaking boils, throwing out globs of that un-D.T. to fall anywhere and grow into some degenerate cancerous life-form, reproducing a hideous random image."[78]

Freedom within Salvation

Beat poetics began to develop along the lines of mysticism in that the act of writing became the means of submission and an avenue of transcendence. Like their masochism, it was a mysticism that possessed a social conscience. The Beats' confessional approach to art stressed not only liberation from social constraints but also, as Rimbaud paradoxically wrote, "freedom within salvation."[79] In that regard, Beat poetics developed along two channels: Kerouac's (and later Ginsberg's) ideal of spontaneous sketching as a way of transcending the civilized self and Burroughs's "factualism," a technique used to transcribe reality without necessarily transcending one's material conditions. Both were mystical endeavors in that writing became an encounter with the most inscrutable truths of existence—the source of the world's being and the limits of human understanding. Although Beat descriptions of that ground of reality resembled Spengler's effusions on the world of Spirit, each writer understood the significance of the experience in somewhat different terms.

For Kerouac and Ginsberg, the confessional strategy was a way to realign the self with the cosmos through the drama of introversion—"submissive to everything"—in order to become less aware of oneself as a separate entity. It was a disciplined spontaneity that sought dissolution into the "cosmic beat," thereby replicating and adhering to the divine logos. Confessional honesty would diffuse any obstacles or internal conflicts and allow the writer to attune himself to, and participate in, the rhythms of the universe. Kerouac and Ginsberg reflected the fundamental assumptions, attitudes, and goals of their Spenglerian theology of experience in claiming that only those utterances based wholly on instinct were guaranteed to circumvent the machinations of the Faustian social filter. In Spengler's words, each man viewed the process of writing as "a spontaneous method by which one is enabled to feel at home in one's world."[80] This current of nostalgia, a yearning for something lost, ran through their poetics. The goal of each writer was a form of compositional immanence—to dissolve the ego into the "cosmic current of being," as one wrote, in order to become intimate with its waters.[81] In that state there were neither separations nor limits, no subject and no object. It was an oceanic existence, in Georges Bataille's words, "that is essentially on a level with the world in which it moves like water in water."[82]

The difference in Burroughs's mystical poetics centered around his chosen means of realigning self with world. For him, writing meant an intense focus on the surrounding environment in order to render multiplicity more vivid and see the guiding logic of the universe. His goal was not to dissolve into numinous waters but to ride atop them with no destination other than the accumulation of insight. Nostalgia did not become a part of Burroughs's poetics. There were no pure origins, no pastoral home, to which to return. Freedom was a matter of clear perception rather than transcendence. Unlike Kerouac and Ginsberg, Burroughs submitted to the cosmic flux during writing to escape from the more immediate forces of control. He sought to demarcate a personal space from which he could see more clearly, to secure a more strategic position from which to defend the self, and, eventually, to counter those working against him. Like the medicine men of Peru, Burroughs's goal was "to foretell the future, locate lost or stolen objects, to diagnose and treat illness, to name a perpetrator of a crime."[83] The physical act of writing allowed him to confront the world head-on and gain knowledge of and power over it. As a magical practice, writing became a form of manipulation. It did not invoke a world elsewhere but delineated limits within this world in order to consider them more clearly.

For Kerouac and Ginsberg, the new vision of literature was predicated on heightened awareness of the body, an awareness that would allow them to resist and eventually overcome socially imposed ideals. The style of each writer was characterized by an attentiveness to the physical senses and the "amazing richness of experience."[84] The fluidity of spontaneous composition, first practiced by Kerouac, was direct expression of the goal of reverting to more physically based poetics. Kerouac's and Ginsberg's understanding of their poetics in holistic terms not only reflected their desire to allow the body to organize and give meaning to their experience but also echoed Spengler's criticism of "Faustian man" for viewing the body as merely "the vessel of the soul."[85] In "Song" (1954), Ginsberg articulated that desire to recover a recognition of human experience as an embodied experience:

yes, yes
that's what
I wanted
I always wanted. I always wanted,
to return
to the body
where I was born.[86]

The association between human origins and the body underscored a desire to mine the unconscious for its musicality in order to participate once again in the natural rhythms of the universe. In Kerouac's words, such participation meant tapping into "the living American melodic symphony that rings in my brain continually and is the great chord of the key."[87] Because of their romantic sensibilities, to Kerouac and Ginsberg the unconscious became the reservoir of authenticity—"the flow that already exists intact in the mind."[88] It was not only an epistemological source for American culture but also a physical reality, a realm of knowledge manifest in the movement and senses of the body. Ginsberg, for example, assumed that writing must correspond to the "human universe" if it was to have any meaning whatsoever: "If the voice is completely separated from the body, it means that the rhythm will be fucked up, it means the affect will be fucked up, it means it no longer has any human content, actually. It probably means it doesn't mean anything, even, finally—by mean, anything that could be connected back to the physical universe or the human universe."[89]

In order to "mean" something, Kerouac and Ginsberg each attempted to condense their literature and experience, language and biology, into one fluid mode of expression. Both men used Wilhelm Reich's theories of orgasm to search for a language lodged in "the mystery in the bones themselves and not the shadows of the mind," that is, in physical experience rather than merely mental cognition.[90] They came to view verbal improvisation, like sex, as a spontaneous, instinctive act that frees the body from social inhibitions.[91] In Reich, Kerouac and Ginsberg found a way to define the body and the unconscious in the same terms. First, spontaneous composition was a disciplined, physical activity aimed at replicating the natural flow of cosmic energy as it pulsed through the individual. In Kerouac's words, spontaneity was a way to shed light on those shadowy recesses of the unconscious—a physical "struggle to sketch the flow that already exists intact in the mind." As Ginsberg once explained, that corresponding harmony was embodied in the example of the North American fellaheen—"a recovery of natural tongue of speech forms that are real rather than literary forms, and recovery of body movement and song and dance. . . . Like Neal and Jack driving around listening to black rhythm and blues."[92] The new mode of expression was organized around the organic flux of the physical body and the rhythms of the cosmos. Spontaneous prose became a form of bodily confession, a muscular expression of one's connection with the "human universe."

Kerouac viewed the aesthetic of spontaneity as a way of perceiving universal truth, what he called "the undisturbed flow" of the "pre-literary mind." In accordance with Spenglerian principles, such mysticism positioned the sentient body at the center of organic patterns of flux, mediating between microcosm and macrocosm. It followed that by viscerally experiencing that mediation an individual would become fully cognizant of "the secret relationship between microcosm and macrocosm."[93] Kerouac stressed his ability to express ontological clarity "as jazz musician" by writing "in accordance with Great law of timing." "'Getting it' in jazz" meant escape from linear constructions of time and exploring the rhythmic interface between self and world. Time ceased to exist as he found "the mystic or the music." Regardless of which he found, his words soon dissolved into sensual yet "meaningless" gibberish: "yhr mydyiv gtrnxy og yhr eiyvhfovyot." As Kerouac described the state of physical receptivity and sensitivity that transcended rational thought and linguistic selectivity, "If possible write 'without consciousness' in semitrance (as Yeats' later Trance writing) allowing subconscious to admit in its own uninhibited interesting necessary and so 'modern' language what conscious art would censor, and write excitedly, swiftly, with writing-or-typing-cramps, in accordance (as from center to periphery) with laws of orgasm, Reich's 'beclouding of consciousness.' Come from within, out—to relaxed and said." His goal was to establish a connection with the rhythms of the "cosmic current of being." "Nothing is muddy that *runs in time* and to laws of *time*," he continued. "Tap from yourself the song of yourself, *blow!—now!—your* way is the only way . . . spontaneous, 'confessional' interesting."[94] Like Rimbaud, Yeats, and American jazz musicians, Kerouac was inventing a language accessible to all the senses.

For both Kerouac and Ginsberg, the "honest frenzy" of jazz improvisation informed the search for the deepest, most fundamental level of human expression. Specifically, the jagged melodies, asymmetrical style, and rhythmic complexity of bebop became literary revelations. In scanning the syncopated phrasings of bebop for poetic and ontological insights, they discovered an aesthetic that embodied the physiological laws of sexual expression. Both men viewed Beat poetics in terms of organic and orgasmic expression—a masturbatory surge of creativity in which a writer would become a conduit for universal forces.[95]

Just as Walt Whitman had found inspiration in the black preachers and orators in antebellum New York, so, too, did Kerouac and Ginsberg find in the revolutionary élan of black jazz musicians a model for their own romantic mysticism. Identifying with a racial underclass reflected their anxiety about status as well as their desire to see themselves as outsiders to the literary establishment. As white males assuming the subject position of black artists, they questioned the authenticity of the white middle class. Their "cross-race identification" also enabled them to challenge official literary culture from the inside because of their race and elite educations and from the outside because of their choice in literary models.[96]

Despite the fact that they sometimes patronized them, both Kerouac and Ginsberg earnestly admired bebop musicians such as Charlie Parker, Dizzy Gillespie, and Lester Young for the way in which they used breathing techniques while composing. Viewing bebop rhythms as ascribing ontological primacy to the unconscious, instinctual act of improvisation, Kerouac and Ginsberg developed their own poetics of breath. Many of their pronouncements on writing opposed the limitations of dualistic thought and equated the textuality of their work with an effusion of feeling that was immaterial despite its physical origins. As Kerouac wrote in "Essentials of Spontaneous Prose," "*Blowing* (as per jazz musician). . . . Blow as deep as you want."[97] Ginsberg later acknowledged his debt to that insight. He asserted that in the "really great poetry I wrote I was able to chant, and use my whole body. . . . So from that point of view, poetry becomes . . . a physiological thing. Something where you actually *use* your body, use your breath, use your full breath . . . poetry when you're really into it can become an expression of the whole body, 'single body, single mind.'"[98] By emphasizing breath, Ginsberg, like Kerouac, could locate the primary site of subjectivity, not necessarily in the words describing the experience but in the physical processes that made the words possible.

For Kerouac and Ginsberg, the act of writing was an attempt to experience hidden modes of awareness by grounding epistemology in the workings of individual perception. As Michael Davidson observes, their poetics did "not represent the mind thinking; it [was] the thinking itself."[99] By collapsing form and content, they sought to overcome any discrepancy between conscious intellect and subjective experience, perception and reality, by eliminating intermediary levels of abstraction. Writing became a way "to think to see, outside, / in a tenement the walls / of the universe itself." "The poem itself," Ginsberg wrote in 1949, was "my way of speaking out, not / declaiming of celebrating, yet, / but telling the truth."[100]

In his attempt to mobilize a visionary consciousness during composition,

Kerouac created a timeless moment of intense feeling and unadulterated attention, what he called *"deep* form . . . the way the consciousness *really* digs everything that happens."[101] That state represented a recovery of the essential characteristics of perception. As Kerouac noted in a 1952 letter, the technique was "beyond the arbitrary confines of the story . . . into the realms of revealed Picture . . . revelated prose. . . . Wild form's the only form holds what I have to say—my mind is exploding to say something about every image and every memory in." Such claims to mystical vision suggested the immediate comprehension of the cosmos—for Ginsberg, a "total consciousness . . . of the complete universe."[102]

In the spring of 1953, Ginsberg began a cursory study of Chinese history and painting, haiku, and Zen Buddhism. While reading about the "various dynasties and epochs of art and messianism and spiritual waves of hipness" he became interested in the idea of satori as a "specific flash of vision." He also took inspiration from Zen koans and determined to write poetry that would enable him to see "anew the universe." The blurring of spiritual and material boundaries in Eastern philosophy resonated with Ginsberg, who had immanentist leanings. So, too, did the aesthetic attitude of the haiku, in which a writer enters a state of readiness and receptivity and becomes able to perceive the essence of the world through intense scrutiny of its surfaces. For Ginsberg, Buddhism provided the mental formulas to explain his Blake visions and the desire to combine an experience with words that describe that experience. The goal was to "exhaust words" and become aware of the physical operations of perception: "Such craft or art there is, is in illuminating mental formations, and trying to observe the naked activity of my mind. Then transcribing that activity down on paper. So the craft is being shrewd at flash-lighting mental activity. Trapping the archangel of the soul, by accident, so to speak. The subject matter is the action of my mind."[103] According to Ginsberg, a poet's mind becomes a microcosmic reflection of the macrocosm. Therefore, by increasing the intensity and alertness of consciousness, it is possible to comprehend the vast and intricate workings of the universe.

Unlike Kerouac and Ginsberg, Burroughs believed that even the most spontaneous prose contained particular social and moral investments unknown to its author. "To speak is to lie," he wrote, "to live is to collaborate."[104] Neither the written nor the spoken word are ever transparent inscriptions of the individual. Viewing language as the preeminent mechanism of physical enslavement, Burroughs did not share the romantic demeanor of Kerouac or Ginsberg or the assumption that ecstatic confessions were, necessarily, a song of oneself. For Burroughs, writing did not produce a record of a coherent self but rather a chronicle of subjection to invisible forces of control. Consequently, confessions that did not compensate for the capacity of language to turn against its user were inherently unreliable. For example, in *Queer*, even as the primary character, William Lee, attempts to be forthright and honest, he cannot confess his true feelings to another without following a "script." Consequently, even a heartfelt confession of homosexuality is subject to external manipulation. Lee's desperate plea for love becomes a manipulative scheme to seduce, reflecting how all communication inevitably devolves into a mechanism of power.[105]

Unlike Kerouac and Ginsberg, Burroughs believed that language could not encompass the full range of experiences but could only distort them. He did not seek to express himself in terms of unity and oneness because written words imposed premature closure and subjected the writer to their discursive logic. He spoke of the "falsifications" inherent in "Western languages," particularly "the IS of identity." "The word BE," Burroughs stated, "contains, as a virus contains, its precoded message of damage, the categorical imperative of permanent condition. To be a body, to be nothing else, to stay a body."[106] Burroughs welcomed the liberation of a shifting identity as long as it furthered his cause against external forces of control that imposed "permanent" conditions on individuals. Because the authentic visions of the individual were, by definition, unspeakable, Burroughs's language is never secure (a fact evidenced by his constant revision of his work even after initial publication).

Beginning in the late 1940s, Burroughs modeled his writing around the continual flux between internal and external reality, a "fact" obscured by the either-or conflict formula embedded in the English language. Through writerly observation he sought heightened awareness of the flux of particularities between self and environment, the visible and the invisible, the mundane and the ultimate. He believed the present state of confusion to be due to the fundamental error of ignoring the fluid, dynamic, and invisible world of cosmic forces and seeking truth in the rigid world of historical traditions, ethical labels, and preexisting categories of thought. As Spengler claimed, "The master of fact, for his part, is content to direct imperceptibly that which he sees and accepts as plain reality. This does not seem very much, yet it is the very starting-point of freedom, in a grand sense of the word."[107] For Burroughs, every thing, person, or event was connected, not necessarily by the same internal logic but through participating in the logic of the macrocosm. As he wrote to Ginsberg in 1948, "Myself I am about to annunciate a philosophy called 'factualism.' All arguments, all nonsensical considerations as to what people 'should do' are irrelevant. Ultimately there is only fact on all levels, and the more one argues, verbalizes, moralizes, the less he will see and feel of fact. Needless to say, I will not write any formal statement on the subject. Talk is incompatible with factualism." As is the case with mystical programs, Burroughs could not adequately describe factualism through formal language. That was precisely the point: Words too often come "between us and the fact" of the macrocosm, negating knowledge of any particular situation by hindering a more general apprehension of cosmic flux.[108] In one sense, the very word *factualism* enabled Burroughs to ground composition in the authority of science, an irony not lost on someone who had come to writing relatively late and who questioned the authority of science at almost every turn.

Factualism greatly influenced Burroughs's approach to writing, so much so that he began to see writing as the means to a mystical, liberatory knowledge—"freedom, in a grande sense of the word." In *On the Road,* Kerouac described Burroughs as always exploring "the facts of life" and "looking for the facts" as he read "Spengler and the Marquis de Sade."[109] And it was Burroughs's literal reading of Spengler that complemented his attraction to the messianic appeal of Korzybski's General Semantics, particularly Korzybski's call for reexamination of thought processes. Burroughs's description of factualism echoes Korzybski's words: "Before we can adjust ourselves to the new conditions of life, created in the main by science, we must first of all revise our grossly antiquated methods of orientation. Then only shall we be able to adjust ourselves properly to the new facts."[110]

What Burroughs found convincing in Korzybski's theory was that words were not only inadequate in accounting for empirical reality but also that the structure of language affects the functioning of the nervous system. As Korzybski wrote, "A language, any language, has at its bottom certain metaphysics, which ascribe, consciously or unconsciously, some sort of structure to the world . . . these structural assumptions are inside our skin."[111] As a writing praxis, factualism enabled Burroughs to expose the ways in which words create illusions, hinder thought, and misdirect action. Factualism was at once a physiognomic enterprise—an intense scrutiny of surfaces—and an interrogation of the assumptions that lie behind the philosophical and scientific traditions of the West.

Following the leads of Spengler and Korzybski, Burroughs conceived of factualism as "the organization of the non-obvious." Spengler had asserted that only one epistemological avenue was left in the "present-day West," a mode of inquiry resembling the Classical Scepticism of the ancient Greeks. He claimed to be practicing that "negation of philosophy," an "unphilosophical philosophy" whose only assumption was that "truths are truths only in relation to a particular mankind." Like Spengler's claim that truth could only be derived by viewing all reality (including the observer and the observed) "as an organism," Burroughs assumed a relativistic orientation toward truth. He renounced "absolute standpoints," in Spengler's words, in order to approach "the secret of the world."[112]

The analytical features of factualism resembled a Protestant theological method. In particular, it shared much with the doctrine of technologia, what Perry Miller called "the true metaphysic of Puritanism." Miller found traces of that doctrine in the thought of writers from Jonathan Edwards through Nathaniel Hawthorne, the Transcendentalists, and Henry Adams. Much in fashion at Burroughs's alma mater during the seventeenth century, technologia was concerned with distinguishing and defining the logic of the divine as it appeared in the particulars of existence. Through intense contemplation of specific objects, the endless search for differences among them would signal the unfathomable totality of the divine. Such scrutiny, however, would also provide a means of establishing "durable bases for scientific knowledge in a world created by the wisdom which could not be sounded."[113]

⌐⌐

Burroughs's first two novels, *Junky* and *Queer,* were experiments in factualism that confronted words as obstacles to this numinous sphere. Each work portrayed an underworld of American society that was an exaggerated reflection of what it lies beneath. In *Junky,* Burroughs depicted his struggle to kick a heroin addiction as he wandered through the world of crime and narcotics. As he later commented, "The only benefit to me as a writer . . . came to me after I went off [junk]. What I want to do is to learn to see more of what's out there. To look outside, to achieve as afar as possible a complete awareness of surroundings."[114] Subsequently, Burroughs believed that drug addiction "teaches the user facts of general validity" because dependence on narcotics is an exaggerated instance of addiction to Faustian Civilization.[115] In the underworld, junk is the ultimate parasite that consumes users without allowing them to create, negating sociability to the extent that they can only wait for the next fix.

Burroughs extended Korzybski's semantic paranoia and incorporated it into the cycle of addiction and healing. Like drugs, words were contextual and prevented users from transcending a particular reality. Language like junk was a virus—a mechanism of control—that must be confronted on its own terms. To be healed, therefore, was to escape its grasp and transcend regular cognitive sanction, a religious world of pure potentiality. At the end of *Junky,*

Burroughs includes a glossary of "junk lingo" that provides insight into the potential revolutionary quality of his language. As he warned, words may dictate a certain reality but are ever-evolving and always subversive: "It should be understood that the meanings of these words are subject to rapid changes and that a word that has one hip meaning one year may have another the next. The hip sensibility mutates. . . . Not only do words change meanings but meanings vary locally at the same time. A final glossary, therefore, cannot be made of words whose intentions are fugitive."[116] Burroughs sought to restore language to a medium of communication rather than one of manipulation. By granting words their "fugitive" status, humans could confront them head-on—strategically and economically—for the purpose of manipulating them.

As a companion piece to *Junky*, *Queer* further explored the power of language by investigating its insidious effects on the emotional level. It details the continuing quest of William Lee to find "freedom from the claims of the aging, cautious, nagging, frightened flesh." While *Junky* is concerned primarily with the individual, *Queer* is a more direct meditation on community. While working on the book in 1952, Burroughs wrote to Ginsberg that "on junk you are concerned primarily with self, so first person is best instrument; but off the junk you are concerned with relationships and 1st person is not adequate to say what I have to say."[117] At the end of *Junky* Burroughs had written of his desire for a relationship "on the nonverbal level of intuition and feeling."[118]

In *Queer*, set in the liminal environs of Mexico and South America, he described the effort of his alter-ego William Lee to achieve a state of "telepathic contact" with the character of Eugene Allerton: "In any relation of love or friendship Lee attempted to establish contact on the non-verbal level of intuition, a silent exchange of thought and feeling." The shift from the first-person narrative to the third in *Queer* marks a refinement in factualism and is emblematic of Burroughs's increasing sense of distance from his work. Personal disengagement while writing was a necessary precursor for seeing the facts. As he later commented, "While it was I who wrote *Junky*, I feel that I was being written in *Queer*."[119] In other words, what he described in his writing did not derive from "Normal Consciousness" but from documentary attention to the epistemological process. He sought "direct recording of certain areas of psychic process."[120]

By the time Burroughs moved to Tangier in 1954 and began to compose what later became *Naked Lunch*, his writing practice had become part of a complex ethic. Known as "El Hombre Invisible" by the locals, he blended into the environment so completely that boundaries between subjectivity and objectivity began to fade. As he wrote in *Naked Lunch*, he regarded his "body impersonally as an instrument to absorb the medium" in which he lived.[121] By merging with his environs so fully he hoped to break down barriers to apprehension and enter a state of pure psychic and physiological attentiveness. *Naked Lunch* marked the culmination of factualism, a radical critique of Cartesian modes of subjectivity. Timothy S. Murphy points out that during this period Burroughs came to understand subjectivity as a "form of addiction to language, to the 'I' of self consciousness and identity as an instrument of control." Under the guise of factualism Burroughs sought to penetrate the egotistical surface of things, what Thoreau called "hearsay" and Charles Olson referred to in 1950 as the "lyrical interference of the individual as ego."[122] In bringing such intensity to his writing, sometimes with the aid of drugs or during periods of withdrawal, Burroughs tried to achieve a reliable, neither subjective nor objective, account of the world.

Like Spengler and Korzybski, Burroughs sought to discover an enduring reality by working through the present state of metaphysical confusion. In order to clear a path for the future he had to transcend language by going through it. Consequently, it was necessary to penetrate the surface reality that language had created in order to experience the space beyond words. As Spengler wrote, such moments "beyond language" in which "words would only disturb the harmony" constituted "deliverance from the waking-consciousness."[123] As Emerson had proposed in *Nature*, Burroughs viewed language as the nexus between the individual and the cosmos. As an obstacle, language could obfuscate. As the means to access the ground of being, it could enable one to influence and control empirical reality. According to that understanding, Burroughs viewed the construction of social reality as dependent on language and therefore susceptible to his manipulations. Working within a Spenglerian view of correspondence, he sought to penetrate the pasteboard masks of postwar society—to cut through the words, advertising labels, moral norms, and political demagoguery and perceive the immutable laws of history.

Unlike Kerouac and Ginsberg, Burroughs's primary goal was not necessarily to experience the mystery of correspondence by submitting to cosmic forces during the act of writing. Instead, he sought to better his lot in the world. Burroughs's writing was not a matter of choosing cosmic harmony but of violent action against obstacles—words and images in particular—that prevented such a state. "In my writing," he noted with more than a hint of frontier swagger, "I am acting as a map-maker, an explorer of psychic areas . . . and I see no point in exploring areas that have been thoroughly surveyed."[124] The "psychic areas" were internal as well as dependent upon interaction with the outside world. Composed as a stream of consciousness,

Naked Lunch is an unmediated recording of experience, a moment-by-moment interpenetration of subjectivity and objectivity, the mechanism that drives experience. It was the creation and expression of Burroughs's entire consciousness and characterized by his role as a "recording instrument."[125] The act of writing his inner consciousness was not merely a severe form of introspection but a way of looking inward by looking out upon the rich thicket of reality. Consequently, Burroughs's intensive self-psychologizing was to gather wild facts about the external world—"some new and *usable* techniques"—in order to gain epistemological leverage over it.[126]

In the spirit of technologia, through factualism Burroughs could get behind words. It was a constructive skepticism that laid the foundation for his later experiments in "cut-up" and "fold-ins." Those techniques, developed near the end of assembling *Naked Lunch,* were aimed at revealing hidden meanings by rearranging various texts by either splicing them or folding them together. As an analytical method of metaphysical clarification, factualism was an attempt to intuit the divine order of things as defined by Spengler, Korzybski, and Reich and to "invent" a world on negative premises.[127] In Burroughs's case, the primeval order of things was most often obscured by the materiality of language. Because "every Fact is incarcerate" behind language, his attempt to verbalize the facts could not "be expressed direct." Finding solace in the space between the familiar and the unseen something beyond it, his "language-scape" was a "mosaic of juxtaposition like articles abandoned in a hotel drawer, defined by negatives and absences."[128]

As in the doctrine of technologia, Burroughs assumed that by distinguishing both the contents of and relations between the particulars of reality (in his case, words) he could "feel" the universal law behind everyday experiences. By asserting that nothing is true and everything is permitted, he affirmed the existence of an enduring truth despite (and in spite of) a world that trafficked in appearances. Radical skepticism led him to assume the existence of a world of absolute alterity, of absolute possibility, so different as to be beyond existing categories of thought. Through the power of negative thinking Burroughs appealed to a numinous sphere beyond negativity in order to write its contents.[129]

Spiritual Intercourse

Reminiscent of Thoreau's notion of experiential discipline, Burroughs, Ginsberg, and Kerouac viewed self-exploration in terms of a Spenglerian metaphysics of discovering the natural rhythms of cosmic flux. As Ginsberg once noted of his poetics, "It's the old Thoreau tradition. The reason for that is that if you don't do it yourself you are a prisoner of the robot state, the electric company, the transportation company, the food monopolies and the chain stores. You live in a suspended state where you don't even know where your power comes from."[130] Although it is highly oppositional in tone, Ginsberg's point is not about writing against society but about writing through it in order to "know where your power comes from." As a counterpoint to an emphasis on the solitary act of writing, however, Beat writing was much more than a mystical practice with a strong social conscience. It was premised on direct social engagement that enabled the writer to tap the source of creative power and allow emotional energy to pass through him and into a reader.[131]

By never losing sight of the surrounding culture, the Beats attempted not only to catalyze natural creativity through the discipline of writing but also to reveal sacred realities—"exactly what is"—in the name of society, cutting through the thicket of gossip that concealed self and world. Although the "democratic state" may not have been as present in their writing as John Crowe Ransom imagined, a democratic impulse governed how each Beat understood his task as a writer. Under a Spenglerian guise, the politics of writing was elevated to the metaphysical plane. To penetrate the interiority of a reader was a logical extension of the mystical desire to transcend distinctions between subject and object. As Spengler wrote, "It is by some 'thou' that we first came to the knowledge of an 'I.' 'I,' therefore, is a designation for the fact that a bridge exists to some other being."[132] That concept of a writerly self was not premised on isolation or uniqueness, nor did it depend on physical proximity to a reader. Instead, it was a fluid subjectivity—volatile, mysterious, democratic, and distinctly American.

Beat writing sought to create an appropriate context for its reception, a mindset that would prepare readers for its religious gravity. Before completing *On the Road,* Kerouac wrote that he wanted "to work in revelations, not just spin silly tales for money. I want to fish as deep as possible into my own subconscious in the belief that once that far down, everyone will understand because they are the same that far down." He believed that these revelations would precipitate "a great world religion based on the hopes and images of childhood and made into the form in the rational vigor of adulthood." He once even compared himself to a "shortwave radio" who picked up the frequencies of America's collective consciousness: "It's all in the air, and is still there for me to grasp another day, and I hope to, I want to, I know I will."[133]

The Beats refused to accept the inevitable isolation that writing entails. As Burroughs noted to Ginsberg, while "political action fails . . . the whole existing system can be *dreamed away* if we get enough people dreaming." He hoped to avoid a discourse whereby the self is divided into author and audience. "I have to have a receiver," he said, otherwise the "routine turns back on me like [a] homeless curse and tears me apart."[134] Each Beat, however, maintained authority over his imagined audience, for revolutionary potential lay in a writer's knowledge of "the original relation between a waking-microcosm and its macrocosm."[135] If the ontological discovery of a writer was manifest in words on a page, the words themselves, vibrating with cosmic energy, would enlighten readers of their connection to that writer—a shared humanity and co-participation in the macrocosm.

The Beats' new vision of literature contained a strong evangelical strain, both in regard to an emphasis on conversion experience and a desire to precipitate that same experience in others. This evangelical impulse invested their political concerns with religious import and blurred the boundary between political engagement and religious awakening. Furthermore, a Spenglerian understanding of language tempered the evangelical impulse. As Spengler noted, poetic methods were the most effective means of communication among humans: "Words . . . evoke images, likenesses—the only language of spiritual intercourse that man has discovered to this day. . . . The real language of souls. . . . The poetic word as utterance, as poetic element, may establish the link, but the word as notion, as element of scientific prose, never."[136] For Spengler, poetry was a form of "spiritual intercourse"—the vehicle of personal expression, the way in which to participate in the organic process of life, and, most important, a means to communicate with others. Ginsberg spoke of such verbal intimacy in terms of a mystical sexuality: "Imagine being able to talk and illustrate Time & Eternity right in everybody's living room. My desire to do so now might merely be snoopiness, but in time I will be making love to everybody in amerca right in their own homes." In order to achieve such honest communication, Kerouac envisioned his writing to be a direct conversation with a close confidant. In *Visions of Cody,* he informed readers, "Now what I'm going to do is this—think things over one by one, blowing on the visions of them and *also* excitedly discussing them as with friends . . . I must . . . communicate to people instead of just appeasing my lone soul with a record of it." Showing similar concern, Burroughs wrote to Ginsberg, "I think all writers write for an audience. There is no such thing as writing for yourself."[137]

Emboldened by Spengler's call to arms, the Beats employed various techniques to carry out the traditional tasks of prophets: revelation and renewal. Just as they sought through writing to dissolve the boundaries between self and macrocosm, they structured much of their work around the possibility of mobilizing the same awareness in readers. By thinking in social, even political, terms, the Beats invested their work with transformative potential.

As Kerouac explained, they sought to influence social reality, not merely describe it: "The whole idea was to *stun* people into . . . *realization*." Beat literature separated readers from the indicative, everyday reality of dominant culture and moved them into the "subjunctive antistructure of the liminal process." Transported from microcosm to macrocosm, they experience motion sickness, as Burroughs suggests in *Naked Lunch,* but awaken to a Spenglerian world. In 1949 Ginsberg wrote, "If one is unconsciously wearying of the world of time and thought, and reads a poem supercharged with rock-like indications of the way to bleak eternity, it may be that eternity opens up in some circumstances, that is, that the reader suddenly opens his eyes." In other words, readers were no longer bounded by limitations of objective fact and social pronouncement. They were introduced into a psychological realm of "wish, desire, and possibility," where potential existed to follow alternative modes of understanding and social relations.[138] "Cosmic consciousness" was a panoramic awareness of space and time and the realization of the interconnectedness of the universe. It was, as Kerouac wrote in 1949, a subjective confirmation of a dynamist metaphysics in which "the truth" could not be defined with any static formula. It existed only in the movement "from moment to moment incomprehensible, ungraspable, but terribly clear."[139]

As a group, the Beats believed they could induce a cognitive shift in readers through manipulations of language. Presenting *Naked Lunch* as "revelation and prophecy," Burroughs was the most self-conscious and commanded readers to "see smell and listen" in order to achieve "a condition of total exposure."[140] He urged his audience to undergo initiation into a world where "nothing is true, [and] everything is permitted," a liminal psychological environment designed to discover "what words actually are, and exactly what their relationship is to the human nervous system."[141]

Burrough's didactic style in *Naked Lunch* stems from an intense desire to make contact with readers, as evidenced by his direct address to the "Gentle Reader" and such enticements as "you want to take a look around with honest Bill?" and "room for one more inside." He does not, however, merely want to transmit his message directly. Skeptical of the conduit theory of communication in which words retain their initial meanings, Burroughs "unlocked" his "Word Hoard" in order to enable readers to participate in the construction of meaning with him. "Every pupil must learn a different lesson," he wrote. Through demystifying the authority of language, Burroughs cast a line of communication to his audience that would make the liberating effects of his vision accessible. "This may not be the best of all possible universes," he commented, "but it may well prove to be one of the simplest. If man can *see*."[142]

At the heart of Burroughs's agenda was the desire to free readers from the authority of words—any and all words, even his as well as those of his readers. Salvation came only through silence, through the continual scrutiny of words and the meanings attributed to them. Burroughs's maternal grandfather, a Methodist circuit rider from Georgia, had preached across the postbellum South.[143] As an itinerant preacher of the mind, Burroughs's goal was to alleviate enslavement, not to sin but to the shackles of late Civilization. In order to become liberated from the manipulative system of Western linguistics and thought, he admonished readers to realize that "the way OUT is the way IN" (that is, through language itself).[144]

Naked Lunch was a head-on attack on the conventional structures of metaphor and morality and sought to expose the hidden assumptions of Western philosophical discourse. The text would defy and destroy these oppressive systems in order to cure the "image addiction" and "morality addiction" of postwar society. By laying bare the abstract mechanisms by which conventional metaphors and morals infiltrate our thinking, Burroughs demonstrated their inherent instability and groundlessness. His goal was to remove all those filters imposed on consciousness in order to launch readers into a horizontal world of associative meanings.[145]

The book was designed to propel readers into a "subjunctive" domain by dislodging notions of hierarchy and objectivity that prevented participation. The structure of *Naked Lunch* defies any order other than that of a reader's choosing. As Burroughs states, "You can cut into *Naked Lunch* at any intersection point." By revealing new epistemological strategies, he enabled readers to question traditional criteria of certainty, identity, and truth that supported mind-body opposition, subject-object dichotomies, and moral dualism. Appealing to readers to undergo an awakening, Burroughs wrote: "*Naked Lunch* is a blue print, a How-To-Book . . . How-To extend levels of experience by opening the door at the end of the long hall. . . . Doors that only open in *Silence* . . . *Naked Lunch* demands Silence from the Reader. Otherwise he is taking his own pulse." The book was conceived as an initiation manual that reflected its author's commitment to transform social reality rather than describe it. Burroughs depicts a "NAKED Lunch—a frozen moment when everyone sees what is on the end of every fork," thereby promoting reexamination of the central values of society through a constructive transformation in a reader's consciousness.[146] What he called for was communal introspection and repentance on the strength of his own example, a politics of writing reminiscent of Spengler's claim that "the true statesman" must be "an educator—not the representative of a moral or a doctrine, but an exemplar in doing."[147]

Ginsberg also sought to instigate a revelatory experience for readers, enabling them to confront the crisis of America and become aware of their compromised state. In 1947 he wrote of his desire to assume "a violent / and messianic voice, inspired at / last, dominating the whole room."[148] After his Blake visitation in 1948, Ginsberg wrote that he "immediately saw poetry as a hermetic or secret way of talking about experiences that were universal, cosmic, that everybody knew about, but nobody knew how to refer to, nobody knew how to bring it up to front brain consciousness, or to present it to social consciousness." The problem, after "having attained realization," was "how to safely manifest it and communicate it." Ginsberg believed that dominant literary conventions and language were inadequate for communicating a cosmic perspective. "Anybody who wants to hang on to traditional metrics and values," he noted, "will wind up stultified and self-deceived."[149]

Although lamenting the inability of most people to come to terms with self-deception, Ginsberg nevertheless continued to advocate the exposition and excision of forces that suppressed "contemplative individuality."[150] His goal was to empower readers by exposing the sources of psychological repression, thereby enabling them to overcome Faustian-imposed neurosis. Equating psychological conditioning with violent but invisible manipulation, Ginsberg asserted that the only way to protect oneself from such Procrustean forces was to make them visible—that is, to eliminate them through confrontation.

In Zen koans and the paintings of Paul Cézanne, Ginsberg saw a blueprint for inducing "cosmic vibrations" in readers.[151] Both Zen philosophy and Cézanne used paired tensions—whether ideas or colors—to create a third, seemingly unrelated, entity. Loosely based on the haiku form, Ginsberg viewed the practice of ellipsis as constitutive rather than descriptive.[152] Although poets such as Ezra Pound, T. S. Eliot, and W. H. Auden would leave out a word (or several words) in order to achieve more compact expression, Ginsberg sought readers' subjective recognition by creating, rather than recording, a version of reality. The principle and practice of ellipsis was essential to "Howl," so much so that Ginsberg invoked it by name at the end of Part One and alluded to the transformative social power of the poet as priest: "Who dreamt and made incarnate gaps in Time & Space through images juxtaposed, and trapped the archangel of the soul between 2 visual images and joined the elemental verb and set the noun and dash of consciousness together jumping with sensation of Pater Omnipotens Aeterna Deus."[153]

Absurd phrases such as "hydrogen jukebox" were intended to precipitate moments for readers when instinct trumped tradition, when gaps of awareness were filled by knowledge that had previously been unconscious and unknown. "Hydrogen jukebox," for example, enabled his audience to discern the relationship between mass culture and political manipulation. The onslaught of juxtapositions in the poem also allowed readers to renegotiate isolated meanings and perceive continuities where there had been only barriers.

Given his "secret ambition to be a tremendous life-changing prophetic artist," Kerouac viewed his art as a revelatory vehicle precisely because it possessed ordinariness and experiential honesty.[154] Like radical empiricists such as William James and John Dewey, he believed that the only authority was experience itself. The primary assumption of radical empiricism was that in addition to the five senses, people harbor the valuational senses of repulsion, attraction, and quality. James wrote that the objective, material world comes to the observer "with definite direction" and goal, a vector of palpable energy from which to derive value. For Kerouac, however, words could be felt empirically, as James put it, inducing "bodily effects upon us, alterations of tone and tension, of heartbeat and breathing, of vascular and visceral action."[155]

Kerouac located his art within the basic philosophical conundrum of the twentieth century—how to move beyond language in and through language. Given his deep yet eclectic religious faith, he believed that the limits of human understanding were not linguistic. "The new vision can be achieved in art," he wrote. "Art, commonly assumed to employ the six senses, may in itself be a sense, or a system of sense, potentially capable of transmitting universal forces as yet blind and numb for the six senses."[156] In other words, Kerouac held firmly to the romantic belief in the transcendent capacities of language.

Given Kerouac's romantic sensibility, poets were not only priests but also possessed the power to regenerate culture sexually. By recovering "universal forces" for readers, Kerouac attempted to precipitate a social reality of communitas and, in Ginsberg's words, challenge the paradigms of society by "generating new philosophical systems, scientific hypotheses, political programs, art forms, and the like—among which reality testing . . . will give form to new contents of social relations."[157] He understood his writing to be something more than language and an endless series of signifiers because he believed language to have an erotic capacity. In a 1949 journal entry Kerouac sounded like an orgiastic revival preacher: "People aren't interested in facts, but in ejaculations. That is why straight naturalism fails to express life. Who wants Dos Passos' old camera eye? Everybody wants to *Go!* So must the author, oblivious to all petty details, huffing and puffing in that heat of his fiery soul, go!"[158] Kerouac, like Emerson before him, equated the expression of the secret of correspondence with the ejaculation of an imaginative writer. The process of writing became a sexual act—"man-to-man communication"—disseminating the essence of creation through words.[159]

Conclusion

As each Beat made a sustained effort to make his work an organic extension of his life, the act of writing took on religious significance. It held the possibility for personal as well as social transformation because it was the most immediate way to set the Spenglerian worldview in action. It cultivated the soil of self and Culture in equal measure. The Beats were no longer satisfied with the traditional function of imaginative literature to limn fictional, unknown horizons. Instead, they demanded that the process of art become a springboard into a world elsewhere. Paradoxically, that did not necessitate passage from one world to another but remaking and revisioning this one. Writing became, in Burroughs's words, a matter "of putting down in some sequence what is already there."[160]

The Beats did not seek to transcend above or across while writing. They went downward into the mystery of America. Composition became a means of transcendence that implied not a separation but rather a return, in the Thoreauvian sense, to the fertile ground of a "bottomless" tradition of macrocosmic truth. Kerouac and Ginsberg envisioned their writing in mystical terms—the goal being to experience the inexhaustible depths of self and an intimate connection to the universal. Burroughs, however, employed the scientific rhetoric of factualism instead of romanticism in attempting to cleanse his mind of nonfactual elements, that is, those unwarranted assumptions that would hinder perception of cosmic forces.[161] Despite their differences, the Beats shared a goal of making writing a revolutionary act, as Spengler put it, *"to create a tradition,* to bring on others so that one's work may be continued with one's own pulse and spirit, to release a current of like activity that does not need the original leader to maintain it in form."[162]

Writing became a search for intimacy between writer and self and writer and world. Such intimacy, whether it had been lost or had never existed to begin with, was associated with a certain level of violence and destruction. Given the Faustian siege against each American, neither expression nor communication could be achieved without aggression. Viewing themselves as the avant-garde of Culture, Kerouac and Ginsberg attempted to rally the American spirit, from the recesses of their unconscious to those of their audience. Burroughs, however, saw his role as the exterminator of Faustian Civilization and sought to dismantle it from the inside, at all times adhering to Spengler's dictum that "we are civilized . . . we have to reckon with the hard cold facts of *late* life."[163]

In either case, to break down barriers between self and other, whether self-consciousness, nature, or another person, required a form of violent reduction of the other. The Beats constantly tried to tap into that reckless, bohemian passion as a source of creative inspiration. According to Kerouac, it was a poet's task to channel such energy at the beginning of a Culture cycle:

> A kind of lyrical ecstasy possesses certain young Americans in the springtime, a feeling of not belonging in any one place or in any one moment, a wild restless longing to be elsewhere, everywhere, right now! The air is balmy and springlike, redolent with so many musics from everywhere, everything seems to describe dizzy circles, there are illimitable thoughts of long spaces and long voyages, it is strange, maddening but still as yet ecstatic feeling of irresponsible wanderlust of the soul, responding to everything at the moment—"I don't *give* a damn!"[164]

Consequently, the act of writing straddled the line between irresponsible mayhem and positive sexual energy. The Beats conceived it as an aggressive action taken against the worldly self in order to break through the wall that separates the self from the outside. The desire to consummate the relationship between self and other, be it a world or a person, was often premised on forms of self-destruction.

Violence and sex, masochism and dominance, negation and affirmation—each depended on the other as the Beats developed a strategic vision of writers in America. Such dialectics invested the poetics of Burroughs, Kerouac, and Ginsberg with political and religious urgency. As Kerouac announced, a writer should be "submissive to everything, open, listening."[165] Consequently, the Beats, like Rimbaud, were desperate to learn how to sacrifice themselves daily and what structures, both internal and external, to dismantle in the process. The time of the assassins was upon them. "War is the primary politics of *everything* that lives," wrote Spengler, "so much so that in the deeps battle and life are one, and being and will-to-battle expire together."[166] As Ginsberg wrote in "Paterson," he would crucify himself for America—"crawl on my naked belly over the tincans of Cincinnati . . . crowned with thorns in Galveston, nailed hand and foot in Los Angeles, raised up to die in Denver." Such sacrifice would be redemptive: "pierced in the side in Chicago, perished and tombed in New Orleans and resurrected in 1958 somewhere on Garret Mountain." Upon returning, however, Ginsberg would assume the role of a premillennial Christ, sacrificing himself yet again in order to rid the temple at last of Faustian money-changers, "screaming and dancing in praise of Eternity annihilating the sidewalk, annihilating reality . . . blood streaming from my belly and shoulders, flooding the city with its hideous ecstasy . . . leaving my flesh and my bones hanging on the trees."[167]

chapter

4

TABLE I.

	INDIAN (from 1500)			
ʼRING.	I. BIRTH OF A MYTH OF THE GRAND STYLE, EXPRESSING A NEW GOD–FEELING. WORLD–FEAR. WORLD–LONGING			
ral-intuitive. Great tions of the newly-kened dream-heavy . Super-personal y and fulness)	1500–1200 Vedic religion	1100–800 Hellenic-Italian "Demeter" religion of the people Homer	0–300 Primitive Christianity (Mandaeans, Marcion, Gnosis, Syncretism (Mithras, Baal) Gospels. Apocalypses	
	Aryan hero-tales	Heracles and Theseus legends	Christian, Mazdaist and pagan legends	
	II. EARLIEST MYSTICAL–METAPHYSICAL SHAPING OF THE NEW WORLD–OUTLOOK ZENITH OF SCHOLASTICISM			
	Preserved in oldest parts of the Vedas	Oldest (oral) Orphic, Etruscan discipline	Origen (d. 254), Plotinus (d. 269), Mani (d. 276), Iamblichus (d. 330)	Thomas Aquinas (d. 1274), Duns Scotus (d. 1308), Dante (d. 1321) and Eckhardt (d. 1319)
		After-effect; Hesiod, Cosmogonies	Avesta, Talmud. Patristic literature	Mysticism. Scholasticism
ʼM M E R.	III. REFORMATION: INTERNAL POPULAR OPPOSITION TO THE GREAT SPRINGTIME FORMS Orphic movement. Dionysiac religion. "Numa" religion (7th Century)			

"Storming the Reality Studios"
Beat Remythologies

Previous page, from table 1, "'Contemporary' Political Epochs," in Oswald Spengler, *Form and Actuality,* volume 1 of *The Decline of the West.*

Mighty world events meant virtually nothing to him, they were not real enough, and he was certain that his wonderful joyous visions of super-spiritual existence and great poetry were "realer than all."
   —Jack Kerouac, *The Town and the City*

the government of America also will fall but how can America fall
I doubt if anyone will ever fall anymore except governments
fortunately all the governments will fall
the only ones which won't fall are the good ones
and the good ones don't yet exist
But they have to begin existing, they exist in my poems.
   —Allen Ginsberg, "Death to Van Gogh's Ear"

These things were revealed to me in Interzone.
   —William S. Burroughs, "Word"

The Beats reached an artistic peak during the 1950s. The new vision matured and assumed more definitive contours. Literary experimentalism gave way to expertise, and Kerouac, Ginsberg, and Burroughs each began to wield a patience that he had not possessed earlier. Their implicit criticism of the dominant ideology—the "American way of life" in all its consumer and technological grandeur—became explicit even as it became more nuanced. Although American exceptionalism became dominant—increasingly politicizing culture and registering its effects in a prescribed worldview—that did not necessarily mean everyone accepted it uncritically or acted within the norms it imposed. On the contrary, many harbored a dissident mentality and recoiled from majority values, including civil rights activists; bebop musicians; various members of the avant-garde, from the Black Mountain poets to the schools of Jackson Pollack and William de Kooning; maverick intellectuals such as C. Wright Mills and Herbert Marcuse; writers as diverse as James Baldwin, Mary McCarthy, and William Gaddis; and a host of Americans outside the public purview. Furthermore, the postwar years were characterized by a conflict between the authoritative ideals of the past and those now appearing on the televised horizon or associated with trends in consumption and the fashions of youth. Because multiple renditions of America circulated in the public sphere like electrons orbiting a nucleus, the possibility of experiencing their heterogeneous and even contradictory imperatives was considerable.[1] For the Beats as well as other Americans, myth provided an experiential ground from which to move forward, backward, or even sideways—in other words, away—from standards that authoritative ideals had set.

While the "official" America of Eisenhower, McCarthy, and nuclear domesticity canvassed the material world in its residue, it was haunted by ghostly presences that threatened to unravel its coherence and undo its assumptions. Myth was the graveyard where the dead were buried, where tradition was interred; it was also where memories still lingered, alive and present, waiting to be invoked. These memories—democratic equality, unfettered individualism, and the pastoral dream—continually forced the Beats into action that was often at odds with the official purveyors of these patriotic ideals. America, as it was popularly conceived, no longer made sense to the Beats "on the ground," that is, as they experienced it. In order to envision, let alone create, a corresponding America, they first had to adjust existing definitions to fit their experiences. Consequently, although each Beat formulated his own ideal within the confines of American culture, it was precisely the internal friction that allowed for radical departures from the status quo. "It is society," Emile Durkheim once observed, "that, by drawing [one] into its sphere of action, has given him the need to raise himself above the world of experience, while at the same time furnishing him the means of imagining another."[2]

As the Beats lived through their contemporary America, they experienced a crisis of cultural authority. Because America's "cowboys" (as Ginsberg termed them) had not yet read Spengler, the tradition that supported America's geopolitical and domestic agendas was tragically misconstrued. As they searched for a new tradition under Spenglerian precepts, Burroughs, Kerouac, and Ginsberg each sensed the nagging falsity at the heart of everyday social reality. They perceived the claims of truth and authority made on behalf of America to be lies. The claims were distortions naturalized through propaganda and disseminated to an unassuming populace, a public secret that insisted that the world was not as it seemed. Roland Barthes, whose treatise on myth in the mid–1950s resembled the Beats' position, wrote that people perpetuate the magical spell they are under and perform a "conjuring trick" by looking myth head-on and then quickly turning away. If, according to Barthes, myth "turned reality inside out" and "emptied it of history and . . . filled it with nature," the Beats turned postwar reality inside out once again, redefining in their work what passed for natural as well as history. In response to a "perceptible absence" at the core of cultural reality, the Beats had unleashed a torrent of literary activity by the mid–1950s. Their output was as a collective re-presentation of America, an invocation of Spengler's ghost on American soil.[3]

Kerouac's *On the Road* and *Visions of Cody,* Ginsberg's *Howl and Other Poems,* and Burroughs's *Naked Lunch* pitted a newfound ideal against American myths that sanctioned the status quo. In doing so, the Beats were simultaneously rebellious and beholden to the mythic language of America, suspicious of its contemporary content but committed to its general form. By recasting America's mythic heritage in a Spenglerian light, they used their literature to question the dominant culture, that is, the system of generalized goals and values that maintained social order. They were also rehearsing the American jeremiad in Spenglerian terms. Having committed themselves to a millennial history of America even as they questioned its present state, they looked to personal experience in order to lay claim to its potential. Their observations and confessions made their work adversarial yet also gave it pathos. Theirs was a violent and personal repossession of American history. They displaced the past by wrenching it away from the realm of stability and anonymity. Using biography, autobiography, and the starkness of the Mexican landscape—coopting anything and everything at their disposal—they ripped the historical fabric apart to force repentance. They made it bleed to prove it was alive and therefore malleable and also to purify and cleanse it of sin. The impetus for their literature was a desire to change the way things were, to alter the present situation by reinventing the past and therefore changing the future.

Criticizing one's own culture is a precarious endeavor, particularly when attempting to reimagine its mythic inheritance. When pointing out faults and exploring uncharted possibilities there is always the danger of reaffirming that which is being criticized as one succumbs to the pressures of living inside culture and its mythic canopy. Theodor Adorno once spoke of the "flagrant contradiction" inherent in that form of cultural criticism: "The cultural critic is not happy with civilization, to which alone he owes his discontent. He speaks as if he represented either unadulterated nature or a higher historical stage. Yet he is necessarily of the same essence as that to which he fancies himself superior."[4] Barthes, in a similar gesture, wrote that "it is extremely difficult to vanquish myth from the inside: for the very effort one makes in order to escape its stranglehold becomes in its turn the prey of myth."[5] For both Adorno and Barthes, a question remained: If an outside perspective cannot be secured, from what position does one begin to renegotiate the myth in question? How should one come to terms with, let alone challenge, prevailing ideological codes when one is subject to them?

The Beats were aware of such theoretical dilemmas. While editing *Naked Lunch,* for example, Burroughs confided to Ginsberg that the novel dealt with the "basic conflict between . . . spontaneous, emergent life—and the West, representing control from without, character armor, death." Despite his critical stance, Burroughs was careful not to fall victim to that which he critiqued. "It is difficult to know what side anyone is working on," he wrote, "especially yourself."[6]

As early as 1948 Kerouac had begun to confront the paradoxical nature of cultural criticism, questioning the existence of society as well as the possibility of getting outside it in order to effect change: "What do we mean by 'society' if we don't mean some ambiguous idea we either seek to honor by strict conformity or 'get around' one way or the other? What is society? Can there be reality without society?" Kerouac, like Burroughs (and unlike Adorno and Barthes), saw middle ground between conformity and escapism. Whereas Adorno and Barthes left little room for the imaginative transcendence of one's cultural context, Kerouac put aside such limitations by approaching the notion of transcendence as a mode of penetration rather than as one of overcoming. He believed that culture could be transformed through "revolution," that is, a return to the ground of humanity (what he called the "fundamental life"). In spurning the political, social, economic, and "religious revolutions" of the past, he did not advocate a return to prerevolutionary traditions but sought to get behind them in order to discover the basis of tradition. He sought an "actual breakthrough to the 'conditions' of the Garden of Eden . . . a world where it is finally admitted that we want to mate and love, eat and sleep, and bask in the days and nights of our true, fundamental life."[7]

The Beats' critical stance toward America was not a mere refutation of that which already existed but an attempt to reinvest, via Spengler, American mythos with a proper metaphysical ground. Kerouac, like Ginsberg and Burroughs, assumed the role of cultural critic in order to engage America on moral grounds—not only to judge but also to show what was possible, and therefore necessary, given unfavorable cultural conditions. They re-narrated America, modifying its details in order to change the sentiments it evoked.[8]

The Beats made no attempt to dissolve the "flagrant contradiction" of which Adorno and Barthes spoke but instead implicated themselves (showing neither vanity nor condescension) in America's crisis situation. By self-consciously using the language of American myth against itself, their literature was not just a reflection of America but a reflection upon it. Through cultural criticism they expressed empathetic understanding and the desire to embrace America for the purpose of mutual healing. Because the nation's problems were also theirs, the Beats, in Ginsberg's memorable line, sought to "hug and kiss the United States under our bedsheets the United States that coughs all night and won't let us sleep."[9]

What country, exactly, was beneath the sheets? For which American constituency were the Beats speaking and to whom? By definition, their audience was imaginary, an extrapolated cross-section of families, friends, acquaintances, and bystanders, innocent or otherwise—from Lionel Trilling to Dean Acheson to Herbert Huncke to Dizzy Gillespie. They hoped to reach all of America's many publics by extracting what each had in common and returning the nation to its rightful and proper place in the Spenglerian cosmos.

Like their romantic forebears, the Beats distanced themselves from the majority not by providing alternative solutions to contemporary problems but by conceiving those issues from a different perspective. From that unique vantage point, they did not merely revel in the fact that the majority culture was a social construction. On the contrary, they translated its claims into a new language, expanded the range of what America meant and included, and stormed the "reality studios" (as Burroughs called them) in order to invent an American tradition that accorded with their experiences.

The Beats envisioned utopia, an imaginary world and ideal state both infinitely remote and immanently present. It may have been literally "nowhere," a world elsewhere that could neither be retrieved nor realized, but it was nevertheless glimpsed in the imaginative confines of their literature. As the focus of this chapter shifts from poetics to the narrative content of their most defining work of the 1950s—Burroughs's *Naked Lunch,* Kerouac's road novels (*Visions of Cody* and *On the Road*), and Ginsberg's *Howl and Other Poems*—it will explore how the Beats engaged postwar society through the religious imagination, specifically on the discursive terms of public religion. Those works elicit emotional sympathy with the respective protagonists no less than with the author, who is searching for an alternative way of life against the current of the cultural majority. Even Burroughs, for whom "utopian" seems an odd moniker, emphasized what was absent in America and therefore what was possible, even as he denounced its present state as a pernicious lie. As cultural critics, the Beats forged a new mythology for the nation by reinvigorating the existing language of myth in their respective works and applying their experiences to the domesticated reservoir of religious symbols.

Mexican Pastorals and Fellaheen Ambulances

During the late 1940s and early 1950s, Mexico held a special place in the Beats' imagination. It was a place for introspection and decadence, where myth and reality converged in stifling heat and the haze of marijuana smoke. The Beats' initial attraction was largely because of Burroughs's interest in Mayan codices, but as they read Spengler's descriptions of Mexican history the country began to assume a mythic hue. They began to see the vast, ancient terrain as casting a prophetic shadow on contemporary America. In *Decline,* Spengler spoke of the "violent death" of the Aztec and Mayan civilizations, which were overwhelmed by the "expansion-power of the Western Soul." Those societies were "not starved, suppressed, or thwarted," he wrote, "but murdered in the full glory of [their] unfolding, destroyed like a sunflower whose head is struck off by one passing."[10]

As an example of pseudomorphosis and cultural extinction, the Beats looked to Mexico as an ominous portent of America's future. At the same time, however, they saw contemporary Mexico as a land of Edenic innocence because it no longer could be characterized as a Civilization. It represented the pastoral ideal on which America was founded and the state of cosmic harmony to which it could once again return. Given Spengler's penchant for racial exoticizing, the Beats could imagine Mexico as existing in a state of nature, no longer subject to its Faustian oppressor. Consequently, each writer traveled to Mexico in order to garner knowledge about America, resolve the tension between his ideal of America and its reality, and undergo a ritual of purification and initiation into a new, American consciousness.

Mexico became an experiential landscape where ideas were worked out, happenstance yielded new ideas, and mythic renderings were put to the test. Burroughs, Kerouac, and Ginsberg each made extended visits to Mexico in order to confirm their Spenglerian understanding of cosmic reality. Imagining themselves to be participants in an apocalyptic drama, Mexico either supported the utopian promise of America or sounded its death knell. In both cases, Mexico became a source of self-validation. As the Beats searched for America in Mexico, what each found depended largely on what he sought. Mexico became the ground beneath America, lurking behind its public facade—a referent whose history foretold America's future. Kerouac and Ginsberg viewed the inhabitants of Mexico as a fellaheen remnant who had survived the decline of Civilization and were now living in a post-apocalyptic age. They understood Mexican Indians, like the nomadic shepherds of Arabia from whom Spengler derived the term, as a people without history, possessing neither past nor future but only the immediacy of the present. These people, by virtue of the cosmic potency of their blood, embodied the source and ground of all life.

Burroughs believed that Mexicans had been forever corrupted by their historical experience—not only by the "expansion power of the Western Soul" but also by the totalitarian legacy of Mayan civilization and its ritual calendar. He had initially fled to Mexico in 1949 in order to avoid drug and weapons charges in New Orleans. He found the environment corrupt politically, but the country was nonetheless a hospitable place to pursue his interests. Burroughs remained in Mexico until 1953. At first young boys, drugs, and guns were readily available, and his monthly stipend provided a degree of luxury not available to him in the United States. Even as he came to despise Mexico's resemblance to the United States, Mexico remained a wasteland where he could learn much about conditions within America.[11] His studies of the Mayan language and codices deepened his appreciation for the ways and means of control in Mayan culture. As Eric Mottram has pointed out, Burroughs became fascinated with how Mayan priests wielded absolute political power over the public, albeit indirectly, through religious rituals.[12] In *Naked Lunch*, he referred to a clarity of vision achieved "when you cross the border into Mexico." "Something falls off you," he wrote, "and suddenly the landscape hits you straight with nothing between you and it, desert and mountains and vultures."[13] In a 1951 letter to Kerouac he attempted to disabuse him of his "idyllic" and romantic conceptions of Mexico: "[It] reflects two thousand years of disease and poverty and degradation and stupidity and slavery and brutality and psychic and physical terrorism."[14] For Burroughs, Mexico was in a perpetual state of corruption and degeneration that was already underway in the United States

In Mexico, Burroughs envisioned the future of America, a depraved atmosphere of corruption and random violence. "Murder," he wrote, "is the national neurosis of Mexico."[15] Burroughs soon encountered that neurosis. In September 1951, he and his common-law wife Joan Vollmer went to a friend's house in order to sell a cache of guns. After some drinking and negotiating, Burroughs and Vollmer decided to perform a "William Tell act" with a .380 automatic. Tragically, he missed the highball glass balanced atop Vollmer's head and shot her instead. Burroughs was devastated by Vollmer's death and attempted to rationalize it by claiming to have been possessed by a spirit of external control.

Burroughs later wrote that Joan Vollmer's death had led him to see writing as a form of "inoculation": "I am forced to the appalling conclusion that I would never have become a writer but for Joan's death . . . I live with the constant threat of possession, from Control. So the death of Joan brought me in contact with the invader, the Ugly Spirit, and maneuvered me into a lifelong struggle, in which I have had no choice except to write my way out." Burroughs felt that he had confronted the full onslaught of the "Ugly Spirit" in Mexico, the same one that had invaded America. "My concept of possession," he wrote, "is closer to the medieval model than to modern psychological explanations, with their dogmatic insistence that such manifestations must come from within and never, never, never from without." He soon put his faith behind yage as the instrument that would "inoculate" him from Faustian infection, "a definite possessing entity."[16]

After beginning to write his "way out" with *Queer*, Burroughs made another excursion into South America to continue his quest for yage, a shamanic, hallucinogenic plant he believed to be "the final fix." As documented in the *Yage Letters*, Burroughs regarded yage as the "bitter Soul Vine of the Amazon."[17] After his disappointing experience with the yage elixir he turned almost completely to writing as end and means of his flight from control.

Ginsberg made his first trip to Mexico in 1950 with Lucien Carr and returned alone in early 1954, traveling across the Yucatan Peninsula. During the trek he met Karena Shields, an archeologist who was excavating the Mayan ruins of Palenque. Accepting Shields's invitation to stay on her *finca*, Ginsberg took part in the daily activities of the cocoa plantation and learned much about Mayan cosmology and symbolism from Shields.[18]

As he surveyed the Mayan ruins of Palenque, Ginsberg began to compose his most ambitious meditation to date on the destiny of America, an "anachronistic valentine" to the Mayans and an urgent appeal to "the nation over the border." By focusing on the collapse of the Mayan civilization and the "ruins of time," "Siesta in Xbalba" was Ginsberg's Spenglerian reading of America's position in the grand scheme of historical cycles. Spengler had written of Palenque and other Mexican city-centers that marked "the culminating point of a grandiose architecture, which thereafter produced no style."[19] Ginsberg's poem was equally enigmatic.

In Mayan mythology, Xibalba was simultaneously the Place of Death and the Place of Regenerative Powers.[20] Likewise, Ginsberg envisioned the underworld of Civilization even as he held out hope that something would emerge, reborn, from the death and decay he relentlessly described. Upon arriving in Chichen on New Year's Day 1954, Ginsberg wrote in his journal: "I want to escape to some great future with Bill Jack Neal Lucien, cannot do and in loneliness forming an imaginary movie . . . set in background of Europe in the rain and decay, a Spenglerian movie." "Siesta in Xbalba" was his solitary response. The ruins of Mexico, as Ginsberg wrote, "woke up in me nostalgia for the unseen old continent of ruins." In the "last sweet days of memory before the ultimate night of war," he envisioned "the last fantastic elements of civilization."[21] This was the end, Ginsberg declared, and consequently his poem became a documentary of the apocalypse, both past and present.

The poem is a hero's journey. Like the Mayan king Lord Pacal, who ruled Palenque for sixty-four years, Ginsberg journeys into the underworld of Xibalba, struggles to overcome death, and returns to the earthly level spiritually renewed. He begins the poem with an attempt to read his natural environment like a book of revelation:

Late sun opening the book,
blank page like light,
invisible words unscrawled,
impossible syntax
of apocalypse—[22]

To obtain the vision that he desires, Ginsberg lets his "mind fall down" into the Mayan underworld, described as both the graveyard for past Civilizations and "the culture of my generation." As he leans against the world tree of Mayan cosmology, he begins to have "moments" of "nocturnal thought / and primitive illuminations." Reminiscent of Spengler's comparison of "the full glory of Palenque and Piedras Negras" to the pinnacle of Western Civilization, Ginsberg sees "Palenque, broken chapels in the green . . . Piedras Negras buried again."[23] The lesson he takes from the ruins is to discard the "god / dying in America" and instead look beyond the present, into both the past and future, toward

an inner
anterior image
of divinity
beckoning me out
to pilgrimage.

To reach that undefined future, the "unimaginable God," the poet must undergo the ordeals of the underworld and overcome "the problem" of "isolation." Ginsberg continually laments the solitude he has "inherited"—a solitude of visionary isolation. How to convey that prophecy to America when it is only he who has been transformed by what he has seen? How to become a cultural savior akin to Lord Pacal? Perhaps by returning to the United States "armed with New Testament" and "satisfying Whitman" with a message of millennial bliss. Such comforting lessons, however, are not the currency of a prophet in the wilderness. "Enough!" Ginsberg interjects at the end of the poem, no longer able to contain his anger and visionary wrath:

> The nation over the border
> grinds its arms and dreams
> of war: I see
> the fiery blue clash
> of metal wheels
> clanking in the industries
> of night, and
> detonation of infernal bombs.

The outburst is calculated for optimum effect. Despite his rage, the symbolism gives way to an underlying hope: "and the silent downtown / of the States / in watery dusk submersion." After the flood, after America has been cleansed of its sins, the future awaits. Upon his return to the United States, Ginsberg noted in his journal that he had been cleansed and was now ready to apply the lessons he had learned from his experiences in Mexico. As he noted, he stood "alone naked with knapsack, watch, camera, poem, beard," materially impoverished but spiritually rich.[24] For Ginsberg as for Burroughs, Mexico was a ritual testing ground, a springboard for a writerly journey home.

Kerouac, too, saw Mexico as a rite of passage, an imaginative journey that would crystalize his understanding of America. After *The Town and the City* received polite but disappointing reviews, he made his first visit to "the magic land at the end of the road."[25] In early 1952, after completing what ultimately became *Visions of Cody,* he visited Burroughs in Mexico City and began work again on *Doctor Sax,* a novel he had begun in the late 1940s. For Kerouac, Mexico was a land of promise, and he found imaginative exhilaration there, particularly in the "great, grave" Mexican Indians.[26] Mexico became a jeremiadic referent in a more traditional sense as well, an imaginary space on which he projected his cultural fantasies (and in a later novel, *Tristessa,* his sexual ones). It symbolized the purity and innocence of the past and the ruggedness of a utopian future. "I know that I will someday live in a land like this," wrote Kerouac. "I did long ago."[27] He was an ardent proponent of the spiritual vitality of Mexico and its fellaheen inhabitants. Only they had not been corrupted by the authoritative claims of Faustian Civilization. And only they were untouched by industry and consumer capitalism, technology, and the social institutions that eliminated contact with the ordinary and everyday.

Although Kerouac often romanticized Mexican Indians and made them the subject of his primitivist desires, such racial exoticizing must be seen in terms of Spengler's volkisch concept of race as a spiritual presence. For Kerouac, race was an ontological as well as a geographical category defined by "duration" and "the cosmic-plantlike side of life . . . rooted in a landscape." It was "something cosmic and psychic," as much a part of human identity as where one was born and lived. "The power of the landscape" determined racial makeup.[28] Kerouac's musings on the fellaheen seem more social when viewed in that light. As he wrote in *On the Road*, Mexican Indians "were not fools, they were not clowns . . . of silly civilized American lore." In *Visions of Cody*, he expressed the same sentiment by poking fun at one of the architects of the American Century, Secretary of State Dean Acheson. Evoking the connection between the policy of containment and its implicit agenda of racial purity, Kerouac preempted Acheson's response ("false nonsense") with his own foreign policy dictate: "You've got to legalize the Fellaheen."[29]

Working within the jeremiadic tradition, Kerouac continually used the innocence of Mexico and the fellaheen to condemn America's sins. At one point in *Visions of Cody*, he self-consciously assumed the role of a biblical prophet condemning other Americans from the "Biblical plateau" of Mexico. From his seat in the "Jeremiacal hobos lounge" he could "see the hand of God." The revelation was, "The future's in Fellaheen." Kerouac's vision of the future, however, was intimately tied to an idyllic past. He wanted to return to a time "when America was America, when people pulled together and made no bones about it." For him, Mexico held the secret to America's cultural survival. As Kerouac made clear in his road novels, that secret motivated his continuous pilgrimage across America and Mexico. In *Visions of Cody*, for example, as he and Cody drive through Mexico they notice that "all the Indians along the road want something from us." Neither have anything to offer because they are themselves cultural beggars: "We wouldn't be on the road if we had it."[30]

Projecting his search for authenticity onto a racial other, Kerouac depicts Mexican Indians as "the essential strain of the basic primitive" and "the source of mankind and the fathers of it." Within Spengler's cyclical view of history, the traditionalism of the fellaheen fulfilled Kerouac's insistence on spontaneity, originality, and self-creation. "As essential as rocks in the desert are they in the desert of 'history.' . . . For when destruction comes to the world of 'history' and the Apocalypse of the Fellahin returns once more as so many times before, people will still stare with the same eyes from the caves of Bali, where it all began and where Adam was suckled and taught to know." The metaphorical reference to Adam reflected Kerouac's belief that the fellaheen embodied a natural orientation to the universe, a pastoral ideal desperately needed in America. "The Fellaheen Ambulance is coming!" he asserts in *Visions of Cody,* its "siren howling" as it weaves around "American and West European" traffic.[31]

Following Spengler's dictum to "reckon with the hard cold facts of a *late* life," Kerouac became an artist on the margins. He placed faith in the future on those who would inherit the new America by virtue of having already seen God in the form of the "cosmic beat." They were the true artists in the Spenglerian sense, harbingers of a new Cultural reality. After dedicating *Visions of Cody* to Charles Atkison, translator of *Decline,* it is no coincidence that the transcripted section ("Frisco: The Tape") was framed with allusions to Spengler's claim of offering "a glimpse of life and not a definition."[32] The section begins, "—and during the night he said 'I'm an artist!',", a reference to Kerouac's position as an artist at the close of the Faustian cycle. It ends 130 pages later with a call-and-response sermon of an African American preacher, the embodiment of the intersubjective loop:

> Preacher [screeches]: WE KNOW HOW TO PRAY!
> People: PRAY! . . . .
> Preacher: AFTER AWHILE THEY KEPT UP ON PRAYIN
> People: YEAH!
> Preacher: AFTER AWHILE!!
> People: AFTER AWHILE!!

Such ecstatic frenzy is a form of positive and necessary violence that keeps the devil at bay and does battle with forces that prey upon the world. For Kerouac, an avant-garde artist whose kingdom was "not of this world," it was an allegory for the cultural revival that would take place through an appeal to oppressed modalities of consciousness and marginalized subcultures. "I HEEEEEEEEEEEEEEEEEEERD!" screams the preacher, announcing the religious discovery of a new, uncorrupted America.[33] Kerouac's Spenglerian longings also extended to his views of African Americans. "The future lies in the Negro," he wrote in his journal. "I know it now. It is the simplicity and raw strength, rising out of the American ground, that will save us."[34]

Among the Beats, Kerouac was most prone to what one critic has called "cross-race identification"—a "melancholic romanticization of otherness" that was both a critique of the white male subject and an anxious response to perceived incursions upon his social authority.[35] Although that may be so—each Beat castigated the predominantly white male public culture—he also found in the racial other a community ideal and the history he sought. Burroughs and Ginsberg also displayed such pastoral vision, ignoring socioeconomic realities and opting instead for the metaphorical capacity of race. Although their visions are less articulate than Kerouac's position, both believed, like Spengler, that "in race there is nothing material but something cosmic and directional, the felt harmony of a Destiny, the single cadence of the march of historical Being."[36]

In 1953 Burroughs described to Ginsberg a yage vision of the emergence of a cosmic race, projecting freedoms of the unconscious onto a racial other: "Yage is space-time travel, the room seems to shake and vibrate with motion. The blood and substance of many races, Negro, Polynesian, Mountain Mongol, Desert Nomad, Polyglot Near East, Indian—new races as yet unconceived and unborn, combinations not yet realized pass through your body."[37] Ginsberg shared that penchant for espousing a romanticized and psychologized version of the melting pot theory. He saw America as a land of cosmic immigrants yet ignored the nightmares of racial violence that were part of the historical record. In a 1955 journal entry he described America's Edenic innocence amid world Civilizations and its potential for expansion: "America is New. Here in America we are gathered independent of one's soil's history and begin anew with the dreamlike arrival of strangers gathering and propagating on a continent newly created and historically empty (for them) at their arrival. No Fall to disorganize us therefore also no symbolic trauma no nightmare no tragedy no wisdom."[38]

Although such musings on race were, in James Baldwin's words, "offensive nonsense," they nonetheless turned the word *civilization* on its head at a time when it was a code for erasing the racial other and keeping it inferior in the story of American expansion. Baldwin's comment that the Beats' racial nostalgia was laced with "real pain" and "real loss" is true enough. So, too, is his statement that this discourse "does not refer to reality, but to a dream."[39] Even as they replicated the patronizing attitudes of the dominant culture, the Beats recoded the meaning of racial others as a nexus into the future instead of consigning them to the past.

The Fundamental Life

Along with other Americans during the 1950s, Beats faced incessant cultural pressure to progress, leave the past behind, and become new. Given the Faustian nightmare at the heart of the American Dream as it was popularly conceived, they dreamed of a different America that was new yet approachable. Living in Mexico enabled them to begin thinking about their ideal Americas and how they would sound, look, smell, taste, and feel. Each came to realize that his ideal America fell inside the real—a world elsewhere right under his feet. Favoring, in Kerouac's words, "subterranean excitement" instead of "artificial newness," the Beats did not embrace the "vicious novelties of America."[40] On the contrary, in order for them to move forward they needed to invent a tradition from which to move at all. What they needed, as it were, was to make the kabbalah bop. What, then, was the substance of this tradition and where should it be sought? According to their reading of Spengler, much, including the future, depended on the local, the vernacular, and the "rootedness" of experience. Consequently, the Beats first grounded themselves. By turning the act of composition into a physically rigorous process, they were able to reinvent their present context by experiencing it in a radically different way. Through such "naked" experience, they would dig to the cleavage point between past and future—the "bellybottom strain," in Kerouac's words, "lurking in our souls all our lives."[41] There they hoped to discover neither a usable past nor even a new tradition but the basis of tradition on which to construct a new Culture.[42]

In works such as *Naked Lunch, On the Road, Visions of Cody,* and "Howl," the Beats created a new mythology. The recombined traditional religious symbols, mythic tropes, and a Spenglerian philosophy of culture in the hope of communicating the values of a new cultural order. This America of prophecy was as much Oswald Spengler's as it was John Winthrop's or any other Puritan luminary's. The Beats' millennial kingdom must be seen in light of Spengler's description of the spiritual birth of a new Culture and its people: "The great religion of every Springtime . . . begins in every case, like a great cry . . . this change is felt and welcomed as an inward rebirth. . . . It traverses the chosen spirits of the time like a grand light, which dissolves all fear in blissful love and lets the invisible appear, all suddenly, in a metaphysical radiance."[43]

Although some of the best minds of their generation had been destroyed in the pursuit, the Beats had discovered the promise that was America as well as the reasons for the nation's desecration. Consequently, underlying much of their literature was a desire for radical social change. They wanted to dislodge "the chosen spirits of the time," whether metaphysical assumptions, contemporary social and moral codes, or the conventions of the literary establishment. Their respective works during the 1950s all had a mythic tenor, self-consciously invoking the form of a hero's journey into the unsettled wilderness while reconceiving the content and meaning of the story. They were counter-myths, renarrations of a well-worn story (the innocent protagonist versus an unforgiving society) that Americans continually told themselves.

Secure in their religious understanding of the world, the Beats engaged society on its own terms, "storming the reality studios" in order first to re-examine and reconstruct the definition of human potential and then to remake society in that image. Subsequently, the oppositional and subversive character of Beat literature was more surgical than belligerent and a process of selection rather than outright negation. Their works depict a contest over the wealth of American symbols, not a simple reproach of nation. As Burroughs proclaimed, his enemy was the "malevolent telepathic broadcast stations" of the West.[44] His battle cry was, "This is war to extermination—Shift linguals—Cut word lines . . . Photo falling—Word falling—Break through in grey room—Calling Partisans of all nations—Towers, open fire."[45]

It was a peculiar sort of battle. Drawing on the work of Barthes, Dick Hebdige has asserted that such struggle between opposing definitions and symbolic meanings is "always, at the same time, a struggle within signification: a struggle for possession of the sign."[46] For Burroughs as for Kerouac and Ginsberg, America was a "sign," indistinguishable from the language that described its character or prescribed its social virtues. The Beats were self-proclaimed wordsmiths, and their criticism of American culture often occurred on the level of signification, that is, on the level on which historical contingency is transformed into nature, description into explanation, and ideas into truths. Barthes spoke of that "metalanguage" as "myth," a "type of speech" defined not by "the object of its message, but by the way in which it utters the message."[47] Burroughs, Kerouac, and Ginsberg—each in his own way—sought to translate the "second-order language" of America into an unfiltered language of pure experience that spoke directly and restored the nation's context in its "metaphysical radiance."

Because the "sign" of America after the war was surfeited with religious assumptions, as the Beats contested the idea of America they also interrogated the meaning of ultimate reality.[48] To question that mythic discourse was to position oneself religiously, staking out claims for America and in the process making claims about God, self, and salvation. In turn, to challenge the fundamental religious assumptions of the American way of life was to question the social, political, and economic principles on which the country was founded. In questioning what America stood for and what it meant to be an American, the Beats were trying to reinvest the nation's second-order language with immediacy and clarity. As David Savran notes, even as the Beats imagined themselves as outcasts in contemporary America "they could not help but be seduced by the insurrectionary vision of the artist as cowboy, rebel, entrepreneur. And so they used writing to try to negotiate a way out, imagining that writing contained and expressed all they so desperately desired."[49]

As forays into cultural criticism, *Naked Lunch*, Kerouac's road novels, and "Howl" were also material representations of self. They were a written record of an "American self," as each man conceived that term. Personal experience became a point of critical leverage in their work. Through recourse to the mysterious depths of their souls, human interaction, physical expression, and the burgeoning currency of everyday life—popular culture—each writer was able to engage America on moral grounds, juxtaposing a "secret mythology" against more official versions.[50] As Ginsberg once noted, the works of Kerouac and Burroughs (as well as his own) were "autobiographies of the psychological or spiritual history, . . . visionary panoramas."[51] That is no less true for their work during the 1950s, which were textual distillations of their lives, renditions of their America as they had experienced it. By integrating life into the praxis of art, the Beats self-consciously mythologized themselves and their activities. On the level of content, confessional honesty challenged the exceptional America of unparalleled geopolitical stature, military might, economic growth, and consumption of leisure activities. Even as they maintained the basic form of American mythos, they critiqued its content by the force of their example. In the process, they subjected the canopy of American myth to radical alteration. They performed cautious incisions, pulled at the seams, and ripped it into a number of pieces, only to reassemble it, reshape it, and mold its contours into a Spenglerian design. Such is the tradition of the subversive.

The Police-Poet

Throughout the 1940s, Burroughs impressed Korzybski's lessons upon both Kerouac and Ginsberg and encouraged them to put forth their counter-legends of America, their rendition of the "facts," in words. Burroughs's preaching about the power of propaganda also had a source closer to home. Ivy Lee, his uncle and an 1898 Princeton University graduate, had been known as the "father of public relations" for his role as press agent for various industrialists and robber barons. His greatest success came as a public relations consultant to the Rockefellers after the 1914 Ludlow Massacre, a dispute between miners and management at a Rockefeller mine during which the Colorado state militia killed thirteen people. An expert on the formation of public opinion, Lee revived the Rockefeller name after a turbulent period of muckraking and reform. Nicknamed "Poison Ivy" by Upton Sinclair for his skillful manipulation of the media, Lee believed that the most effective strategy of persuasion was through "symbols and phrases" not reasons and evidence.[52] His preference for image over substance soon backfired, however. In 1933 he was publicly denounced and humiliated after an ill-advised decision to act as press liaison for the newly elected Nazi regime in Germany. In

1934, six months after the House Un-American Activities Committee labeled him a press agent for Hitler, Lee died of a cerebral hemorrhage in New York.[53]

Like his uncle, Burroughs was media-savvy and sensitive to the hegemony that public rhetoric could potentially wield. Encountering the various forms of mid-century propaganda, he attempted to silence such manipulation by jamming the signals of perceived enemies and offering a counter-broadcast of his own. His goal was to hunt down and exterminate the forces of control that compromised freedom. Despite the tragic fall of his uncle, Burroughs took artistic inspiration from his example and derived from him the names of his control-fighting alter egos in *Junky, Queer,* and *Naked Lunch.* Burroughs even compared his work to advertising: "Like the advertising people we talked about, I'm concerned with the precise manipulation of word and image to create an action, not to go out and buy a Coca-Cola, but to create an alteration in the reader's consciousness."[54] He believed himself to be a New World artist who would create a new cultural reality by first depicting (that is, creating) that reality on a page.

Burroughs was in exile when he began to assemble what would become *Naked Lunch* in 1953 (the title came at Kerouac's suggestion). With warrants out for his arrest on narcotics charges, he emigrated to Tangier, then an international zone in Morocco and still under colonial rule by French, Spanish, and British administrators. Tangier was hospitable and provided for Burroughs's needs, but its political situation was eerily reminiscent of pseudomorphosis as in America—a literal invasion and colonization by Faustian Civilization. For Burroughs, Tangier was a place where "everybody has both feet in your business." Given his penchant for confronting the forces of control directly, it was also the "prognostic pulse of the world . . . a frontier between dream and reality—the 'reality' of both called into question."[55] By taking up residence in Tangier, Burroughs could learn and write about America as both participant and observer, a "patroller." As he wrote, "No matter how tight Security, I am always somewhere *Outside* giving orders and *Inside* this straightjacket . . . stamped with the seal of alien inspection."[56]

His increasing paranoia was not entirely delusional but grounded in social fact. In addition to Burroughs's run-ins with the law, institutional power bases were consolidated into an elite economic and political power structure during the period of rapid growth and expansion after the war. This corporate liberal ideology strove to eradicate differences within American society through a hegemonic push for national consensus.[57] Such "bureaucratic control," which concentrated real social power at the top of pyramidal institutional hierarchies, gradually became the foremost means of ensuring social cohesion during and after World War II.[58] The persuasive rule of this cultural formation "engaged in the adjustment of conflicts that were not ever allowed to fully engage public consciousness."[59] Through the advent of television-mediated propaganda, the "American way of life" came to be defined by a complementary combination of scientifically managed work, mass leisure, an ethnocentric celebration of American technology, and the suburban "standard of living."[60] That drive toward a universal American culture did not respect traditionalistic or personal distinctions of any sort but, for the most part, demanded only competency and efficiency for its maintenance.[61] Those developments only added fuel to Burroughs's conspiratorial fire.

Naked Lunch was both a chronicle of an imprisoned America and a manifesto for cultural as well as individual liberation from "alien" history. For Burroughs, it was necessary to conceive of a new kind of hero, and, because of the dire situation at hand, he believed that he must put forward a new kind of American adventure as well. In January 1955 he wrote a blurb for the then-unfinished work: "This book is a must for anyone who would understand the sick soul, sick unto death, of the atomic age."[62] Echoing Barthes's notion of a revolutionary political language that "makes the world" and does not merely describe it, Burroughs believed he was putting forth a philosophy of life—a new religious program that would counter the ones that had eradicated "the myth of other-level experience."[63]

A month after writing the blurb, Burroughs explained the impetus behind his writing. "The novel is taking shape," he reported to Ginsberg, "something even more evil than atomic destruction is the theme—namely an anti-dream drug which destroys the symbolizing, myth-making, intuitive, empathizing, telepathic faculty in man, so that his behavior can be controlled and predicted by the scientific methods that have proved so useful in the physical sciences."[64] Burroughs was writing a manifesto inspired by his scientific-like pursuit of facts. His counter-theory of interpretation would explain (and explain away) the Faustian forces of control that had straightjacketed America.

Since writing "Twilight's Last Gleaming" in 1938, Burroughs had continually questioned the terms of American mythos, testing the ideals inherited by postwar Americans against insights he had gleaned from various parts of the underworld and junkie havens. The basic "fact" he learned was that "junk" was "a prototype of invasion. That is, junk replaces the user's cells until he *is* junk." Seeing "drug addiction as a microcosm of life, pleasure, and human purpose," Burroughs concluded that "morality (at this point an unqualified evil), ethics, philosophy, religion, can no longer maintain an existence separate from the facts of physiology."[65]

For Burroughs, the body was a site of manipulation as well as potential liberation. Applying those insights to contemporary America, he found the liberatory promises of consumer culture to be physically debilitating, a process whereby psychological desires internalized mechanisms of control. As the organizing principle of postwar society, the mythology of capitalism wielded control by producing desires through words and images, desires that by definition remained unfulfilled and thus subject to manipulation. Because these mediated promises were always deferred, they reduced individuals to a state of constant anxiety, imprisoning them within a storehouse of desire. In *Naked Lunch* Burroughs parodied that situation through an "American Housewife" who discovers that the kitchen appliances she once lusted after have turned against her: "the Garbage Disposal Unit snapping at me, and the nasty old Mixmaster keep trying to get up under my dress."[66]

While the ethic of capitalism, represented abstractly in the free market, spoke of the autonomous individual, Burroughs saw something more sinister at work. According to Karl Marx the ideal of possessive individualism enslaved subjectivity by reducing it to yet another commodity form, a process Marx referred to as "the fetishism of commodities."[67] Derived from the Portuguese *fetiço*—"that which is made in order to make"—Marx employed the concept of the fetish to explain how, when humans become alienated from their work, they begin to ascribe agency to the products of their labor. Burroughs was no Marxist, but *Naked Lunch* has many affinities with Marx's materialist critique and his insight into how ordinary objects, when commodified, acquire "phantom objectivity," a transcendent character beyond the immediate grasp of the senses. As Timothy S. Murphy points out, *Naked Lunch* "constitutes an exacting critique both of the social organization of late capital and of the logic of representation or textuality that abets it."[68]

Indeed, Burroughs did attempt to debunk the universal claims of capitalism that rendered any alternatives to possessive individualism wholly unnatural. He assailed the religious character of the capitalistic social contract by affirming an alternative, material, and untranscendable reality that did not subject individuals to the causal reasoning of the marketplace. His critique, however, must be seen in a Spenglerian light, for Burroughs, unlike Marx, believed this reality to be decidedly otherworldly in daily operation. Spengler spoke of the "present-day world-economics" as an "exclusively Western-dynamic, anything but common-human." As such, "Faustian money-thinking" yielded an imperialistic "*force* distilled from economy-dynamics of the Faustian brand" that incessantly told the individual that he is "inwardly constituted to represent a part of this force, or that he is, on the contrary, nothing but mass to it."[69]

Spengler's critique of capitalism, unlike Marx's, held that animate energy coursed through the physical universe. And Burroughs's invocation of Marxist insights into commodity fetishism, particularly in his concept of the Algebra of Need, confirmed what Marx intended to negate: The material universe, including the body, has a mystical character and is subject, for better or worse, to the invisible forces of the macrocosm. Burroughs neither denied nor debunked the power of the commodity fetish but instead called for a strategic manipulation of that power. In other words, the objectivity of the material world was real precisely because the phantoms were real. Because the visible and the invisible cannot be separated, the "facts" of existence can never be exhausted empirically.

Burroughs's trenchant critique of capitalism was linked to his practice of cutting through linguistic obstacles that overlaid any sort of fundamental, sensuous reality. His was a religious critique intended not to desiccate the religious residue left in the wake of capitalism but to illuminate its true nature and macrocosmic source and empower individuals through such illumination. According to Burroughs's Manicheanism, words prevent people from taking charge within the "magical universe." "In the magical universe," he notes, "there are no coincidences and no accidents. Nothing happens unless someone wills it to happen. The dogma of science is that the will cannot possibly affect external forces, and I think that's just ridiculous."[70]

Naked Lunch is an intense investigation into the use and function of language. In particular, it is concerned with how cultural conceptions of reality are reflected in language, and, more ominously, how words dictated and continued to legitimate those conceptions. Burroughs believed that "words—at least as we use them—tend to hide non-physical experience from us." His goal was to discover and diffuse the "word-locks" that had locked up Western "civilization for a thousand years."[71] By "storming the reality studios" of Faustian civilization Burroughs hoped to aid in dismantling it, thereby intuiting the more benign forces that animated the universe. He also envisioned himself as a New Age Moses, leading the way to a promised land beyond language. "I say open the Door and the whole universe will rush in," he lectured in letter to Ginsberg. "Go on the nod and dream of a square universe. I stand with THE FACTS."[72]

⌐⌐

Naked Lunch takes place in the hyper-real world of Interzone, a satirical mirror-image of Burroughs's America. It is the "carny world . . . a kind of mid-western, small-town, cracker-barrel, pratfall type of folklore, very much my own background. That world was an integral part of America."[73] Due to

Faustian corruption and pseudomorphosis, "the stench of spiritual vileness" hangs in the air of Interzone "like a green cloud." Following a model of Spenglerian correspondence—as above, so below—the contamination of "old rotten replica cultures" visits the community. There is no rule of law in Interzone save for the Algebra of Need and the hegemonies constructed around the addiction to control, both to assume and be subsumed by authority. As a composite city of addiction, Interzone is the end-game of consumer desire, a capitalist dystopia "where all human potentials are spread out in a vast silent market."[74]

Burroughs had described Interzone's real-world referent, Tangier, in terms of fetishization, a place where the human form and commodity form were all but blurred: "There is an end of the world feeling in Tangiers, with its glut of nylon shirts, Swiss watches, Scotch and sex and opiates sold across the counter. Something sinister in complete *laissez faire*. And the new police chief up there on the hill accumulating dossiers. I suspect him of unspeakable fetishistic practices with his files."[75] In the section entitled "The Market," Burroughs depicts the "sinister" nature of Interzone's City Market in a way reminiscent of Marx's association of commodity fetishism and "the mistenveloped regions of the religious world." He juxtaposes the desecration of "human potentials" with "The Prophet's Hour," implicating everyone from Jesus, Buddha, and Confucius in the "New Religion": "Mohammed? Are You kidding? He was dreamed up by the Mecca Chamber of Commerce."[76]

Burroughs equated rampant capitalism with a form of totalitarian control buttressed, in Marx's words, by "metaphysical subtleties and theological niceties."[77] Spengler (as well as Marx) believed capitalism to be the "hallmark of a politic of Civilization," investing the power of political decision making in an unnamed elite and concealing them from view. "The decisions," he wrote, "lie elsewhere. A small number of superior heads, whose names are very likely not the best-known, settle everything, while below them are the great mass of second-rate politicians—rhetors, tribunes, deputies, journalists—selected through a provincially-conceived franchise to keep alive the illusion of popular self-determination."[78] In an ironic nod to his paternal grandfather, inventor of the adding machine in the 1880s, Burroughs labels this franchise the "Algebra of Need." Distilling the capitalist system into a metaphor of drugs (commodity), dealer (producer), and addict (consumer), he uses that metaphor to define the social dynamic of addiction. For him, "Junk yields a basic formula of 'evil virus': The Algebra of Need. The face of evil is always the face of total need. You would lie, cheat, inform on your friends, steal, do anything to satisfy total need. Because you would be in a state of total sickness, total possession, and not in a position to act any other way. . . . Junk is the mold and monopoly of possession." According to Burroughs, junk is "ideal product . . . the ultimate merchandise. No sales talk necessary." Like Spengler's description of "the money-spirit," "the mold and monopoly of possession" has "penetrate[d] unremarked the historical forms of the people's existence."[79]

Here Burroughs's thinking aligns with Marx's on the commodity fetish. As David Savran notes, Burroughs's conception of junk is entirely fetishistic, "an object of such intense (and unsatiable) desire [that] it ends up objectifying the user."[80] As a fetish, junk is "endowed with life." It is inseparable from its production value but conceals its social substance from view. It has no trace of human history and is thus "surrounded by magic and taboos, curses and amulets." Junk can only be consumed, and in the act of consumption it establishes a parasite-host relationship with the consumer by severing all ties among fellow consumers. "The junk merchant," writes Burroughs, "does not sell his product to the consumer, he sells the consumer to the product." In Marxian terms, junk mysteriously acquires "an objective character" because of its addictive potency and refusal to acknowledge complicity in a monopolistic system of control. "There are no accidents in the junk world"; there are only "junk pyramids feeding on peoples of the world."[81] In the end, the life-energy of junk is not so much that of a primitive totem but that of the virus, an animate force that invades and feeds on the human race and uses the human form to reproduce more of itself.

For Burroughs, the Algebra of Need and its bureaucratic manifestations are the only true evils in society—"the mist that covers the Zone in the winter months like a cold Turkish Bath."[82] In *Naked Lunch,* he attributes the pyramids of power associated with the Algebra of Need to the philosophical inheritance of the Enlightenment, particularly its progressive conquest of the natural realm and its disabling of the physical senses. In depicting institutional excess on a human scale, Burroughs saw the epistemological systems of Enlightenment thought mapped onto the human body's internal desires. As such, Interzone is a ghoulish version of Eliot's Wasteland. It is devoid of any understanding of vital cosmic forces and meaningful myths about them. Having undergone the social equivalent of the biological process of addiction and possession, the "myth-making, intuitive" faculties of its human inhabitants have been destroyed. In Interzone, everything has become commodified and subject to manipulation and exchange, even the body. As in the European quarter of Tangier, "everyone looks you over for the price tag, appraising you like merchandise."[83]

The cultural criticism in *Naked Lunch* focuses on the rational mechanisms that imprison the body within an abstract, mechanized universe. In the last days of Civilization, the Cartesian *cogito* has turned against itself and legitimizing one's existence is no longer an act of producing the self in performance but one of endless material consumption. In order to resist claims made upon the body, Burroughs sought to expose the mechanism of control that prevented "non-body experiences" and to realign both self and society with the true intentions of the material world, those animate forces reflected in the microcosm. Only then would clear vision of present circumstances ensue.[84]

As a record of Burroughs's addiction to opiates, his treatment, and his eventual cure, *Naked Lunch* dramatizes biography in the figure of William Lee, the "agent" who "is taking the junk cure."[85] A central theme of *Naked Lunch* is the journey and pursuit of Agent William Lee through the American dystopia of Interzone—from his initial comment that he "can feel the heat closing in" to his killing of his nemeses Hauser and O'Brien and ultimate escape from Interzone. Reminiscent of the hero's journey, Burroughs depicts his alter-ego as self-reliant and on his way to becoming self-motivated. He runs into the eye of the Faustian storm to attack the forces of control, institutional and otherwise: "So we stock up on H, buy a second-hand Studebaker, and start West." Agent Lee is a member of the Factualist Party, aligned against the three other parties of Interzone. One, the Liquefactionists, plans to eliminate everyone but themselves "by a process of protoplasmic absorption." The Senders, another party, seek to control everyone from within. The Divisionists plan to take over the world through self-replication. The character of William Lee outwits these forces of control solely by his own resources—his "word horde" and a collection of books and manuscripts. As he negotiates the terrain of Interzone, "a maze of penny arcades and dirty pictures," Agent Lee's actions derive from an ability to assess a situation clearly.[86] He discerns that everyone is a junky or control addict in some sense, dehumanized with "no escape from external time, no place to go. [They] can only wait."[87] There is no personal history in Interzone, no room for creation in a world following the declining path of the West.

Lee's archenemy is the mysterious Doctor Benway, a "pure scientist" who is continually improving and perfecting mechanisms of control. He is a "manipulator and coordinator of symbol systems, an expert on all phases of interrogation, brainwashing and control." Benway, the Faustian spirit personified, first appeared in "Twilight's Last Gleamings." As a link between Rotwang, the inventor in Fritz Lang's Weimar classic *Metropolis* (1926) and Stanley Kubrick's *Dr. Strangelove* (1962), Benway resonates with cold war paranoia about mad scientists who are excessively rational and bent on world destruction. The Benway character also reminds one of the Gnostic demiurge, who, shielding himself from detection, has developed a system for imprisoning humans within their own bodies. As Benway declares, "The naked need of control addicts must be decently covered by an arbitrary and intricate bureaucracy so that the subject cannot contact his enemy direct." Consequently, Lee's quest for liberation is premised on direct engagement with the enemy, an engagement made difficult by Benway's subtle machinations. "I deplore brutality," he proclaims. "It's not efficient. On the other hand, prolonged mistreatment, short of physical violence, gives rise, when skillfully applied, to anxiety and a feeling of special guilt."[88]

In the novel's "final" scene, Agent Lee confronts the two narcotics detectives, Hauser and O'Brien, who have come to arrest him for the "crime of separate life." In an act of cold calculation, Lee murders them. As he escapes from Interzone, he calls the Narcotics Bureau to check on the status of the investigation into the murder and is told the detectives do not exist. As Lee surmises what has happened, "I had been occluded from space-time like an eel's ass occludes when he stops eating on the way to Sargasso. . . . Locked out. . . . Never again would I have a Key, a Point of Intersection. . . . The Heat was off me from here on out . . . relegated with Hauser and O'Brien to a landlocked junk past where heroin is always twenty-eight dollars an ounce." Lee is no longer subject to Interzone's laws of correspondence and no longer an addict in a world based on the Algebra of Need. Instead, he has fulfilled the "myth of other-level experience" and is able to create a meaningful world. As Burroughs writes in the "Atrophied Preface," "The way OUT is the way IN." The moral is that only through the continual act of individual creation can the forces of external control be held at bay. Retreat from confrontation is a junkie's mistaken solution, a self-destructive path that leads, ironically, further and further from the self. As the disembodied voice comments at the end of *Naked Lunch,* "They are rebuilding the City." "Yes . . . Always," Lee agrees. And in a remark aimed at those who believe they have found refuge from the decline of the West in exotic philosophies, Burroughs advises, "Either way is a bad move to The East Wing."[89]

In the journey of Agent William Lee, Burroughs puts forth a factualist myth to deflate the public myths of America. His goal is to exterminate the everyday assumptions brought to the table of social life, specifically that one makes decisions for oneself and that choosing freely makes a choice an expression of free will. Burroughs, a confidence man, reveals the incongruity between actual and ideal through a liberating form of deception. A junkie's unstable world of excess, manipulation, and the grotesque is presented as real, whereas the reader's is assumed to be a comforting ideal. "Bill's Naked Lunch Room. . . . Step right up," he announces. "Good for young and old, man and bestial. Nothing like a little snake oil to grease the wheels and get a show on the track Jack. Which side are you on?" Wearing whatever mask suits his purpose, the author assumes the role of trickster only to reveal the real snake oil of capitalistic America: media-generated expectations, signals, and images that preached that identity was a matter of assertive consumption. Such clarification—the replacement of the mirror by which we come to know ourselves—is needed because the real cancer is "at the door with a Singing Telegram."[90] Burroughs unmasks verbal manipulations even as he performs them in the hope of inducing a state of silence, the ground of subjectivity from which true exploration of facts can begin. "Nothing but fact can save us."[91]

In *Naked Lunch*, Burroughs uses factualism as a method of cultural criticism, pointing out the many forms of addiction and revealing that "they all obey basic laws." Invoking the authority of science, he quotes Heisenberg: "This may not be the best of all possible universes but it may well prove to be one of the simplest." He then adds, "if man can *see*."[92] Burroughs's goal as a cultural critic was not just to question reality but to delineate the possibilities that existed at his particular cultural moment. He saw himself as both defender of the "human image" and innovator of new ways of living. "When the Human Image is threatened," he wrote, "The Poet dictates forms of survival. Dream police of poetry protect us from The Human Virus. The human virus can now be isolated and treated. This is the work of The new POLICE-POET. . . . . This is the latest revelation and way of action."[93]

What threatened the most, according to Burroughs, were American social institutions infected by the heritage of the Enlightenment. Bureaucracy in *Naked Lunch* is both virus and cancer, in both cases a parasite that annihilates its host. In America, bureaucratic structures have taken over a once-healthy social body and degraded it in order to fill their needs. Like Spengler's "money-spirit," the virus is the "form of intellectual energy in which the ruler-will, the political and social, technical and mental, creative power, the craving for a full size life, [were] concentrated." Burroughs attacks that hegemonic franchise and its logic of consensus through consumption in vehement, overtly political terms. Echoing Spengler's idea that the Faustian "imperial age . . . signifies the end of the political mind," he does not indict the ideals of American democracy but rather its corrupted form: "The end result of complete cellular representation is cancer. Democracy is cancerous, but bureaus are its cancer. . . . Bureaus cannot live without a host, being true parasitic organisms. . . . Bureaucracy is wrong as cancer, a turning away from the human evolutionary direction of infinite potentials and differentiation and independent spontaneous action to the complete parasitism of a virus."[94] Although skeptical of the potential to erect an enduring democratic state,

Burroughs does not just condemn that philosophy. Rather, he condemns the institutionalization of democratic ideals of egalitarianism as parasitical, suffocating "infinite potentials" of humans and destroying them entirely.

At the same time, the critique of culture was profoundly religious. Burroughs uses sarcasm, hyperbole, and phantasmagoria to depict not a world of stasis and absolutes but rather one of shifting totality and anchored in the stability of the macrocosm. Over and against capitalistic and bureaucratic social forms, he affirms an alternative reality of Spenglerian proportions. Within that "magical universe," the self is constituted not through autonomous choice but through recourse to a living community that is itself a reflection of the macrocosm. Revelation depends on acts of destruction. As he admits, parody is a condition of truth—the only way he can "achieve complete sincerity."[95]

Burroughs undermined all moral pretensions; blurred the distinctions between nature and society, sacred and profane, visible and invisible, and subject and object; and created a world of total possibility through negation. His negation was, however, an affirmative social act, for it led him to assume the existence of others. In creating a new myth for America, Burroughs may have been "condemned," in Barthes's phrase, "to live in a theoretical sociality." The community Burroughs envisioned resided in his moral code of always speaking the truth in accordance with the "facts." He believed, as Barthes's mythologist believed, that "tomorrow's positivity [was] entirely hidden by today's negativity" and that the future lay in "the most profound apocalypse of the present."[96]

In practicing that political gesture, Burroughs viewed himself as evolving toward a new communal frontier quite different from Whitman's vision of "fervent comradeship" embodied in Kerouac and Cassady's late-night bull sessions or in Ginsberg's mystical retreats into the depths of the soul. Although Cassady's sacralization of everyday moments and his affinity for group celebrations personified the sacred connections of communitas, Burroughs's ethic preserved group relations on a different plane. That form of communal interaction was achieved in the privacy of the mind.[97]

Burroughs modeled his "new mythology for the space age" on a "nonsubservient model of human nature" in which each individual would be free from the conditioning of an authoritarian society.[98] That belief did not dictate a radical and isolating individualism but it did maintain individual freedom within a group dynamic. "All codes of conduct that have any validity," Burroughs wrote, "are based on the relations between individuals."[99] In that sense, *Naked Lunch* negatively limns the basis of an indigenous American political tradition. By describing the new American frontier in terms of religious naturalism, Burroughs affirmed the potential to silence institutional hearsay. He put forth a notion of radical democracy, a social relationship defined by unadorned acknowledgment, respect, and admiration for one another and instilled with egalitarianism and emotionless compassion. It was, however, a relationship that occurred in total seclusion in space: "To achieve complete freedom from past conditioning is to be in space. Techniques exist for achieving such freedom. These techniques are being concealed and withheld. . . . You must learn to exist with no religion no country no allies. You must learn to live in silence. Anyone who prays in space is not there."[100]

The forms of solitary communitas that Burroughs proposes are metaphysical union of consciousness, mutual recognition, and sharing a worldview that enables survival in a corrupt and conspiratorial society. As Spengler wrote, "The deeper and more intimate a spiritual communion, the more readily it dispenses with signs and linkages through waking-consciousness. . . . The purest symbol of an understanding that has again got beyond language is the old peasant couple sitting in the evening in front of their cottage and entertaining one another without a word being passed, each knowing what the other is thinking and feeling." Such withdrawal precipitates emancipation from the imposed structural relations of the world. The techniques were profoundly religious in that Burroughs was attempting to move past the logic of Western metaphysics into the "pulse-beat of Being" and experience "a real faith [that] is silent altogether."[101] That contact could potentially form the basis from which a more egalitarian society could be constructed—a democratic America not "loused up by literacy, advertising, TV and drive-ins."[102]

A Vertical Metaphysical Study

Burroughs was the most self-conscious mythologist among the Beats, but Kerouac also wrote against public myths of America, even as he wrote a local version of his own. In April 1951 he retreated to a Manhattan apartment and embarked upon a twenty-day, Benzedrine-driven typing session that would become the first full draft of his road novel. On a roll of teletype paper smuggled out of the New York headquarters of the United Press by Lucien Carr, Kerouac produced an eighty-six-thousand-word paragraph with no commas. After many revisions, the manuscript yielded both *On the Road* and *Visions of Cody*.[103]

Kerouac's focus on the local was evident not only in his preferred method of solitary composition but also in his interest in all things American, a search for a Cultural essence that would later manifest itself as a conservative form of nationalism. In an 1947 letter to Hal Chase, a former Columbia University student and member of the Beats' inner circle, Kerouac claimed that his life's project was to study "the face of America itself" in order to recover its original innocence. "My subject as a writer," he confirmed, "is of course America, and simply, I must know everything about it."[104]

That insatiable lust, the nostalgia for the real America, was satisfied only by recourse to details. In *Visions of Cody,* for example, Kerouac describes himself sitting at a diner on the shore of Staten Island: "I only know, that is, I *strictly* know what I know . . . my own complete life, an endless contemplation, is so interesting, I love it so, it is vast, goes everywhere." Upon grounding himself in a local version of America, he muses on the multitude of things he has "re-discovered"—"gulls, wild hungers, voices of workers, figures crossing rainy supply dumps with umbrellas, black wires, poles, masts of ships." The secret is to sharpen perception in order to experience inexhaustible mystery in the "great gray mist of America and American things." Only by tapping the spirituality of the material world can one forge a new America out of the old, leaving the past behind like a "boy headed for prepschool but so much more."[105]

Kerouac's symbolic revisioning of national character was intended to reconnect America to its wilderness origins and its living soul—to perform miracles of resurrection in the American "cemetery," where "the dead are laid out in the suburbs row by row."[106] Reminiscent of Huckleberry Finn's search for the good society, Kerouac's narratives are attempts to salvage paradise before it becomes a distant memory. In *On the Road,* he evokes that sense of disconnection in a conversation between the narrator, Sal Paradise, and the character of Old Bull (Burroughs): "Our sad drama in the American night . . . I wanted to sit on the muddy bank and dig the Mississippi River; instead of that I had to look at it with my nose against a wire fence. When you start separating the people from their rivers what have you got? 'Bureaucracy!' says Old Bull."[107]

Burroughs's answer to a Spenglerian question confirms Sal's sentiments of suppression and cleavage. The American people have become detached from land and their natural selves—an ominous sign of conformity signaling the death-throws of the "American Night." Spengler's description of "Caesarism" outlines how such detachment occurred during the final stages of Civilization, when the struggle over mastery of all forms of nature ends and Caesar establishes a universal imperium over society. Under his manipulative leadership, individual life is characterized by general uniformity and anomie.[108] For Kerouac, however, Caesar was not a particular individual but had become embedded in the framework of American psychology.

In "dictating forms of survival" for a new America, Kerouac's work was informed by a utopian drive to construct a distinct community grounded in the affirmation of experience. As Ginsberg later commented, "No other author not even Tolstoi had to contend with the Decline of the West; the vision in the Cracks of the American sidewalk."[109] As America was being paved over with Civilization, Kerouac looked to cracks in the pavement as a source of wilderness vitality. Most saw only weeds, but he saw the essence of his hero, Neal Cassady (Dean Moriarty in *On the Road* and Cody Pomeray in *Visions of Cody*), "who represents all that's left of America for me."[110]

In one sense, Kerouac's account of Cassady challenged the American myth of postwar consensus by creating a new one. "Dedicated to America, whatever that is," he wrote in the preface to *Visions of Cody*, calling into question America's public facade with his "vertical, metaphysical study of Cody's character and its relationship to the general 'America.' " Kerouac's intent was to dig deep into Cassady's personality—"mad with a completely physical realization of the origins of life-bliss"—and create "an enormous paean which would unite my vision of America."[111]

A common interpretation of Kerouac's road novels deals with his obsession with the loss of spiritual values and the decline of America in a picaresque mode.[112] In general terms, that reading is correct. What is lacking in such critical assessments, however, is an eye for detail, particularly Spenglerian detail. Like Burroughs, Kerouac distinguished between the private and the public America, between the volkisch core of America and its compromised form. The latter, according to Kerouac, was a thief who had stolen the communal essence of the land and was "wanted by the police, pursued across Kentucky and Ohio." Because of the crime, the country had become a place "where you're not even allowed to cry for yourself . . . where people, people, people are weeping and chewing their lips in bars as well as lone beds and masturbating in a million ways . . . where people wait, wait, poor married couples sleep on each other's shoulders on worn brown benches while the nameless blowers and air conditioners and motors of America rumble in the dead night." The identity of America, its "human image," has been usurped. "America, the word," Kerouac lamented, "is the sound of my unhappiness, the pronunciation of my beat and stupid grief." A "police-poet" like Burroughs, Kerouac's duty was to retrieve that which had been stolen—the ideal, mysterious version that "has a more personal smaller more tittering secret name." What Kerouac pursued was the ability to create meaning—"the great moment of discovering my soul." "I'm in love with my life," he wrote, "and I'm sticking to it—I mean the belief in it." Upon retrieving that confidence through his "paean" to Neal Cassady, Kerouac takes on the false gods of America and assumes the role of a competing American mythologizer. "Gods, if not help me, if instead barb me, be careful of me," he warns with the passion of Ahab. "I can catch thunderbolts and pull you down and have done it before. Adieu!"[113]

The fictionalized Cassady is representative man in both an Emersonian and a Spenglerian sense. Like Emerson's depiction of nature, it is Cassady's example that sets the terms of salvation for postwar America. Kerouac not only humanized nature in his depiction of Moriarty/Pomeray but also portrayed him as a Spenglerian hero—the "prime symbol" of a new Culture and a receptive channel of the macrocosmic spirit. Spengler's idea of a prime symbol referred to the unique spiritual orientation of a fellaheen group that had achieved a unitary conception of their world. This encompassing symbol "blossoms up, wholly plantwise, from mother earth" and informs their activities, art, religion, philosophy, economics, politics, mathematics, and even warfare. According to Spengler, the emergence of the prime symbol signaled the first stage of cultural development: "Every culture actualizes here its prime symbol. Each has its own sort of love—we may call it heavenly or metaphysical as we choose—with which it contemplates, comprehends, and takes into itself its godhead . . . the deep urge of the soul is governed always by the prime symbol of the particular culture and no other."[114]

Kerouac saw in and through Cassady the panorama of America. "I saw him with eyes of fire or on fire," he wrote, "and saw everything not only about him but America, all of America as it has become conceptualized in my brain."[115] It is no surprise that Kerouac wrote those words in the attic of the Cassady household in San Francisco. While revising his road manuscript, Kerouac would spend evenings with the Cassady family, listening to the radio and reading aloud passages from *Decline of the West*.[116]

Given the Spenglerian context of the road novels, Cassady embodied the universal trait of all emerging Cultures, faith: "Dean was tremendously excited about everything he saw," wrote Kerouac in *On the Road*, "everything he talked about, every detail of every moment that passed. He was out of his mind with real belief."[117] That aspect of Kerouac's portrayal resonated with Spenglerian metaphysics as well as the American tradition of searching for a higher authority by which to define itself. According to Spengler, it was an affirmation of belief that "is the great word against metaphysical fear, and at the same time it is an avowal of love." Kerouac's description of Moriarty in *On the Road* symbolized the essence of belief that "in its primitive, unclear condition, acknowledges superior sources of wisdom . . . such as prophetic words, dreams, oracles, sacred scriptures, the voices of the deity."[118]

With numerous Spenglerian allusions, Kerouac proposed that Moriarty embodied the new authority: "He was out of his mind with real belief, 'And of course now no one can tell us that there is no God. We've passed through all forms. . . . Everything is fine, God exists, we know time. Everything since the Greeks has been predicated wrong. You can't make it with geometrical systems of thinking. It's all *this!*' He wrapped his finger in his fist."[119] Through a sexualized gesture, Moriarty discounts Faustian abstraction and its philosophical inheritance of skepticism.[120] He instead affirms the redemption of America through the ability to convert others to his optimistic stance. Moriarty is a confidence man, "talking and conning somebody all day," as Kerouac described him.[121] But his deception, like that Burroughs employed in *Naked Lunch,* has a higher purpose—rallying populist sentiment around America's sacred promise.

The emotional reliance on confidence as an instrument of achieving power or security has continually been a motif of the American mythos. From republican independence, to Jeffersonianism, to the *Democratic Vistas* of Whitman, confidence in self and others has always been at the forefront of attempts to renew the structure of society.[122] Kerouac's Spenglerian valence and penchant for mythology were fully intertwined in his use of the metaphor. As Moriarty assures Sal in *On the Road,* faith in a knowledge of America is all that is needed: "As we roll along this way I am positive beyond doubt that everything will be taken care of for us. . . . Furthermore we know America . . . I know the people, I know what they do."[123]

As a Yankee peddler selling confidence, Cassady embodied the notion of a communal faith that had been eroded by the development of Civilization. In *On the Road,* Kerouac alludes to the lost spirit of communitas by contrasting Moriarty's primitive nature with a bustling but lonely crowd on a cable car. The Faustian incursion upon that natural spirit is symbolized by Moriarty's injured thumb (the opposable thumb being the characteristic that emphasizes his humanity). He excitedly runs to the nearest cable car, through "a mass of men and suitcases with that enormous bandaged thumb sticking up in the air." By juxtaposing Cassady's ecstatic joy with the somnolent masses, Kerouac not only exposes the isolation endemic to America's business culture but also positions Moriarty as a martyr, sacrificing himself for the sake of the same masses. "That thumb became the symbol of Dean's final development," Kerouac points out. "He no longer cared about anything (as before) but now he also cared about everything in principle; that is to say, it was all the same to him and he belonged to the world and there was nothing he could do about it."[124]

Although Burroughs's alter-ego Agent Lee had explored a wilderness devoid of meaning, Cassady embodies the romantic rediscovery of the var-

ious wildernesses of America, from highways to hobo subcultures and popular culture in particular. Instead of autobiography, Kerouac uses biography
to mold a national hero from the detritus of mid-century America—the
characters, personalities, and sentiments of popular comic books such as *The
Shadow* and *The Green Hornet* and radio serials. W. T. Lhamon, Jr., notes that
Kerouac employed "poplore" to signify impatience with more established
traditions, an impatience that also reflected his hope of becoming a myth-
maker for the masses. "Kerouac's work," Lhamon observes, "gives good instance of avant-garde techniques primarily progressing from an urge to
match poplore practice rather than to pursue ever more esoteric tendencies
in late modern tradition."[125]

In much of his early work, Kerouac tapped the inchoate traditions in the
media to connect his mythic renderings to something more experientially
tangible than Puritan doctrine, democratic decrees, or even the hermetic
traditions of either Pound or Eliot. He took seriously radio programs, car-
toons, film stars, and the silliness of popular culture because in them he saw
a common denominator of American experience. Kerouac identified the
sources of "beat" with the frivolity of childhood heroes in American popular media. They included the most accessible and pervasive conduits of the
mythical realm—"the completely senseless babble of the Three Stooges, the
ravings of the Marx Brothers." For Kerouac, the imaginary state of boyhood
embodied psychological virginity and ready acceptance of the magic and
power he deemed lost in contemporary America.[126] As Spengler wrote of such
childhood faith, "Only youth has a future, and *is* Future, that enigmatic syn-
onym of directional Time and Destiny. *Destiny is always young.*"[127] That the-
matization only reinforced Kerouac's nostalgic longings.

Kerouac found the personification of this youthful media vernacular in
the kinetic Neal Cassady. His admiration stemmed from Cassady's openness
to the currents of popular culture swirling around him. Lhamon suggests that
Kerouac crowned Cassady "the perverse poplore American king," a multi-
faceted, complex, contradictory, and distinctly American figure of "protean
extremes."[128] Cassady's sexual escapades, both hetero- and homosexual, are
described in graphic detail in *Visions of Cody*. Kerouac also muses on his capacity for tenderhearted camaraderies and penchant for selfish indulgence.
A figure of pure transgressive potential, Cassady embodies the negativity of
the sacred, what Michael Taussig has termed the "worshipful negative." He
is the conduit of the range of human experience, "the dizzying logic unleashed as the negative negatively defines something ineffable."[129] In that
respect, Kerouac portrays Cassady as a homegrown archetype not afforded
a proper place amid the people. As an "American saint" who remains spiri-

tually vital and uncorrupted in a Faustian world devoid of such values, Cassady is compared to the Three Stooges, W. C. Fields, Caesar, Jesus, and the Greek heroes Oedipus and Odysseus. Cassady, Kerouac maintains, "Out-Marxes Marx" by replacing abstract theories with the slapstick quality of the American experience. He is a cipher of universal values, because they have been filtered through his essential Americanness. Kerouac muses that he and Cassady are "great Homeric warriors . . . just like that, Cody and Me, only American."[130]

Moving fluently from one symbol of cosmic populism to the next, Kerouac also envisions Cassady as a Christ figure whose destiny extends beyond his immediate environment onto the universal plane. Cassady embodies the religious faith and compassion of Jesus, but his divinity is not based on otherworldly origins. On the contrary, through Kerouac's reading of Spengler's detailed account of Jesus, Cassady belongs "to the world." As Spengler noted, "Jesus never lived one moment in any other world but this. He was no moralizer, and to see in moralizing the final aim of religion is to be ignorant of what religion is."[131]

Cassady possesses divine qualities because of his amorality and worldliness. "I suddenly realized," Kerouac wrote, "that Dean, by virtue of his enormous series of sins, was becoming . . . the Saint of the lot." It is precisely because of Moriarty's groundedness that he is continually misunderstood by both the general public and his friends. Like Herbert Huncke, Cassady has characteristics of the persecuted fellaheen, continually suffering for the inabilities and inadequacies of others. Kerouac remarks that many friends had "lost faith in Dean" and describes how his message of salvation fell on deaf ears and his self-sacrifice went unnoticed.[132]

Integrating his Catholic heritage, American myth, and Spenglerian metaphysics, Kerouac describes Cassady in terms of being a fellaheen and his Christ-like persecution, transvaluing his suffering from a form of self-sacrifice to a form of martyrdom that is culturally redemptive.[133] At one point in *On the Road,* Kerouac attributes Moriarty's suffering to a breakdown in communication and then interprets it as a martyrdom of New Testament proportions. In describing that shift, Kerouac alludes to the rejection of the prophetic revelations of Jesus:

> Then a complete silence fell over everybody; where once Dean would have talked his way out, he now fell silent himself, but standing in front of everybody, ragged and broken and idiotic, right under the light-bulbs, his bony face covered with sweat and throbbing veins, saying, "Yes, yes, yes," as though tremendous revelations were pouring into him all the time now, and I am

convinced they were, and the others suspected as much and were frightened. He was BEAT—the root, the soul of Beatific. What was he knowing? He tried in all his power to tell me what he was knowing.[134]

That Moriarty's friends misunderstand him suggests Jesus' crucifixion and martyrdom. By the conclusion of the passage, *On the Road* has moved from being a hagiography of Cassady to a gospel account of his life. Moreover, the narrator, Sal Paradise (Kerouac), assumes the role of Pontius Pilate in describing his failure to understand Dean: "'We're going to Italy,' I said, I washed my hands of the whole matter." Spengler wrote that the encounter between Jesus and Pilate was "overwhelming in its symbolism" in that it portrayed the opposition between "fact" and "truth." For Kerouac as for Spengler, religious faith could not be comprehended "in the midst of an alien, aged, and sick world."[135]

Kerouac extended the metaphor of Christ's persecution to demonstrate America's search for a blessing from divine authority. The subplot that generates much of the action in *On the Road* concerns the search for Moriarty's father, a quest that ends unfulfilled. Playing terms of Freudian analysis against the Trinity, Kerouac attributes a disconnection from America's father (that is, Moriarty's father) as the source of its neurotic state. In the final pages of *On the Road,* Sal denies Moriarty and does not allow him to ride to Penn Station with Sal and his friends, who are in a Cadillac and on their way to a Duke Ellington concert at the Metropolitan Opera. Sal's friend Remi "wouldn't have it, he liked me but he didn't like my idiot friends." The rejection of Moriarty in favor of his "gentleman" friends leaves Sal forlorn and guilty. Kerouac metaphorically describes the consequences of this act for America, equating Sal's action with America's denial of its paternal source with regard to its ignorance of Moriarty's message:

So in America when the sun goes down and I sit on the old broken-down river pier watching the long, long skies over New Jersey and sense that all that raw land that rolls in one unbelievable huge bulge over to the West Coast, and all that road going, all the people dreaming in the immensity of it, and in Iowa I know by now the children must be crying in the land where they let the children cry, and tonight the stars'll be out, and don't you know that God is Pooh Bear? The evening star must be dropping and shielding her sparkler dims on the prairie, which is just before the coming of complete night that blesses the earth, darkens all rivers, cups the peaks and folds the final shore in, and nobody, nobody knows what's going to happen besides the forlorn rags of growing old, I think of Dean Moriarty, I even think of Old Dean Moriarty the father we never found, I think of Dean Moriarty.[136]

That passage of natural imagery and twilight conjures up Spengler's description of the twilight of civilization and highlights an inevitable apocalypse due to the American nation's refusal to embrace the values and vitality of Dean Moriarty.

In contrast to the tragic quality of *On the Road, Visions of Cody* offers a more hopeful portrait of America's future. Even before beginning work on his road novels, Kerouac had received a letter from Ginsberg imploring him to continue his quest to become a famous writer by retaining his focus on the redemptive powers of Cassady: "Find Neal's heart, not his gut or his cock or wig; stretch his heart over America, crucify him in Texas, crown his head with thorns in Manhattan, pierce his side in Denver, moan for him in Mexico, tomb in 1949 and resurrect his trembling eyes on the Pacific. Neal is Christ walking in the doubts of the Garden of Whores. Enough to make me weep."[137]

Kerouac heeded that advice. The final pages of *Visions of Cody* resemble those of *On the Road* in natural imagery. But instead of lamenting the entropic organicism of nature, Kerouac emphasizes the notion of rebirth in the "December spring" in which "everything was alright." Much more hopeful than *On the Road, Visions of Cody* affirms the inevitability of cultural rebirth and its source of rejuvenation, Neal Cassady:

> Now flights of doublecrossing blackbirds come winging across the paleness of the East, the morning-star lips in that pale woodshed sky, she shudders and shits sparks of light and waterfalls of droop and moistly hugens up a cunt for cocks of eyes crowing across the fences of Golden Southern America in her Dawn.
>
> Goodbye Cody—your lips in your moments of self-possessed thought and new found responsible goodness are as silent, make as least a noise, and mystify with sense in nature, like the light of an automobile reflecting from the shiny silverpaint of a sidewalk tank in this very instant, as silent and all this, as a bird crossing the dawn in search of the mountain cross and the sea beyond the city at the end of the land.
>
> Adios, you who watched the sun go down, at the rail, by my side, smiling—Adios, King.[138]

Ginsberg has referred to this passage as an "explanation & prayer for innocence" in that it acknowledges death, but it is only a death like the setting sun. The darkness and the stars reveal procreative potential as Cody smiles at the twilight, anticipating the advent of the dawn, a new American culture. In this cosmic fade-out, Kerouac positions Cody as both American savior and representative American. He is on a mission toward sacred reality; *a dios* means "to God." Choosing to follow Cody, America will undergo a spiritual rejuvenation by reconnecting with the ground of being, what Spengler termed the "proto-soul."[139]

"Putting His Queer Shoulder to the Wheel"

For Ginsberg, the early 1950s were years of increasing optimism. He became more self-assured in life and his art, more comfortable with his sexuality, and more confident in his poetic vocation. Even as he spoke in 1950 of "this unreligious age," fearing that "the light is gone . . . the god is gone," he could still hold out the promise of a new America. Ginsberg thought it his duty to "create a poetic world not depending on gods." That world no longer depended on the master narratives of social progress and Christian moralism but on the poet's ability to clear a space where humanity took precedence over its civilized accouterments. As Ginsberg looked back he was also looking forward. He rejected the fear-laden nostalgia of the cold war years and the "poor poor self pitying sentimental years" in order to "build new, anew, modernly" from the ground up.[140]

After his initial correspondence with William Carlos Williams in 1952, Ginsberg began to revise his conception of the poetic calling. Now more than ever he unabashedly claimed that poets were priests, a romantic force whose mission was to evangelize America and spread a new gospel of mystical truth "not depending on gods." After his travels in Mexico, Ginsberg moved to San Francisco,

> armed with New Testament
> . . . satisfying Whitman, concerned
> with a few Traditions,
> metrical, mystical, manly.[141]

It was in San Francisco that Ginsberg met the man who would be his lover for the next thirty years, Peter Orlovsky, and committed himself to Walt Whitman's religious, profoundly homoerotic vision of America. As he worked on what would become *Howl and Other Poems,* Whitman was ever-present, appearing in "Love Poem on Theme by Whitman," "Supermarket in California," "Many Loves," and in an early draft of "Howl" (along with Spengler). After publication, Ginsberg claimed that "the poems are religious and I meant them to be and the effect on audience is . . . a validation of this. It is like 'I give the primeval sign' of Acceptance, as in Whitman."[142]

Although Ginsberg maintained poetic ties to the spirits of William Blake, Guillaume Apollinaire, and Christopher Smart, Walt Whitman became his inspiration of choice. In him, Ginsberg had found a muse of Spenglerian optimism, later referred to as the "innovator of many of these breaths and visions . . . breakthrough out of the crust of hyper-industrialized conscious-ness."[143] Ginsberg's days as a pessimistic "black priest" were long past. The American apocalypse was now something to be fostered not bemoaned, a revelatory event that promised a religious renewal of Culture on a par with his celebration of homosexuality.

In addition to its sexual themes, much of the symbolic economy of *Howl and Other Poems* focused on the mythical resolution of the conflicts between nature and civilization, between an original state of affairs and its institution-alization, and between the individual soul and society. For example, at the beginning of "Sunflower Sutra" Ginsberg sits beside Kerouac, thinking "the same thoughts of the soul, bleak and blue and sad-eyed, surrounded by the gnarled steel roots of trees of machinery." By the end of his meditation, a revelatory vision occurs: "We're not our skin of grime . . . we're all golden sunflowers inside, blessed by our own seed & hairy naked accomplishment-bodies."[144]

As Whitman had done in *Song of Myself,* Ginsberg sought to resolve inherent tensions through mythogenesis, that is by demonstrating the sacred-ness of the human spirit by interpreting felt experience within a mythic par-adigm. He wanted to invest corporeality with transcendence. In the magi-cal-realist "Supermarket in California," Ginsberg imagines a harmonious solution to the apparent contradiction between body and soul. "Dreaming of the lost America of love" in a grocery store, Walt Whitman at his side, Ginsberg yearns for an America free from the impositions of Civilization and the concomitant reduction of human experience to the abstract realm of ideas. Celebrating both the sensuality of the everyday world and their cama-raderie, he and Whitman run from "the store detective" and refuse to shop "for images." Instead, they stroll down "the open corridors together in our solitary fancy tasting artichokes, possessing every frozen delicacy, and never passing the cashier."[145]

Ginsberg's self-conscious romanticism seemed to reflect the climate of the times. During the early stages of the cold war there was widespread de-sire to reformulate a perception of America as symbolic garden space of vast potentialities and somehow mediate the gap between natural origins and civilization.[146] Occurring simultaneously was a search for its representative inhabitant—innocent yet experienced in sin, ever hopeful for new adventures yet grounded in the rich traditions of the past. From the celluloid heroes played by James Dean, John Wayne, and Marlon Brando to Norman Mail-er's White Negro and Ralph Ellison's Invisible Man, the mythic archetype was under radical reconstruction as intellectuals and artists alike contemporized the Adamic tradition of "the simple genuine self against the whole world." In *The American Adam* (1955), R. W. B. Lewis reflected the trend of recovering "the authentic American as a figure of heroic innocence" in order to divinely grant a "second chance for the human race, after the first chance had been so disastrously fumbled in the darkening Old World."[147] As Ginsberg engaged such mythic longings, his conception of the new world man, and the new world itself, contrasted starkly to the hetero-masculinity at the center of the Adamic tradition. Like Whitman, he was "resolved to sing no songs henceforth but those of manly attachment."[148]

Ginsberg's celebration of "manly attachments" revisioned the Adamic tradition, a political gesture that complemented the physicality of his compositional method and its emphases on breath, voice, and sexual expression. Both polis and poetics were colored by his heroic ideal of masculinity, a gendered subjectivity defined by sexual prowess and physical contact between men. Ginsberg made a sharp distinction between the "populist, humanist, quasi-heterosexual, Whitmanic, bohemian, free-love, homosexual" and the "privileged, exaggeratedly effeminate, gossipy, moneyed, money-style-clothing-conscious, near-hysterical queen."[149] In doing so, his masculine ideal was opposed not only to heterosexual norms but also to an increasingly feminized domestic sphere of suburban isolation and leisure consumption.

Using both the Whitmanic tradition and Spengler to counter what he perceived to be a society distrustful of personal experience, Ginsberg (as Kerouac before him) conceived of Neal Cassady as the "American Adam" whose presence eradicated cultural and personal oppression. He and Cassady had begun an affair shortly after they met in 1947. Despite Cassady's heterosexual exploits, the affair was liberating for Ginsberg, who at the time had not come to terms with his homosexuality. "Neal Cassady," he wrote in 1956, "was my animal: he brought me to my knees / and taught me to love his cock and the secrets of his mind."[150]

Within a culture of rabid homophobia, Cassady allowed Ginsberg to love the secrets of his mind and see his sexuality in terms of cultural redemption. Cassady embodied communitas qualities such as "emotional generosity and adhesiveness" that Ginsberg believed had been eradicated. In Cassady, he saw a recovery of "the portion of Adam which had been extirpated from American public life, and even from private consciousness, in the years between Thoreau and Whitman and the postwar generations, through the development of a competitive macho capitalistic selfish ethic. So Cassady was a recovery of that tradition of generosity of emotion and magnanimity of body and soul."[151] In terms of both personal biography and political manifesto,

Ginsberg celebrated Cassady's unbridled sexuality as the basis for a new frontier experience.

Just as Cassady had left Ginsberg lying "naked in the dark, dreaming," America could, by embracing its secret identity, recover a sense of promise and possibility.[152] Ginsberg's regenerative metaphor of "putting his queer shoulder to the wheel" appeared in his poem "The Green Automobile" (1953), a commemoration of his affair with Cassady. Viewing Cassady's sexuality as a literal "vehicle" for cultural procreation, Ginsberg envisions himself and Cassady riding around the country, sexually renewing America:

> If I had a Green Automobile
> I'd go find my old companion
> in his house on the Western ocean . . .
>
> He'd come running out
> to my car full of heroic beer
> and jump screaming at the wheel
> for he is the great driver . . .
>
> Neal, we'll be real heroes now
> in a war between our cocks and time:
> let's be the angels of the world's desire
> and take the world to bed with us before we die . . .
>
> We will go riding
> over the Rockies, we'll go on riding
> all night long until dawn.[153]

"The Green Automobile" is Ginsberg's poetic rendition of Kerouac's *On the Road*. The theme of Cassady as cultural redeemer recalls Kerouac's declaration that "Dean Moriarty and I was off on another spurt around the road," implying the regenerative nature of their adventures.[154] As Michael Davidson notes, Beat celebrations of homosociality were a response to the increasing alienation males felt at mid-century. Physical camaraderie, whether or not it implied homosexual contact, was a declaration of an alternative form of community against a bureaucratic society defined by "giant, anonymous corporations, a new class of technical and intellectual expertise, [and] a consensus ideology in institutional life."[155]

Seeking a "practical apocalypse," Ginsberg believed his poetry would reveal this world elsewhere, an America community liberated from Faustian shackles.[156] As he composed "Howl" (whose "secret hero" was Cassady),

Ginsberg confirmed his apocalyptic mindset in a letter to Kerouac. He saw his unfinished poem as a form of counter-myth to American militarism and corporate liberalism, a vision of democracy founded on individuals working in isolation, each a skilled cog in a larger bureaucratic structure. Echoing Spengler's dual emphasis on decline and rebirth, Ginsberg wrote, "There's too many poems to finish and not one done. . . . And the possibility now after Indo China and Ike's admission that U.S. contingency policy would be replaced by a weaker more limited policy of cold war—are we losing? . . . Is the Fall of America upon us? The Great Fall we once prophesied. . . . So the possibility of a prophetic poem, using ideas of politics and war and calling on love and reality for salvation."[157]

In "Howl," Ginsberg assumes the role of Jeremiah, celebrating the indigenous exceptionalism of America while lamenting the tragedy of its denial within a Spenglerian framework. He constructed the poem around the physical suffering and subsequent canonization of individuals—"angelheaded hipsters . . . starving hysterical naked"—who by their nonparticipation in dominant institutions retained transcendent qualities and exhibited an unsystematic, spontaneous, and natural sense of community.[158] In their attempt to forge an American culture, they have been martyred by Moloch—the "cannibal dynamo" and symbol of "Faustian being" on American soil, a character partly inspired by the industrial dystopia of Fritz Lang's *Metropolis*.[159]

In Part One of "Howl," specific examples of personal suffering result from America's compromised identity and the ruthless, institutional oppression of average people. But Ginsberg frames that suffering as a necessary step in America's struggle for independence. Consequently, he depicts the suffering of the fellaheen as a graphic reflection of America's split identity as well as source of healing:

> [who] rose reincarnate in the ghostly clothes of jazz in the goldhorn shadow
> of the band and blow the suffering of America's naked mind for love into
> an eli eli lamma lamma sabachthani saxophone cry that shivered the cities
> down to the last radio.

Ginsberg's reference is to the power of Christian martyrdom as a vehicle for personal purgation and cultural renewal. It is a means to recognize the natural ground of "America's naked mind" and an authentic self. By repossessing and rearticulating the redemptive suffering of Christ through a jazz-inspired transvaluation, Ginsberg uses "Howl" to express a philosophy of culture, a spiritual vision, and a new poetic mode that will cause the walls (and radios) of America to shake. Upon reading the Old Testament for the first time, Ginsberg had described it to Kerouac as a narrative of "Spenglerian degeneration, all told in detail, whoring and queerness and worship of moloch . . . I am beginning to see how important Christ is in relation to old Testament—he just turns it upside down, revokes the old God-spoken holy laws in person."[160]

With the notion of the redemptive, Christ-like suffering of the fellaheen structuring the entire poem, "Howl" may be read as an origin myth of a new American culture. Although it is the fellaheen who are sacrificed in attempting to challenge Moloch, they eventually will rise "reincarnate" to claim final victory: "They broke their backs lifting Moloch to Heaven! . . . to Heaven which exists and is everywhere about us!" Part One depicts the initial sacrifice of the "best minds" of Ginsberg's generation,

> who ate fire in paint hotels or drank turpentine in Paradise Alley, death, or
>   purgatoried their torsos night after night . . .
> who burned cigarette holes in their arms protesting the tobacco haze of
>   Capitalism.

In Part Two of "Howl," Ginsberg exposes the false god of America who has caused innumerable sufferings. Moloch is not a demonized other but the enemy within. Moloch is a multilayered symbol representing a Faustian inheritance: capitalism ("Moloch whose blood is running money!"); industrialization ("Moloch whose smokestacks and antennae crown the cities!"); the nuclear age ("Moloch whose fate is a cloud of sexless hydrogen!"); militarism ("Moloch whose fingers are ten armies!"); technological drive ("Moloch whose love is endless oil and stone!"); McCarthy-era politics ("Moloch the crossbone soulless jailhouse and Congress of sorrows!"); reason and abstraction ("Moloch whose poverty is the specter of genius!"); stagnant religious orthodoxies ("Moloch who frightened me out of my natural ecstasy!"); the atomization of the individual ("Moloch in whom I sit lonely!"); and social conditioning ("Moloch the incomprehensible prison!").

Because Moloch is not organically related to America, Ginsberg speaks of its insidious nature by likening it to a parasite: "Moloch whose name is the mind! . . . Moloch who entered my soul early!" According to a Spenglerian logic, Faustian Civilization is not intimately connected to America, and consequently Moloch is only an acquired characteristic: "Moloch who entered my soul early! . . . Moloch whom I abandon! Wake up in Moloch!" Employing mythology from the Hebrew scriptures, Ginsberg equates America's acceptance of these characteristics to those Jews who turned from Yahweh to false idols.[161] Instead of protesting the symbol of Faustian Civilization, however, Ginsberg reveals the revolutionary capacity that Moloch has covered and suppressed. Consequently, while portraying the horrific consequences of psycho-cultural struggle, he affirms its transcendental capacity:

> who bared their brains to Heaven under the El and saw Mohammedan angels staggering on tenement roofs illuminated . . .
> who fell on their knees in hopeless cathedrals praying for each other's salvation and light and breasts, until the soul illuminated its hair for a second.

Although Moloch represents the internalized source of this disruption, Ginsberg alludes to the liberating potential of abandonment. After "'ten years' animal screams and suicides," he mythologizes the final apocalyptic victory of the fellaheen over the symbol of physical and psychological oppression, a triumph that will end in the dawning of a new Culture. As the fellaheen rise "reincarnate," so does a new cultural reality: "They broke their backs lifting Moloch to Heaven! Pavements, trees, radios, tons! lifting the city to Heaven which exists and is everywhere about us!"

Part Three of "Howl" is more personal in tone and was Ginsberg's attempt "to expound terms of spiritual revolution."[162] His eulogy for Carl Solomon, a fellow patient at Columbia Presbyterian Psychiatric Institute, representative martyr, and muse for cultural awakening, attests not only to Ginsberg's belief in alternative constructions of reality but also to his acknowledgment of the anguish that accompanies such a catharsis. Even as he attempts to forge a new America, Ginsberg acknowledges that he must leave one behind. He affirms solidarity with Solomon, for example, in order to "plot a revolution against the United States" and "hug and kiss the United States under our bedsheets the United States that coughs all night and won't let us sleep." That aggressive but compassionate stance reflects his eagerness to drop his "angelic bombs," a desire to be both destroyer and redeemer. "Footnote to Howl" is the final testament to the victory of redemption and destruction and an ecstatic celebration of apocalyptic purification. As Ginsberg celebrates the "bop apocalypse," an incipient reality emerges. It is an American democratic reality in which "everything is holy! everybody's holy! everywhere is holy! everyday is an eternity! Everyman's an angel!"

The religious dimension of Ginsberg's cultural vision, expressed through the struggle of the fellaheen, posited that the nature of the universe contains the deepest truths, ones that necessitated living in harmony with the universe and thereby illuminating all human life as sacred. But such harmony had been disrupted by contemporary society. As Spengler remarked, the Faustian soul's tendency to project its ego against the natural world had resulted in an "immense sense of guilt which runs throughout these centuries like one, long, desperate lament."[163] The goal, then, was to allow the macrocosm to dictate the reality of the microcosm. In Ginsberg's America there was potentially no break between the sacred and profane because everything was grounded on the prior, and greater, pattern of the cosmos. The meter of "Howl" reflects the values adopted through a metaphysics of correspondence and based on the experience of that correspondence. Breath became the hinge between micro- and macrocosm. Ginsberg perceived "Howl" as part incantation and part autobiography, which allowed him to engage in the sacrality of the "mystical experience" while simultaneously communicating it.[164]

In a letter to *New York Times* critic Richard Eberhart shortly after the publication of "Howl," Ginsberg noted, *"Howl* is an affirmation of individual experience of God, sex, drugs, absurdity etc. . . . [It is] an affirmative act of mercy and compassion, which are the basic emotions of the poem." That declaration implied a critical assessment of contemporary America and affirmed the self as America: "The criticism of society is that 'Society' is merciless. The alternative is private, individual acts of mercy. The poem is one such. It is therefore clearly and consciously built on liberation of basic human virtues. . . . Its force comes from positive 'religious' belief and experience. It offers no 'constructive' program in sociological terms—no poem could. It does offer a constructive human value—basically the experience— of the enlightenment of mystical experience—without which no society can long exist."[165]

Despite the tendency "to vulgarize the renaissant spirituality of what we had proposed," Ginsberg believed the words of "Howl" communicated actual values and experiences rather than just ideas. Like Emerson, he thought that his words had their own architecture.[166] As a romantic wordsmith, Ginsberg would not so much cause the walls of the city to shake as he would restore them, brick by brick and using his personal experience for mortar.

The restoration is evident in the poem "America," in which Ginsberg rehearses the origin myth of "Howl" on a personal level and exposes the dominant ideology as having been foisted upon his consciousness through psychological conditioning. In jettisoning these "imports from England," Ginsberg hopes to perform a unique blend of psychoanalysis and cultural engineering.[167] In "America," Ginsberg asserts that the strategies of confrontation, confession, and recovery initiate the processes of self-unification and cultural renewal.[168] The poem reveals America's compromised status by creating an internal dialogue between the poet and the country from which he is in exile, a conversation that alternates between the diasporic voice of Ginsberg and the Faustian voice of the dominant culture: "America when will we end the human war? / Go fuck yourself with your atom bomb. / I don't feel good don't bother me." The two sides of the antagonistic dialogue are not clearly demarcated because both America and its corrupted element are within the poet: "America I've given you all and now I am nothing," the poem begins. "I can't stand my own mind." After dissolving his ego, the poet no longer possesses a separate identity and must engage America on its own terms in order to regain a coherent identity for both. The dissolution illuminates their shared status. More important, it reveals the potential for stabilization and congruence of identity through a joint confession initiated by Ginsberg: "America stop pushing I know what I'm doing." Speaking from a position within America's fractured identity, Ginsberg appeals to that part of the nation that has denied its true nature and cloaked itself with European hand-me-downs: "I won't write my poem until I'm in my right mind. / America when will you be angelic? / When will you take off your clothes?" At this point neither poet nor country are in their right (that is, American) mind. Ginsberg's analysis soon becomes a pretense for seduction. By requesting that America remove its clothes and slough off its Faustian exterior, he is urging it to take the same mystical step he has—stand naked and in harmony with the macrocosmic universe.[169]

"America" concludes with Ginsberg's confession of his true Americanness and an assertion of the social virtues of his "contemplative individuality." In the denouement of the poem he confesses, "It's true I don't want to join the Army or turn lathes in precision parts factories" and reveals that "I'm nearsighted and psychopathic anyway." Thus he comes to reject the militaristic and technoeconomic terms of the American Century and demonstrates his aversion to philosophical abstraction, a complete inability to rationalize according to the Enlightenment tradition. Putting his "queer shoulder to the wheel," he transforms the terms of deviance into terms of American citizenship, rejecting the part of himself that has become infected. Furthermore, he becomes empowered through confession, claiming that it is only his most personal characteristic, his vilified sexuality, that qualifies him for a leadership role.

Conclusion

Consistency was not the Beats' forte in re-presenting American culture at mid-century. In their major works of the 1950s—*Naked Lunch, On the Road, Visions of Cody,* and *Howl and Other Poems*—they selected which cultural values they chose to oppose and which of Spengler's ideas they would emphasize. Not always acknowledging continuities among themselves and the beliefs and values of the majority culture, they exaggerated discontinuities for their own purposes. Having approached Spengler for answers to their personal crises, the Beats found in his text a self-serving mechanism for projecting personal issues onto a cultural matrix. Thus, Beat literature assumed that America, and life, had definitive meaning. How, they continually asked, would both have to look in order to correspond to the larger patterns of the macrocosm?[170]

The Beats' fictionalized America, strategic and enabling, was also Spengler's. It allowed them not only to live within an American drama but also to participate in its unfolding. The dramatic tension rested upon the struggle between the corrupted present and the promise of past and future. The Beats assumed the dual roles of social critic and visionary, challenging normative definitions of America by asserting a Spenglerian reading of its sacred history. Unlike more mainstream critics who spoke from positions of institutional power, they adopted the prophetic strategy of "crying in the wilderness" and positioned themselves on the margins of society. They claimed the moral high ground and cast aspersions, both calumnious and holy. Like many religious outsiders before them, the Beats re-sacralized the symbolic meaning of America in order to reimagine themselves at its center. They looked to their particular construction of America to provide the symbolic currency needed to negotiate the terms of their salvation.

In attempting to ameliorate what they perceived as the cultural ills of the postwar era, the Beats used religious strategies instead of political procedures, generating symbol systems instead of casting ballots. They were the counter-mythologists of postwar America: Burroughs reenchanted a capitalist dystopia, Kerouac made pastoral claims, and Ginsberg envisioned, in the words of Whitman, the spiritual democracy of "still-to-be-form'd America."[171] Although never manifesting themselves as an institutionalized reform community, the Beats were a resistant subculture and ardent defenders of Spengler's America—the utopian counterpart to his vision of inevitable decline. From their position of cultivated marginality, they engaged in a power struggle over ideological and religious terrain. They articulated counter-myths of American exceptionalism, transvalued the dominant codes of symbols and modes of behavior, and dislodged dominant metaphysical assumptions. They reenvisioned America on a symbolic level and also expressed the nation's mythic themes in terms of their own experiences, rewriting the past in energetic terms of the present. They did not so much subvert or displace the religious inheritance of America as they repossessed it by getting beneath its Faustian exterior.[172]

Burroughs, Kerouac, Ginsberg, and Cassady had planned a rendezvous in San Francisco during the summer of 1954. Burroughs even suggested that they all go down to Mexico in order to work on their various projects. But the meeting never happened. Burroughs, with warrants still out for his arrest, traveled to Tangier, and Ginsberg and Kerouac drifted toward San Francisco. Even ten years after their meeting, however, their friendship was a source of creative inspiration. The new vision was still incomplete, and the fame that would descend on each of them during the next few years remained a sought-after ideal. Little did they know the extent to which their story would become part of America's mythological inheritance. As Kerouac wrote to Carolyn Cassady, who was married to Neal, "I want to go back to California this September if Allen is still there and my God if Burroughs goes there I'm sure to come on the fly. Wouldn't it be wonderful for Neal, Allen, Bill, me and you to be all together talking at night; Bill and me with your wine, Allen with his upheld index finger, Neal with his oolong, and you with your pizza pies . . . and wine."[173]

Although they condemned the present, the Beats still possessed organic optimism. Their utopian vision may not have come to pass, but its restless energy dissipated and assumed new forms. It was precisely that restlessness, that inability to accept America as it was handed to them, that eventually turned their stories into mythic fodder for future generations.

Conclusion

The Seduction of Tradition

Previous page, banner for "Beat Culture and the New America: 1950–1965, " Walker Art Center, Minneapolis.

Nowadays only the teaheads have any idea what Democracy
   means
Only the bop musicians seem to glimpse a Presence among us
Man listen to that band of Angels swing.
   —Allen Ginsberg

Stop the hoax
what's the hex
where's the wake
how's the hicks
take my golden beam.
   **—Allen Ginsberg, Jack Kerouac, and Neal Cassady
   "Pull My Daisy" (1949)**

When art leaves the frame and page but the frames and pages
of assigned categories, a basic disruption of reality occurs. The literal realization of art. Success will write "apocalypse" across the sky.
   —William S. Burroughs, "Apocalypse"

Ginsberg, Kerouac, and Burroughs each attained celebrity status during the
1950s. After Ginsberg's Six Gallery reading of "Howl" in 1955, the publication
of Kerouac's *On the Road* in 1957, and the voyeuristic interest in Burroughs
generated by his inclusion in both of the latter—a disembodied notoriety—
everything changed. The Beats were no longer anonymous; no longer were
they considered ordinary Americans who ate pizza or drank wine by the fire.
The literary establishment, for the most part, dismissed their work as "puer-
ile sniveling and self righteous braggadocio." The mainstream media excori-
ated them for being "disengaged" rebels without causes, "model psychopaths,"

"chronic manic-depressives," and "strident practitioners" of "tongue-clucking outrage." Their religious agenda was reduced to a hedonistic quest for "the Kingdom of kicks" found in "drinks, drugs, jazz, and chicks."[1]

Yet it was precisely the sensationalistic verve of such condemnations that invested the Beats with authenticity. They were counter-cultural anti-heroes, the real thing (or so it was thought) and not the feigned subversion of American mores projected on film or emanating from pelvic gyrations on the Ed Sullivan show. For them, subversive character could not be separated from religious agenda. Their criticism of American culture was a complicated matter, metaphysical yet grounded in everyday experience. That aspect transformed the criticism into a platform for belief and action. It was a religious sensibility aimed at repossessing something they had never possessed in the first place.

Throughout the 1940s and early 1950s, Kerouac, Ginsberg, and Burroughs each pursued the "new vision" on his own terms while maintaining an insular and creative (albeit sometimes imaginary) community. The new vision evolved in a number of directions as the Beats' constellation grew to include Gregory Corso and John Clellon Holmes on the East Coast and—given the Western migrations of Kerouac and Ginsberg in the mid–1950s—the poets associated with the San Francisco Renaissance (Gary Snyder, Michael McClure, and Lawrence Ferlinghetti, among others). In Paris, Burroughs collaborated with Brion Gysin in a series of cut-up experiments that would extend his new vision of literature to its breaking point. And on the West Coast, poets such as Kenneth Rexroth, Robert Duncan, and William Everson were cultivating a religious ground for their work to make the arrivals of Ginsberg and Kerouac hospitable.

Even as the original "libertine circle" of Kerouac, Ginsberg, and Burroughs began to disperse and insularity became ever more imaginary, the previous decade of intense collaboration continued to generate results. Despite the glare of the spotlight, the Beats managed to continue the religious journey they had begun together in 1944. Although the totality of their original message became fragmented as it was carried across the media, an earnestness remained. Despite public misconceptions and the personal crises that came from publicity, they did not cease in their pursuit of an ever-elusive ultimacy.

In January 1959, Robert Frank, whose collection of photography, "The Americans" (1958), had won critical acclaim, began filming *Pull My Daisy.* The short film, based on the third act of Kerouac's unpublished play *The Beat Generation,* in Frank's hands became cinema verité that depicted an "ordinary" evening in a New York City Beat pad. Together in 1949, Ginsberg, Kerouac, and Cassady had collaborated on the poem "Pull My Daisy." Underneath its playfulness and sexual innuendo lay a serious challenge:

Pull my daisy
tip my cup
all my doors are open . . .
Silk my garden
rose my days
now my prayers awaken.[2]

In the same spirit, the film follows Ginsberg, Peter Orlovsky, and Gregory Corso as they smoke, drink, and converse the evening away at the home of Neal Cassady, ("Milo," played by the painter Larry Rivers). Reminiscent of Kerouac's sketching method, the camera angle repeatedly shifts yet remains focused on the action in the room. The camera pans from left to right and cuts up and down as Frank tries to capture everything that is happening. There is no sound except for Kerouac's spontaneous voice-over of the conversations, which was recorded as the final, twenty-eight-minute version neared completion. Assuming the voices of narrator and characters, Kerouac describes his friends in the apartment as "laying their beer cans out on the table, bringing up all the wine, wearing hoods and parkas, falling on the couch, all bursting with poetry."[3] Despite the jazz cadences of the lines, Kerouac's words betray his exhaustion. His melancholy meanderings seem to have lost youthful zest, yet they retain poignancy if one acknowledges the Spenglerian currents that lie beneath them.

"Early morning in the universe," whispers Kerouac as the film begins, framing the story as a cosmic folktale. After the opening sequence, Milo informs the others that "the bishop" is planning to stop by for conversation. Although bishops symbolized an authority to be reckoned with as well as feared before Vatican II, this bishop hails from the Liberal Catholic Church, a theosophically oriented denomination whose High Mass had a Gnostic subtext concerning an impersonal absolute and an esoteric interpretation of Christian doctrine.[4]

Given the bishop's antinomian credentials, the men are unphased by the announcement. In fact, their bawdy behavior seems to crescendo. "Act a little better on behavior there because you don't want to hang the bish-op up you understand," orders Milo. Ignoring his pleas, Ginsberg, Corso, and Orlovsky become noticeably excited about the prospect of discussing their spiritual insights with a religious "specialist."

When the bishop enters the apartment, sister and mother in tow, Corso barrages him with questions: "Bishop, bishop, I want to ask you some questions about Buddhism, which I understand you know all about." The bishop agrees to listen. "Is it true that we're all in heaven now and that we don't know it? And that if we knew it we would still know it. But that because we don't know it we go around and act just the way that we do when we know it. But isn't it strange to realize that Buddhism is all involved with the fact that you don't have to get one way or the other about anything and you can do anything you want really?" The bishop is perplexed by this litany of non-sequiturs, but the koan quality of Corso's monologue leads him to question his own religious authority:

> It's a kind of strange and interesting evening, says the bishop.
> The bishop says, Ah, but I don't know anything.
> Well, I thought you knew something that you could say.
> And he says, Well there's one thing that I don't know what to say and that is to say what I really mean.

In confronting the bishop with the strangeness of their world, Ginsberg, Corso, and Orlovsky are seducing him and strategically needling him about his repressed desires. "Have you ever played baseball and seen girls with tight dresses?" inquires Orlovsky. "Well, I've seen—yes, I suppose so," the bishop nervously answers. The conversion through seduction climaxes when Ginsberg unleashes a final barrage of questions celebrating the sacrality of everyday life: "Is the world holy? Is glasses holy? Is time holy? Is all the white moonlight holy? Empty rooms are holy? You holy? Come on bishop, tell us. . . . Izza american flag holy? . . . What is holy? Holy, holy, holy, holy, holy?" The bishop is clearly becoming uncomfortable. The "apocalyptic orgasm" that Norman Mailer used to misidentify the Beat sensibility in 1957 finds a proper context—revelation through continual stimulation.[5]

The chagrined bishop looks to his mother and sister, signaling that they are leaving. Neither, however, are paying attention to him. "Is the organ of man holy?" Ginsberg blurts out. "What, holy, holy?" the stuttering bishop replies incredulously. Desperately trying to change the subject, he turns to the piano in the corner of the room and declares, "Oh, my mother wants to play the organ." But his mother has already been seduced by Ginsberg's religious banter. "Holy, yes," she confirms, "but I want to play a little music here."

As a confrontation between religious inquisitiveness and institutional authority, even one that is patently liberal, *Pull My Daisy* is a movie microcosm of the experiential opening of the American religious field in the postwar years. In the film, that spiritual curiosity is celebrated as a distinctly American trait—a pragmatic yearning that eschews doctrine in favor of mental ambulation. After the disconcerting encounter, the bishop stands outside the apartment and begins to read from the Sacraments. A large American flag blusters in the wind, draping his face and preventing him from seeing the words on the page. The mysterious excess of nature, embodied here in the preeminent symbol of America, has engulfed the rule of religious law. Just as the exotic tastes of Ginsberg, Corso, and Orlovsky overwhelmed the bishop's sense of religious propriety with everyday concerns, so, too, does the reality of a rapidly changing economy, proliferation of atomic anxieties, and an increasingly global world exact a toll on the authority of the American mainstream and subsequently on the master narrative of American religious history.

Fifteen years before the film was made, however, Burroughs, Kerouac, and Ginsberg had already set upon a journey of religious exploration. They had identified a religious space that had always existed in America, from the Algonkian Indians to New Age channelers, the space for the repossession of tradition. It was a place of sanctuary—an imaginary plane where one could practice the subversion of tradition through the tradition of subversion.

Pull My Daisy

> Oh, we're the men of Texaco.
> We work from Main to Mexico.
> There's nothing like this Texaco of ours . . .
> I wipe the pipe, I pump the gas,
> I rub the hub, I scrub the glass.
> I touch the clutch, I mop the top.
> I poke the choke, I sell the pop.
> I clear the gear, I block the knock.
> I jack the back, I set the clock.
> So join the ranks of those who know
> And fill your tank with Texaco.
> **—from theme song of Milton Berle's**
> **Texaco Star Theatre (1949–55)**

The word *subversion* is not one-dimensional, nor does it suggest closure. It is not quantifiable because it is an ongoing process of the back-and-forth of making meaning. Subversion implies fluidity, strategy, interspersed moments of silence, exile, and cunning. It involves neither absolute negation nor wholesale appropriation on the part of those who practice it. Subversion is always happening to everyone and everything, sometimes openly and sometimes not. It is a form of seduction, an act of persuasion in which personal intentions are masked and those of others are redirected or replaced, all in the name of personal gratification or empowerment. No matter how alluring an argument, however, the position or person being seduced rarely abandons all it stands for or all it has stood against. The act of seduction implies strategic compromise and adapting persuasiveness to a specific situation. Every seducer is, in some way or another, seduced. There is no such thing as a zero-sum game.

After World War II, most Americans worked through a common fund of public symbols and emotions, appropriating them for their own needs even as they were seduced by them. For some, that process became a localized, and therefore incomplete, internalization of the mores of the status quo. For the Beats, however, the "American way of life" and its religious assumptions were reinterpreted to such a degree, with such imaginative transgression, as to appear almost unrecognizable. They not only reflected the cultural milieu but also refracted it.

The Beats' America, however, still bore some resemblance to the America they sought to transform. Confronted with a set of cultural norms, they worked through them in a distinctive way. It was a religious style neither more interesting nor important than those of their peers but imbued with remarkable passion. Like other postwar Americans, the Beats were trapped within the dominant ideological sphere yet capable of transcendence. "Dominant" did not necessarily mean "dominating," for in such imaginative moments they constructed a religious world. Although their religious ideals were never institutionalized, the energy of these ideals never wholly dissipated.

What I have referred to as the "tradition of subversion," Catherine L. Albanese has identified as a process of religious "combinativeness," a strategy of continually grounding religious belief and praxis in the stuff of everyday life, where instincts and influences swirl in pragmatic harmony. As she notes, "The shape and operation of American religious life—all of it—is best described under the rubric of religious combination."[6] The "combinativeness" of Burroughs, Kerouac, and Ginsberg seems to be an exaggerated version of this trait of the American imagination. In an era when church attendance soared and theological debate raged, their example demonstrates how American religious history may find a voice through artists and works of art, not solely in those places where religion is self-consciously practiced or proclaimed as the subject of inquiry or contemplation. The most explosive examples of religion are often the most secretive, quietly transgressing even the most accepted truths that a particular culture holds dear. The Beats were, to borrow Gary Snyder's phrase, the "American incarnation of the

Great Subculture . . . of illuminati [that] has been a powerful undercurrent in all higher civilizations."[7]

Style, then, comes to be a defining characteristic of any religious world, whether on the personal level or the social. Burroughs's pragmatic phantasmagoria, Kerouac's wild improvisations on America, and Ginsberg's prophetic rants clearly had social significance. As T. J. Clark has stressed, a work of art may have a particular ideological perspective as its material. What gives it new form that "in itself is a subversion of ideology" is how the artist "works that material."[8]

The way in which the Beats worked the material of literature and life defines their religious creativity and mode of repossession. They collectively developed a theology of experience, a poetics, and a philosophy of culture as many postwar Americans gained increased awareness and interest in things religious. Although each was often thought to be moving against the grain of the postwar "turn toward religion," midwestern Protestant, immigrant Catholic, and leftist Jew moved across it and participated fully in it. Indeed, Burroughs, Kerouac, and Ginsberg used religious strategies for personal empowerment as well as leverage for their cultural criticism. Their response to a perceived religious crisis was distinct yet intimately related to the cultural milieu. Far from anarchists and agitators, they effectively used outsider rhetoric to create their own definition of Americanness. In the process, they critiqued the status quo from the inside.[9] By manipulating the symbol of America and not dismissing it, they fabricated opposition in order to delineate, personally and culturally, the possibilities of the present. Standing at the edges of a sacred canopy that constituted and legitimated a dominant theory of reality for most Americans, they added layers of meaning. They pulled the canopy outward, cut it up, and folded it in, all in the name of understanding the notion of America and explaining what it meant.

Scientologist, Buddhist, Psychedelic

Burroughs, Kerouac, and Ginsberg never expressed the new vision in a completely uniform manner, but as the 1950s progressed the personal idiosyncrasies that had always existed became increasingly apparent as each writer gravitated toward more individual projects. As their new visions developed, each assimilated a number of influences, including traditions that were expressly religious. Burroughs became interested in L. Ron Hubbard's "Dianetics" (later renamed "Scientology") after completing *Naked Lunch;* by late 1953 Kerouac had immersed himself in Buddhism; and Ginsberg undertook a Burroughs-like investigation into the literary and political potential of hallucinogenic drugs. As their stories became more complex, so did America's. "Scientologist, Buddhist, Psychedelic," the rhythm of the phrase was no longer straightforward and no longer rolled off the tongue as "Protestant, Catholic, Jew" had done. The mode of the music, for both the Beats and America, was beginning ever so slightly to change. Even as their Spenglerian vocabulary began to fade, the way in which they wrote over it was an extension of their religious past and emblematic of America's future. As ever, provocation continued to follow provocation.

The stories of Burroughs, Kerouac, and Ginsberg as they unfolded during the 1960s are significant. What they accomplished during their season of collaboration, and how they accomplished it, sheds light on larger trends in American religious history and American history in general. Their example made inroads into public consciousness. More important, their religious style of eclectic assimilation later became the modus operandi of a significant portion of America. Although direct links between literature and cultural change are difficult to quantify, the Beats were a nexus between two Americas. In one, most Americans looked to institutions to provide the building blocks of a religious world. In the late 1940s and early 1950s, church affiliation increased dramatically as Americans searched for sources of authority in religious traditions. At the dawn of the nuclear and television ages, "other-directedness" seemed a sound religious strategy when, according to a 1954 Gallup poll, most Americans were suspicious of personal faith and distrusted the subjective nature of individual experience.[10]

The other America was fast approaching, a rising tide of public skepticism directed at the public sphere itself. The America that came of age during the 1960s was one of controlled paranoia and quiet conspiracy. It differed from an earlier time not so much in how people constructed their religious worlds as it did in the material they used to do so. It became publicly acceptable, if not preferable, to look beyond the institutional horizon for religious direction. Although the American religious imagination had always been active, after World War II it became more restlessly integrative, less likely to announce itself as having arrived at a definitive resting point. Since the 1960s, an increasing number of Americans have looked to personal experience as a model of authority, not merely to supplement tradition but to challenge it and in some cases to usurp institutional authority altogether. The promise held out by experience, long present in American religious circles of antinomianism, began to eclipse the promise held out by institutions (even when the promise was fulfilled within an institutional setting). The potential for personal ecstasy went a long way in seducing the staid American mainstream.

In many ways, the Beats were transitional figures in American religious history. They did not single-handedly change the ways and means of religion as it was practiced, but the force of their example allowed others to look beyond religious orthodoxies, stagnant or otherwise.

Religion, far from being a curious subtext of the Beats' literary production and cultural sensibility, was the central principle that organized their beliefs and activities. Before Kerouac encountered Buddhism, Ginsberg hallucinogenics, and Burroughs Scientology, they had already collaborated in creating both a religious outlook on the world and a practice within it. While sharing an underlying framework of ideas, the development of their religiosity after the period of intense collaboration involved individual processes of translation. Those translations were catalyzed by the inadequacy of a present religious apparatus to deal with experience—intellectual, emotional, and moral. Such translations were not marked by cycles of deconversion and conversion. On the contrary, the Beats' forays into new religious terrain were quests for new meanings for the historical moment as well as efforts to apply existing ones. Even as they were seduced by new religious idioms, their religious language was steeped in the Spenglerian tradition.

When considering the religious consciousness of any individual, an interpreter must take into account two related operations: the way in which religious ideas color other aspects of lived experience and the development, through time, of that individual's meaning-making method. On the one hand, religion operates through categories of thought and modes of behavior, translating ordinary events and experiences as they occur and integrating them into a deeply felt framework. On the other hand, religious ideas and practice evolve constantly, repeatedly undergoing processes of translation. Yet the translation process is not one of strict mimesis. As new metaphysical templates for describing reality are created through combination, they always draw nourishment from the old. They retain original concerns yet inflect them with different meanings. As Kerouac became attracted to the Buddhist principle of anatman ("all unreal and impermanent, a vanishment, a dream, a temporary imaginary arbitrary manifestation from the mind which is not your mind"), for example, he approached it in terms of Catholic tendencies toward self-denial.[11] But his use of anatman was neither a Catholic appropriation nor a strict Buddhist understanding of the doctrine. Reflecting his spiritual development, Kerouac translated this aspect of Buddhism into an existing religious language of Spenglerian subtleties. In the process of rewording, his religious language was altered.

Because every translation issues from the afterlife, it is, by definition, a ghost, a haunting, or a special continuation of that which came before it. Kerouac's example demonstrates how, as an individual's religious orientation develops, the metaphysical template for describing reality becomes more and more of a palimpsest. In viewing the religious consciousness of the individual as a haunted text—a document that has been written over several times, often with remnants of earlier, imperfectly erased translations still visible—religiosity is not misjudged as a seamless whole. Personal religiosity is always an uneven layering of past and present interpretations, a build-up of meanings that converge as well as create intratextual tensions.

Previous interpreters of Beat religiosity in the mid-to-late-1950s have been of two camps. One views their exotic interests as mere extensions of childhood faiths. That occurs most often in the case of Kerouac. Some have interpreted his Buddhist interests solely in terms of an anti-triumphalist Catholicism that emphasizes suffering and redemption. That ignores the possibility for intellectual growth and religious creativity on the part of an individual writer and assumes instead that all experience is reduced to an original mental template inculcated during the early years. Such interpretations assume that ideology is a black hole and that the Beats' literature and lifestyles did not escape the gravitational pull of a childhood understanding of the world. The other interpretive camp assumes that the Beats' specific interest in religion occurred in a vacuum, a spontaneous embrace of alternative traditions in protest against a hegemonic culture. Such a view holds the romanticized misconception that the Beats were in a constant state of rebellion and reacting against any and all forms of tradition.

Neither camp accounts for the actual terms of interpretation, terms that were fluid, open to change, and possessing their own history of development. Each fails to acknowledge the evolving presence of Spengler and thus reduces the Beats' interest in religion during the 1950s to a static formation. By attributing their religious exploration to either a Freudian return to the womb or a retreat from a dominant paradigm, both interpretations fail to account for the messy business that is religion—an imaginative creation of new forms out of old, delineation of personal as well as cultural possibilities, and circumvention of ideological traps that carry determinative weight. Similarly, in order to understand the Beats' interest in Buddhism, Scientology, or psychedelic drugs, one must engage the terms of engagement, which requires attention to minute particulars of individual psychologies, historical change, and the ghostly presence of the past. It is also necessary to engage the creative friction generated by unending contradictions, themselves generated as individuals attempt to make a coherent and meaningful world.

Burroughs, Scientology, and "American Policy"

After completing *Naked Lunch,* Burroughs moved to Paris and became friendly with Brion Gysin, a painter who previously had been "expelled" from the Surrealists by Andre Breton. Gysin was responsible for introducing Burroughs to the "cut-up" method as well as to L. Ron Hubbard's "science of mental health." In a series of letters to Ginsberg in October 1959 Burroughs announced his discovery of both a "new method of writing" (the cut-up method) and the "method of directed recall" (Scientology).[12]

The cut-up method was a mechanical technique of cutting passages from text and reassembling them at random. Gysin attributed the method's origin to a Dadaist poet, Tristan Tzara, who had composed poems on stage at the Cabaret Voltaire in Zurich by pulling words at random out of a hat. The following is an excerpt from a cut-up piece in *Minutes to Go* (1960), a collaborative work by Burroughs, Gysin, Corso, and Sinclair Beiles:

Words	Death by	William Lee Dealer
No	house percentage	CUT
FUNCTION	WITH	BURROUGHS	EVERY MAN
AN AGENT		CUT

In THEE beginning was THE word.. The word was a virus.. "Function always comes before form" L Ron Hubbard. Virus made man.. Man is virus.. Kick that virus habit MAN.[13]

The literary version of collage was similar to the technique of juxtaposition he had used in *Naked Lunch,* but Burroughs now made it the centerpiece of his literary praxis and his battle against the forces of control and addiction. The cut-up method was a functional, materialistic approach to writing, but unlike his previous method of spontaneous juxtaposition it became a weapon to be used against texts and authors to reveal hidden messages and motivations. It was a form of guerrilla warfare against the authority of language, a way to "make explicit a psycho-sensory process that is going on all the time anyway" but inhibited by its inevitable expression in words.[14] In 1959, when he explained the cut-up method to Samuel Beckett in a Paris cafe, Burroughs informed him that he had even used some of Beckett's own writing in his experiments. "You can't do that!" Beckett ordered indignantly. "You can't take my writing and mix it up with the newspapers." "Well," Burroughs responded, "I've done it."[15]

In short succession at the beginning of the 1960s, Burroughs produced

The Soft Machine, The Ticket That Exploded, and *Nova Express,* a trilogy that extended themes introduced in *Naked Lunch* and developed a comprehensive mythology using the cut-up method. From the beginning of Burroughs's use of the cut-up principle, he related it directly to his interest in Dianetics. Burroughs was never an ardent supporter of either Dianetics or Scientology and by 1970 had severed all ties with the church. He still sympathized with some of its main contentions but was in "flat disagreement with its organizational policy."[16] In the early 1960s, however, he had found Scientology more than useful in confirming his already strong notion of Spenglerian correspondence between the individual and the cosmos. Scientology also augmented Burroughs's eclectic theories of mind control and provided a vocabulary for extending his already radical notions of literature and culture.[17] As Burroughs inscribed Scientology onto existing beliefs and methods, his spiritual practice gained a dimension of intellectual clarity it had not previously possessed.

L. Ron Hubbard began formulating a theory he called "Dianetics" in the late 1940s after a brief involvement with Jack Parsons, himself a follower of Aleister Crowley, a notorious occultist, heroin addict, and early-twentieth-century popularizer of sex "magick." In 1950 Hubbard published *Dianetics,* which quickly gained popularity in a culture saturated with pop psychologisms. "The hidden source of all psycho-somatic ills and human aberrations," he claimed, "has been discovered and skills have been developed for their invariable cure."[18]

In Dianetics, the mind is likened to a computational device. Through a focus on the "anatomy of the mind," Dianetics seeks to render it "clear." As an applied religious philosophy, Dianetics views all past traumas, physical or mental, as obstacles to rational behavior, spiritual development, freedom, happiness, and success. These traumas ("engrams") prevent a person from taking an active position in relation to matter, energy, space, and time (MEST) and from being liberated from the material universe. Engrams are recorded and stored in the "reactive mind," that part of the mind that corresponds roughly to the psychoanalytic concept of the unconscious.[19]

In 1952 Hubbard gained control over the Dianetics community by establishing the "official" church of Scientology in Phoenix, Arizona.[20] He attributed the consolidation to a new revelation that transcended the psychotherapeutic teachings of Dianetics by incorporating a strong element of cosmic correspondence. Scientology differs from Dianetics in that it is interested not only in achieving full human potential but also in attuning each individual to the spiritual world. That coincides with Hubbard's belief in an externally existing aspect of human nature that is spirit rather than matter, what he calls the "thetan." "The thetan is the 'I' the individual," Hubbard wrote, "that force, not a part of the physical universe, which is directing the organism."[21] The aspect of Scientology mythology designated the "immortal aspect of self" existed before the origins of MEST but has since become enmeshed in the phenomenal world. According to Hubbard, everyone is a thetan and has acquired engrams during every stage of their previous lives. The purpose of Scientology is to restore the thetan to its original capabilities and, consequently, gain spiritual power and control over the body and environment.

Scientology differs from psychoanalysis in that it does not stress insight into the unconscious workings of the mind as an essential component of therapy. Long suspicious of traditional forms of psychoanalysis, Burroughs was attracted to the fact that Scientology confirmed his belief that consciousness is akin to a tape recording that can be rewound, fast-forwarded, or even erased. In October 1959 he described the importance of this discovery to Ginsberg: "The method of directed recall is the method of Scientology. You will recall I wrote urging you to contact a local chapter and find an auditor. They do the job without hypnosis or drugs, simply run the tape back and forth until the trauma is wiped off. It works. I have used the method, partially responsible for recent change in management, and policy." Unlike psychoanalysis, Scientology does not interpret or evaluate psychological material but only acknowledges it. Furthermore, it stresses recounting incidents to the point where they can be expunged completely.[22]

"Scientology can do more in ten hours," Burroughs claimed, "than psychoanalysis can do in ten years." Scientology's therapeutic emphasis allowed him to integrate the scientific and therapeutic dimensions of his writing under a single strategy of achieving correspondence between the individual mind and its spiritual counterpart, the thetan. According to Hubbard, such correspondence is achieved by transcending the limitations of MEST as well as the words and images the thetan has recorded. To become clear is to increase awareness of one's spiritual capacities to such a degree as to become an active agent upon the environment rather than a passive participant.[23] Becoming clear refers to the key on a calculator that clears the machine of previous entries and the buildup of depressed numbers, erasing all systematic inaccuracies and assuring the accuracy of future computations. The erasure of these engrams and "locks" takes place in the reactive mind—"that portion of the mind which files and retains physical pain and painful emotion and . . . *thinks only in identities.*"[24]

Burroughs used Scientology techniques in order to locate and erase contradictory engrams from the reactive mind, thus eradicating their deleterious effects upon mind, body, and soul. He even suggested that the reactive mind is located in the hypothalamus, describing it as "an artificially constructed and highly disadvantageous regulatory system grafted onto the natural regulatory center." Burroughs believed that "reactive commands can be inserted in advertisements, editorials, newspaper stories" in order to present an individual with a series of "contradictory commands." The reactive mind, as theorized by Hubbard, gave further justification (and clarification) to Burroughs's notion that language is not only a physically invasive virus but also not of this world. "The R.M. [reactive mind] as expounded by Mr. Hubbard is of considerable antiquity . . . manifesting itself through all modern languages," Burroughs explained, "consequently it must refer to a *symbol system*." The reactive mind, he believed, is susceptible to outside control systems that manipulate by way of imposed contradictions. "Contradictory commands are an integral part of the modern industrial environment" that disable an individual from taking positive action—he or she can only react against.[25]

In Scientology, the erasure of engrams is accomplished through the "E-meter," a form of skin galvanometer that measures resistance to a current that passes between two terminals. Resistance is measured in terms of "body-reads," the results of increased body temperature and sweat. Resistance occurs when the person being audited reacts against certain words, phrases, ideas, or questions. Such reactions are interpreted as signs of internal contradiction, an inorganic tension between the analytic mind and the reactive mind and between the true nature of the thetan and the limitations imposed by MEST. Hubbard claimed that through repeated isolation, via the E-meter, such obstacles could systematically be erased.

Always open to new areas of psychic investigation, Burroughs learned much from Scientology. As he explained, "Techniques exist to erase the Reactive mind and achieve a complete freedom from past conditioning and immunity against such conditioning in the future. Scientology processing accomplishes this."[26] Of greatest interest was Scientology's intense concern with language, including a preoccupation with neologisms and insider rhetoric. Hubbard's theories on how the reactive mind "thinks in identities" was due, in part, to Korzybski, who asserted that the source of psychosomatic illness, as well as emotional tension, is the misguided tendency to think in terms of identification.[27] Given Burroughs's fluency in Korzybski's General Semantics, Scientology offered him a corresponding theory of communication that confirmed the neurological effects of words and their capacity to condition the human nervous system. Scientology reinforced Burroughs's belief that language is a control system that locks people into patterns of thinking and behavior. In the "Appendix to the Soft Machine" he included Scientology, the metabolic regulation of apomorphine, and Reich's orgonic theories in the panoply of weapons for use against the forces of control.

The Soft Machine, first published in Paris by Olympia Press in 1961, was the first work to emerge from notes that remained after Burroughs had edited and compiled *Naked Lunch.* Its major theme was that reality is a reel-to-reel tape, looped through the human body (the "soft machine") and various control systems that produce the tape. Through video and audio stimuli, the body is behavioristically programmed on the cellular level. In response, Burroughs called for total resistance: "This is war to extermination—Fight cell by cell through bodies and mind screens of the earth."[28]

The only way an individual can regain control of the "reality" process is to take over the control machine, turning it against itself through newspaper cut-ups and photomontage—in effect, rewinding the reality tape and diffusing its power through exposure in order for an individual to become the sole source of meaning production. Cut-ups, as Robin Lydenberg has noted, began "as an exercise in negativity," extinguishing the ideological freight that language carries within itself—its original "context, its author, its signifying function." A cut-up text no longer possesses a history of ownership and consequently can be interpreted anew without recourse to the dictates of authorial intent.[29] Burroughs's plan called "for total exposure" as he urged readers to "wise up all the marks everywhere Show them the rigged wheel—Storm the Reality Studio and retake the universe."[30]

In one sense, the cut-up method was the evangelical counterpart of Scientology in that it was intended to alter a reader's consciousness. Burroughs urged readers to "do it for yourself," that is, use cut-up in order to become aware of their own power to dictate reality and "lighten [their] own life sentence."[31] Because Burroughs's work demanded interpretive effort, readers could potentially become co-collaborators with him in the creation of meaning. For Burroughs, consciousness was the generative source of reality, possessing the capacity to resist the external controls of both the body and language. Due to the conditioning power of words, however, consciousness is prevented from wielding that potential. Cut-ups promised liberation, a way out from under the oppression of Western thought. In a three-part process, cut-ups enabled both Burroughs and his readers to see the enemy directly. First, they could reduce language to a state of naked materiality, which would then allow for unencumbered investigation into a nexus involving language, mind, and body. Finally, they could expose the mechanisms of conditioning.

As Lydenberg notes, Burroughs practiced cut-up in order to exorcise "habitual conditioned responses" inculcated by Western Civilization, a "deliberate and conscious abdication of control which aims at an escape *from* controls— controls imposed from within or without."[32] As the means to become clear, both Scientology and the cut-up method were ways to expose word controls in order to free a subject from their determinative effects.

Through the cut-up method, Burroughs sought to expose the arbitrary nature and manipulative power of all linguistic systems. The method not only exposed word "locks" but also revealed a new world through the accidental combinations of words. Burroughs's Calvinist disposition assumed that events were prewritten and prerecorded, so "the future leaks out" when the cut-up method is applied. He came to believe that his cut-up experiments would be a transport into a world beyond words, outside time and space where universal forces were at work. "My most interesting experience with the earlier techniques," he commented, "was the realization that when you make cut-ups you do not get simply random juxtaposition of words, that they do mean something, and often that these meanings refer to some future event."[33]

Burroughs believed he had found a way to access the "space between," a universal, subliminal level of consciousness where one could see clearly the past as well as the future. Burroughs sought to reveal the means of access to this world beyond in (as well as through) his writing. As he wrote in *The Soft Machine*, "I have just returned from a thousand-year time trip and I am here to tell you what I saw—And to tell you how such time trips are made—It is a precise operation—It is difficult—It is dangerous—It is the new frontier and only the adventurous need apply—But it belongs to *anyone* who has the courage and know-how to enter—It belongs to *you*."[34]

His message was religious in form as well as content. A faith in "the possibility of mass deconditioning" through clear vision countered his experience of a declining West—a fallen world of confusion and suffering.[35] Burroughs's faith was still that of the American Jeremiah. Embedded in his method of disorientation was a clear voice, crying in the wilderness:

"phantom cleavage is Un-American."
[]
"This is not American policy"
[]
CUT THE IN LINES
CUT THE JUNK LINES
LOOK OUT TO SPACE. . OUT FLAG IS STILL THERE.[36]

Kerouac, Buddhism, and *The Climax of German Thought*

Kerouac's publications in the late 1950s have often been ignored by religious historians as either examples of religiously inspired literature or as sources of America's increased interest in Buddhism following World War II. In the hands of literary critics, religion is often inscribed into Kerouac's poetics and not given its place as a generative force behind his artistic consciousness. Although there have been a number of interpretations of Kerouac's Buddhist period, few have accounted for how Buddhism confirmed previous beliefs while denying others and extended certain practices while translating others into radically new forms. Some critics, such as Ann Charters and Richard S. Sorrell, view all of Kerouac's religious explorations as functions of his childhood Catholicism. As Sorrell writes, "Catholicism was always his dominating moral and ideological motivating force."[37]

Such interpretations mistake omnipresence for omnipotence and reify Kerouac's religious consciousness into something readily understood without reference to either personal biography or intellectual context. More perceptive critics, such as Paul Giles and Stephen Prothero, see a link between Kerouac's Catholicism and Buddhism. Yet they, too, fail to account fully for either his Spenglerism or the nuances of the translation process. Only James T. Jones has attempted to discover the internal logic guiding Kerouac's religious bricolage of Catholicism, Spenglerism, and Buddhism. He is one of the few critics to acknowledge Spengler's profound influence on Kerouac's writing, although Spengler's influence went beyond mere aesthetics. Put another way, Kerouac's aesthetics went beyond the written page. Jones's analysis of *Mexico City Blues* is insightful as a literary critique, but because of its textual emphasis it fails to account for the symbolic process that led to Kerouac's hybridized and ever-evolving religious discourse.[38]

Kerouac's religiosity was constant in focus yet unstable, complex, and even contradictory in mood and motivation. His interest in Buddhism was a continuation and rejection of his past beliefs, both Spenglerian and Catholic. In his most frequently cited "Buddhist" work, *The Dharma Bums,* written in November 1957, he seems to have replaced Neal Cassady ("Moriarty/ Pomeray") as Spenglerian hero with a newfound faith in the Zen poet Gary Snyder ("Japhy Ryder"). "Ryder," Kerouac wrote, "is a great new hero of American culture."[39] Even the name of Kerouac's character, Ray Smith, seems to imply resignation, as Kerouac no longer attempts to salvage paradise but is content with the imperfect banality of this world. Ryder's pronouncements on Buddhism and "Zen Lunacy," however, as well as the lessons Smith learns from his new mentor, bear resemblance to beliefs previously held by Kerouac.[40]

Ryder's vision of a "rucksack revolution" and his expectation of "how truly great and wise America will be, with all this energy and exuberance and space focused into the Dharma" are reminiscent of the ancient wisdom of the fellaheen. Even as he dismisses Smith's evocation of medieval mystics as "European gloom and crap," Ryder proclaims, "I want my Dharma Bums to have springtime in their hearts." Smith's Buddhist insight—"it's with your six senses that you're fooled into believing not only that you have six senses, but that you can contact an actual outside world with them"—resonates with Kerouac, who had a penchant for immanental mysticism.[41]

Although it is easy enough to identify the overlapping territory between Kerouac's Catholicism and Buddhism, it is much more interesting and vital to see how that terrain was altered and inflected during the translation process. As Alan Miller has insightfully commented, "Perhaps it is enough to say that for Kerouac the religious quester, neither analytic distinctions nor creedal labels were appropriate to his actual religious experience."[42]

By the time Kerouac discovered Buddhism in late 1953, his religious disposition consisted mainly of the interface between Catholicism and Spenglerism. He achieved a momentary balance in religious consciousness in 1951, just two years before beginning studies of Buddhism. Even as Kerouac began to read Spengler in a more pessimistic light, he hoped that the Catholic Church could expressly accommodate Spengler's theories of inevitable decline. In a letter to Neal Cassady, he announced that he was "done sneering at any part of [the church]" and expressed desire for it to become a "refuge for the poor, the humiliated, and the suffering" from a corrupt and declining "civilization." Seeking solace from the negativity of Spengler's prophecies, Kerouac reached an uneasy resolution: "I wished all mankind could gather in one immense church of the world, among the arcades of the angels, & when it came time to take of bread, I wished Jesus would reach out his hand to a single loaf and make of it two billion loaves of every single soul in the world. What else would we need besides the bread for our poor unfortunate bodies? And then someday we could all become pure souls—not animals and not even mortal men, but angels of heaven."[43]

That hope would soon fade as Kerouac descended ever deeper into depression over his spiritual health and that of the country he loved so dearly. By 1952, after completing *Visions of Cody,* he had come to realize the futility of his grandiose Faustian plan to "extend" himself. He subsequently fell back into an even more despairing Spenglerism. As he wrote to Ginsberg:

I thought I was beyond Darwin's chain,
A phosphorescent Jesus Christ in space, not a champion
    of the Fellaheen night
    with my French Canadian mind.[44]

In May and June of 1952, Kerouac completed *Doctor Sax: Faust Part Three,* a fantasy rendering of a mythic battle between a hero, "Doctor Sax of the North American Antiquity," and his nemesis "Count Condu, impeccably dressed, just-risen from the coff of eve, the Satin Doombox with its Spenglerian metamorphosed scravenings on the lid." But even as Kerouac's novel was a mythic reversal of the trajectory of Western (that is, American) decline, Doctor Sax, like the author, "had knowledge of death . . . a mad fool of power a Faustian man."[45]

The tensions created by Kerouac's utopian hope, Faustian guilt, and realistic assessment of his literary credentials became steadily more apparent. By the end of 1953, he was increasingly insecure and depressed and felt he had become too involved in the politics of writing. He justified his professional retreat through an even more pessimistic reading of Spengler. From Richmond, New York, he wrote to Carolyn Cassady in December 1953 of his existential despair: "God is alone, and I'm better off because of it. It'll be more important for me to know—in the Apocalypse of the Fellaheen to come, when all culture & civilization are done—that the shallow-eyed potato is the best potato, then t'would be for me to know the sum of my Advance, what J. Roger Critic said, and the politics of reprint rights."[46]

It was during this period that Kerouac reread *Walden* and found comfort in Thoreau's rejection of and retreat from society. He followed up on Thoreau's references to Eastern philosophies and soon obtained *The Life of Buddha* by Ashvaghosha the Patriarch from the local library. Kerouac immediately found solace in Buddhism's discussion of illusions and dreams, and the existential gravity of his situation seemed to lessen. In August 1954 he thanked Malcolm Cowley for helping arrange for an excerpt from *On the Road* to be published in *New World Writing.* In a postscript he added, "Since I saw you I took up the study of Buddhism and for me it's the word and the way I was looking for. All things are imaginary and in a state of suffering due to Ignorance."[47]

In February 1954, when Kerouac had traveled to California, his career as a writer had become almost nonexistent, his alcoholism was becoming more severe, and he was no longer surrounded by supporters because Ginsberg and Burroughs were out of the country. Making matters worse was Kerouac's disappointing reunion with Neal Cassady, from whom he sought reassurance about the validity of his new Buddhist ideas. Instead of finding comfort, he was troubled by Cassady's obsession with Edgar Cayce and Cayce's theories on reincarnation and karma. Although he was sympathetic to Cayce's prophetic pronouncements on imminent catastrophes, Kerouac viewed Cassady's Caycean faith in the immortality and uniqueness of the individual soul as exactly the Faustian obstacle he was trying to overcome in his own life. Kerouac was extremely disappointed with Cassady's evangelical fanaticism and called him "Billy Graham in a suit." That spring, as arguments between the two men became more heated, Kerouac renewed his Buddhist studies at the San Jose Public Library.[48]

Kerouac found an affinity between antitriumphalist Spenglerism and the Buddhist teachings he found in books such as Dwight Goddard's *The Buddhist Bible* and Paul Carus's *The Gospel of Buddha*. Both presented Buddhism within a Christian religious matrix. Despite Goddard's insistence that his text was compiled very differently than the Christian Bible, the name of the compendium hints of ecumenicism.[49] Carus, a speaker at the World's Parliament of Religions in 1893, argued for broadening the parameters of Christianity to include other religious traditions as well as science; otherwise, Christianity was "destined to disappear with the progress of civilization."[50]

Given the evangelical subtext informing Kerouac's sources, his energetic witnessing to friends is unsurprising. In a May 1954 letter to Ginsberg, he included a bibliographical study guide of Buddhist texts and volunteered himself as spiritual advisor. "For your beginning studies of Buddhism," he instructed, "you must listen to me carefully and implicitly as tho I was Einstein teaching you relativity or Eliot teaching the Formulas of Objective Correlation on a blackboard in Princeton."[51]

When Burroughs learned that Kerouac had taken up a self-taught Buddhist program in early 1954, he expressed immediate disapproval to both Kerouac and Ginsberg in a series of letters. Displaying a deep-seated Spenglerism, Burroughs believed that Buddhism was "not for the West" because it was neither indigenous nor a form of active engagement with the facts: "So my conclusion [is] only for the West to *study* as *history,* that is it is a subject for *understanding.* . . . But it is not, for the West, *An Answer,* not *A Solution.* We must learn by acting, experiencing, and living: that is, above all, by *Love* and *Suffering.* A man who uses Buddhism or any other instrument to remove love from his being in order to avoid suffering has committed, in my mind, a sacrilege comparable to castration . . . Buddhism frequently amounts to a form of psychic junk." Believing Kerouac's *"Catholic* Buddhism" to be "an intellectually disreputable bastard," Burroughs urged him not to retreat from the task of cultural change and discovery of an organic alternative to put forth after the decline of the West. Denouncing those who take up Eastern practices as "a sorry bunch of psychic retreaters from the dubious human journey," Burroughs affirmed that "human life has direction. Even if we accept some Spenglerian Cycle routine, the cycle never comes back to exactly the same place, nor does it exactly repeat itself." Reminding Kerouac that "we must evolve our own solutions," he urged him not "to sit on the sidelines [because] there are no sidelines. Whether you like it or not, you are committed to the human endeavor."[52]

In December 1953, Kerouac began to keep a notebook to document his Buddhist studies. What began as lists of the Four Noble Truths and the Eightfold Path rapidly became larger in scope, with prayers, poems, short stories, metaphysical dialogues, personal letters, journal entries, and drawings. Completed in March 1956, *Some of the Dharma* maps Kerouac's journey through Buddhism during a highly volatile period of his life.[53] In order to portray accurately his evolving religious consciousness, however, it is necessary to understand the mental categories, attitudes, and motivations that brought him to Buddhism and also consider how they were translated into a new religious language as his studies developed.

Kerouac began his journey into Buddhism by confirming the existence of a corresponding realm of spiritual refuge. In the opening pages of *Some of the Dharma*, he wrote, "Buddhism is a return to the Original mind" and a few pages later that "BUDDHA AND JESUS BOTH FREED THEMSELVES OF THE SUBCONSCIOUS DREAMFLOOD WHICH IS THE SOURCE OF 'RELIGIOUS VISION' AND AVAILABLE TO ANY DOZING MAN."[54] The Spenglerian notion of the universal macrocosm was translated into the Buddhist notion of Universal Mind, clarifying for Kerouac the connection between the individual and the cosmos. Because both the individual and the universal are connected through the mind, Kerouac's goal was no longer to reveal his deepest subconscious thoughts but to free himself from them. The method and the results of his writing remained the same as before, but the motivation behind it had changed. Where once he had worked under the assumption that the subconscious contains the deepest truths of humanity, he now conceived of the ground of humanity as a purified and empty mind.[55]

Before the winter of 1953, Kerouac moved toward Buddhism as he attempted to align his Catholic and Spenglerian faiths. As he refined his practice of spontaneous composition, he came to see "sketching" as a regenerative act that heightens subjective awareness to the point of achieving an original orientation toward the cosmos. In opposition to the rational drive toward certainty deplored by Spengler, the sketching method depicts a timeless moment in which Kerouac silently meditated on the fluctuating associations that constituted subjective reality. During the early 1950s he continued his quest for an artistic technique that would lead to "self-actualization," a term Spengler used to denote the revelation of timelessness and "the secret relationship between microcosm and macrocosm."[56] Reflecting this sentiment, Kerouac had begun *Doctor Sax,* written in the middle of 1952, with an invocation of the sketching method.[57] "THE OTHER NIGHT I had a dream that I was sitting on the sidewalk on Moody Street, Pawtucketville, Lowell, Mass., with a pencil and paper in my hand saying to myself 'describe the wrinkly tar of this sidewalk, also the iron pickets of Textile Institute, or the doorway where Lousy and you and G.J.'s always sittin and dont stop to think of words when you do stop, just stop to think of the picture better—and let your mind off yourself in this work.'"[58] The opening paragraph integrates four layers of reality: the physical world, a dream of the physical world, an artistic representation of the physical world in a dream, and an artistic representation of the dream representation of the physical world.[59] Kerouac begins with subjective assertion and concludes with an objective account of himself as just another aspect of a larger fictional creation.

The sketching method not only provided such a means but also resonated with his Catholic upbringing, specifically the interpretive mode of anamnesis. Primarily used as a tool for recalling the mystery of the Eucharist, anamnesis implies both a subjective and an objective element of understanding. Under the assumption that bodily death is actually rebirth, anamnesis is a representation of events that have shaped, and continue to impinge upon, the present. For Kerouac, it was a mode of remembering that brought the past into the present. "I struggle in the dark with the enormity of my soul," he wrote, "trying desperately to be a great rememberer redeeming life from darkness."[60] Through the practice of sketching, Kerouac sought to attend to the present moment and dissolve the self into the current of being, thereby becoming ever-present as the subject of memory and mysteriously invisible as the object to be memorialized. Such mystical vision suggested an immediate comprehension of the cosmos, where life, dreams, and art converged by the emptying of the self.

While anamnesis was but one aspect of the sketching method, it nonetheless represented an important nexus between Kerouac's Catholicism, Spenglerism, and Buddhist turn in late 1953.[61] Inflected by Spengler and a Catholic metaphysics, sketching was a self-forgetful mode he used to empty himself in order to remember his true identity as participant in the universal macrocosm. He employed sketching to experience the Spenglerian dictum that "we ourselves are Time."[62]

As he read *The Surangama Sutra,* Kerouac found that the bodhisattvas he admired "answered questions spontaneously with no recourse to discriminating thinking." As Goddard's translation reads: "It is because of the straight-forwardness of their minds and the spontaneity of their mentations that the Tathagatas have ever remained, from beginningless time to endless time, of one pure Suchness, undisturbed by any complexity within their minds nor any rising thoughts of discrimination." Just a few months earlier Kerouac had compiled the "Essentials of Spontaneous Prose," which listed many insights he sought and confirmed through Buddhism. "Blow as deep as you want," he wrote, affirming that all writing should be "honest, ('ludicrous'), spontaneous, 'confessional' interesting, because not 'crafted.'" His statement that "craft is craft" would acquire deeper resonance when he read in *The Surangama Sutra* that Ananda declared, "I may attain to self-mastery and become emancipated from the lure of evil myself, and be able to free all heretics from the bonds of their false ideas and craft."[63]

Kerouac was attracted to the Mahayanan strain of Buddhism, which extended the concept of no-self to mean that all things were not just transitory but were, in a certain sense, unreal. Mahayana also emphasized the importance of the exercise of compassion before enlightenment. As Gerald Nicosia has noted, Kerouac's self-identification with both a Tathagata and a Bodhisattva appealed to the combination of selfishness and compassion in his character.[64] As a Tathagata, Kerouac could follow his own path through the world without any attachments. As a Buddha-to-be, he could justify helping others on the path to enlightenment. The personal identification with the historic Buddha resembled his previous identification with the fellaheen, those earthly entities also in touch with the ground of being. That identification is evident throughout *Some of the Dharma* and is the leitmotif of *Mexico City Blues,* a book of poetry written in 1955. As Kerouac wrote in *Some of the Dharma,* his belief in the social value of art was renewed through his Buddhist studies: "I am Buddha come back in the form of Shakespeare for the sake of poor Jesus Christ and Nietzsche . . . I'll become an Intuitional farmer."[65]

The majority of references in *Some of the Dharma* are from Goddard's *Buddhist Bible;* consequently, the themes Goddard stressed colored Kerouac's own appraisal of Buddhism. "The theme of the Buddhist Bible," Goddard declared, "is designed to show the unreality of all conceptions of a personal ego." Kerouac found comforting logic in Goddard's interpretation of Buddhism, particularly his emphases on the theme of anatman and the possibility that suffering could be alleviated through abandoning the individual ego. "Nothing to worry about," he wrote to Carolyn Cassady in 1954. "Biggest trouble is hang-up on self, on ego-personality. I am not Jack, I am the Buddha now."[66]

According to Kerouac's reading of *The Buddhist Bible,* everything in the universe is subject to change, including what is commonly referred to as the self. Suffering originates in the desire to cling to an eternal *I* over and against the impermanence of the material world. Ironically, Goddard's instructions only legitimated Kerouac's penchant for narcissistic contemplation, a tendency that would alternate with severe bouts of depression to plague him throughout his life. If anything, *Some of the Dharma* is a record of intensive self-analysis in keeping with Goddard's commands. As Goddard wrote, the purpose of his book was "to awaken faith in Buddhahood as being one's true self-nature. . . . The true response to the appeal of this Buddhist Bible is not in outward activities, but in self-yielding, becoming a clear channel for Buddhahood's indrawing compassion."[67]

Given Goddard's directives, Kerouac viewed Buddhism as a means to reinvigorate his literary creativity as well as a spiritual path. The irony, however, was not lost on Kerouac. "I'll go down to Mexico someday and live my own kind of healthy life," he wrote, "a self-sufficient practising Dhyanist in Mexico—a selfish religionist resting . . . only on trips to New York or home headquarters of family and publishers shall I revert to the Machine Age Orgonic Writer with the New Ribbon."[68]

Despite Kerouac's attempt to move away from the pessimism of Spengler's authoritative historical schema, particularly as it had influenced his Faustian desire for transcendence, Spengler's influence remained even as it was consciously negated. Under Goddard's instruction, Kerouac retained belief in mystical intuition and the accompanying knowledge of the "laws of time." Now, however, he conceived of them in relation to the Buddhist law of impermanence (*anitya*). By reinterpreting Spenglerian cycles in terms of devolution and anatman, Kerouac used his new Buddhist vocabulary to lend coherence to Spenglerian prophecies: "Civilization takes us one more step removed from intuitive realization of what has been made manifest in this we call our life—American know-how is not savior of world but its curse in the struggle to understand emancipation from suffering." The way in which to adhere to Spengler's notions of correspondence and decline was to realize the futility of escaping them. Accepting "loss forever," Kerouac could "believe in the holy contour of life" but not in its substance. On the same page, he boldly wrote:

NOTHING'S ALIVE
FOR THE UNIVERSE
IS A DREAM
ALREADY ENDED.[69]

Kerouac also found Goddard's position to be in line with his Spenglerian quest to find an alternative to Faustian Civilization. Goddard, for example, observed, "In these days when Western civilization and culture is buffeted as never before by foreboding waves of materialism and selfish aggrandizement both individual and national, Buddhism seems to hold out teachings of highest promise. . . . It may well be the salvation of Western civilization."[70] In a 1954 letter, Kerouac wrote that the "Western 'work' idea is essentially Faustian and it is Faustian Totalitarianism." In its place he sought "self-realization or highest perfect wisdom, ecstasy of transcendental insight."[71]

In one sense, a "Goddardized" Buddhism offered Kerouac release from the anxiety that his Spenglerian idealism had caused. As a counterargument to his previous belief that a new Culture could be forged, he found relief in the notion that sense perceptions are illusions and meaningless ("Spengler did not understand Tao, it was in his nature not to"). Because all is illusion, there is nothing to do except exist and "accept the wonder of illusion, to be kind to all who were afflicted by it and to know that death marks the end of it and a return to the perfect void."[72]

No translation process is ever seamless, consequently, Kerouac's new-found Buddhist language sometimes complicated his Spenglerian orientation. The fact that he was reinterpreting Spengler is evident in a passage from *Some of the Dharma:*

> *The Decline of the West* as a work should really be called *The Climax of German Thought* . . . the sound of boots is in it always, something alien from the nebulous cloud and far below it . . . a concern with everlasting details of history . . . but in all the myriad assyamkas of kalpas of innumerable millenniums how many details, how many grains of dust, in this HISTORY? Not one. This is Tao—
> A reality which can only be explained ahistorically, is where Spengler is now, in death, in truth, in void.[73]

For Kerouac, Buddhism was not an outright rejection of Spengler but a sympathetic reconfiguration. Through Buddhism, he translated Spengler's morphology and emphasis on cultural creation into new terms of personal meditation: "The Spring phenomenon becomes the Winter noumenom— The gist of Buddhism: neither grasp nor reject, but take what's given you."[74]

Paradoxically, Kerouac's drift away from a Spenglerian orientation reaffirmed his peasant romanticism, but in a new language. Although he began to depend less and less on Spenglerian terms to legitimate his spiritual project, he maintained much of the attitude and many of the motivations that had generated his earlier work. As he wrote of his mystical path in *Some of the Dharma:*

But I'm too sad to care that I understand everything.
Lowell is a happy dream but just a dream.
All's left, I must go now into my own monastery
wherever its convenient
My life went from culture of Town, to civilization of
City, to neither of Fellaheen.

Kerouac continued to align himself with the margins of society in order to carry out a religiously based cultural program. Mystical insight could only "be achieved in solitude, poverty, and contemplation—and in a gathering of homeless brothers."[75] As he wrote in the fall of 1954, "Buddhism is a Fellaheen thing.—Fellaheen is Antifaust Unanglosaxon Original World Apocalypse. Fellaheen is an Indian Thing, like the earth. Jean-Louis the Fellaheen Seer of New North America.—The Unfaust, the Antichrist . . . Unsquare, Ungothic."[76] He also identified Buddhism in terms of a Catholic universalism and continued to perceive himself as a leader of the fellaheen, bringing a salvific message for a "New North America."[77]

After publication of *On the Road* in 1957, Kerouac began a slow withdrawal from the glare of the spotlight, a retreat with his mother to Florida and a spiral into alcoholism and depression.[78] As he experienced both misplaced adulation and critical scorn and began to comb through Spengler once again for insights into his predicament, his Buddhism became written over by Spengler. Kerouac came to see the fellaheen as part of the last gasp of Western Civilization (the "second religiousness" as Spengler had described it) rather than the first breaths of a new Culture. He adopted a more Burroughsian reading of Spengler yet did not have the religious constitution to maintain Burroughs's solitary disposition. In a 1958 interview with Mike Wallace, Kerouac articulated his position and its emotional costs:

Wallace: You mean beat people are mystics?
Kerouac: Yeah, it's a revival prophesied by Spengler. He said that in the late movements of Western civilization there would be a great revival of religious mysticism. It's happening.
Wallace: What do the mystics believe in?
Kerouac: Oh, they believe in love . . . and . . . all is well . . . we're in heaven now really.
Wallace: You don't sound happy.
Kerouac: Oh, I'm tremendously sad, I'm in great despair.
Wallace: Why?
Kerouac: Oh, it's a great burden to be alive.[79]

As Kerouac became known as the "King of the Beat Generation," his quest for meaning accelerated downward—a vertiginous slide toward a childhood Catholicism and xenophobic conservatism. Believing that his literary achievements were becoming obscured by adulation, he recoiled. Never again did he feel comfortable with the terms of success. As he traveled down the road of uncertainty, he seemed to be always looking up, toward heaven perhaps yet always falling further and further away.

Ginsberg, LSD-25, and Spengler's Ghost

While Ginsberg dabbled in Buddhist philosophy during the 1950s, what he took from his conversations with Kerouac was the notion that life is illusory and that social reality is constructed. Initially, he was reticent to adopt Eastern spirituality as Kerouac had done. In a 1955 journal entry, Ginsberg complained in jest that "Zen Buddhists [are] all egotists."[80] Before he immersed himself in the study of Hinduism, Tibetan Buddhism, and Indian literature on a trip to India in 1962, Ginsberg first pursued the expansion of individual consciousness through various experiments with drugs, including not only marijuana, peyote, mescaline, and morphine but also lysergic acid (LSD-25).[81]

Of the Beats, Ginsberg became the most politically active. His visibility in New Left causes brought him ever-increasing fame as a poet, agitator, and celebrity rabble-rouser. In the 1960s he became a psychedelic Transcendentalist while continuing his Spenglerian prophecies, believing that changing the consciousness of society's members would necessarily lead to a change in society. In a 1966 public address given at the Arlington Street Church in Boston, Ginsberg proposed that "everybody who hears my voice, directly or indirectly, try the chemical LSD at least once: every man woman and child American in good health over the age of fourteen . . . may everybody in American turn on, whatever the transcient law—because individual soul development (as once declared by a poet in jail in this city) is our law transcending the illusions of the political state."[82] Ginsberg still considered himself the "Father of the American Revolution."[83] The details of his revolutionary agenda may have become more expressly political, but his pharmaceutical experiments now redrew the boundaries of his religious vision. As he wrote in "Laughing Gas" late in 1958:

High on Laughing Gas
I've been here before
the odd vibration of
the same old universe.[84]

After the publication of *Howl and Other Poems* in 1956 garnered significant public attention and some much-needed revenue, Ginsberg first sailed to the Arctic Circle aboard the USNS *Sgt. Jack J. Pendleton* and then traveled to Tangier with Peter Orlovsky to help Burroughs compile *Naked Lunch*. From Tangier, Ginsberg set off on a tour of Europe, exploring the "classic stations of the earth," including Venice, Paris, Amsterdam, and London.[85] Upon returning to the United States, he assumed the public role that had been handed to him, traveling across the country to give readings, writing editorials, and pushing the work of his friends onto sympathetic publishers. Because of Aldous Huxley's *The Doors of Perception*, Ginsberg became increasingly curious about chemically induced states of consciousness. "What I'm interested in," he explained, "is states of altered perception, widened consciousness, deepened feeling . . . In our society ecstasy is considered 'immoral.' . . . The highly organized conditions of modern civilization preclude certain free sexual and emotional responses basic to human physiology, basic to human desire."[86] The indigenous romanticism of Ginsberg's early years had been given a new twist. The same scientific imagination that had once corrupted America's spiritual state could now "open the door to God." For Ginsberg, drugs could accomplish exactly what he had tried to accomplish through poetry—to induce a state of cosmic awareness and make people realize that "the ways of this world / are the ways of Heaven."[87]

In the spring of 1959, Stanford researcher Gregory Bateson invited Ginsberg to participate in LSD experiments being conducted at the Mental Research Institute in Palo Alto, California. Ginsberg became excited about the mystical possibilities of the hallucinogenic, not necessarily about its effects on the creative process but about its political ramifications. While interacting with the researchers, he began to adopt their vocabulary. As his language became more psychoanalytic, Ginsberg continued experimenting with chemical substances, including laughing gas, believing them to be the key to revealing the subconscious of America and to experiencing the secret of correspondence. More than ever, he believed that America was in need of a psychological exorcism:

America is schizophrenic . . .
the subconscience of US filled with poison gas,
　　secret bombs, nerve electricity, angeless
　　noises, buzzing of death
The populace afraid to know afraid to find out
　　the secret.[88]

In 1960 Ginsberg continued to follow in Burroughs's analytic footsteps and conducted his own search for the yage vine in South America. Later that year he met Timothy Leary, a Harvard University researcher who was experimenting with the ritualistic aspects of hallucinogens. The friendship buoyed Ginsberg about the political possibilities of psilocybin. After their first experimental session together, they "started planning the psychedelic revolution." Ginsberg took a stash of "mushroom pills" from Leary's Boston home and began distributing them to his friends and fellow artists, including Burroughs and Kerouac as well as Charles Olson, Robert Lowell, Thelonius Monk, and Dizzy Gillespie.[89]

In the midst of his drug experiments, Ginsberg continued to position himself as a social critic and prophet of doom ("I am the Defense Early Warning Radar System / I see nothing but bombs"). He also viewed himself as a conduit of a rediscovered set of social norms and cultural values ("The day of the publication of the true literature of the America body will be day of Revolution"). When Ginsberg claimed "Poet is Priest" in "Death to Van Gogh's Ear," he was proclaiming his affinity to the romantic tradition of expressing an essential, spiritual self.[90] By 1959 he had "founded the Church of Poetry," positioning himself as a spokesperson for aesthetic and spiritual but not necessarily institutional discovery.[91] "I long for a Yes of Harmony to penetrate / to every corner of the universe" wrote Ginsberg in "Lysergic Acid" (1959), a paean to psychedelica. "A Yes there Is . . . a Yes I Am . . . a Yes You Are . . . a We."[92] In order for America to affirm this "we" and "discover itself," Ginsberg prescribed drug-induced introspection in order to promote a national "nervous breakdown":

> To get America into a situation and sense of understanding that would actually provide peace would be a complete change of values—I'm not talking moral or political values—those are just ideas—but a change of inward understanding of themselves on the part of masses of individuals—a sort of breakdown of our habit of identifying ourselves with property, external property, and realization that value is inside and needs no excuses or properties to prove it—and this would amount to a series of personal changes as violent as a nervous breakdown.[93]

The solution of psychological violence harkened back to Ginsberg's theorizing about the exorcistic qualities of confessional poetry. In that sense, drugs reaffirmed Ginsberg's view of art as a vehicle for social change and a way to grasp the macrocosm superstructure of this world. Yet Ginsberg's Spenglerian romanticism, his promotion of hallucinogenics, and his psychological vocabulary undermined, to a certain degree, the efficiency of his political engagement. As his politics became more and more personal, his poetry became more inner-directed and lacked the mythic resonance of "Howl" or "America."

Ginsberg continued to don the mantle of bearded and psychedelic prophet and American Jeremiah well into the 1960s. As the most visible artist in the political campaigns of the New Left, his legacy of the 1950s directly influenced much of the strategy that radicals of the 1960s would come to employ. In testimony before a Senate Judiciary Subcommittee in 1966, Ginsberg advocated LSD in terms of participatory democracy. "I am taking the word from our prophet, Walt Whitman," said Ginsberg, who was attired in a new Brooks Brothers suit for the occasion. "This is the tradition of the Founding Fathers, this is the true myth of America, this is the prophecy of our most loved thinkers—Thoreau, Emerson, and Whitman. That each man is a great universe in himself, this is the great value of America that we call freedom."[94] The romantic aspect that he imparted to the 1960s' counterculture was as much Spengler as it was Whitman. In assuming a Spenglerian version of correspondence and the implicit notion that individuals could dictate the terms of their environment, Ginsberg continued to put forth a version of Spengler's aesthetic view of history, reducing his historical experiences to products akin to works of art.[95] As he had always done, Ginsberg sought to induce political change through an appeal to the individual imagination, to "create as divine a world as we can imagine." He had written optimistically of that process in 1954: "Fortunately art is a community effort—a small but select community living in a spiritualized world endeavoring to interpret the wars."[96] When that political stance was adopted by ideologues of the 1960s, however, it seemed to have lost authority, religious grounding, and the grassroots authenticity that Ginsberg had brought to such pronouncements.

Ginsberg cannot be faulted for the terms of his appropriation, but the cultural politics of the New Left, particularly as practiced by the disaffected, white, middle-class youths of Students for a Democratic Society, had a current of romantic anti-intellectualism that in many ways undermined the agenda to eliminate racism and institutional imperialism. In its struggle for radical democracy, the New Left employed a strict dualism betwen artifice and nature.[97] In representing Ginsberg's political spirituality as a spiritualized politics something was lost. The New Left's symbolization of political and economic realities, as well as the individualistic thrust of its dissent during these halcyon (and televised) days of protest, prevented members from constructing an effective plan of reform or engaging in a practical discussion of pressing social problems. Burdened by the anonymous ghost of Spengler's mythic framework, radicals of the 1960s perceived themselves in an artistic vein, engaging in a symbolic struggle for their own souls as well as America's. Such emphasis on subjectivity did not allow them to engage the discourse of capitalism and materialism on its own terms. The Faustian death cloud of which Ginsberg spoke in 1944 had become the faceless monolith of the military-industrial complex. In translation, the institutionalization of Spengler's "morphology of history" became devoid of any historical referent save for a vague and somewhat vulgar Marxism.

Ginsberg had long before intuited the pitfalls associated with the transition from religion to politics. Even before he assumed the political spotlight, he had slowly begun to distance himself from the apocalyptic tirades gleaned from Spengler. Maintaining a measured optimism as well as a sense of irony about his earlier reading of *Decline of the West,* Ginsberg was still impatient with America. In a 1957 journal entry, for example, he regretted that America's cowboys had not yet read Spengler and admitted that the nation's cultural promise had yet to be fulfilled.[98] The jeremiadic formula was still operative. Similarly, in 1960 Ginsberg acknowledged that "we missed the boat to the New World" and asked, "The ships are leaving for the moon, / Have we anything to export to the universe / but a few dead prophets and a basketful of cranky Formulae for Electricity?"[99]

Despite his increasing distance from an earnest apocalypticism (later referring to it as "Apocalypse Rock, End of History Rag"), it still carried rhetorical weight, just as it had done for seventeenth-century Puritan divines.[100] Even as Ginsberg became more self-deprecating, he did not concede defeat or relinquish faith in precipitating a cultural transformation. Instead, he invoked his muse and asserted a sense of comedy and optimism despite increased resistance to Beat proselytizing:

Spengler makes sense in 1000 years
in the Harz Mts., retired he listened to Beethoven Deaf quartets
I could have stretched out the oomph at least or wobbled the cycle—But the
   Police took over the poetry & music cafes and charged Admission . . .
Vain tho my activity, I did strike a chord—
I banged my own bell, and a thousand alarm clocks began ringing
but that's not enuf to wake the Expanding Population,
all they want to do is fuck & play with Chevrolets, gibber in the Supermarket
   over Frozen lobstertails.[101]

It was precisely Ginsberg's humor and playfulness in the face of such absurdity that confirmed his creativity and enduring hope. Never relinquishing the Spenglerian lessons of his youth, he did not ignore the role of the human confrontation with nature and the sphere of the ordinary. He reveled in the absurdity of the everyday, ever refusing to reduce experience to the abstract realm of ideas. Through his artistic output and insistence on the social and religious value of that art, a more mature Ginsberg continued to skewer the pretensions of those who would deny the religious seriousness of play. His poetry still pushed readers to account for the symbolic dimensions of their experiences, to qualify them in terms of culture in order to eventually see beyond "the narcotic tobacco haze of capitalism."[102]

Demythology

More than a half-century after their initial collaboration, the legacy of the Beats continues to be defined in binary terms. Ginsberg, Kerouac, and Burroughs, even more so than their individual works, still evoke derision as well as hagiography. Neo-reactionary accounts from the Left view the Beats' self-promotion during the late 1950s and early 1960s as willful acts of commodification—"breaking rules, pissing off the suits, shocking the bean counters." They differ from the initial wave of tirades only in what cultural turf they are defending.[103] A Whitney Museum exhibit entitled "Beat Culture and the New America: 1950–1965" (1995), a Web-site entitled *Literary Kicks,* and *The* Rolling Stone *Book of the Beats* (1999) all indicate that hagiography is growing more common, yet such celebrations often obscure as much as they illuminate. They cast a wide net and include almost anyone who had something critical to say about Eisenhower's America under the category of "Beat." Hagiography can sometimes be an unintended act of slander and diminish that which it chooses to canonize. Ironically, just as the Beats engaged their America in terms of myth, the American public, detractors as well as acolytes, have returned the favor. That is not to say that the Beats, having been assumed into the pantheon of popular culture, are woefully misunderstood. It is to say, however, that they have only been understood. Writing from France on the eve of the Beat phenomenon in America, Roland Barthes described such an ambiguous form of knowledge: "Myth hides nothing and flaunts nothing: it distorts; myth is neither a lie nor a confession: it is an inflexion."[104]

In this volume I have attempted to turn the distortion against itself and demythologize the origins of the Beat movement by transforming the "natural" facts about the Beats back into history. Ironically, doing so has required entering the mythic world the Beats fashioned. Ginsberg, Kerouac, and Burroughs shared a complex religious vision informed by Oswald Spengler's *The Decline of the West.* Beginning in 1944, Spengler's ethereal hand was an integral part of their collaborative efforts to envision an America of mythic proportions and "total metaphor." Northrop Frye once argued that myth "operates at the top level of human desire" and is "apocalyptic in the sense of that word already explained, a world of total metaphor, in which everything is potentially identical with everything else, as though it were all inside a single body."[105] The Beats' America was a revelation, an aesthetic creation rising from the depths of their desires and given shape by their collective imaginations. It was an America of their own invention yet one that demanded proper belief and action during and after the fact. Together, the Beats began to develop this new way to live, think, and write in their New York City apartment during the mid–1940s. They framed both ontological questions and cultural concerns in the same Spenglerian language, supplementing this religious idiom with everything from the theories of Wilhelm Reich and Alfred Korzybski to drug experiences, their religious backgrounds, and the rhythms of bebop. Despite their differences, they would soon establish a vision of literature that encompassed not only the salvation of the individual artist but also that of American culture. The vision was expressed in the content of their most controversial works of the 1950s and in the way they composed them. Although it may be too much to say that the Beats embodied a systematic religious program, their lives and works were pieces of a religious whole "all inside a single body." Like the self and the America they envisioned, that whole could never be fully and completely realized within the confines of the real.

The Beat's disdain for institutional structure limited their cultural program to a nebulous outburst of religiosity that did not coherently endure past the 1960s. Although failing to institute "religions of perception" in the legislature, they did have profound influence in shaping not only the religious climate of the 1960s but also the expansion of religious strategies into other areas of American culture, specifically the symbolic, individualistic politics of the New Left and the stylized alienation of youth culture. The Beats were precursors of the institutional changes that came about during the 1960s. They helped usher in a new public religiosity, redefining the notions of American exceptionalism and creating new possibilities for what it meant to be an American. Because of the popular media and increased sensationalism, their legacy managed to "stop the hoax" and alter the story Americans continually told themselves about themselves. The Beats managed to cause many Americans to reevaluate their everyday lives and religious orientations. The world was changing rapidly, and the Beats held out a viable model of belief and action. Although not many took up their lifestyle, Burroughs, Kerouac, and Ginsberg remained a highly visible standard of religious dissent.

The most "effective" religious legacy of the Beats may be that created for them in and by popular imagination. They have become commodities and acquired phantom objectivity, even in death.[106] Yet another revival of Beat sensibility in popular culture occurred during the 1990s: eulogies for Herbert Huncke, Ginsberg, and Burroughs; Gap advertising featuring a smiling, khaki-wearing Jack Kerouac; a spate of biographies, memoirs, and recordings (Ginsberg's *Holy Soul Jelly Roll, The Best of William Burroughs,* and a Kerouac tribute CD, *Kerouac—kicks joy darkness* in 1997); a revival of spoken-word poetry and slam competitions; highbrow literary celebrations at the Ninety-second Street Y in New York City; academic studies and conferences; documentaries and film chronicles such as David Cronenberg's *Naked Lunch,* Jerry Aronson's *The Life and Times of Allen Ginsberg,* and Chuck Workman's mesmerizing documentary *The Source;* a host of Web-sites dedicated to any number of Beat-related items; and last but not least, a "Beat Generation Catalog." Enveloped in the theatrics of contemporary cultural trends, their legacy remains a potent yet somewhat ambiguous force in contemporary culture.

Given such rampant commercialization, what remains of the Beats' religious vision? As Walter Benjamin once noted, fashions of today, even commodified and costumed images of the past, remain politically vital because "the confrontation with the fashions of the previous generations is a matter of far greater importance than we ordinarily suppose."[107] As the Beats become a permanent fixture in popular culture, the religious energy they once generated is still present, albeit in a different form than it possessed. When the past desire for apocalypse meets its present manifestation the Beats acquire something even more than objectivity. They begin to speak in our voices and become vehicles for our utopian wishes. In that sense, they have become ciphers for the religious desires of others and yearnings for a world elsewhere in which revolution is completely severed from any sense of historical contingency. Popular culture is a symbol factory, what Greil Marcus, one of Benjamin's most astute readers, calls "a product-show, a spectacle, a channeling of suppressed wishes into marketable form" as well as an "impulse—a production of suppressed wishes that once released can call their own tune."[108]

Despite efforts by others to "call the tune" of the Beats' legacy, the nature of their message—to resist that which is given you and create a world as divine as possible out of everyday materials—continues to resonate. Their influence is anything but direct, yet embedded in Burroughs's "word horde," Kerouac's "spontaneous bop prosody," and Ginsberg's prophetic wails are seeds of change. Due, in part, to the incoherent dissemination of their ideas via the media, the Beats were both an index and shapers of the 1960s. Because that dissemination was always incomplete, they remain so. Protestant, Catholic, and Jew represent a significant nexus between the postwar "turn to religion" and the continuing evolution of America's religious pluralism, an evolution accompanied by weakening public faith, expanding moral attitudes, and an emphasis on spiritual life. As this evolution continues, America may once again become, in Kerouac's words, "a permissible dream."[109]

notes

Introduction

1. DeLillo, *Underworld*, 76.

2. "You and the Atomic Bomb," New York State Civil Defense Commission, 1951, cited in Jonas and Nissenson, *Going, Going, Gone*, 38.

3. Quoted in Schumacher, *Dharma Lion*, 141.

4. Recently, scholars have turned their attention to "Beat" poets of the 1950s and 1960s—particularly minority and women writers such as Ted Joans, Joyce Johnson, and Hettie Jones, among others. See, for example, *Women of the Beat: The Writers, Artists, and Muses at the Heart of a Revolution* (1996), edited by Brenda Knight, and *A Different Beat: Writings by Women of the Beat Generation* (1997), edited by Richard Peabody. Unlike some more general treatments, this study is primarily concerned with the evolution of a particular historical moment and not the loosely organized movement to which this moment gave rise. Mine is a specific use of the term *Beat*. I do not wish to deny the canonicity of Joans, Johnson, or Jones, or even those writers such as Gregory Corso and John Clellon Holmes associated with the core contributors to the "new vision." On the contrary, I believe it does disservice to those on the periphery of the "libertine circle" when their work is immediately contextualized in terms of their more famous friends.

5. "You and the Atomic Bomb," New York State Civil Defense Commission, 1951, cited in Jonas and Nissenson, *Going, Going, Gone*, 38.

6. Kerouac, *The Town and the City*, 417.

7. Victor Turner has described this ideal state of bonding outside the purview of social institutions as *communitas*, a charged moment of communal interaction that blends "lowliness and sacredness . . . homogeneity and comradeship." *Ritual Process*, 96–97.

8. Ginsberg, "Terms in Which I Think of Reality," 50; Kerouac, *Visions of Cody*, 17–18; Harris, ed., *Letters of William S. Burroughs*, 70. This paranoid fantasy was first brought to Burroughs's attention by his wife, Joan Vollmer. He became "convinced . . . that her [atomic] kick contained a solid core of reality." For reference to this "atomic disease," see Kerouac, *The Town and the City*, 375.

9. Long, "Human Centers," 77.

10. Feather, *The Book of Jazz*, 93. Bebop emerged in New York City in the early 1940s

among musicians such as Charlie Parker, Dizzy Gillespie, Kenny Clarke, and Thelonius Monk. As Frank Tirro notes, the word *bebop* originated in the practice of singing or vocalizing instrumental melodic lines with nonsense syllables (266). Consequently, bebop phrases were characterized by abrupt endings that in turn allowed for more radical innovations. Implicit in this new style, whose standard procedure was to perform without written music, was a critique of the written arrangements of the big band orchestras of Glenn Miller, Benny Goodman, and Tommy Dorsey among others. Richard Wang's comparison of swing and bebop resonates with how I am distinguishing between stabilizing and destabilizing modes of religion. "A comparison of the two styles," writes Wang, reveals that "swing phrases are more uniform in length, more symmetrical in shape, and more congruent with the harmonic phrases that those of bebop; swing rhythm patterns are less varied, more even-flowing, and less disrupted by shifting accents than those of bebop; bebop, on the other hand, is more complex, full of greater contrasts, has more rhythmic subtilties, and makes a greater and more expressive use of dissonance" (quoted in Tirro, *Jazz,* 268).

11. Geertz, "Religion as a Cultural System," 123.

12. Kerouac, *On the Road,* 254.

13. Geertz, *Islam Observed,* 2.

14. Ginsberg, "A Mad Gleam," 16.

15. See Geertz's definition of religion in "Religion as a Cultural System," 90.

16. Benjamin, "Imagination," 280–82; Harris, *The Letters of William S. Burroughs,* 397.

17. Burke, *The Rhetoric of Religion,* vi; Kerouac, *The Subterraneans,* 52; Langer, *Philosophy in a New Key,* 41. I am also indebted to Giles Gunn for this insight into religion and language.

18. Long, "Conquest and Cultural Contact in the New World," 108.

19. Taussig, "Transgression," 352.

20. Ginsberg, "A Blake Experience," 123.

21. Geertz, "Religion as a Cultural System," 89–90, 112.

22. Spengler, *Form and Actuality* and *Perspectives of World-History.*

23. Spengler, *Form and Actuality,* 3.

24. Kerouac, *On the Road,* 287.

25. For the most part, Spengler has been invoked in passing or else used as an interpretive window into a particular aspect of Beat literature. See, for example, Robert Holton's discussion of Kerouac's racial discourse in "Kerouac among the Fellahin." The only exception to the critical neglect of Spengler in relation to the Beats is James T. Jones, *A Map of* Mexico City Blues. Although Jones focuses solely on Kerouac's epic poem *Mexico City Blues,* he has been the only scholar so far to discern Spengler's influence in a meaningful way. His reliance on Spengler as a critical wedge is evidence of his deep familiarity with the life and work of Kerouac and distinguishes his study from the numerous biographies and critical assessments that treat *The Decline of the West* in a perfunctory and cursory manner.

26. Spengler, *Form and Actuality,* xiv.

27. Ibid., 5.

28. Ahlstrom, *A Religious History*, 483.

29. Emerson, "The Poet," 335.

30. Petros, interview with Allen Ginsberg.

31. Tytell, *Naked Angels*, 3.

32. Ibid., 4.

33. McClure, *Scratching the Beat Surface.*

34. Rumaker, "Allen Ginsberg's 'Howl'," 38.

35. Merrill, *Allen Ginsberg*, 106.

36. Prothero, "On the Holy Road."

37. Holmes, "This Is the Beat Generation."

38. Burroughs, *Letters of William S. Burroughs*, 145.

39. Ginsberg, "Howl," 132.

40. Examples include Watson, *The Birth of the Beat Generation;* Turner, *Jack Kerouac;* Charters, ed., *Portable Beat Reader;* Mahoney, "Back in Black"; George-Warren, ed., *The* Rolling Stone *Book of the Beats;* and Workman, *The Source.*

41. Sisk, "Beatniks and Tradition."

42. Davidson, *San Francisco Renaissance*, 28–29; Thoreau, *Walden*, 213

43. See, for example, O'Neil, "The Only Rebellion Around," quoted in Davidson, *San Francisco Renaissance*, 61.

44. Rexroth, "Disengagement"; see also Mailer, "White Negro."

45. Ginsberg, "To John Hollander," 175. "Lame" sociological interpretations include Hollander, "Review of *Howl and Other Poems*," and Podhoretz, "A Howl of Protest."

46. Podhoretz, "The Know-Nothing Bohemians."

47. O'Neil, "The Only Rebellion Around," 114–15.

48. Bercovitch, *American Jeremiad*, 204; see also Bercovitch, *The Rites of Assent.*

49. Marcus, "The Bob McFadden Experience"; Will, "The Ginsberg Commodity." Marcus uses the Beats' ambitions against them and reduces their literature and lives to self-parodies of revolutionary change. "They wanted to be larger than life," he writes. "They wanted fame. They wanted everyone to be like them—which is not the same as wanting to change the world." The Beats were, in Marcus's words, "about mystification, myth-making, and making it" ("The Bob McFadden Experience," 112). Truth be told, religion and the desire for popular success are not mutually exclusive categories. The Beats did, in fact, want to change the world. Specifically, they wanted to change how they experienced the world. The literary production of their small community not only reflected an intense concern with inner spirituality and metaphysical realities but also with social realities. In their literature, the Beats demanded both self-reflection and reader engagement. Consequently, their literature acted as a meditative vehicle for themselves as well as a conduit for readers to enter into a sacred, communal reality. Because their myth-making concerned not only themselves but also the whole of America, they did not want "everyone to be like them" so much as they wanted everyone to view America from the same mythic perspective.

50. Quoted in Schumacher, *Dharma Lion*, 273.

51. Kerouac, *On the Road,* 245.

52. Prothero, "On the Holy Road," 205.

53. McLoughlin, "Introduction," x.

54. Hudnut-Beumler, *Looking for God,* 1. Stephen J. Whitefield notes that in 1910 and 1920 church membership in the United States had remained constant at 43 percent of the population. By 1940 it had risen to 49 percent, then 55 percent by 1950, 62 percent by 1956, and 69 percent by 1960. Cited in *The Culture of the Cold War,* 83, 87.

55. For a treatment of this "underground" religious economy, see Ellwood, *The Fifties Spiritual Marketplace.*

56. Durkheim, *Elementary Forms of Religious Life,* 425.

57. Herberg, *Protestant, Catholic, Jew.*

58. Ahlstrom, *A Religious History,* 8, 12, 1079–96. See also Bercovitch, *American Jeremiad* and *Rites of Assent.*

59. Ellwood, *The Fifties Spiritual Marketplace,* 160–71.

60. van der Leeuw, *Religion in Essence and Manifestation,* 609. As van der Leeuw writes, "Every religion is perpetually *reformanda*—to be reformed—although it is always already reformed—*reformata*—also. The dynamic of life compels religion continually to change its form; while it is living it is being reformed; and it is impossible to connect the occurrence of reformations merely with certain definite conflicts" (613).

61. Robinson, *American Apocalypses,* xi. I am also indebted to Richard Hecht for this insight.

62. Kerouac, *Visions of Cody,* 371.

63. Frye, *Anatomy of Criticism,* 136.

64. The Beats sought to unmake the present world in terms of myth and to refashion a "new mythology" in accordance with their personalities and emotional requirements. Regrettably, their social ideal patronized African Americans and women. In part because of a Spenglerian infrastructure, much Beat literature depicts minorities as an enduring source of "primitive" values whose identities remain stable and static. Similarly, women, if mentioned at all, function primarily to support white male activity and development.

65. Burroughs, *Naked Lunch,* 20, 195.

66. Because of the Beats' Spenglerian valence, their wish to recover an "authentic," American self became a commitment to social engagement. As they understood *Decline,* Spengler outlined not only the self to be attained but also the America. Paul Breslin (*The Psycho-Political Muse*) and Daniel Belgrad (*Culture of Spontaneity*) have patiently explored the correspondence between the Beats' emphases on psychological liberation and social change. Both studies however, rely too much on interpretive models grounded in depth psychology and ignore the Spenglerian nexus that bound the Beats' personal and social concerns. According to the Beats' Spenglerian assumption, the problems of America were also visited upon themselves. Consequently, the Beats used Spengler to diagnose both America and self as having repressed their true natures and, furthermore, to prescribe a program of healing for

both. From the beginning of the Beats' partnership, the personal was always political, the political always religious. Belgrad's volume is the more exhaustive and accessible of the two. Although Belgrad is concerned with the entire spectrum of the postwar avant-garde, his discussion of the Beats contains a number of insights that are fundamentally correct and which I have attempted to contextualize throughout this study.

67. Hagedorn, *The Bomb That Fell on America*, 32.

68. Ibid., 7, jacket.

69. Ginsberg, "Two Sonnets," 5.

70. Danforth, "A Brief Recognition," 199.

71. See Miller, "Errand into the Wilderness." Bercovitch's assessment of the Puritan jeremiad recasts Perry Miller's classic essay "Errand into the Wilderness," itself part of Miller's ongoing revisionary project that situated the Puritans at the center of America's intellectual and cultural heritage. Although both Miller and Bercovitch agree that the defining characteristic of the jeremiad is its ambiguity, they differ in the way they understand how the competing impulses within the jeremiad operate. Miller claims that the jeremiad, an apparent call for restoration, works against its conservative surface by encouraging progressive action. According to Miller, "The exhortation to a reformation which never materializes serves as a token payment upon the obligation, and so liberates its debtors" (9). He suggests that it was under the guise of the jeremiad, "this mounting wail of sinfulness, this incessant and never successful cry for repentance, the Puritans launched themselves upon the process of Americanization" (9). This liberation of conscience resulted in changes, both in consciousness and history: "adaptations to environment, expansion of the frontier, mansions constructed, commercial adventures undertaken" (9). These changes, in turn, guaranteed the primacy of experience as both continuing source of innovation and redefinition of cultural norms. In the end, Miller identified the jeremiad as the Puritan literary form that allowed them to assume the roles of existential heroes and sole creators of America as both idea and place, utopian ideal and pragmatic space.

While Miller viewed the jeremiad as liberating rehearsals of declension and thus precipitating a certain type of rugged individualism, Bercovitch sees the jeremiad as initiating a different sort of Americanization. The literary form of the jeremiad involves "use of ambiguity," but, as opposed to Miller's existentialist reading, Bercovitch writes that this ambiguity "is not divisive but progressive—or more accurately, progressive because it denies divisiveness—and which is therefore impervious to the reversals of history, since the very meaning of progress is inherent in the rhetoric itself" (*American Jeremiad* 17). For Bercovitch, the primary effect of the jeremiad was an unreflective consensus of ideas, emotions, and social practice. It bound Americans together not in light of a shared quest for individuation nor in how they collectively missed opportunities to change either themselves or their country for the better, but in their collective inability even to notice the opportunities they were missing. In other words, the jeremiad was the source of a Puritan version of middle-class "false consciousness."

72. Turner, "Social Dramas," 161, 165.

73. Kerouac, *On the Road*, 133–34.

74. Spengler, *Form and Actuality*, 5; Kerouac, *On the Road*, 132, 113, 204.

75. White, *Content of the Form*, 81.

76. James, "What Pragmatism Means," 146.

77. Passaro, "The Forgotten Killer," 71.

78. Deleuze and Guattari are only partially correct and overly pessimistic when they write that Kerouac and Ginsberg are "men who know how to leave, to scramble the codes, to cause flows to circulate, to traverse the desert of the body without organs. They overcome a limit, they shatter a wall, the capitalist barrier. And of course, they fail to complete the process, they never cease failing to do so." *Anti-Oedipus*, 132–33.

79. Kerouac, *Visions of Cody*, 87.

Chapter 1: Anxiety and Influence in Postwar America

1. All references to "America" taken from recorded composition of "America," 18 March 1956.

2. Ginsberg, *Journals Mid-Fifties*, 78, quoted in Miles, *Allen Ginsberg*, 210.

3. Kerouac, *Vanity of Duluoz*, 211, quoted in Morgan, *Literary Outlaw*, 91.

4. Nicosia, *Memory Babe*, 276. As Spengler writes, "Each Culture possesses its own standards, the validity of which begins and ends with it. There is no general morale of humanity." *Form and Actuality*, 345; see also Kerouac, *Visions of Cody*, 257.

5. Ginsberg, *Howl*, 23.

6. Campbell, *Hero with a Thousand Faces*, 389; Howe, "Religion and the Intellectuals," 472; Whyte, *The Organization Man*, 5, 14.

7. Spengler derived his four stages of culture from Goethe's "four epochs of the human spirit," what he called the ages of poetry, theology, philosophy, and prose. Heller, *The Disinherited Mind*, 91. While Goethe's influence (as well as that of Leo Frobenius) accounts for Spengler's apparent cyclicism, Northrop Frye argues that Spengler's cyclical view of history is only an illusion because he does not specifically propose a superorganic mechanism. That may be literally true, but Spengler's language is sufficiently vague as to find easy justification for such a supreme order of existence. Frye makes this point to counter Spengler's appropriation by Yeats and Pound, begging the question of why readers found a superorganic principle despite its supposed absence. Frye, "Spengler Revisited," 185–86.

8. Spengler, *Form and Actuality*, 31.

9. Ibid., 424, 31.

10. For discussion of classification of cultural formations and modes of production see Williams, *Sociology of Culture*, 62–70.

11. Stackelberg, *Idealism Debased*, 12–13; also see Laqueur, *Young Germany*. Given the fact that Herder declared that every nation was an individual in a universal and all-encompassing harmony, the path between Herder's romantic nationalism and Nazism was anything but direct.

12. Woods, *Conservative Revolution,* 3; Stern, *Politics of Cultural Despair,* xxix.

13. Herman, *Idea of Decline,* 241–45; Stackelberg, *Idealism Debased,* 153; Stern, *Politics of Cultural Despair,* 238–39.

14. Spengler, *Perspectives of World-History,* 361, 413.

15. Quoted in Woods, *Conservative Revolution,* 30.

16. Ominously, the Nazis appropriated such rhetoric to justify their politics of domination. Assertions that "socialism means power, power, and yet again power" were distilled to form a politically expedient and abstract version of Spengler's thesis (Herman, *Idea of Decline,* 248). Testifying to the interpretive fluidity of Spengler's text, the Nazis read him as the historical validation of their lust for power. Before his death in May of 1936, Spengler renounced such appropriation and distanced himself from the Nazis.

17. Benjamin, "Theories of German Fascism," 315–16.

18. Spengler, *Form and Actuality,* 5, emphasis in the original; Fischer, *History and Prophecy,* 8.

19. Laqueur, *Young Germany,* 116.

20. Ellwood, *Mysticism and Religion,* 58.

21. Hughes, *Oswald Spengler,* 60.

22. Spengler, *Form and Actuality,* 22; Frye, "Spengler Revisited," 180 (quotation); Spengler, *Perspectives of World-History,* 174.

23. Spengler, *Form and Actuality,* 3.

24. Ibid., 3.

25. Ibid., 343, emphasis in the original.

26. Quoted in Watt, *Myths of Modern Individualism,* 196, 193.

27. Spengler, *Form and Actuality,* 354; Spengler, *Perspectives of World-History,* 292.

28. Spengler, *Perspectives of World-History,* 504, emphasis in the original.

29. Hughes, *Oswald Spengler,* 97.

30. Kazin, *On Native Grounds,* 270.

31. Pound quoted in Stromberg, *After Everything,* 1; Campbell quoted in Larsen and Larsen, *A Fire in the Mind,* 214.

32. Frye, "Spengler Revisited," 191. Ernst Cassirer, who emigrated to the United States in 1941, sensed this mimetic quality of *Decline.* "Spengler's book," wrote Cassirer, "was, as a matter of fact, an astrology of history—the work of a diviner who unfolded his somber apocalyptic visions." *Myth of the State,* 290.

33. Quoted in May, *Homeward Bound,* 90.

34. Hughes, *Oswald Spengler,* 96.

35. Aaron, *Writers on the Left,* 139.

36. Dakin, "American Communiqué," 333, 350, 15. In 1957 Max Lerner offered a similar, albeit more discerning, assessment of Spengler. "I do not deny a degree of force in Spengler's contention that inner homologous structures may be 'contemporary,' even when they are far removed in time and place," he wrote. "Yet I must reassert that America is not Rome but itself." Lerner, *America as a Civilization,* 936.

37. Luce, *American Century,* 37–38.

38. Luce "Ethical Problems," 2–3, 13.

39. Carpenter, *Revive Us Again,* 177–78.

40. Luce "Ethical Problems," 11, 14–15. Luce issues the challenge to acquire such "moral capital" as the most important in "American Life." Without a hint of irony, he claims, "It is not the poverty which is now the great challenge but the wealth. Not the weakness but the power. Not the illiteracy but the literacy. Not the disease, but the health. Not the back-breaking toil, but the play and the pleasure. Not the squalor but the lights. These are the great challenges—these American triumphs and achievements" (15).

41. Quoted in Caute, *The Great Fear,* 15.

42. May, *Homeward Bound,* 104–6; Jonas and Nissenson, *Going, Going, Gone,* 39.

43. Graham, *Revival,* 71, quoted in Whitefield, *Culture of the Cold War,* 81, 77.

44. Graham, *Revival,* 70.

45. Quoted in Ellwood, *The Fifties Spiritual Marketplace,* 48.

46. For an overview of Fulton Sheen, see Williams, "Fulton J. Sheen."

47. Quoted in Marty, *Modern American Religion,* 91.

48. McLoughlin "Introduction," ix; Howe, "Religion and the Intellectuals."

49. For an in-depth discussion of Will Herberg's dual role as apologist for the "American Way of Life" and his roots as a leading theorist of the Communist Party in the 1920s, see Nelson, *Culture of Confidence.*

50. Herberg, *Protestant, Catholic, Jew,* 260.

51. Riesman, Glazer, and Denny, *The Lonely Crowd,* 19–24. Despite popular misinterpretations, Riesman did not see the social conformity resulting from "other-directedness" as an inherent problem, for he took conformity as a given need of every society. What Riesman did see as the problem of his age was that this predominant psychological disposition did not enforce social norms from within. A society interested in conforming its members to itself had taken over that fundamental task. Peers and mass media had replaced Americans' "internal gyroscope" with subservience to public opinion. His solution was to eliminate the social model of personalism, replacing it with the "autonomous" individual who maintained a certain amount of free will while simultaneously participating in an organic and—in Riesman's view—traditional sense of American nationalism. Riesman, *The Lonely Crowd,* 304–7; Hudnut-Beumler, *Looking for God in the Suburbs,* 87–91; Nelson, *Culture of Confidence,* 207–8.

52. Mills, *White Collar,* xvi, xv.

53. Kerouac, *Visions of Cody,* 31; Clark, *Jack Kerouac,* 103. Kerouac and Mills appear to have been on the same page in 1951, but their political sensibilities would diverge radically by the end of the decade. As Kerouac drifted farther and farther to the political right, Mills went in the opposite direction. His "Pagan Sermon to the Christian Clergy" (1958) attacked both the propagandist nature of civil religion and the political fear-mongering of anticommunism. He accused the nation's religious leadership of accommodating themselves and their religions to political expediency—what he called the "crackpot metaphysics of militarism" (199). He proclaimed the

"moral death of religion in North America" and castigated those who used religious ideas for legitimating economic and military agendas (200). Mills did not call for a revival of faith but rather called for a different sort of awakening: a reevaluation of the complicity of American religion in creating a morally reprehensible nationalism. His enemy was not a demonized other but the complacency of religious leaders in handling this crisis. "As a social and as a personal force," wrote Mills, "religion has become a dependent variable. It does not originate; it reacts. It does not denounce; it adapts. It does not set forth new models of conduct and sensibility; it imitates . . . religion has generally become part of the false consciousness of the world and the self" (200). For Mills, the universalization of religion under a patriotic banner had resulted in an alarming misappropriation of religious ideas for nonreligious, self-serving, even totalitarian ends. Mills, "Pagan Sermon."

54. Niebuhr, *Moral Man and Immoral Society,* xii.

55. Niebuhr, *Irony of American History.*

56. For historical perspective on this "age of anxiety," see Susman, "Did Success Spoil the United States?"

57. Weaver, "Original Simplicities and Present Complexities," 232.

58. Hutchison, *The Modernist Impulse,* 289; Ahlstrom, *A Religious History,* 935.

59. Kerouac, *Vanity of Duluoz,* 211.

60. In a 1944 journal entry headed "Burroughs Memorabilia," Ginsberg noted "Procedure—Needle; alcohol" and "Reading." In addition to Spengler's *Decline of the West,* the list includes "parlor tricks—card tricks—formulas," "Egyptian grammar," "hypnoanalytic study," William Blake, Arthur Rimbaud, and Melville's *Moby-Dick.* Journal entry, 1944, Allen Ginsberg Papers, 1937–1994, Stanford University, Palo Alto, Calif.

61. Kerouac, *Vanity of Duluoz,* 208; Ginsberg, "Prose Contribution," 137.

62. Morgan, *Literary Outlaw,* 83, 87.

63. Schumacher, *Dharma Lion,* 11–12, 21.

64. Ibid., 23, 28.

65. Kerouac, "My Generation, My World," 228; Nicosia, *Memory Babe,* 66. At Horace Mann, Kerouac had written a music column for the school newspaper in which he often spoke of his love for Harlem jazz and the improvisational dynamic in which the soloist expressed himself.

66. Kerouac, "Beauty as a Lasting Truth," 226–27.

67. Fisher. *The Catholic Counterculture,* 207.

68. Sorrell, "Sentinelle Affair," 72.

69. Nicosia, *Memory Babe,* 59.

70. Kerouac, *Selected Letters,* 37. In the same letter to a friend, Kerouac states that the politicized America of ideological rhetoric must be included if one hopes to enjoy commercial success. With an air of regretful determination he writes, "Today's writers have to combine both Americas, if they choose of course to be in some sense timely. It is their choice, it is my choice for the time being—and I don't deny the reason: I would like, for a change, to have my stuff published. It has always seemed

to me a great injustice that the artists of the world are expected to produce, along with their 'great' works, the commodities for consumption which all non-artists are expected to produce." Ibid.

71. Kerouac, *Visions of Cody*, 260.

72. Spengler, *Form and Actuality*, 40–41; see also Kerouac's rephrasing of Spengler's invocation in *The Subterraneans*, 29.

73. Albanese, ed., *Spirituality of the American Transcendentalists*, 8, 21.

74. Ginsberg, "Metaphysics," 33.

75. Kerouac, *Town and the City*, 22.

76. Spengler elucidates this point by stating that "great Cultures are entities, primary or original, that arise out of the deepest foundations of spirituality, and that the peoples under the spell of a Culture are, alike in their inward form and in their whole manifestation, its products and not its authors. . . . The people of Athens is a symbol not less than the Doric temple, the Englishman not less than modern physics. . . . World-history is the history of the great Cultures, and peoples are but the symbolic forms and vessels in which the men of these Cultures fulfill their Destinies." *Perspectives of World-History*, 170.

77. Spengler, *Form and Actuality*, 106.

78. Ibid., 424.

79. Kerouac, *Selected Letters*, 107–8; Kerouac, *Doctor Sax*, 160; Ginsberg, *Journals: Early Fifties*, 34.

80. Spengler, *Form and Actuality*, 106, 209 (first quotation), 212 (second quotation); Spengler, *Perspectives of World-History*, 189 (third quotation).

81. See, for example, Kerouac, *Visions of Cody*, 386.

82. Ross, *No Respect*, 46.

83. In an illuminating article, Michael Davidson makes a similar point in terms of containment rhetoric and the ideological frame inhabited by a variety of postwar poets. See "From Margin to Mainstream."

84. Kerouac, *Visions of Cody*, 252.

85. Ginsberg, "Poetry, Violence, and the Trembling Lambs."

86. Ginsberg, "Death to Van Gogh's Ear" and "Howl."

87. Burroughs, "Word," 137, 159.

88. Burroughs, *Naked Lunch*, 122.

89. Burroughs, "Twilight's Last Gleamings."

90. In addition to the purely technological aspects, Spengler warned that the "scientific worlds" and philosophy of Europe were "superficial worlds, practical, soulless" and that life within them was "no longer to be lived as something self-evident— hardly a matter of consciousness, let alone choice." *Form and Actuality*, 353.

91. Burroughs, *Naked Lunch*, 23.

92. Quoted in *Seeds of the Sixties*, ed. Eyerman and Jamison, 14, 20.

93. Elaine Tyler May attests to the intrusion of a scientific paradigm into all aspects of postwar life: "The postwar years marked a heightening of the status of the professional. Armed with scientific techniques and presumably inhabiting a world above

popular passions, the experts had brought us into the atomic age. Physicists developed the bomb, strategists created the cold war, and scientific managers built the military-industrial complex. Science and technology seem to have invaded virtually every aspect of life, from the most public to the most private." "Explosive Issues," 155–56.

94. Ginsberg, Untitled.

95. Spengler, *Perspectives of World-History,* 97.

96. Kerouac, *Visions of Cody,* 260, quoted in Nicosia, *Memory Babe,* 275.

97. Kerouac, *Town and the City,* 369–70.

98. Spengler, *Perspectives of World-History,* 119.

99. Ginsberg, "An Exposition," 134–35.

100. Spengler, *Form and Actuality,* 159.

101. Interview with John Sampas, 15 Feb. 1999.

102. Kerouac, *Selected Letters,* 65–70.

103. Clark, *Jack Kerouac,* 56; Kerouac, *Town and the City,* 368, 360, 367. As Spengler writes, "The rootless city-mass that has replaced the People, the Culture-folk that was sprung from the soil and peasantlike even when it lived in towns." *Form and Actuality,* 359.

104. Kerouac, *Visions of Cody,* 393.

105. Kerouac, *Town and the City,* 69–72; see Spengler, *Perspectives of World-History,* 327.

106. Quoted in Nicosia, *Memory Babe,* 162.

107. Kerouac, *Town and the City,* 14–15, 11, 54.

108. Ibid., 138, 18, 121. In the novel, Panos is more a Cassandra than a Jeremiah. He was intensely sensitive, emotional, and "proud and noble in his poverty." He was also given to fits of melancholy and ecstasy and "was not of this world" (134–35).

109. Ibid., 210–11.

110. Ibid., 317.

111. Ibid., 3.

112. Ibid., 5. As Spengler notes in *Perspectives of World-History,* "The town, too, is a plantlike being, as far removed as a peasantry is from nomadism and the purely microcosmic. Hence the development of a high-form language is linked always to a landscape. Neither an art nor a religion can alter the site of its growth; only in the Civilization with its giant cities do we come again to despise and disengage ourselves from those roots" (90).

113. Kerouac, *Town and the City,* 3; Spengler, *Form and Actuality,* 32, emphasis in the original.

114. Kerouac, *Town and the City,* 498–99.

115. Kerouac, *Visions of Cody,* 94.

Chapter 2: The Spenglerian Strain of Piety

1. Kerouac, *Selected Letters,* 81; Spengler, *Form and Actuality,* 191. For a recounting of this incident, see McNally, *Desolate Angel,* 73.

2. Bourdieu, *Outline of a Theory of Practice*, 78.

3. Ginsberg, "Poetry, Violence," 24–25.

4. Spengler, *Form and Actuality*, 191.

5. Emerson, "Divinity School Address," 87.

6. For an exception to this neglect, see Hall, ed., *Lived Religion in America*.

7. Kerouac, *The Town and the City*, 450.

8. Morgan, *Literary Outlaw*, 86–90.

9. Rimbaud, *Season in Hell*, 89.

10. Kerouac, *Vanity of Duluoz*, 265.

11. Quoted in Charters, *Kerouac*, 63.

12. Yeats, *A Vision*, 261. Yeats writes, "A few months after the publication of the first edition of *A Vision* a translation of Spengler's *The Decline of the West* was published, and I found there a correspondence too great for coincidence between most of his essential ideas and those I had received before the publication of his first German edition."

13. Quoted in Schumacher, *Dharma Lion*, 34.

14. Ginsberg, "New Consciousness," 81.

15. Ibid., 82.

16. Quoted in Schumacher, *Dharma Lion*, 51–52.

17. Albanese, *America*, 3–7. Albanese's definition of religion understands ordinary powers as those found within the boundaries of human society. Extraordinary powers are those that approach the transcendent in being outside the boundaries of society, what she terms "objective realities."

18. Burroughs, *Letters of William S. Burroughs*, 97, 227, 85, 25, emphasis in the original.

19. Kerouac, *Selected Letters*, 191. Kerouac's letter was a response to Burroughs's letter of March 15, 1949, in which Burroughs wrote, "Because in the end people will do what they want to do, or the species will become extinct. That is what I believe." Burroughs, *Letters of William S. Burroughs*, 42.

20. Ginsberg, "New Consciousness," 71–72.

21. Slotkin, *Gunfighter Nation*, 321.

22. Ibid., 11–12.

23. For details of this incident, see Schumacher, *Dharma Lion*, 42–47; Morgan, *Literary Outlaw*, 102–9; Nicosia, *Memory Babe*, 127–29; and Grauerholz and Silverberg, eds., *Word Virus*, 10–13.

24. Schumacher, *Dharma Lion*, 49.

25. Kerouac, *Selected Letters*, 81–82.

26. Ginsberg, "Paterson," 40.

27. Ginsberg, "New Consciousness," 70.

28. Kerouac, *The Subterraneans*, 87–88; Burroughs, *Letters of William S. Burroughs*, 321.

29. Spengler, *Form and Actuality*, 353.

30. Morgan, *Literary Outlaw*, 71.

31. Korzybski, *Science and Sanity*, 51, ii.

32. Grauerholz and Silverberg, eds., *Word Virus*, 9; Nicosia, *Memory Babe*, 104; Miles, *Allen Ginsberg*, 117–19.

33. Belgrad, *Culture of Spontaneity*, 310.

34. Kerouac, *On the Road*, 8.

35. Quoted in Kerouac, *Selected Letters*, 210.

36. Ginsberg, "Refrain," 11.

37. Ginsberg, "Bop Lyrics," 43. In a 1945 letter to Ginsberg, Kerouac wrote of the strength of their "mad" community: "It has suddenly been revealed to me, the extent of our common madness, and I mean not only you or me, but all of us. . . . C'est une chose formidable." *Selected Letters*, 100.

38. Cassady, *Off the Road*, 223.

39. Kerouac, *On the Road*, 114, 10.

40. Rosenthal, "Poet of the New Violence," 29–31; see also Lipton, *Holy Barbarians*.

41. Regrettably, such oppositional language has subsumed most discussions of the Beats, despite their distance from this particular mode of discourse.

42. Spengler, *Perspectives of World-History*, 4.

43. Spengler, *Form and Actuality*, 346, emphasis in the original.

44. Kerouac, *Selected Letters*, 81–82.

45. Quoted in Ball, ed., *Allen Verbatim*, 34.

46. Spengler, *Perspectives of World-History*, 5.

47. Kerouac, *The Town and the City*, 5. Spengler's cosmic explanation must have had special relevance for Kerouac, for it offered an alternative explanation for the death of his brother Gerard at the age of nine. For Kerouac, never able to rest comfortably with the Catholic theodicy of original sin and glorified suffering, here was the notion that sin could be overcome. Although it made sense of such tragedies, it offered the promise of overcoming them by overcoming the "discordant cycles." The explanation, however, blurred the boundary between joy and sadness. For Kerouac, both emotional states were a response to the same cyclical reality. Although he tried to wrest a certain happiness from such awareness ("it's a joy to know that life is life and death is death"), he was often unable to appreciate such joy in his own life.

48. James, *The Varieties of Religious Experience*, 388.

49. Kerouac, *Selected Letters*, 100.

50. Ibid., 364.

51. Ginsberg, *Journals: Early Fifties*, 8; Ginsberg, "Paterson," 40.

52. Burroughs, *Junky*, 127.

53. Emerson, "Nature," 3.

54. Rose, *Transcendentalism*. Among other things, Rose discusses the Transcendental social vision and argues that reform was the lifeblood of Transcendentalism. She posits that Emerson and Thoreau were attempting to transform society by way of personal example.

55. Kerouac, *Selected Letters*, 194.

56. Thoreau, *Walden,* 150; see also 1 Corinthians 3:16; Emerson, "Self-Reliance," 166.

57. Peale's books were consistently top-ten bestsellers in the category of nonfiction during this decade. Whitefield, *Culture of the Cold War,* 84.

58. Burroughs, *Junky,* 112.

59. Spengler, *Perspectives of World-History,* 5, emphasis in the original.

60. Belgrad, *Culture of Spontaneity,* 149, 211.

61. Reich, *Cancer Biopathy,* 11.

62. Reich, *Cosmic Superimposition,* 12.

63. Morgan, *Literary Outlaw,* 141.

64. Burroughs, *Letters of William S. Burroughs,* 11.

65. Ibid., 70.

66. Reich, *Cancer Biopathy,* xx. In *The Subterraneans,* Kerouac writes of his "sudden illuminated glad wondrous discovery of Wilhelm Reich [and] his book The Function of the Orgasm." The religious form of knowledge is decidedly Spenglerian and masculine—a clarity that was "Germanic, beautiful, true—something I'd always known . . . here magnified and at the same time microcosmed and pointed in and maled into" (57–58).

67. Ibid., 402–3.

68. Ibid., 3, 405, 413.

69. Burroughs, *Letters of William S. Burroughs,* 52.

70. Reich, *Cancer Biopathy,* 405.

71. Spengler, *Form and Actuality,* 154.

72. Ginsberg, "Poetry, Violence," 24.

73. Spengler, *Form and Actuality,* 129.

74. Ibid., 117, emphasis in the original.

75. Ibid., 152, 388.

76. Ibid., 389.

77. Spengler, *Perspectives of World-History,* 15.

78. Spengler, *Form and Actuality,* 8.

79. Ibid., 119, 126, 353 (quotation).

80. Kerouac, *The Town and the City,* 20, 70, 155.

81. Burroughs, "Portuguese Mooch," 7–8.

82. Ginsberg, "The Terms," 50.

83. Spengler, *Form and Actuality,* 7.

84. Kerouac, *Doctor Sax,* 56, 91–92.

85. Kerouac, *On the Road,* 127.

86. Spengler, *Form and Actuality,* 394, 122. In "Howl" (129), Ginsberg lamented those who have courageously attempted to separate time from space, thus internalizing it, only to have their alternative temporal system negated by the dominant ideology of American politics: "who threw their watches off the roof to cast their ballot for eternity outside of Time, & alarm clocks fell on their heads every day for the next decade." The act of removing one's watch symbolized the attempt to overcome the spatialization of time. Ginsberg eulogizes those who have striven to eradicate both

the physical and psychological barriers preventing the immediate and unmediated appreciation of experience.

87. Spengler, *Form and Actuality*, 121.

88. Ginsberg, "America," 146–47.

89. A certain form of immortality is achieved by such realization. See, for example, Ginsberg, "In Death, Cannot Reach What Is Most Near" (34): "It is amazing to think that / thought and personality / of man is perpetuated in / time after his passage / to eternity. And one time / is all Time if you look / at it out of the grave."

90. Kerouac, *The Town and the City*, 417.

91. Kerouac, *Visions of Cody*, 351. Earlier in the novel, Kerouac laments the loss of this communalism within postwar America, in part due to the trends of suburbanization that took place shortly after the postwar boom: "The sins of America are precisely that the streets . . . are empty where their houses are, there's no sense of neighborhood anymore, a neighborhood quarter or a neighborhood freeforall fight between two streets of young husbands is no longer possible except I think in Dagwood Bumstead and he ain't for real—he couldn't—beyond this honesty there can only be thieves" (261). In a 1952 letter to Neal Cassady, Kerouac attributed the current tension in their relationship to the interference of abstractions that had prevented full apprehension and appreciation of the other: "Many's the time I wanted to hold your hand or kiss you, merely as acknowledgment that we were all in the car heading for the world unknown, but felt the jealousy kick . . . this is the fault with accepting balloons of abstract possibility become real fact with bannerline headlines we put across the mind . . . confusing the level of reality with level of imagination . . . or 'value' (jealousy is a hassle over value, which is an abstract idea)." Kerouac, *Selected Letters*, 364.

92. Burroughs, *Letters of William S. Burroughs*, 239. Burroughs's admiration for the white Brubeck contrasted with Kerouac's and Ginsberg's romanticizations of black jazz musicians. For Kerouac and Ginsberg, jazz was an inspiration not only for the vitality of its form but also for its value as a symbol of marginalized community. Burroughs, however, did not thematize his status as a marginalized outsider in terms of race, but in terms of homosexuality, criminality, and addiction.

93. Spengler, *Perspectives of World-History*, 8.

94. Quoted in Robinson, *The Freudian Left*, 24–25.

95. Kerouac, *On the Road*, 200.

96. Reich, *Selected Writings*, 113.

97. Ginsberg, "A Blake Experience," 128–29.

98. Kerouac, *Selected Letters*, 92.

99. Spengler, *Form and Actuality*, 165.

100. Kerouac, *On the Road*, 208–9, emphasis added.

101. Spengler, *Perspectives of World-History*, 4–5, emphasis in the original.

102. Kerouac, *On the Road*, 206–8, emphasis in the original; see also *The Town and the City*, 44–45.

103. Hebdige, *Subculture*, 129–30.

104. Michael Davidson's term *compulsory homosociality* aptly describes the Beats' rejection of the domestic ideology of the nuclear family in which male authority held sway. Even in their ready acceptance, even celebration, of homosexuality, the Beats replicated the public culture's dismissal of female authority and recalibrated the misogynist fantasy of cold war masculinity. Davidson, "Compulsory Homosociality."

105. Ginsberg, "New Consciousness," 85. Speaking of Beat relationships, Ginsberg continues: "The point is that in our private relationship we found the whole spectrum of love if not convenient at least tolerable and charming. And that was a world of private sociability and discourse which was the inverse of the lack of adhesiveness and the lack of recognition of Person, the objectification, reification, depersonalization, mechanization of Person."

106. Reich, *Selected Writings,* 102–3. Referring to the neurotic consequences of sexual repression, Reich states: "the natural instincts are *biological* facts which can neither be affected from the earth nor be basically altered. Like everything living, man needs first of all satisfaction of his hunger and gratification of his sexual instinct. Society as it is today, impedes the first and denies the second. That is, there is a *sharp conflict between natural demands* and certain *social institutions.* Caught as he is in the conflict, man gives in more or less to one side or the other; he makes compromises which are bound to fail; he escapes into illness or death; or he rebels—senselessly and fruitlessly—against the existing order."

107. Kerouac, *On the Road,* 4.

108. Whitman, "Over the Carnage Rose Prophetic," 250. In "Democratic Vistas" (505), Whitman celebrated "the personal and passionate attachment of man to man— which, hard to define, underlies the lessons and ideals of the profound saviors of every land and age, and which seems to promise, when thoroughly develop'd, cultivated and recognized in manners and literature, the most substantial hope and safety of the future of these states."

109. Ginsberg, "Howl," 128.

110. For a discussion of Beat misogyny and male friendship, see Stimpson, "The Beat Generation."

111. Ginsberg, "New Consciousness," 85. Ginsberg goes on to note that the "interesting thing about *On the Road* and *Visions of Cody* is Kerouac's approach to Neal as a Whitmanic lover to another man and the books are real love songs of a very ancient nature. They are not to be categorized as homosexual because Jack and Neal never made love genitally, they never had sexual relations. But they had a very noble, thrilling, love tenderness, heart palpitations for each other which is characteristic of normal masculine relationships and, as I keep saying, is almost obliterated in modern culture."

112. Kerouac, *Visions of Cody,* 261.

113. Although he did not consider himself homosexual, nor did others around him, Kerouac did engage in homosexual activity with Ginsberg as well as with others. Nicosia, *Memory Babe,* 150, 154–55.

114. Burroughs, *Naked Lunch*, 34, emphasis in the original; Burroughs, *Letters of William S. Burroughs*, 119.

115. Ginsberg, "New Consciousness," 85.

116. Kerouac, *On the Road*, 106.

117. Belgrad, *Culture of Spontaneity*, 230.

118. *On the Road* once had the working title of *Souls on the Road*, and Kerouac's continual references to "souls" point to its metaphysical orientation. Nicosia, *Memory Babe*, 345.

119. Ibid., 155–56.

120. Miles, *Ginsberg*, 30.

121. Whitman, "Democratic Vistas," 515–16, 515. For similarities in language, see the opening paragraph of Wolfe, *Look Homeward, Angel*, 3: "A Destiny that leads the English to the Dutch is strange enough: but one that leads from Epsom into Pennsylvania, and thence into the hills that shut in Altamount over the proud coral cry of the cock, and the soft stone smile of an angel, is touched by that dark miracle of chance which makes new magic in a dusty world." Kerouac repeatedly looked to this book while composing *The Town and the City*.

122. Spengler, *Form and Actuality*, 40.

123. Korzybski, *Science and Sanity*, 49.

124. Ellwood, *The Fifties Spiritual Marketplace*, 85; Kierkegaard, *Fear and Trembling*, 70.

125. Spengler, *Form and Actuality*, 159.

126. Ibid., 159.

127. Burroughs, "Twilight's Last Gleamings," 9.

128. Kerouac, *Mexico City Blues*, 36.

129. Spengler, *Perspectives of World-History*, 84, 105, 107.

130. Spengler, *Form and Actuality*, table 1.

131. Spengler, *Perspectives of World-History*, 105.

132. Holmes, *Nothing More to Declare*, 82.

133. Kerouac, *Selected Letters*, 226.

134. Kierkegaard, *Fear and Trembling*, 70.

135. Kerouac, "Origins of the Beat Generation," 69.

136. The Beats adopted the language of the street precisely in order to question the dominant culture's epistemological system and concomitant language. They viewed such modes of communication as not only more real and authentic but also superior in the dominant culture's terms of institutionalized efficiency: "It was a new language," Kerouac wrote, "actually spade (Negro) jargon but you soon learned it, like 'hung up' couldn't be a more economical term to mean so many things." Kerouac, "Origins," 72.

137. Kerouac, *Selected Letters*, 345, 354. In this letter, Kerouac describes the Indians as "Huncke-like," referring to one "in big sombrero but with downturned Huncke-like Indian face and scornful eyes." He muses if there "was a secret underground Indian hipster organization of revolutionary thinkers (all of them scornful of Amer-

ican hipsters who come down among them not for shit or kicks but with big pretenses of scholarship and superiority, this is what Scornful indicated) and not with pure Allen Ginsberg–like friendship on the corner on Times Square is what these Indians of course want, see, no bullshit, and they need Hunckes."

138. Ginsberg, "On Huncke's Back," 20–21; see also Prothero, "On the Holy Road," 213.

139. Ginsberg, "On Huncke's Back," 20–21.

140. Ibid., 20–21. The perspective of the hipster as existential hero has often been equated with the Beats through a misguided reference to Norman Mailer's 1957 essay "The White Negro."

141. Spengler, *Form and Actuality*, 32, quoted in Schumacher, *Dharma Lion*, 64. In 1945 Ginsberg wrote a poem, "The Character of the Happy Warrior, or Death in Violence," and dedicated it to Burroughs, based partly on his conversations with Huncke. In it, Ginsberg attempted to outline the potential for individual agency within "a particularly unpleasant culture." While arguing that "it is difficult to conceive of any man escaping the evil effects of his culture by purely intellectual liberation, or by exile," he came to believe that the hipster persona provided the only viable means of attaining both individualism and happiness. Quoted in Schumacher, *Dharma Lion*, 63–64.

142. Tytell, *Naked Angels*, 14.

143. Slotkin, *Gunfighter Nation*, 349, 402.

144. Burroughs, *Letters of William S. Burroughs*, 26.

145. Ibid., 25.

146. Burroughs, "Lee's Journals," 71.

147. Huncke, "From *Guilty of Everything*," 72.

148. Delattre, "The Culture of Procurement," 130.

149. Burroughs, *Junky*, xv.

150. Skerl, *William S. Burroughs*, 12.

151. Burroughs, *Junky*, xvi.

152. Kerouac, *Visions of Cody*, 387; Kerouac, *Selected Letters*, 347–53.

153. Quoted in Nicosia, *Memory Babe*, 325–26.

154. Kerouac, *On the Road*, 10, 132. Kerouac continues, "A western kinsman of the sun, Dean. Although my aunt warned me that he would get me in trouble, I could hear a new call and see a new horizon."

155. Burroughs's original reaction to Kerouac and Ginsberg's fascination with Cassady reveals the critical pessimism behind his conception of the new vision. In a 1949 letter to Ginsberg, he offers a Spenglerian critique of Cassady, whom he calls the "very soul [a] voyage into pure, abstract, meaningless motion. He is the Mover, compulsive, dedicated, ready to sacrifice family, friends, even his very car itself to the necessity of moving from one place to another." Burroughs, *Letters of William S. Burroughs*, 37.

156. Spengler, *Perspectives of World-History*, 89, emphasis in the original.

157. Kerouac, *Selected Letters*, 69.

158. Kerouac, *On the Road,* 207–8.

159. Spengler, *Perspectives of World-History,* 35.

160. Quoted in Schumacher, *Dharma Lion,* 94.

161. Most often, however, these visionary moments occurred with the aid of drugs. See, for example, Kerouac's discussion of "It" in *On the Road,* 127–29, 206–11.

162. Ginsberg, "A Blake Experience," 122, 123.

163. Albanese, *Corresponding Motion.*

164. Ginsberg, "A Blake Experience," 123–24.

165. Burroughs, *Letters of William S. Burroughs,* 68, emphasis in the original.

166. See the discussion of Burroughs's "factualism" in chapter 3, 159–64.

167. Burroughs, *Letters of William S. Burroughs,* 68.

168. Spengler, *Form and Actuality,* 106.

169. Kerouac, *Vanity of Duluoz,* 265–67.

170. Nicosia, *Memory Babe,* 139; Ginsberg, "New Consciousness," 69.

171. Spengler, *Form and Actuality,* 102.

172. Kerouac, *The Town and the City,* 424.

173. Quoted in Miles, *Ginsberg,* 47, emphasis added.

174. Williams, *America's Religions,* 435.

175. Geertz, "Thick Description," 16.

Chapter 3: The Utopia of Beat Language

1. Kerouac, *Visions of Cody,* 303, emphasis in the original.

2. Quoted in McNally, *Desolate Angel,* 79.

3. Kerouac, *The Town and the City,* 115.

4. Kerouac, "Belief and Technique for Modern Prose," 67.

5. Kerouac, *Selected Letters,* 98.

6. Burroughs, *Letters to Allen Ginsberg,* 50, emphasis in the original.

7. Emerson, "The Poet," 320.

8. Burroughs, *Letters of William S. Burroughs,* 25.

9. Spengler, *Perspectives of World-History,* 499.

10. Bataille, *Theory of Religion,* 98.

11. Emerson, "The Poet," 317.

12. Kerouac, *Selected Letters,* 293.

13. Spengler, *Perspectives of World-History,* 445.

14. Ibid., 344.

15. Ibid., 441, emphasis in the original; Ginsberg, "The New Consciousness," 76.

16. Quoted in Nicosia, *Memory Babe,* 251.

17. Spengler, *Perspectives of World-History,* 294.

18. Albanese, ed., *Spirituality of the American Transcendentalists,* 20.

19. Spengler, *Perspectives of World-History,* 152, 150.

20. Burroughs, *Letters of William S. Burroughs,* 44, 226–27.

21. Korzybski, *Science and Sanity,* 51, emphasis in the original.

22. Ibid., 50.

23. Burroughs, *Naked Lunch*, 207.

24. Ibid., 63.

25. Kerouac, *On the Road*, 40.

26. Ginsberg, *Allen Verbatim*, 29–30.

27. Spengler, *Perspectives of World-History*, 311.

28. Ransom, *World's Body*, xi.

29. Ibid., 329.

30. As Alan Golding points out, these critics were not so much "New" in contrast to a previous group but rather the first to possess a standard definition of literature and a set of interpretive principles to ground their discussion and debate. See *From Outlaw to Classic*, 71.

31. Ransom, *World's Body*, 335.

32. Quoted in Golding, *From Outlaw to Classic*, 77–78.

33. Ginsberg, "Notes on the Final Recording of 'Howl,'" emphasis added.

34. Spengler, *Perspectives of World-History*, 134–37, emphasis in the original.

35. Kerouac, *Visions of Cody*, 265.

36. Burroughs, *Naked Lunch*, 69.

37. Ibid., xv.

38. Brooks, *Modern Poetry*, 71–72, 76n.

39. Ginsberg, "It's a Vast Trap!" 79.

40. In 1952 Burroughs wrote to encourage Ginsberg to pursue his literary friendship with William Carlos Williams. Burroughs, *Letters of William S. Burroughs*, 112.

41. Ginsberg, "An Exposition," 135; Ginsberg, "The New Consciousness," 71.

42. Miles, *Allen Ginsberg*, 126–27; Ginsberg, *Journals: Early Fifties*, 10.

43. Ransom, *World's Body*, x; see also Bercovitch, ed., *Poetry and Criticism*, 286, 311.

44. Spengler, *Form and Actuality*, 41.

45. Kerouac, *Visions of Cody*, 153, 249.

46. Lhamon, Jr., *Deliberate Speed*, 156–69; Kerouac, *Visions of Cody*, 48.

47. Rieff, *Triumph of the Therapeutic*.

48. See Kerouac, *The Town and the City*, 116.

49. Belgrad, *Culture of Spontaneity*, 229, 232.

50. Kerouac, *Visions of Cody*, 393.

51. Kerouac, *Selected Letters*, 96.

52. Kerouac, *The Town and the City*, 370.

53. Kerouac, *Dr. Sax*, 160.

54. As with everything, the Beats were selective in what they borrowed and what they left behind. Considering Reich's blend of Freudianism and Marxism, Burroughs explained what he found stimulating in a 1949 letter: "Reich's social and political theories, and his polemics, bore me. What interests me is his factual discoveries particularly about the nature of the cancer process, and the use of the [orgone] accumulator in the treatment of cancer." Burroughs, *Letters of William S. Burroughs*, 57–58.

55. Spengler, *Form and Actuality*, 302n.

56. Kerouac, *Selected Letters*, 167. Kerouac continues: "Nature Boy is only an American beginning of the last human preoccupation—the position of the soul among all the souls in the Forest of Arden of the world, the crux of life." He and Ginsberg believed that Shakespeare had used the Forest of Arden as a metaphor for the ideal human existence. As Kerouac once explained the phrase "Forest of Arden" to John Clellon Holmes, it seemed to represent the unity of humanity: "Dense masses of people going about all their ways of being." Quoted in Nicosia, *Memory Babe*, 237.

57. Kerouac, *Visions of Cody*, 92.

58. Hayakawa, *The Use and Misuse of Language*, ix. For this distinction see Breslin, *Psycho-Political Muse*, 47.

59. Korzybski, *Science and Sanity*.

60. Kerouac, "Belief and Technique," 68; Kerouac, *Selected Letters*, 356.

61. Kerouac, *Visions of Cody*, 15.

62. Belgrad has noted that the formal structural innovation associated with intersubjectivity is that dialogue was often not a mere plot device but the fulcrum of Beat writing. Belgrad, *Culture of Spontaneity*, 209.

63. Kerouac, *On the Road*, 42; John Clellon Holmes to Allen Ginsberg, 14 June 1949, Allen Ginsberg Papers, 1937–1994, box 1, folder 32, Stanford University, Palo Alto, Calif., emphasis in the original.

64. Kerouac's privileging of communal discourse over plot is further epitomized in *Visions of Cody* when he juxtaposes transcripts of recorded dialogues with his own accounts of these conversations. These, in turn, were juxtaposed, and participants in the dialogues read transcripts of previous conversations, attempting to pick up on earlier associations and strains of thought. Daniel Belgrad has noted (*Culture of Spontaneity*, 209–10) that the dialogues consisted of the two men sharing their memories of a common event, following up on the associations of each other like bebop soloists improvising on a common theme. The accumulation of dialogue creates a social realm in which each individual voice is subsumed within a conversational dynamic, breaking down hierarchies that preclude full communication among selves. As Cassady laments to Kerouac in the transcript, moments of cosmic reciprocity required discipline. Even drugs, Cassady notes, do not guarantee the dissolution of the self into the group: "I think the both of us are going around containing ourselves, you know what I mean, what I'm saying is, ah, we're still aware of ourselves, even when we're high." Kerouac, *Visions of Cody*, 128–29.

65. Kerouac, *Selected Letters*, 356, 200.

66. Ginsberg, "The Terms in Which I Think," 51.

67. Kerouac, *Visions of Cody*, 79. Kerouac uses the term *unspeakable* throughout that volume, particularly in the second section (48, 50, 79, 81, 82, 86). It signifies his strategy of rendering the full gamut of reality beyond objective and subjective categories. Such is the way in which Kerouac conceived the central paradox of his prose and the purpose of his style—to put in words that which could not be expressed through words alone. Korzybski writes of the "un-speakable objective level" to refer to that which is "not words, can not be reached by words alone." Korzybski, *Science and Sanity*, 34.

68. Reich asserted that the determinism of an Enlightenment worldview had enveloped people in "character structures," preventing them from emitting or receiving "orgone energy." He wrote that deep introspection was a viable means to cut through the "character armor" imposed by the homogenizing forces of mass society. On the level of Reichian allegory, the Beats sought to shed these "character structures" and tap this energy through the physical act of writing. Reich, *Selected Writings*, 470.

69. Ginsberg, *Howl*, 152.

70. Breslin, *From Modern to Contemporary*, 97.

71. Ginsberg, *Journals Mid-Fifties*, 36.

72. Kerouac, *On the Road*, 176.

73. Kerouac, *Visions of Cody*, 28, 96, emphasis in the original.

74. Burroughs, *Letters of William S. Burroughs*, 285–87.

75. Quoted in Morgan, *Literary Outlaw*, 51.

76. Burroughs, *Naked Lunch*, xii, 218–19, emphasis in the original; Burroughs, *Junky*, xv.

77. Burroughs, *Letters of William S. Burroughs*, 289. For an excellent discussion of the masochistic dimension of Beat poetics, see Savran, *Taking It Like a Man*, 79–84, 98–103.

78. Burroughs, *Naked Lunch*, xvii, 200, 209, 33, 121, emphasis in the original; see also Ginsberg, "On Burroughs' Work," 114.

79. Rimbaud, "Bad Blood," in *A Season in Hell*, 22. Spengler also expressed such a sentiment: "'Liberation' is a fundamental word in every religion and an eternal wish for every waking-being. In this general, almost pre-religious sense, it means the desire for freedom from the anxieties and anguishes of waking-consciousness; for relaxation of the tensions of fear-born thought and search; for the obliteration and removal of the consciousness of the Ego's loneliness in the universe, the rigid conditionedness of nature, the prospect of the immovable boundary of all Being in eld and death." Spengler, *Perspectives of World-History*, 266.

80. Ibid., 499.

81. Ibid., 265.

82. Bataille, *Theory of Religion*, 42, 25 (quotation).

83. Burroughs, *Naked Lunch*, 100.

84. Spengler, *Perspectives of World-History*, 499.

85. Spengler, *Form and Actuality*, 260.

86. Ginsberg, "Song," 112.

87. Kerouac, *Visions of Cody*, 328–29.

88. Kerouac, "Belief and Technique For Modern Prose," 68.

89. Ginsberg, *Allen Verbatim*, 28.

90. Kerouac, *Visions of Cody*, 341. Reich posits (*Character Analysis*, 312) that "intellectual activity" often avoids "facts" and "really detracts from reality" rather than illuminates it.

91. Belgrad, *Culture of Spontaneity*, 149.

92. Kerouac, "Essentials of Spontaneous Prose," 68; Ginsberg, "The New Consciousness," 76.

93. Kerouac, *Selected Letters,* 384, emphasis in the original; Spengler, *Perspectives of World-History,* 271.

94. Kerouac, "Essentials of Spontaneous Prose," 67, 66; Kerouac, *Visions of Cody,* 358, 265.

95. As Ginsberg wrote in a journal during the 1940s, "Creation is an organismic process, it works by itself: it cooks itself." "Notes on a Book of Doldrums" [undated], Allen Ginsberg Papers, 1937–1994, box 3, folder 17, Stanford University, Palo Alto, Calif.

96. For a psychoanalytic reading of the Beats' "cross-race identification," see Savran, *Taking It Like a Man,* 62–63.

97. Kerouac, "Essentials of Spontaneous Prose," 65–66.

98. Ginsberg, "First Thought, Best Thought," 106.

99. Davidson, "Palimtexts," 80. For a discussion of Ginsberg's poetics, see Portuges, "Allen Ginsberg's Paul Cézanne."

100. Ginsberg, "After All, What Else Is There to Say?" 29, emphasis in the original.

101. Quoted in Holmes, *Nothing More to Declare,* 78.

102. Kerouac, *Selected Letters,* 371; Ginsberg, "A Blake Experience," 125.

103. Gifford, *As Ever,* 140–42; Portuges, "Allen Ginsberg's Paul Cézanne," 151.

104. Burroughs, *Nova Express,* 7.

105. Burroughs, *Queer,* 39, 40.

106. Quoted in Oldier, ed., *The Job,* 200.

107. Spengler, *Perspectives of World-History,* 445.

108. Burroughs, *Letters of William S. Burroughs,* 24, 166.

109. Spengler, *Form and Actuality,* 41; Kerouac, *On the Road,* 143.

110. Korzybski, *Science and Sanity,* v.

111. Quoted in Hayakawa, ed., *Use and Misuse of Language,* ix.

112. Spengler, *Perspectives of World-History,* 446; Spengler, *Form and Actuality,* 45–46, 374. This "unphilosophy" also had political implications. As Spengler wrote, "The fact-man is immune from the risk of practising sentimental or program politics. He does not believe in the big words. . . . The born statesman stands beyond true and false. He does not confuse the logic of events with the logic of systems. 'Truths' or 'errors'—which here amount to the same—only concern him as intellectual currents, and in respect of *workings.* He surveys their potency, durability, and direction, and duly books them in his calculations for the destiny of the power that he directs." Spengler, *Perspectives of World-History,* 442.

113. Miller, *The New England Mind,* 161–63.

114. Knickerbocker, "William Burroughs," 23.

115. Burroughs, *Junky,* xvi.

116. Ibid., 158. On the assumption of linguistic "identification" (the assumption that there is a direct correspondence between signifier and signified), Korzybski writes that it "makes general sanity and complete adjustment impossible. . . . As in infec-

tious diseases, certain individuals, although living in infected territory, are somehow immune to this disease. Others are hopelessly susceptible." Korzybski, *Science and Sanity*, lxxix.

117. Burroughs, *Letters of William S. Burroughs*, 122.

118. Burroughs, *Junky*, 152.

119. Burroughs, *Queer*, 58, xiv.

120. Burroughs and Ginsberg, *The Yage Letters*, 59; Burroughs, *Naked Lunch*, 221.

121. Burroughs, *Naked Lunch*, 61.

122. Murphy, *Wising Up the Marks*, 58; Thoreau, *Walden*, 1; Olson, "Projective Verse," 247.

123. Spengler, *Perspectives of World-History*, 137.

124. Quoted in Mottram, *William Burrroughs*, 13.

125. As Jennie Skerl notes, its content is autobiographical (the protagonist William Lee is Burroughs's alter ego). The plot represents his inner conflicts, the structures of the work are his actual experiences filtered through his mind, the texture consists of his individual perceptions, and the themes represent his search and discovery of an internal reality. Skerl, *William S. Burroughs*, 144.

126. Burroughs, *Letters of William S. Burroughs*, 129. "Factualism" was premised on the interconnectedness of reality. As Burroughs wrote (333) to Ginsberg, "Everybody and everything is in this universe together. If one explodes we all explode." Burroughs hoped to discover that interconnectedness for himself.

127. Korzybski, *Science and Sanity*, 50.

128. Burroughs, *Naked Lunch*, 105.

129. Miller, *The New England Mind*, 167; Gunn, *Culture of Criticism*, 50.

130. Ginsberg, "The New Consciousness," 90.

131. In a 1949 letter Ginsberg described this desire to communicate clearly despite "the problem of language": "Value, or feeling, is what I'm after." Allen Ginsberg to John Clellon Holmes, July 1949, Allen Ginsberg Papers, 1937–1994, box 1, folder 32, Stanford University, Palo Alto, Calif.

132. Spengler, *Perspectives of World-History*, 115.

133. Quoted in Nicosia, *Memory Babe*, 325–26; Kerouac, *Selected Letters*, 281.

134. Burroughs, *Letters of William S. Burroughs*, 398 (emphasis in the original), 201.

135. Spengler, *Perspectives of World-History*, 499.

136. Spengler, *Form and Actuality*, 300.

137. Gifford, ed., *As Ever*, 52; Kerouac, *Visions of Cody*, 98, 107; Burroughs, *Letters of William S. Burroughs*, 138.

138. Kerouac, *On the Road*, 130, emphasis added; Allen Ginsberg to John Clellon Holmes, July 1949, Allen Ginsberg Papers, 1937–1994, box 1, folder 32, Stanford University, Palo Alto, Calif.; Turner, "Social Dramas and Stories," 163.

139. Quoted in Nicosia, *Memory Babe*, 279. This sense of interconnectedness is also expressed in a letter to Neal Cassady dated December 28, 1950: "I discovered my soul; that is to say, I looked about for the first time and realized I was in a world and not just myself." Kerouac, *Selected Letters*, 249.

140. Burroughs, *Naked Lunch*, 208, xvi.

141. Quoted in Mottram, *William Burroughs*, 38.

142. Burroughs, *Naked Lunch*, 208, xvi.

143. Morgan, *Literary Outlaw*, 20.

144. Burroughs, *Naked Lunch*, 208; see also Lydenberg, *Word Cultures*. Commenting on the damaging effect of classical philosophical thought, Burroughs claims, "It's completely outmoded, as Korzybski, the man who developed general semantics, has pointed out, the Aristotelian 'either-or'—something is either this or that—is one of the great errors of Western thinking, because it's no longer true at all. That sort of thinking does not even correspond to what we know about the physical universe . . . I would agree emphatically that Aristotle, Descartes, and all that way of thinking is extremely stultifying and doesn't correspond even to what we know about the physical universe, and particularly disastrous in that it still guides the whole academic world." Quoted in Oldier, ed., *The Job*, 48–49.

145. Lydenberg, *Word Cultures*, x, 3. Burroughs invites readers to the realm beyond cognitive sanction, beyond even miracles, to the realm of pure fact: "Come in, please! Come in, please! Can't move a cell of my body without got the Word. . . . Nobody know my trouble, and especially not Jesus, the miracle artist. Something he don't like? Go make with the miracle, James, I show you how. Now the perpetrating of miracles constitute a brazen attempt to louse up the universe. When you set up something as MIRACLE, you deny the very concept of FACT, establish a shadowy and spurious court infested by every variety of coyote and shady fixer, *beyond* Court of Fact" ("Word," 173).

146. Burroughs, *Naked Lunch*, 203 (first two quotations), ix (third quotation).

147. Spengler, *Perspectives of World-History*, 443.

148. Ginsberg, "In Society," 3.

149. Quoted in Portuges, "Poetics of Vision," 135; Ginsberg, "A Blake Experience," 129, quoted in Ginsberg, *Howl*, 153.

150. Ginsberg, "Poetry, Violence, and the Trembling Lambs," 25.

151. Schumacher, *Dharma Lion*, 95.

152. In the fall of 1955 Ginsberg compared ellipsis to "naked haiku" and defined haiku as "objective images written down outside mind the results is inevitable mind sensations of relations." Ginsberg, *Journals: Early Fifties*, 95.

153. Ginsberg, "Howl," 130.

154. Kerouac, *Selected Letters*, 274.

155. Quoted in Dean, *American Religious Empiricism*, 27.

156. Quoted from Kerouac, *A Jack Kerouac ROMnibus*.

157. Ibid.; Ginsberg, *Allen Verbatim*, 32.

158. Kerouac, "On the Road Again," 59, emphasis in the original.

159. Kerouac, *Visions of Cody*, 99.

160. Burroughs, *Letters of William S. Burroughs*, 109.

161. Kerouac, *On the Road*, 143. Ginsberg, showing Burroughs's influence on his thoughts, wrote to Neal Cassady in 1948: "The poetry should be a literal statement,

in common and not classic language, of unspeakable mysteries. These things (the mysteries) will have to become not mysterious but spiritual *facts* to me." For Ginsberg, fact meant something experienced, or rather known through experience. Quoted in Gifford, *As Ever,* 52.

162. Spengler, *Perspectives of World-History,* 444, emphasis in the original.

163. Spengler, *Form and Actuality,* 40, emphasis in the original.

164. Kerouac, *The Town and the City,* 89.

165. Kerouac, "Belief and Technique For Modern Prose," 67.

166. Spengler, *Perspectives of World-History,* 440, emphasis in the original.

167. Ginsberg, "Paterson," 40–41.

Chapter 4: Beat Remythologies

1. Montrose, "New Historicisms," 414. The appropriation of cultural norms may produce unexpected results as well as a reflexive knowledge of one's position among conflicting myths of America. As Montrose points out (415), "The very process of subjectively living the contradictions within or among ideological formations may allow us to experience facets of our own subjection at shifting internal distances— to read, as in a refracted light, one fragment of our ideological inscription by means of another." Such friction is created when an individual receives conflicting messages, both supposedly originating from a univocal ideological position.

2. Durkheim, *Elementary Forms of Religious Life,* 425.

3. Barthes, *Mythologies,* 142–43.

4. Adorno, "Cultural Criticism," 19.

5. Barthes, *Mythologies,* 135.

6. Burroughs, *Letters to Allen Ginsberg,* 88.

7. Quoted in *A Jack Kerouac ROMnibus,* 1 Dec. 1948.

8. Lincoln, *Discourse and the Construction of Society,* 25.

9. Ginsberg, "Howl," 133.

10. Spengler, *Perspectives of World-History,* 46, 43.

11. Burroughs, *Letters of William S. Burroughs,* 65–69.

12. Mottram, *William Burroughs,* 67–68.

13. Burroughs, *Naked Lunch,* 14–15.

14. Burroughs, *Letters of William S. Burroughs,* 91.

15. Burroughs, *Queer,* 21.

16. Ibid., xxii, xix.

17. Burroughs, *Naked Lunch,* 199.

18. Schumacher, *Dharma Lion,* 162.

19. Gifford, ed., *As Ever,* 182; Spengler, *Perspectives of World-History,* 45.

20. Carrasco, *Religions of Mesoamerica,* 118.

21. Ginsberg, *Journals: Early Fifties,* 34, 62–63.

22. All references to the poem are from Ginsberg, "Siesta in Xbalba," 97–110.

23. Spengler, *Perspectives of World-History,* 45.

24. Ginsberg, *Journals: Early Fifties*, 71.

25. Clark, *Jack Kerouac*, 88; Kerouac, *On the Road*, 276.

26. Kerouac, *On the Road*, 281.

27. Kerouac, *Visions of Cody*, 380.

28. Spengler, *Perspectives of World-History*, 113, 119.

29. Kerouac, *On the Road*, 280; Kerouac, *Visions of Cody*, 387.

30. Kerouac, *Visions of Cody*, 380.

31. Kerouac, *On the Road*, 281; Kerouac, *Visions of Cody*, 384.

32. Spengler, *Form and Actuality*, 330.

33. Kerouac, *Visions of Cody*, 119, 247.

34. Kerouac, "On the Road Again", 54.

35. Savran, *Taking It Like a Man*, 62–64.

36. Spengler, *Perspectives of World-History*, 165.

37. Burroughs, *Letters of William S. Burroughs*, 182.

38. Ginsberg, *Journals Mid-Fifties*, 133.

39. Cited in Savran, *Taking It Like a Man*, 330; see also Baldwin, "The Black Boy," 231

40. Kerouac, *Visions of Cody*, 392, 110, 359.

41. Kerouac, *On the Road*, 208.

42. Fredman, *The Grounding of American Poetry*, vii.

43. Spengler, *Perspectives of World-History*, 278–79.

44. Burroughs, *Letters to Allen Ginsberg*, 88.

45. Burroughs, *Nova Express*, 67.

46. Hebdige, *Subculture*, 17.

47. Barthes, *Mythologies*, 115, 119.

48. This methodological point stems from Peter W. Williams's definition of religion and symbolic acts as social phenomena. See Williams, *Popular Religion in America*, 8–9.

49. Savran, *Taking It Like a Man*, 102.

50. Barthes, *Writing Degree Zero*, 10–11. As Barthes writes, "Imagery, delicacy, vocabulary spring from the body and the past of the writer and gradually become the very reflexes in his art. Thus under the name of style a self-sufficient language is evolved which has its roots only in the depths of the author's personal and secret mythology, that subnature of expression where the first coition of words and things take place, where once and for all the great verbal themes of existence come to be installed. . . . It is the private portion of the ritual, it rides up from the writer's mythladen depths and unfolds beyond his area of control."

51. Cited in Savran, *Taking It Like a Man*, 54.

52. Skerl, *William S. Burroughs*, 2–3.

53. Morgan, *Literary Outlaw*, 22.

54. Quoted in Skerl, *William S. Burroughs*, 3.

55. Burroughs, *Letters of William S. Burroughs*, 195, 302.

56. Burroughs, *Naked Lunch*, 200.

57. For a secondary treatment of this issue, see Gleason, "American All." Contemporary social critics were also aware of this trend. See, for example, *The Managerial Revolution,* in which James Burhnam argues that America was quickly becoming a bureaucratic corporatism. In "The Psychopathology of *Time* and *Life*" (1949) McLuhan accuses Henry Luce and his publishing empire of desensitizing Americans to the point that they had become passive political observers, enabling Luce and others to impose self-serving political initiatives upon them. McLuhan cited in Belgrad, *Culture of Spontaneity,* 4.

58. Edwards, *Contested Terrain,* ch. 8, "Bureaucratic Control."

59. Birnbaum, *Radical Renewal,* 15.

60. Belgrad, *Culture of Spontaneity,* 3–5. A sense of togetherness was also striven for from the bottom up after the long-term disruptions of the Great Depression and the fresh memory of wartime nationalism. It was the desire for a national identity that paved the way for such conditioning programs to be enacted. As Jackson Lears points out, the lists of "American" traits compiled by those who sought a national character bore a suspicious resemblance to the values enshrined by the corporate sponsors of the American Way of Life. "Nearly all the traits that were alleged to characterize American culture as a whole," he notes, "were projections of hegemonic values onto a wider population that did not necessarily share them." Lears, "A Matter of Taste," 51.

61. Ginsberg once remarked that Kerouac's life and art were in part motivated by his "tender brooding compassion for bygone scene and Personal Individuality oddity'd therein." Ginsberg, "Visions of the Great Rememberer," 404.

62. Burroughs, *Letters to Allen Ginsberg,* 85.

63. Burroughs, *Naked Lunch,* 203; Barthes, *Mythologies,* 146. For an analysis of Burroughs's mythological imagination, see Stull, "Quest and the Question."

64. Burroughs, *Letters to Allen Ginsberg,* 88.

65. Burroughs, "Ginsberg Notes," 123.

66. Burroughs, *Naked Lunch,* 112.

67. Marx, *Critical Analysis,* 76–87.

68. Murphy, *Wising Up the Marks,* 74–76.

69. Spengler, *Perspectives of World-History,* 469, 485 (emphasis in the original), 493.

70. Quoted in Morgan, *Literary Outlaw,* 236.

71. Oldier, ed., *The Job,* 48–49.

72. Burroughs, *Letters of William S. Burroughs,* 334.

73. Quoted in Knickerbocker, "An Interview," 31.

74. Burroughs, *Naked Lunch,* 168, 126, 96.

75. Burroughs, *Letters of William S. Burroughs,* 215.

76. Marx, *Critical Analysis,* 77; Burroughs, *Naked Lunch,* 96–110.

77. Marx, *Critical Analysis,* 76.

78. Spengler, *Form and Actuality,* 34–35.

79. Burroughs, *Naked Lunch,* x–xi; Spengler, *Form and Actuality,* 34–35.

80. Savran, *Taking It Like a Man,* 100.

81. Marx, *Critical Analysis*, 77; Burroughs, *Naked Lunch*, 7, xi, xiii, x.

82. Burroughs, *Naked Lunch*, 168.

83. Burroughs, "International Zone," 47.

84. Knickerbocker, "An Interview," 23.

85. Burroughs, *Naked Lunch*, 198; Skerl, *William S. Burroughs*, 36.

86. Burroughs, *Naked Lunch*, 3, 9, 147–51, 208, 70.

87. Burroughs, *Junky*, 87.

88. Burroughs, *Naked Lunch*, 31, 20, 21.

89. Ibid., 202, 197, 203, 208, 212–13.

90. Ibid., xvii, 189.

91. Burroughs, "Ginsberg Notes," 123.

92. Burroughs, *Naked Lunch*, xvi, emphasis in the original.

93. Burroughs, *Letters of William S. Burroughs*, 397.

94. Spengler, *Perspectives of World-History*, 484, 432; Burroughs, *Naked Lunch*, 121–22.

95. Burroughs, *Letters of William S. Burroughs*, 272.

96. Barthes, *Mythologies*, 157.

97. The idea of "solitary communitas" is from Miller's discussion of the term in "Ritual Aspects of Narrative"; see also Turner, *Ritual Process*.

98. Quoted in Miles, *William S. Burroughs*, 105. Kerouac was well aware of Burroughs's attentive maintenance of his individuality within any group context and once compared his lifestyle to that of a monk's fending off of the corruption of the outside world. Fisher, *Catholic Counterculture in America*, 225.

99. Burroughs, *Letters of William S. Burroughs*, 79.

100. Oldier, ed., *The Job*, 21.

101. Spengler, *Perspectives of World-History*, 137, 7, 137.

102. Burroughs, *Naked Lunch*, 32. As opposed to Turner's categories of spontaneous, normative, and even ideological communitas, this form of intersubjectivity is the only one that can be realized within Burroughs's philosophical framework. According to Burroughs, any system of group dynamics is futile without first isolating the "junk virus." Without an explicit, mutual recognition of the human condition of bodily dependency, all members become "assimilated." Turner, *Ritual Process*, 155; Burroughs, *Naked Lunch*, 17.

103. Nicosia, *Memory Babe*, 342–43.

104. Kerouac, *Selected Letters*, 107–8.

105. Kerouac, *Visions of Cody*, 98, emphasis in the original.

106. Ibid., 263.

107. Kerouac, *On the Road*, 158.

108. Spengler, *Perspectives of World-History*, 416–35.

109. Ginsberg, "Visions of the Great Rememberer," 426.

110. Kerouac, *Visions of Cody*, 342.

111. Ibid., preface; Kerouac, *On the Road*, 132.

112. See, for example, Weinreich, *The Spontaneous Poetics of Jack Kerouac*, 34.

113. Kerouac, *Visions of Cody*, 90–91, 93.

114. Spengler, *Perspectives of World-History*, 279.

115. Kerouac, *Visions of Cody*, 297.

116. Nicosia, *Memory Babe*, 363.

117. Kerouac, *On the Road*, 120.

118. Spengler, *Perspectives of World-History*, 269, 270.

119. Kerouac, *On the Road*, 120.

120. With respect to faith, Spengler writes, "The critical spirit, on the contrary, wants, and believes itself able, to look into everything for itself. It not only mistrusts alien truths, but even denies their possibility. Truth, for it, is only knowledge that it has proved for itself." Spengler, *Perspectives of World-History*, 270. There is a distinction between Burroughs's factualism and Cassady's stance toward reality.

121. Kerouac, *Visions of Cody*, 361.

122. Nelson, *Culture of Confidence*.

123. Kerouac, *On the Road*, 120–21.

124. Ibid., 188.

125. Lhamon, *Deliberate Speed*, 163.

126. Kerouac, "Origins of the Beat Generation," 71.

127. Spengler, *Form and Actuality*, 152, emphasis in the original.

128. Lhamon, *Deliberate Speed*, 167.

129. Taussig, "Transgression," 349.

130. Kerouac, *On the Road*, 39; Kerouac, *Visions of Cody*, 303.

131. Spengler, *Perspectives of World-History*, 217. As Kerouac once confessed to his priest, he felt that Catholicism enslaved people by telling the poor to accept their suffering because they would have their reward in heaven. He thought that those on the margins should be redeemed in this life and not have to wait for the next. "Christ is joy," he told the priest, "not damnation. That's why He cursed the fucking Pharisees" (quoted in Nicosia, *Memory Babe*, 86). In a 1950 letter to John Clellon Holmes, Ginsberg expressed a similar understanding of the Christian Messiah: "Well that is another idea, a nonreligious Jesus, interesting in this world, asserting himself in this world not for the sake of heaven." Allen Ginsberg to John Clellon Holmes, 13 Dec. 1950, Allen Ginsberg Papers, 1937–1994, box 3, folder 44, Stanford University, Palo Alto, Calif.

132. Kerouac, *On the Road*, 193, 224, 190.

133. For example, Kerouac follows the description of being homeless in San Francisco with a description of Dean's entrance: "That was the way Dean found me when he finally decided I was worth saving." In a passage regarding Cassady's bad drug trip, Kerouac depicts him as being found lying on the bed, "arms stretched out forever." In describing Dean as a "Holy Goof," Kerouac employs references from the Passion narrative and laments that even his "disciples" misunderstood his essential character. Defending Dean from their accusations, "This was not true," Sal states. "I knew better and I could have told them all. I didn't see any sense in trying it. I longed to go and put my arm around Dean and say, Now Look here, all of you, remember just

one thing: this guy has his troubles too, and another thing, he never complains and he's given all of you a damned good time just being himself, and if that isn't enough for you then send him to the firing squad, that's apparently what you're itching to do anyway." Kerouac, *On the Road*, 174, 184, 194.

134. Ibid., 195.

135. The crucifixion metaphor continues when Kerouac asks friends, "'Dean will be dead someday. Then what can you say to him?' 'The sooner he's dead the better,' said Galatea, and she spoke officially for almost everyone in the room." Kerouac, *On the Road*, 195; see also Spengler, *Perspectives of World-History*, 216, 214.

136. Kerouac, *On the Road*, 309–10.

137. Quoted in Tytell, *Naked Angels*, 176.

138. Kerouac, *Visions of Cody*, 397–98.

139. Spengler, *Form and Actuality*, 106. After the publication of *Visions of Cody* in 1972, Ginsberg interpreted this passage more pessimistically than may have been Kerouac's original intent in 1951. Despite his knowledge of the intermediate history, including the deaths of both Kerouac and Cassady (what Ginsberg refers to as the "great betrayal of that manly America of Love"), he still acknowledged the implicit sense of hope expressed in the passage: "The book was a dirge for America, for its heroes' deaths too, but then who could know except in the Unconscious?—A dirge for the American Hope that Jack (& his hero Neal) carried so valiantly after Whitman—an America of pioneers and generosity" ("Visions of the Great Rememberer," 430).

Nicosia notes the similarity of this passage and the ending of Thoreau's *Walden*, pointing to its parallel structure and hopeful sentiment (*Memory Babe*, 386). It is also evidence of Thoreau's Transcendental influence upon Kerouac's religiosity. Thoreau writes in the last paragraph of *Walden*: "I do not say that John or Jonathan will realize all this; but such is that character of that morrow which mere lapse of time can never make to dawn. the light which puts out our eyes is darkness to us. Only that day dawns to which we are awake. there is more day to dawn. the sun is but a morning star." Thoreau, *Walden*, 221.

140. Allen Ginsberg to John Clellon Holmes, 13 Dec. 1950, Allen Ginsberg Papers, 1937–1994, box 3, folder 44, Stanford University, Palo Alto, Calif.

141. Ginsberg, "Siesta in Xbalba," 110.

142. Ginsberg, *Howl*, 152. As Whitman writes in the 1872 Preface to *Leaves of Grass*, "When I commenced, years ago, elaborating the plan of my poems, and continued turning over that plan, and shifting in my mind through many years . . . experimenting much, and writing and abandoning much, one deep purpose underlay the others, and has underlain it and its execution ever since—and that has been the religious purpose . . . not of course to exhibit itself in the old ways, as in writing hymns or psalms with an eye to the church-pew, or to express conventional pietism, or the sickly yearnings of devotees, but in new ways, and aiming at the widest sub-bases and inclusions of humanity" (519).

143. Ibid., 176.
144. Ginsberg, "Sunflower Sutra," 138, 139.
145. Ginsberg, "Supermarket in California," 136.
146. Nelson, *Culture of Confidence*, 74.
147. Lewis, *American Adam*, 1, 5.
148. Ginsberg, "Many Loves," 156.
149. Quoted in Savran, *Taking It Like a Man*, 70.
150. Ginsberg, "Many Loves," 156.
151. Ginsberg, "New Consciousness," 84.
152. Ginsberg, "Many Loves," 158.
153. Ginsberg, "Howl," 128; Ginsberg, "The Green Automobile," 83–86.
154. Kerouac, *On the Road*, 114.
155. Davidson, "Compulsory Homosociality," 199, 201 (quotation).
156. Allen Ginsberg to John Clellon Holmes, 13 Dec. 1950, Allen Ginsberg Papers, 1937–1994, box 3, folder 44, Stanford University, Palo Alto, Calif.
157. Quoted in Schumacher, *Dharma Lion*, 209.
158. All references to the poem are from Ginsberg, "Howl," 126–34.
159. Ginsberg, *Howl*, 140.
160. Quoted in Miles, *Ginsberg*, 210.
161. Leviticus 18:21: "And thou shalt not let any of thy seed pass through the fire to Molech."
162. Ginsberg, *Howl*, 88.
163. Spengler, *Perspectives of World-History*, 192.
164. Ginsberg, "New Consciousness," 77.
165. Ginsberg, *Howl*, 151–54.
166. Emerson, "The Poet," 320.
167. Ginsberg, "An Exposition," 134–35.
168. All references from the poem are from Ginsberg, "America," 146–48.
169. The Beats' propensity for public nakedness can be understood as an exhibition of natural physicality and a symbolic gesture of repossessing the unadorned, uncorrupted self. Through "naked observations," in Ginsberg's words, they would recover the "naked original" mind. For example, when Kerouac describes riding naked down the highway as an act of naturalness and freedom, he questions the legitimacy of the social norm while casting doubt on the authenticity of the framework of social conventionality. As Moriarty shouts, "Disemburden yourselves of all that clothes—now what's the sense of clothes?" Ginsberg, "Visions of the Great Rememberer," 419; Kerouac, *On the Road*, 161.
170. Weber, *Sociology of Religion*, 59.
171. Whitman, 1876 Preface to *Leaves of Grass*, 525.
172. Gunn, *Culture of Criticism*, 185.
173. Kerouac, *Selected Letters*, 427.

Conclusion

1. Podhoretz, "A Howl of Protest," 34; [Anon.], "The Disorganization Man," 54, 55; O'Neil, "The Only Rebellion Around," 116.
2. Ginsberg, "Pull My Daisy," in *Collected Poems*, 24.
3. Nicosia, *Memory Babe*, 584; Kerouac, *Pull My Daisy*, 21–32.
4. Ellwood and Partin, eds., *Religious and Spiritual Groups*, 108.
5. Mailer, "The White Negro."
6. Albanese, "Exchanging Selves," 224.
7. Snyder, *Earth House Hold*, 104–5.
8. Clark, "On the Social History of Art," 253.
9. For discussion of this strategy in American religious history, see Moore, *Religious Outsiders*.
10. Cited in Hudnut-Beumler, *Looking for God*, 41.
11. Geertz has written that religious ideas extend beyond "their specifically metaphysical contexts to provide a framework of general ideas in terms of which a wide range of experience—intellectual, emotional moral—can be given meaningful form." In "Religion as a Cultural System," 123; see also Kerouac, *Some of the Dharma*, 54.
12. Burroughs, *Letters of William S. Burroughs*, 431, 434.
13. Beiles et al., *Minutes to Go*, 59.
14. Knickerbocker, "William Burroughs," 26.
15. Morgan, *Literary Outlaw*, 323.
16. Burroughs, "Naked Scientology," 33, 41.
17. As Brion Gysin would later comment on Burroughs's interest in Scientology, "[Burroughs] must be one of the few people who has made more money from them than they made from him." Quoted in Miles, *William S. Burroughs*, 114.
18. Quoted in Ellwood and Partin, eds., *Religious and Spiritual Groups*, 142.
19. Ibid.
20. Wallis, *Road to Total Freedom*, 91.
21. Hubbard, *Creation of Human Ability*, 286.
22. Burroughs, *Letters of William S. Burroughs*, 431; Wallis, *Road to Total Freedom*, 90.
23. Wallis, *Road to Total Freedom*, 106.
24. Hubbard, *Dianetics*, 56, emphasis in the original.
25. Oldier, ed., *The Job*, 45, emphasis in the original.
26. Ibid.
27. Wallis, *Road to Total Freedom*, 36.
28. Burroughs, *The Soft Machine*, 155.
29. Lydenberg, *Word Cultures*, 44, 48.
30. Skerl, *William S. Burroughs*, 56; Burroughs, *The Soft Machine*, 155.
31. Burroughs and Gysin, *The Third Mind*, 34, 61.
32. Lydenberg, *Word Cultures*, 54, emphasis in the original.
33. Oldier, ed., *The Job*, 28.

34. Burroughs, *The Soft Machine*, 85, emphasis in the original.

35. Oldier, ed., *The Job*, 47.

36. Burroughs and Gysin, *The Exterminator*, 13.

37. Sorrell, "The Catholicism of Jack Kerouac," 192; Charters, *Kerouac*, 199.

38. Jones (*A Map of* Mexico City Blues, 10, 112) argues that Kerouac's "excitement over the newfound vocabulary of Buddhism" resulted in "a balance of Catholicism and Buddhism" in works such as *Desolation Angels* that stabilized his psychic "oscillation between solitude and society." Although there is certainly overlap between these two religious languages, they were never, "in perfect equipoise." Kerouac's Spenglerism continued to motivate his desire for his work to have social meaning as well as social effect.

39. Kerouac, *Dharma Bums*, 32.

40. In a 1956 journal entry, Snyder (*Earth House Hold*, 39) seems to have glossed his Buddhist beliefs with identifiable Spenglerian musings. There "comes a time when the poet must choose," he wrote, "either to step deep in the stream of his people, history, tradition, folding and folding himself in wealth of persons and past; philosophy, humanity, to become richly foundationed and great and sane and ordered. Or to step beyond the bound onto the way out, into horrors and angels, possible madness or silly Faustian doom, possible utter transcendence, possible enlightened return, possible ignominious wormish perishing."

41. Kerouac, *Dharma Bums*, 97–98, 203–4, 33.

42. Miller, "Ritual Aspects," 44.

43. Kerouac, *Selected Letters*, 285, 292.

44. Ibid., 348.

45. Kerouac, *Doctor Sax*, 194, 95, 38.

46. Kerouac, *Selected Letters*, 403–4.

47. Ibid., 430.

48. Nicosia, *Memory Babe*, 457; Cassady, *Off the Road*, 234–36.

49. Goddard, *A Buddhist Bible*, xiii. The three sutras of Goddard's collection that most influenced Kerouac were the *Diamond Sutra*, the *Surangama Sutra*, and the *Lankavatara Sutra*. The Buddhist principles found in these specific texts not only confirmed some of his previous notions but also transposed them into new forms.

50. Quoted in Marty, *Irony of It All*, 20.

51. Kerouac, *Selected Letters*, 415.

52. Burroughs, *Letters of William S. Burroughs*, 226, 394, 226–27.

53. Kerouac, *Some of the Dharma*.

54. Ibid., 5, 9.

55. According to Kerouac (*Some of the Dharma*, 12–13, see also 53), internal peace would never be attained if dualistic conceptions remained: "The thought-material manifested during sleep is still the same material as that during waking, but uncontrolled by mind laws. This disproves the theory of the conscious and subconscious, which is a false duality placing a constraint upon the original intelligence nature, which is contamination causing the perception of dual-mind-sensing (which has no

substantiality of existence) to go on perceiving, so out of opposing conflicting notions come same."

56. Spengler, *Perspectives of World-History*, 271.

57. Belgrad, *Culture of Spontaneity*, 205.

58. Kerouac, *Doctor Sax*, 3.

59. Nicosia, *Memory Babe*, 393.

60. Kerouac, *Visions of Cody*, 103.

61. As Kerouac learned more about Buddhism, he concluded that past and present, subjective and objective should not be evident in his writing. As he wrote in the summer of 1954, "Subjective and Objective are another Western dualism—in dreams what is subjective and what is objective? It's all the same fantastic emanation of scenes and selves. Dreams are either deep or shallow . . . which is subjective? which is objective?" *Some of the Dharma*, 94.

62. Spengler, *Form and Actuality*, 122.

63. Kerouac, "Essentials of Spontaneous Prose," 66; Goddard, *A Buddhist Bible*, 112, 113, 122.

64. Quoted in Nicosia, *Memory Babe*, 458.

65. Kerouac's penchant for retreating into self is evidenced a few pages later: "In America only the silent Buddhahood may be possible . . . the clinging here is so intense and widespread (democracy) the populace is literally unteachable and sees not life as sorrow." Kerouac, *Some of the Dharma*, 41 (quotation in text), 61.

66. Goddard, *A Buddhist Bible*, xvi; Kerouac, *Selected Letters*, 428.

67. Goddard, *A Buddhist Bible*, xvi.

68. Kerouac, *Some of the Dharma*, 32.

69. Ibid., 54.

70. Goddard, *A Buddhist Bible*, xvi.

71. Kerouac, *Selected Letters*, 447.

72. Hipkiss, *Jack Kerouac*, 66.

73. Kerouac, *Some of the Dharma*, 100.

74. Ibid., 53.

75. Ibid., 140; Kerouac, *Selected Letters*, 447.

76. Kerouac, *Some of the Dharma,*, 114.

77. Spengler, *Perspectives of World-History*, 184; Kerouac, *Some of the Dharma*, 114.

78. McNally, *Desolate Angel*, 237.

79. Quoted in Clark, *Jack Kerouac*, 168–69, originally in Wallace, "Mike Wallace Asks Jack Kerouac," 3.

80. Journal entry, "Berkeley 1955–56," Allen Ginsberg Papers, 1937–1994, box 3, folder 12, Stanford University, Palo Alto, Calif.

81. Schumacher, *Dharma Lion*, 295, 376.

82. Ginsberg, "Public Solitude," 126.

83. Ginsberg, *Journals: Early Fifties*, 164.

84. Ginsberg, "Laughing Gas," 189.

85. Schumacher, *Dharma Lion*, 273.

86. Quoted in Lucie-Smith, *Mystery in the Universe*, 5.

87. Ginsberg, "Metaphysics," 33.

88. Quoted in Schumacher, *Dharma Lion*, 313.

89. Ibid., 347; Lee and Shlain, *Acid Dreams*, 79.

90. Ginsberg, "Death to Van Gogh's Ear," 167.

91. Ginsberg, *Journals: Early Fifties*, 100.

92. Ginsberg, "Lysergic Acid," 232.

93. Quoted in Davidson, *San Francisco Renaissance*, 29.

94. Ginsberg, "U.S. Senate Statement," 68.

95. See Adorno's discussion of Spengler in "Spengler after the Decline," 67.

96. Ginsberg, *Journals: Early Fifties*, 78.

97. Rossinow, "The New Left in the Counterculture."

98. Ginsberg, *Journals Mid-Fifties*, 389–90.

99. Ginsberg, *Journals: Early Fifties*, 159.

100. Ginsberg, "Seabattle of Salamis," 288.

101. Ginsberg, *Journals: Early Fifties*, 159–60.

102. Ginsberg, "Howl," 127.

103. Frank, "The Rebel Consumer," 38.

104. Barthes, *Mythologies*, 129.

105. Frye, *Anatomy of Criticism*, 136.

106. For booksellers, "phantom objectivity" has had consequences; a number report that the works of Kerouac, Ginsberg, and Burroughs are the top choices for shoplifters. Running a distant second among book thieves is the Bible. Jensen, "Steal This Book."

107. Benjamin, *The Arcades Project*, 64–65.

108. Marcus, *Lipstick Traces*, 149. As Benjamin wrote in *The Arcades Project*, his secret history of the nineteenth century, "The question of costume reaches deep into the life of art and poetry, where fashion is at once preserved and overcome" (65).

109. Kerouac, *Mexico City Blues*, 51.

works cited

Aaron, Daniel. *Writers on the Left: Episodes in American Literary Communism.* New York: Columbia University Press, 1992.

Adorno, Theodor. *Prisms.* Trans. Samuel Weber and Shierry Weber. Cambridge: MIT Press, 1982.

——. "Spengler after the Decline." In *Prisms,* trans. Samuel Weber and Shierry Weber, 53–72. Cambridge: MIT Press, 1982.

Ahlstrom, Sydney. *A Religious History of the American People.* New Haven: Yale University Press, 1972.

Albanese, Catherine L. *America: Religions and Religion.* 2d ed. Belmont: Wordsworth Publishing, 1992.

——. *Corresponding Motion: Transcendental Religion and the New America.* Philadelphia: Temple University Press, 1977.

——. "Exchanging Selves, Exchanging Souls: Contact, Combination, and American Religious History." In *Retelling U.S. Religious History,* ed. Thomas A. Tweed, 200–226. Berkeley: University of California Press, 1997.

——, ed. *The Spirituality of the American Transcendentalists: Selected Writings of Ralph Waldo Emerson, Amos Bronson Alcott, Theodore Parker, and Henry David Thoreau.* Macon: Mercer University Press, 1985.

Anonymous. "The Disorganization Man." In *On the Poetry of Allen Ginsberg,* ed. Lewis Hyde, 54–55. Ann Arbor: University of Michigan Press, 1984.

Baldwin, James. "The Black Boy Looks at the White Boy." In *Nobody Knows My Name: More Notes of a Native Son,* 216–44. New York: Delta, 1962.

Ball, Gordon, ed. *Allen Verbatim: Lectures on Poetry, Politics, Consciousness.* New York: McGraw Hill, 1974.

Barthes, Roland. *Mythologies.* Trans. Annette Lavers. New York: Hill and Wang, 1972.

——. *Writing Degree Zero.* Trans. Annette Lavers and Colin Smith. New York: Hill and Wang, 1997.

Bataille, Georges. *Theory of Religion.* Trans. Robert Hurley. New York: Zone Books, 1989.

Beiles, Sinclair, William S. Burroughs, Gregory Corso, and Brion Gysin. *Minutes to Go.* Paris: Two Cities, 1960.

Belgrad, Daniel. *The Culture of Spontaneity: Improvisation and the Arts in Postwar America.* Chicago: University of Chicago Press, 1998.

Bell, Catharine. *Ritual Theory, Ritual Practice.* New York: Oxford University Press, 1992.

Benjamin, Walter. *The Arcades Project.* Trans. Howard Eiland and Kevin McLaughlin. Cambridge: Harvard University Press, 1999.

———. "Imagination." In *Selected Writings,* vol. 1: *1913–1926,* 280–82. Ed. Marcus Bullock and Michael W. Jennings. Cambridge: Harvard University Press, 1996.

———. "Theories of German Fascism." In *Selected Writings,* vol. 2: *1927–1934,* 312–21. Ed. Michael W. Jennings, Howard Eiland, and Gary Smith. Trans. Rodney Livingstone and Others. Cambridge: Harvard University Press, 1999.

Bercovitch, Sacvan. *The American Jeremiad.* Madison: University of Wisconsin Press, 1978.

———. *The Rites of Assent.* New York: Routledge, 1993.

———, ed. *Poetry and Criticism, 1940–1995.* Vol. 8 of *The Cambridge History of American Literature.* New York: Cambridge University Press, 1996.

Birnbaum, Nathan. *The Radical Renewal: The Politics of Ideas in Modern America.* New York: Pantheon Books, 1988.

Bourdieu, Pierre. *Outline of a Theory of Practice.* Trans. R. Nice. New York: Cambridge University Press, 1977.

Breslin, James E. B. *From Modern to Contemporary: American Poetry: 1945–1965.* Chicago: University of Chicago Press, 1984.

Breslin, Paul. *The Psycho-Political Muse: American Poetry since the 1950's.* Chicago: University of Chicago Press, 1987.

Brinkley, Alan. "For America, It Truly Was a Great War." *New York Times Magazine,* 7 May 1995, 54–57.

Brooks, Cleanth. *Modern Poetry and the Tradition.* New York: Oxford University Press, 1965.

Burke, Kenneth. *The Rhetoric of Religion: Studies on Logology.* Boston: Beacon Press, 1961.

Burnham, James. *The Managerial Revolution.* New York: John Day, 1941.

Burroughs, William S. "Apocalypse." *Dead City Radio.* Island Records, 1990.

———. *Call Me Burroughs.* Rhino Records, 1995.

———. "Ginsberg Notes." In *Interzone,* ed. James Grauerholz, 117–31. New York: Viking Press, 1989.

———. *Interzone.* Ed. James Grauerholz. New York: Penguin Books, 1989.

———. *Junky.* 1953. Reprint. New York: Penguin Books, 1977.

———. "Lee's Journals." In *Interzone,* ed. James Grauerholz, 63–105. New York: Viking Press, 1989.

———. *Letters to Allen Ginsberg, 1953–1957.* New York: Full Court Press, 1982.

———. *The Letters of William S. Burroughs: 1945–1959.* Ed. Oliver Harris. New York: Viking Press, 1993.

———. *Naked Lunch.* 1959. Reprint. New York: Grove Weidenfeld, 1990.

———. "Naked Scientology." *Los Angeles Free Press,* 6 March 1970, 33, 41.

————. *Nova Express*. New York: Grove Press, 1992.

————. "The Portuguese Mooch." In *Early Routines*. Santa Barbara: Cadmus Editions, 1981.

————. *Queer*. New York: Penguin Books, 1987.

————. *The Soft Machine*. New York: Grove Press, 1967.

————. "Twilight's Last Gleamings." In *Interzone*, ed. James Grauerholz, 3–12. New York: Viking Press, 1989.

————. "Word." In *Interzone*, ed. James Grauerholz, 135–94. New York: Viking Press, 1989.

————. *Word Virus: The William S. Burroughs Reader*. Ed. James Grauerholz and Ira Silverberg. New York: Grove Press, 1998.

Burroughs, William S., and Allen Ginsberg. *The Yage Letters*. San Francisco: City Light Books, 1975.

Burroughs, William S., and Brion Gysin. *The Exterminator*. San Francisco: Auerhahn Press, 1960.

————. *The Third Mind*. New York: Viking Press, 1978.

Campbell, Joseph. *The Hero with a Thousand Faces*. Bollingen series 17. New York: Pantheon Books, 1949.

Carpenter, Joel A. *Revive Us Again: The Reawakening of American Fundamentalism*. New York: Oxford University Press, 1997.

Carrasco, David. *Religions of Mesoamerica: Cosmovision and Ceremonial Centers*. San Francisco: Harper and Row. 1990.

Cassady, Carolyn. *Off the Road: My Years with Cassady, Kerouac, and Ginsberg*. New York: William Morrow, 1990.

Cassirer, Ernst. *The Myth of the State*. New Haven: Yale University Press, 1963.

Caute, David. *The Great Fear: The Anti-Communist Purge under Truman and Eisenhower*. New York: Simon and Schuster, 1978.

Cavell, Stanley. *This New yet Unapproachable America: Lectures after Emerson and Wittgenstein*. Albuquerque: Living Batch Press, 1989.

Charters, Ann. *Kerouac: A Biography*. New York: St. Martin's Press, 1973.

————, ed. *The Portable Beat Reader*. New York: Viking Penguin, 1995.

Clark, Thomas. "Interview with Allen Ginsberg." *Paris Review* 37 (Spring 1966): 13–55. Reprinted as "A Blake Experience" in *On the Poetry of Allen Ginsberg*, ed. Lewis Hyde, 120–30. Ann Arbor: University of Michigan Press: 1984.

Clark, T. J. "On The Social History of Art." In *Image of the People: Gustave Courbet and the 1848 Revolution*, 9–20. London: Thames and Hudson, 1973. Reprinted in *Modern Art and Modernism: A Critical Anthology*, ed. Francis Frascina and Charles Harrison, 249–58. New York: Harper and Row, 1984.

Clark, Tom. *Jack Kerouac: A Biography*. New York: Marlowe and Company, 1984.

Connor, Steven. *Postmodernist Culture: An Introduction to Theories of the Contemporary*. Oxford: Blackwell Publishers, 1989.

Dakin, Edwin Franden. "American Communiqué." In *Today and Destiny: Vital Excerpts from* The Decline of the West *of Oswald Spengler*, ed. Edwin Franden Dakin, 305–50. New York: Alfred A. Knopf, 1940.

Danforth, Samuel. "A Brief Recognition of New England's Errand into the Wilderness." Reprinted in *Early American Writing*, ed. Giles Gunn, 198–207. New York: Penguin Books, 1994.

Davidson, Michael. "Compulsory Homosociality: Charles Olson, Jack Spicer, and the Gender of Poetics." In *Cruising the Performative: Interventions into the Representation of Ethnicity, Nationality, and Sexuality*, ed. Sue-Ellen Case, Philip Brett, and Susan Leigh Foster, 197–216. Bloomington: Indiana University Press, 1995.

———. "From Margin to Mainstream: Postwar Poetry and the Politics of Containment." *American Literary History* 10 (Summer 1998): 266–90.

———. "Palimtexts: Postmodern Poetry and the Material Text." In *Postmodern Genres*, ed. Majorie Perloff, 75–95. Norman: University of Oklahoma Press, 1989.

———. *The San Francisco Renaissance: Poetics and Community at Mid-Century*. New York: Cambridge University Press, 1989.

Dean, William. *American Religious Empiricism*. Albany: State University of New York Press, 1986.

Delattre, Roland A. "The Culture of Procurement: Reflections on Addictions and the Dynamics of American Culture." *Soundings*, no. 1–2 (69): 127–44.

DeLillo, Don. *Underworld*. New York: Scribner, 1997.

Deleuze, Gilles, and Felix Guattari. *Anti-Oedipus: Capitalism and Schizophrenia*. Trans. Robert Hurley, Mark Seem, and Helen R. Lane. Minneapolis: University of Minnesota Press, 1983.

Durkheim, Emile. *The Elementary Forms of the Religious Life*. 1915. Trans. Karen E. Fields. Reprint. New York: Free Press, 1995.

Edwards, Richard. *Contested Terrain: The Transformation of the Workplace in the Twentieth Century*. New York: Basic Books, 1979.

Eliade, Mircea. *Myth And Reality*. New York: Harper and Row, 1963.

———. *Symbolism, the Scared, and the Arts*. Ed. Diane Apostolos-Cappadona. New York: Continuum, 1992.

Ellwood, Robert S. *The Fifties Spiritual Marketplace: American Religion in a Decade of Conflict*. New Brunswick: Rutgers University Press, 1997.

———. *Mysticism and Religion*. Englewood Cliffs: Prentice-Hall, 1980.

Ellwood, Robert S., and Harry B. Partin, eds. *Religious and Spiritual Groups in Modern America*. 2d ed. Englewood Cliffs: Prentice-Hall, 1988.

Emerson, Ralph Waldo. "The Divinity School Address." In *Selected Prose and Poetry*, ed. Reginald L. Cook, 69–88. New York: Holt Rinehart and Winston, 1950.

———. "Nature." In *Selected Prose and Poetry*, ed. Reginald L. Cook, 3–46. New York: Holt Rinehart and Winston, 1950.

———. "The Poet." In *Selected Prose and Poetry*, ed. Reginald L. Cook, 316–40. New York: Holt Rinehart and Winston, 1950.

———. *Selected Prose and Poetry*. Ed. Reginald L. Cook. New York: Holt Rinehart and Winston, 1950.

———. "Self-Reliance." In *Selected Prose and Poetry*, ed. Reginald L. Cook, 165–92. New York: Holt Rinehart and Winston, 1950.

Eyerman, Ron, and Andrew Jamison, eds. *Seeds of the Sixties*. Berkeley: University of California Press, 1994.

Feather, Leonard. *The Book of Jazz: From Then until Now*. New York: Bonanza Books, 1965.

Fennelly, John F. *Twighlight of the Evening Lands: Oswald Spengler—a Half Century Later*. New York: Brookdale Press, 1972.

Ferlinghetti, Lawrence. "Horn on HOWL." *Evergreen Review* 4 (1958): 145–58.

Fischer, Klaus P. *History and Prophecy: Oswald Spengler and the Decline of the West*. Durham: Moore Publishing, 1977.

Fisher, James Terence. *The Catholic Counterculture in America, 1933–1962*. Chapel Hill: University of North Carolina Press, 1989.

Frank, Thomas. "The Rebel Consumer: Why Johnny Can't Dissent." In *Commodify Your Dissent: Salvos from* The Baffler, ed. Thomas Frank and Matt Weiland, 31–45. New York: W. W. Norton, 1997.

Frank, Thomas, and Matt Weiland, eds. *Commodify Your Dissent: Salvos from* The Baffler. New York: W. W. Norton, 1997.

Fredman, Stephen. *The Grounding of American Poetry: Charles Olson and the Emersonian Tradition*. New York: Cambridge University Press, 1993.

Fromm, Erich. *The Sane Society*. Greenwich: Fawcett, 1955.

Frye, Northrop. *Anatomy of Criticism: Four Essays*. Princeton: Princeton University Press, 1957.

———. "Spengler Revisited." In *Spiritus Mundi: Essays on Literature, Myth, and Society*, 179–98. Bloomington: Indiana University Press, 1976.

Geertz, Clifford. *The Interpretation of Cultures*. New York: Basic Books, 1973.

———. *Islam Observed: Religious Development in Morocco and Indonesia*. Chicago: University of Chicago Press, 1971.

———. "Religion as a Cultural System." In *The Interpretation of Cultures*, 87–125. New York: Basic Books, 1973.

———. "Thick Description: Toward an Interpretive Theory of Culture." In *The Interpretation of Cultures*, 3–30. New York: Basic Books, 1973.

George-Warren, Holly, ed. *The* Rolling Stone *Book of the Beats: The Beat Generation and American Culture*. New York: Hyperion, 1999.

Giles, Paul. *American Catholic Arts and Fictions: Culture, Ideology, Aesthetics*. New York: Cambridge University Press, 1992.

Gifford, Barry, ed. *As Ever: The Collected Correspondence of Allen Ginsberg and Neal Cassady*. Berkeley: Creative Arts Book Company, 1977.

Ginsberg, Allen. "After All, What Else Is There to Say?" In *Collected Poems: 1947–1980*, 29. New York: Harper and Row, 1984.

———. Allen Ginsberg Papers, 1937–94. Stanford University, Palo Alto, Calif.

———. *Allen Verbatim: Lectures on Poetry, Politics, Consciousness*. Ed. Gordon Ball. New York: McGraw Hill, 1974.

———. "America." In *Collected Poems: 1947–1980*, 146–48. New York: Harper and Row, 1984. Also recorded 18 March 1956. *Holy Soul, Jelly Roll: Poems and Songs, 1949–1993*. Rhino Records, 1994.

———. "A Blake Experience." In *On the Poetry of Allen Ginsberg,* ed. Lewis Hyde, 120–30. Ann Arbor: University of Michigan Press, 1984.

———. "Bop Lyrics." In *Collected Poems: 1947–1980,* 42–43. New York: Harper and Row, 1984.

———. *Collected Poems: 1947–1980.* New York: Harper and Row, 1984.

———. "On Burroughs' Work." In *Collected Poems: 1947–1980,* 114. New York: Harper and Row, 1984.

———. *Composed on the Tongue: Literary Conversations, 1967–1977.* Ed. Donald Allen. San Francisco: Grey Fox Press, 1980.

———. "In Death, Cannot Reach What Is Most Near." In *Collected Poems, 1947–1980,* 34. New York: Harper and Row, 1984.

———. "Death to Van Gogh's Ear." In *Collected Poems: 1947–1980,* 168–70. New York: Harper and Row, 1984.

———. "An Exposition of William Carlos Williams' Poetic Practice." In *Composed on the Tongue: Literary Conversations, 1967–1977,* ed. Donald Allen, 118–52. San Francisco: Grey Fox Press, 1980.

———. "'First Thought, Best Thought.'" In *Composed on the Tongue: Literary Conversations, 1967–1977,* ed. Donald Allen, 106–17. San Francisco: Grey Fox Press, 1980.

———. "Footnote to Howl." In *Collected Poems: 1947–1980,* 134. New York: Harper and Row, 1984.

———. "The Green Automobile." In *Collected Poems, 1947–1980,* 83–87. New York: Harper and Row, 1984.

———. "Howl." In *Collected Poems: 1947–1980,* 126–33. New York: Harper and Row, 1984.

———. *Howl: Original Draft Facsimile.* Ed. Barry Miles. New York: Harper and Row, 1986.

———. "On Huncke's Back." *The Unspeakable Visions of the Individual* 3 (1973): 20–21.

———. "It's a Vast Trap!" In *On the Poetry of Allen Ginsberg,* ed. Lewis Hyde, 78–79. Ann Arbor: University of Michigan Press, 1984.

———. "To John Hollander 7 Sept. 1958." Reprinted in *Allen Ginsberg in America,* ed. Jane Kramer, 163–77. New York: Random House, 1968.

———. *Journals: Early Fifties, Early Sixties.* Ed. Gordon Ball. New York: Grove Press, 1977.

———. *Journals Mid-Fifties: 1954–1958.* Ed. Gordon Ball. New York: HarperCollins, 1995.

———. "Laughing Gas." In *Collected Poems: 1947–1980,* 189–200. New York: Harper and Row, 1984.

———. "Lysergic Acid." In *Collected Poems: 1947–1980,* 231–34. New York: Harper and Row, 1984.

———. "A Mad Gleam." In *Collected Poems: 1947–1980,* 16. New York: Harper and Row, 1984.

———. "Many Loves." In *Collected Poems: 1947–1980*, 156–58. New York: Harper and Row, 1984.

———. "Metaphysics." In *Collected Poems: 1947–1980*, 33. New York: Harper and Row, 1984.

———. "The New Consciousness." In *Composed on the Tongue: Literary Conversations, 1967–1977*, ed. Donald Allen, 63–93. San Francisco: Grey Fox Press, 1980.

———. "Notes on the Final Recording of Howl." *Allen Ginsberg Reads "Howl" and Other Poems*. Fantasy Records, 1959.

———. "Paterson." In *Collected Poems: 1947–1980*, 40–41. New York: Harper and Row, 1984.

———. "Poetry, Violence, and the Trembling Lambs." *Village Voice*, 25 Aug. 1959, 1, 8. Reprinted in *Casebook on the Beat*, ed. Thomas Parkinson, 24–27. New York: Thomas Y. Crowell, 1961.

———. "Prose Contribution to Cuban Revolution." In *Deliberate Prose: Selected Essays, 1952–1965*, ed. Bill Morgan, 135–45. New York: HarperCollins, 2000.

———. "Public Solitude." In *Deliberate Prose: Selected Essays, 1952–1965*, ed. Bill Morgan, 67–82. New York: HarperCollins, 2000.

———. "Pull My Daisy." In *Collected Poems: 1947–1980*, 24–25. New York: Harper and Row, 1984.

———. "Seabattle of Salamis Took Place off Perama." In *Collected Poems: 1947–1980*, 288. New York: Harper and Row, 1984.

———. "Siesta in Xbalba." In *Collected Poems: 1947–1980*, 97–110. New York: Harper and Row, 1984.

———. "In Society." In *Collected Poems: 1947–1980*, 3. New York: Harper and Row, 1984.

———. "Song." In *Collected Poems: 1947–1980*, 111–12. New York: Harper and Row, 1984.

———. "Sunflower Sutra." In *Collected Poems: 1947–1980*, 138–39. New York: Harper and Row, 1984.

———. "Supermarket in California." In *Collected Poems: 1947–1980*, 136. New York: Harper and Row, 1984.

———. "The Terms in Which I Think of Reality." In *Collected Poems: 1947–1980*, 50–51. New York: Harper and Row, 1984.

———. "Two Sonnets." In *Collected Poems: 1947–1980*, 5. New York: Harper and Row, 1984.

———. Untitled. In *Collected Poems: 1947–1980*, 32. New York: Harper and Row, 1984.

———. "U.S. Senate Statement." In *Deliberate Prose: Selected Essays, 1952–1965*, ed. Bill Morgan, 67–82. New York: HarperCollins, 2000.

———. "The Visions of the Great Rememberer." Afterward to Jack Kerouac, *Visions of Cody*, 399–430. New York: Penguin, 1993.

Gitlin, Todd. *The Sixties: Years of Hope, Days of Rage*. New York: Bantam Books, 1987.

Gleason, Philip. "American All: World War II and the Shaping of American Identity." *Review of Politics* 43 (July 1981): 483–518.

Goddard, Dwight. *A Buddhist Bible.* Boston: Beacon Press, 1970.

Golding, Alan. *From Outlaw to Classic: Canons in American Poetry.* Madison: University of Wisconsin Press, 1995.

Graham, Billy. *Revival in Our Time: The Story of Billy Graham's Evangelistic Campaigns.* Wheaton: Van Kampen Press, 1950.

Grauerholz, James, and Ira Silverberg, eds. *Word Virus: The William S. Burroughs Reader.* New York: Grove Press, 1998.

Grimes, Ronald L. *Ritual Criticism: Case Studies in Its Practice, Essays on Its Theory.* Columbia: University of South Carolina Press, 1990.

Gunn, Giles. *The Culture of Criticism and the Criticism of Culture.* New York: Oxford University Press, 1987.

Hagedorn, Hermann. *The Bomb That Fell on America.* Santa Barbara: Pacific Coast Publishing, 1946.

Hall, David D., ed. *Lived Religion in America: Toward a History of Practice.* Princeton: Princeton University Press, 1997.

Hayakawa, S. I., ed. *The Use and Misuse of Language.* Greenwich: Fawcett Publications, 1962.

Hebdige, Dick. *Subculture: The Meaning of Style.* London: Routledge, 1979.

Heller, Erich. *The Disinherited Mind.* Cleveland: World Publishing, 1959.

Herberg, Will. *Protestant, Catholic, Jew: An Essay in American Religious Sociology.* Garden City: Doubleday, 1955.

Herman, Arthur. *The Idea of Decline in Western History.* New York: Free Press, 1997.

Hipkiss, Robert A. *Jack Kerouac: Prophet of the New Romanticism.* Lawrence: Regents Press of Kansas, 1976.

Hollander, John. "Poetry Chronicle." *Partisan Review* 24 (Spring 1957): 296–304.

Holmes, John Clellon. *Nothing More to Declare.* New York: Dutton, 1967.

———. "This Is the Beat Generation." *New York Times Magazine,* 16 Nov. 1952. Reprinted in Holmes, *Nothing More to Declare,* 113, 115. New York: Dutton, 1967.

Holton, Robert. "Kerouac among the Fellahin: On the Road to the Postmodern." *Modern Fiction Studies* 41 (Summer 1995): 265–83.

Howe, Irving. "Religion and the Intellectuals IV." *Partisan Review* 17 (May–June 1950): 456–83.

Hubbard, L. Ron. *The Creation of Human Ability.* London: Scientology Publications, 1955.

———. *Dianetics: The Modern Science of Mental Health.* 1950. Reprint. Los Angeles: Bridge Publications, 1985.

Hudnut-Beumler, James. *Looking for God in the Suburbs: The Religion of the American Dream and Its Critics, 1945–1965.* New Brunswick: Rutgers University Press, 1994.

Hughes, H. Stuart. *Oswald Spengler: A Critical Estimate.* New York: Charles Scribner's Sons, 1952.

Huncke, Herbert S. "From *Guilty of Everything.*" In *Kerouac and the Beats,* ed. Arthur Knight and Kit Knight, 66–104. New York: Paragon, 1988.

Hutchison, William R. *The Modernist Impulse in American Protestantism.* Cambridge: Harvard University Press, 1976.

Hyde, Lewis, ed. *On the Poetry of Allen Ginsberg.* Ann Arbor: University of Michigan Press, 1984.

Jameson, Fredric. *The Political Unconscious: Narrative as a Socially Symbolic Act.* Ithaca: Cornell University Press, 1981.

James, William. *The Varieties of Religious Experience.* Ed. Martin E. Marty. New York: Penguin, 1983.

———. "What Pragmatism Means." In *William James: Essays in Pragmatism,* ed. Alburey Castell, 141–58. New York: Hafner Publishing, 1966.

Jensen, Joyce. "Steal This Book: What the Bible and the Beats Have in Common." *New York Times,* 19 June 1999, A19.

Jonas, Susan, and Marilyn Nissenson. *Going, Going, Gone: Vanishing Americana.* San Francisco: Chronicle Books, 1994.

Jones, James T. *A Map of* Mexico City Blues: *Jack Kerouac as Poet.* Carbondale: Southern Illinois University Press, 1992.

Kazin, Alfred. *On Native Grounds: An Interpretation of Modern American Prose Literature.* New York: Harcourt Brace, 1995.

Kerouac, Jack. *Atop an Underwood: Early Stories and Other Writings,* ed. Paul Marion. New York: Viking, 1999.

———. "Beauty as a Lasting Truth." In *Atop an Underwood: Early Stories and Other Writings,* ed. Paul Marion, 225–27. New York: Viking, 1999.

———. "Belief and Technique for Modern Prose." *Evergreen Review* 8 (Spring 1959): 57. Reprinted in *A Casebook on the Beat,* ed. Thomas Parkinson, 67–68. New York: Thomas Y. Crowell, 1961.

———. *The Dharma Bums.* New York: Viking Press, 1971.

———. *Doctor Sax: Faust Part Three.* New York: Ballantine Books, 1973.

———. "The Essentials of Spontaneous Prose." *Evergreen Review* 5 (1958): 72–3. Reprinted in *A Casebook on the Beat,* ed. Thomas Parkinson, 65–66. New York: Thomas Y. Crowell, 1961.

———. *The Jack Kerouac Collection.* Rhino Records, 1990.

———. *A Jack Kerouac ROMnibus.* CD-ROM. Produced by Ralph Lombreglia and Kate Bernhardt. New York: Penguin Books USA, 1995.

———. *Mexico City Blues.* New York: Grove Press, 1959

———. "My Generation, My World." In *Atop an Underwood: Early Stories and Other Writings,* ed. Paul Nearion, 228–29. New York: Viking, 1999.

———. "The Origins of the Beat Generation." *Playboy,* June 1959, 31–32, 42, 79. Reprinted in *A Casebook on the Beat,* ed. Thomas Parkinson, 68–76. New York: Thomas Y. Crowell, 1961.

———. *Pull My Daisy: Text Ad-libbed by Jack Kerouac for the Film by Robert Frank and Alfred Leslie.* New York: Grove Press, 1961.

———. *On the Road.* 1957. Reprint. New York: Penguin Books, 1976.

———. "On the Road Again." Comp. Douglas Brinkley. *New Yorker*, 22, 29 June 1998, 46, 48, 50–52, 54, 56, 58–59.

———. *Selected Letters, 1940–1956*. Ed. Ann Charters. New York: Viking Press, 1995.

———. *Some of the Dharma*. New York: Viking Press, 1997.

———. *The Subterraneans*. New York: Avon Publications, 1959.

———. *The Town and the City*. New York: Harcourt Brace, 1950.

———. *Vanity of Duluoz: An Adventurous Education, 1935–46*. New York: Coward-McCann, 1967.

———. *Visions Of Cody*. New York: Penguin Books, 1993.

Kierkegaard, Soren. *Fear and Trembling*. Trans. Alastair Hannay. New York: Penguin Books, 1985.

Knickerbocker, Conrad. "William Burroughs: An Interview." *Paris Review* 35 (Fall 1965): 12–50.

Knight, Arthur, and Kit Knight, eds. *The Beat Vision: A Primary Sourcebook*. New York: Paragon House, 1987.

Korzybski, Alfred. *Science and Sanity: An Introduction to Non-Aristotelian Systems and General Semantics*. New York: International Non-Aristotelian Library Publishing Company, 1933.

Langer, Susanne K. *Philosophy in a New Key: A Study in the Symbolism of Reason, Rite, and Art*. New York: Mentor Books, 1951.

Laquer, Walter Z. *Young Germany: A History of the German Youth Movement*. New York: Basic Books, 1962.

Larsen, Stephen, and Robin Larsen. *A Fire in the Mind: The Life of Joseph Campbell*. New York: Doubleday, 1991.

Lears, Jackson. "A Matter of Taste: Corporate Culture Hegemony in a Mass-Consumption Society." In *Recasting America: Culture and Politics in the Age of the Cold War*, ed. Lary May, 38–57. Chicago: University of Chicago Press, 1989.

Lee, Martin A., and Bruce Shlain. *Acid Dreams: The Complete Social History of LSD: The CIA, the Sixties, and Beyond*. New York: Grove Weidenfeld, 1985.

Lerner, Max. *America as a Civilization: Life and Thought in the United States Today*. New York: Simon and Schuster, 1957.

Lewis, R. W. B. *The American Adam: Innocence, Tragedy, and Tradition in the Nineteenth Century*. Chicago: University of Chicago Press, 1955.

Lhamon, W. T., Jr. *Deliberate Speed: The Origins of a Cultural Style in the American 1950s*. Washington: Smithsonian Institution Press, 1990.

Lincoln, Bruce. *Discourse and the Construction of Society: Comparative Studies of Myth, Ritual, and Classification*. New York: Oxford University Press, 1989.

Lipsitz, George. *Time Passages: Collective Memory and American Popular Culture*. Minneapolis: University of Minnesota Press, 1990.

Lipton, Lawrence. *The Holy Barbarians*. New York: Julian Messner, 1959.

Long, Charles H. "Conquest and Cultural Contact in the New World." In *Significations: Signs, Symbols, and Images in the Interpretation of Religion*, 97–113. Philadelphia: Fortress Press, 1986.

———. "Human Centers: An Essay on Method in the History of Religions." In *Significations: Signs, Symbols, and Images in the Interpretation of Religion*, 65–78. Philadelphia: Fortress Press, 1986.

———. *Significations: Signs, Symbols, and Images in the Interpretation of Religion.* Philadelphia: Fortress Press, 1986.

Luce, Henry. *The American Century.* New York: Farrar and Rinehart, 1941.

———. "The Ethical Problems Facing America." Address to Duke University Divinity School, Durham, N.C., 12 Feb. 1946.

Lucie-Smith, Edward. *Mystery in the Universe: Notes on an Interview with Allen Ginsberg.* London: Turret Books, 1965.

Lydenberg, Robin. *Word Cultures: Radical Theory and Practice in William S. Burroughs's Fiction.* Urbana: University of Illinois Press, 1987.

Mahoney, Maura. "Back in Black: Here Come the Beatniks." In *Commodify Your Dissent: Salvos from* The Baffler, ed. Thomas Frank and Matt Weiland, 57–61. New York: W. W. Norton, 1997.

Mailer, Norman. "The White Negro (Superficial Reflections on the Hipster)." *Dissent* 4 (Summer 1957): 276–93.

Marcus, Greil. "The Bob McFadden Experience: On *The Beat Generation* CD Box Set." In *The Dustbin of History*, 111–18. Cambridge: Harvard University Press, 1995.

———. *The Dustbin of History.* Cambridge: Harvard University Press, 1995.

———. *Lipstick Traces: The Secret History of the Twentieth Century.* Cambridge: Harvard University Press, 1989.

Marty, Martin E. *The Irony of It All: 1893–1919.* Vol. 1 of *Modern American Religion.* Chicago: University of Chicago Press, 1996.

———. *Under God, Indivisible, 1941–1960.* Vol. 3 of *Modern American Religion.* Chicago: University of Chicago Press, 1996.

Marx, Karl. *A Critical Analysis of Capitalist Production.* Vol. 1 of *Capital.* Ed. Frederick Engels. Trans. Samuel Moore and Edward Aveling. New York: International Publishers, 1967.

May, Elaine Tyler. "Explosive Issues: Sex, Women and the Bomb." In *Recasting America: Culture and Politics in the Age of the Cold War,* ed. Lary May, 154–70. Chicago: University of Chicago Press, 1989.

———. *Homeward Bound: American Families in the Cold War Era.* New York: HarperCollins. 1988.

Maynard, John Arthur. *Venice West: The Beat Generation in Southern California.* New Brunswick: Rutgers University Press, 1991.

McClure, Michael. *Scratching the Beat Surface.* San Francisco: North Point, 1982.

McLoughlin, William G. "Introduction: How Is America Religious?" In *Religion in America,* ed. William C. McLoughlin and Robert Bellah, ix–xxiv. Boston: Beacon Press, 1968

McLuhan, Marshall. "The Psychopathology of *Time* and *Life.*" *Neurotica* 5 (Autumn 1949): 5–16.

McNally, Dennis. *Desolate Angel: Jack Kerouac, the Beat Generation, and America.* New York: McGraw Hill, 1979.

Merrill, Thomas F. *Allen Ginsberg.* Boston: Twayne Publishers, 1988.

Miles, Barry. *Allen Ginsberg: A Biography.* New York: Simon and Schuster, 1989.

———. *William Burroughs: El Hombre Invisible.* New York: Hyperion, 1992.

Miller, Alan L. "Ritual Aspects of Narrative: An Analysis of Jack Kerouac's *The Dharma Bums.*" *Journal of Ritual Studies* 9 (Winter 1995): 41–53.

Miller, Perry. "Errand into the Wilderness." In *Errand into the Wilderness,* 1–15. New York: Harper Torchbooks, 1956.

———. *The New England Mind: The Seventeenth Century.* Boston: Beacon Press, 1962.

Mills, C. Wright. "Pagan Sermon to the Christian Clergy." *Nation,* 8 March 1958, 199–202.

———. *White Collar: The American Middle Classes.* New York: Oxford University Press, 1951.

Montrose, Louis. "New Historicisms." In *Redrawing the Boundaries: The Transformation of English and American Literary Studies,* ed. Stephen Greenblatt and Giles Gunn, 392–418. New York: Modern Language Association of America, 1992.

Morgan, Ted. *Literary Outlaw: The Life and Times of William S. Burroughs.* New York: Avon Books, 1988.

Moore, R. Laurence. *Religious Outsiders and the Making of Americans.* New York: Oxford University Press, 1986.

Mottram, Eric. *William Burroughs: The Algebra of Need.* London: Marion Boyars, 1977.

Murphy, Timothy S. *Wising Up the Marks: The Amodern William Burroughs.* Berkeley: University of California Press, 1997.

Nelson, Richard. *A Culture of Confidence: Politics, Performance, and the Idea of America.* Jackson: University of Mississippi Press, 1996.

Nicosia, Gerald. *Memory Babe: A Critical Biography of Jack Kerouac.* Berkley: University of California Press, 1983.

Niebuhr, Reinhold. *The Irony of American History.* New York: Charles Scribner's Sons, 1952.

———. *Moral Man and Immoral Society: A Study in Ethics and Politics.* New York: Charles Scribner's Sons, 1932.

Noble, David W. *The Eternal Adam and the New World Garden.* New York: George Braziller, 1968.

Oldier, Daniel, ed. *The Job: Interviews with William S. Burroughs.* New York: Penguin Books, 1989.

Olson, Charles. "Projective Verse." In *Collected Prose,* ed. Donald Allen and Benjamin Friendlander, 239–49. Berkeley: University of California Press, 1997.

O'Neil, Paul. "The Only Rebellion Around." *Life,* 30 Nov. 1959, 115–16, 119–20, 123–26, 129–30.

Parkinson, Thomas, ed. *A Casebook on the Beat.* New York: Thomas Y. Crowell Company, 1961.

Passaro, Vince. "The Forgotten Killer: The Work of William S. Burroughs, Once Dangerous, Is in Danger Itself." *Harper's,* April 1998, 71–76.

Peale, Norman Vincent. *The Power of Positive Thinking.* 1952. Reprint. Englewood: Prentice-Hall, 1978.

Petros, George. "Groovin' Guru: Beat Laureate Allen Ginsberg Goes Bananas." *Seconds* (1996): 17 pp. Online. Internet. 1 May 1996.

Podhoretz, Norman. "A Howl of Protest in San Francisco." *New Republic,* 16 Sept. 1957.

———. "The Know-Nothing Bohemians." *Partisan Review* 25 (Spring 1958): 305–11, 313–16, 318. Reprinted in *A Casebook on the Beat,* ed. Thomas Parkinson, 201–12. New York: Thomas Y. Crowell, 1961.

Portuges, Paul. "Allen Ginsberg's Paul Cézanne and the Pater Omnipotens Aeterna Deus." In *On the Poetry of Allen Ginsberg,* ed. Lewis Hyde, 141–57. Ann Arbor: University of Michigan Press, 1984.

———. "The Poetics of Vision." In *The Visionary Poetics of Allen Ginsberg.* Santa Barbara: Ross-Erikson, 1979. Reprinted in *On the Poetry of Allen Ginsberg,* ed. Lewis Hyde, 131–40. Ann Arbor: University of Michigan Press, 1984.

Prothero, Stephen. "On the Holy Road: The Beat Movement as a Spiritual Protest." *Harvard Theological Review* 84, no. 2 (1991): 205–22.

Ransom, John Crowe. *The World's Body.* New York: Charles Scribner's Sons, 1938.

Reich, Wilhelm. *The Cancer Biopathy: Volume II of the Discovery of the Orgone.* Trans. Andrew White. New York: Farrar, Straus and Giroux, 1973.

———. *Character Analysis.* Trans. Theodore P. Wolfe. London: Verso Press, 1953.

———. *Cosmic Superimposition.* Rangeley: Orgone Institute Press, 1951.

———. *The Function of the Orgasm: Sex-Economic Problems of Biological Energy.* 1942. Trans. Victor R. Carfagno. New York: Simon and Schuster, 1973.

———. *Selected Writings.* New York: Farrar, Straus and Giroux, 1960.

———. *Selected Writings: An Introduction to Orgonomy.* New York: Farrar, Straus and Giroux, 1973.

Rexroth, Kenneth. "Disengagement: The Art of the Beat Generation." *New World Writing.* New York: New American Library, 1957.

Rieff, Philip. *The Triumph of the Therapeutic: Uses of Faith after Freud.* New York: Harper and Row, 1966.

Riesman, David, Nathan Glazer, and Reuel Denny. *The Lonely Crowd: A Study of the Changing American Character.* New Haven: Yale University Press, 1950.

Rimbaud, Arthur. *A Season in Hell.* Trans. Loiuse Varese. Norfolk: New Directions, 1945.

Robinson, Douglas. *American Apocalypses: The Image of the End of the World in American Literature.* Baltimore: John's Hopkins University Press, 1985.

Robinson, Paul A. *The Freudian Left: Wilhelm Reich, Geza Roheim, Herbert Marcuse.* New York: Harper and Row, 1969.

Rose, Anne C. *Transcendentalism as a Social Movement, 1830–1850.* New Haven: Yale University Press, 1981

Rosenthal, M. L. "Poet of the New Violence." *Nation,* 23 Feb. 1957, 162. Reprinted in *On the Poetry of Allen Ginsberg,* ed. Lewis Hyde, 29–31. Ann Arbor: University of Michigan Press, 1984.

Ross, Andrew. *No Respect: Intellectuals and Popular Culture*. New York: Routledge, 1989.

Rossinow, Doug. "The New Left in the Counterculture: Hypotheses and Evidence." *Radical History Review* 67 (1997): 79–120.

Roszak, Theodore. *The Making of a Counter Culture: Reflections of the Technocratic Society and Its Youthful Opposition*. Garden City: Doubleday, 1969.

Rumaker, Michael. "Allen Ginsberg's 'Howl.'" In *On the Poetry of Allen Ginsberg*, ed. Lewis Hyde, 36–40. Ann Arbor: University of Michigan Press, 1984.

Russell, Charles. *Poets, Prophets, and Revolutionaries: The Literary Avant-Garde from Rimbaud through Postmodernism*. New York: Oxford University Press, 1985.

Savran, David. *Taking It Like a Man: White Masculinity, Masochism, and Contemporary American Culture*. Princeton: Princeton University Press, 1998.

Schumacher, Michael. *Dharma Lion: A Critical Biography of Allen Ginsberg*. New York: St. Martin's Press, 1992.

Sisk, John P. "Beatniks and Tradition." *Commonweal*, 17 April 1959, 74–77. Reprinted in *A Casebook on the Beat*, ed. Thomas Parkinson, 194–99. New York: Thomas Y. Crowell, 1961.

Skerl, Jennie. *William S. Burroughs*. Boston: Twayne Publishers, 1985.

Slotkin, Richard. *Gunfighter Nation: The Myth of the Frontier in Twentieth-Century America*. New York: HarperCollins, 1992.

Snyder, Gary. *Earth House Hold: Technical Notes and Queries to Fellow Dharma Revolutionaries*. New York: New Directions, 1969.

Sorrell, Richard S. "The Catholicism of Jack Kerouac." *Studies in Religion* 11 (Spring 1982): 190–200.

———. "Sentinelle Affair (1924–1929)—Religion and Militant Survivance in Woonsocket, Rhode Island." *Rhode Island History* 36 (Aug. 1977): 67–79.

Spengler, Oswald. *Form and Actuality*. Volume 1 of *The Decline of The West*. Trans. Charles Atkison. New York: Alfred A. Knopf, 1926.

———. *Perspectives of World-History*. Volume 2 of *The Decline of The West*. Trans. Charles Atkison. New York: Alfred A. Knopf, 1928.

Stackelberg, Roderick. *Idealism Debased: From Volkisch Ideology to National Socialism*. Kent: Kent State University Press, 1981.

Stern, Fritz. *The Politics of Cultural Despair: A Study in the Rise of Germanic Ideology*. Berkeley: University of California Press, 1961.

Stimpson, Catherine R. "The Beat Generation and the Trials of Homosexual Liberation." *Salmagundi* 58–59 (Fall 1982–Winter 1983): 373–92.

Stromberg, Roland N. *After Everything: Western Intellectual History since 1945*. New York: St. Martin's Press, 1975.

Stull, William L. "The Quest and the Question: Cosmology and Myth in the Work of William S. Burroughs, 1953–1960." In *The Beats: Essays in Criticism*, ed. Lee Bartlett, 14–29. Jefferson: McFarland, 1981.

Susman, Warren. "Did Success Spoil the United States?" In *Recasting America: Cul-*

ture and Politics in the Age of the Cold War, ed. Lary May, 18–37. Chicago: University of Chicago Press, 1989.

Taussig, Michael. "Transgression." In *Critical Terms for Religious Studies,* ed. Mark C. Taylor, 349–64. Chicago: University of Chicago Press, 1998.

Thoreau, Henry David. *Walden* and *Civil Disobedience.* Reprint. New York: New American Library, 1960.

Tillich, Paul. *Theology of Culture.* New York: Oxford University Press, 1959.

Tirro, Frank. *Jazz: A History.* New York: W. W. Norton, 1977.

Turner, Steve. *Jack Kerouac: Angelheaded Hipster.* New York: Viking Penguin, 1996.

Turner, Victor. "The Anthropology of Performance." In *The Anthropology of Performance.* New York: PAJ Publications, 1987.

———. *Ritual Process: Structure and Anti-structure.* Ithaca: Cornell University Press, 1969.

———. "Social Dramas and Stories about Them." *Critical Inquiry,* 7 (Autumn 1980): 141–68.

Tytell, John. *Naked Angels: The Lives and Literature of the Beat Generation.* New York: McGraw Hill, 1976.

van der Leeuw, G. *Religion in Essence and Manifestation: A Study in Phenomenology.* Vol. 2. Trans. J. E. Turner. New York: Harper and Row, 1963.

van Gennep, Arnold. *The Rites of Passage.* 1908. Reprint. Chicago: University of Chicago Press, 1960.

Wallace, Mike. "Mike Wallace Asks Jack Kerouac What Is the Beat Generation." *New York Post,* 1 Dec. 1958, 3.

Wallis, Roy. *The Road to Total Freedom: A Sociological Analysis of Scientology.* New York: Columbia University Press, 1977.

Watson, Steven. *The Birth of the Beat Generation: Visionaries, Rebels, and Hipsters, 1944–1960.* New York: Pantheon Books, 1995.

Watt, Ian. *Myths of Modern Individualism: Faust, Don Quixote, Don Juan, Robinson Crusoe.* New York: Cambridge University Press, 1996.

Weaver, Jace. "Original Simplicities and Present Complexities: Reinhold Niebuhr, Ethnocentrism, and the Myth of American Exceptionalism." *Journal of the American Academy of Religion* 63 (Spring 1995): 231–47.

Weber, Max. *The Sociology of Religion.* Trans. Ephraim Fischoff. Boston: Beacon Press, 1963.

Weinreich, Regina. *The Spontaneous Poetics of Jack Kerouac: A Study of the Fiction.* Carbondale: Southern Illinois University Press, 1987.

Whitefield, Stephen J. *The Culture of the Cold War.* Baltimore: Johns Hopkins University Press, 1991.

White, Hayden. *The Content of the Form: Narrative Discourse and Historical Representation.* Baltimore: Johns Hopkins University Press, 1987.

Whitman, Walt. "Democratic Vistas." In *Leaves of Grass and Selected Prose,* ed. John A. Kouwenhoven, 460–515. New York: Modern Library, 1950.

———. *Leaves of Grass and Selected Prose,* ed. John A. Kouwenhoven. New York: Modern Library, 1950.

———. "Over the Carnage Rose Prophetic a Voice." In *Leaves of Grass and Selected Prose,* ed. John A. Kouwenhoven, 250–51. New York: Modern Library, 1950.

———. "Preface to *Leaves of Grass,* 1872." In *Leaves of Grass and Selected Prose,* ed. John A. Kouwenhoven, 517–21. New York: Modern Library, 1950.

———. "Preface to *Leaves of Grass,* 1876." In *Leaves of Grass and Selected Prose,* ed. John A. Kouwenhoven, 522–29. New York: Modern Library, 1950.

Whyte, William H. *The Organization Man.* New York: Simon and Schuster, 1956.

Will, George F. "The Ginsberg Commodity." *Washington Post,* 9 April 1997, A21.

Williams, Peter W. *America's Religions: Traditions and Cultures.* New York: McMillan, 1990.

———. "Fulton J. Sheen." In *Twentieth-Century Shapers of American Popular Religion,* ed. Charles Lippy, 387–93. New York: Greenwood Press, 1989.

———. *Popular Religion in America: Symbolic Change and the Modernization Process in Historical Perspective.* Englewood: Prentice Hall, 1980.

Williams, Raymond. *The Sociology of Culture.* Chicago: University of Chicago Press, 1981.

Wolfe, Thomas. *Look Homeward, Angel.* New York: Random House, 1929.

Woods, Roger. *The Conservative Revolution in the Weimar Republic.* New York: St. Martin's Press, 1996.

Workman, Chuck. *The Source.* Calliope, 1999.

Yeats, W. B. *A Vision.* New York: McMillan, 1938.

Index

Acheson, Dean, 49, 179, 185
Adams, Henry, 72, 161
Adams, Joan Vollmer, 86, 134, 181–82, 259n8
Adorno, Theodor, 177, 178–79
Ahlstrom, Sydney, 23
Albanese, Catherine L., 65, 137, 228, 270n17
The American Adam (Lewis), 212
The American Century (Luce), 50
And the Hippos Were Boiled in Their Tanks (Burroughs and Kerouac), 91
apocalypsis, 24–25
apocalypticism, 24–28, 66
Apollinaire, Guillaume, 210
Atkison, Charles Francis, 47, 48, 73, 186
Auden, W. H., 169

Baldwin, James, 176, 182
Barth, Karl, 58, 116
Barthes, Roland, 176–77, 178–79, 189, 192, 200, 254
Basie, Count, 61
Bataille, Georges, 136, 154
Bateson, Gregory, 250
"Beat": as critical term, 20–21, 259; as pejorative label, 18–19; as self-descriptive adjective, 18, 118–21
"Beat Culture and the New America: 1950–65" (exhibit), 254
bebop, 6, 7, 10, 61, 81, 106, 108–19, 144, 156, 157, 214, 255, 259n10, 267n65
Beckett, Samuel, 233
Beiles, Sinclair, 233
Belgrad, Daniel, 145, 262n66, 279nn62, 64
Bell, Daniel, 55
Benjamin, Walter, 44, 256, 294n108
Benzedrine, 98, 100, 201
Bercovitch, Sacvan, 19–20, 23, 28, 263n71

Berle, Milton, 54, 227
Blake, William, 10, 68, 86, 126–27, 158, 169, 210, 267n60
The Bomb That Fell on America (Hagedorn), 26–27
Bourdieu, Pierre, 83–84
Bradford, William, 39
Brando, Marlon, 32, 211
Breslin, Paul, 262n66
Breton, Andre, 233
Brooks, Cleanth, 141
Brubeck, Dave, 108, 273n92
Bruce, Lenny, 36
Brunner, Emil, 58, 116
Buber, Martin, 44
Buddhism, 31, 75, 158, 169, 226, 229, 231–32, 239–48
The Buddhist Bible (Goddard), 242, 245–46, 292n49
Burke, Kenneth, 9
Burnham, James, 286n57
Burroughs, William S.: on Buddhism, 198, 242–43; and the commodity fetish, 193–97; and the cut-up method, 164, 233, 237–38; on dreams, 8, 165–66, 192; and drug addiction, 117, 122–23, 151–52, 161, 192; early friendship with Ginsberg and Kerouac, 4–5, 37–38, 59, 85–87, 89–92, 134–36; evangelical strain, 166–68; and "factualism," 127–28, 153, 159–64, 171, 198–201, 282n126, 288n120; family background, 14, 59–60, 168, 190; on homosexuality, 111–12, 159; on Mexico, 180–82, 220; and "orgone accumulator," 101–2; religious background, 14–15; and Scientology, 233–38; on virus as metaphor, 68–69, 88–89, 139, 159–60, 195–96, 236–37, 281n116, 287n102

311

————, works of: "Apocalypse," 223; *Junky,* 98, 123, 161–62, 191; *Minutes to Go,* 233; *Naked Lunch,* 6, 8, 19, 31, 54, 68, 69, 102, 112, 139, 142, 151–53, 162–64, 167–68, 177, 178, 179, 181, 188, 189, 191–201, 205, 218, 229, 233, 234, 237, 250; *Nova Express,* 234; "The Portuguese Mooch," 104–5; *Queer,* 161–62, 182, 191; *The Soft Machine,* 234, 237–38; *The Ticket That Exploded,* 234; "Twilight's Last Gleamings," 69, 116–17, 192, 197; "Word," 175; *Yage Letters,* 182
Bush, Vannevar, 70

Caen, Herb, 18
Campbell, Joseph, 38, 47
Camus, Albert, 32
The Cancer Biopathy (Reich), 101
Carr, Lucien, 85, 86, 90–92, 129, 135, 182, 201
Carus, Paul, 242
Cassady, Caroline, 220, 241, 245
Cassady, Neal, 29–30, 87–88, 95–96, 98, 114, 124–26, 134, 136, 146, 156, 200, 203–10, 212–13, 225, 239, 240, 241–42, 273n91, 274n111, 276n155, 279n64, 288n133
Cassirer, Ernst, 265n32
Cayce, Edgar, 242
Celine, Louis-Ferdinand, 86
Central Intelligence Agency (CIA), 13, 49
Cézanne, Paul, 169
Chamberlain, Houston Stewart, 43
Chandler, Raymond, 122
Charters, Ann, 239
Chase, Hal, 112, 202
Clark, T. J., 229
Clark, Tom, 51
Clarke, Kenny, 259n10
Commonweal, 17
confessional writing, 136–38, 145–53, 156
containment (policy of), 48–49, 51, 67–69
correspondence (worldview), 63–65, 77, 81–82, 86–87, 97–98, 103–4, 112, 114, 127, 128, 136–38, 149, 156, 158, 163, 170, 217, 234
Corso, Gregory, 15, 224, 225–27, 233, 259n4
Cowley, Malcolm, 241
Critic, J. Roger, 241
Crowley, Aleister, 234

Dakin, Edwin Franden, 49–50
Danforth, Samuel, 28
Davidson, Michael, 157, 213, 268n83, 274n104
Dean, James, 32, 211

The Decline of the West (Spengler): and Alfred Korzybski, 94–95, 102, 138–39, 143, 147, 160–61, 164; as apocalyptic revelation, 24–26; on Destiny, 103–4; and Faustian myth, 45–46, 66–70; on fellaheen, 118–23, 124–25, 155, 184–87, 214–16, 240–41, 245, 248; on history, 39–40, 64–65; and jeremiadic formula, 26, 37–38, 40–42, 63–64; and Karl Marx, 193–96; on "pseudomorphosis," 67–68, 88–89, 95, 139, 180–81, 191, 195; reception in Germany, 43–44; reception in the U.S., 47–50; on "spiritual intercourse," 165–66, 168; and time, 105–7; and Wilhelm Reich, 101–2, 108–9, 146–47, 164; the writing and publication of, 42–48
de Kooning, William, 176
Delattre, Roland, 123
Deleuze, Gilles, 264n78
DeLillo, Don, 3
Democratic Vistas (Whitman), 115
Dewey, John, 55, 170
Dianetics (Hubbard), 234
Donovan, 20
The Doors of Perception (Huxley), 250
Dorsey, Tommy, 259n10
Dos Passos, John, 170
Dostoevsky, Fyodor, 72
Dr. Strangelove (Kubrick), 197
drugs (in general), 7, 98–100, 117, 121–23, 135, 181, 197–99, 228–29, 231, 232, 255, 279n64; *see also* specific drug by name
Duncan, Robert, 224
Durkheim, Emile, 176

Eberhart, Richard, 217
Edwards, Jonathan, 27, 161
Eliot, T. S., 47, 143, 169, 192, 206, 242
Ellington, Duke, 208
Ellison, Ralph, 211
Elvins, Kells, 69
Ellwood, Robert, 23
Eckhart, Meister, 44
Einstein, Albert, 57, 242
Emerson, Ralph Waldo, 3, 10, 12, 17–18, 72, 84, 98–99, 132, 136, 137, 163, 170, 204, 217, 252, 271n54
Esquire, 17
Everson, William, 224

Ferlinghetti, Lawrence, 15, 224
Fichte, Johann Gottlieb, 42

Fields, W. C., 207
The Fifties Spiritual Marketplace (Ellwood), 23
Fisher, James Terrance, 62
Frank, Robert, 223
Freeman, Joseph, 49
Freud, Sigmund, 101
Freyer, Hans, 43
Frobenius, Leo, 264n7
Fromm, Eric, 56
Frye, Northrop, 273, 264n7
Fuller, Margaret, 18
The Function of the Orgasm (Reich), 101

Gaddis, William, 176
Garten, Friedrich, 58
Geertz, Clifford, 7, 10, 291n11
Giles, Paul, 239
Gillespie, Dizzy, 10, 61, 157, 179, 251, 259n10
Ginsberg, Allen: and Buddhism, 158; on critical appraisals, 18, 20; evangelical poetics, 166, 168–70; family background, 60–61; friendship with Burroughs and Kerouac, 4–5, 16, 37–38, 59, 86–92, 134–36, 271n37; and halucinogenics, 249–54; and homosexuality, 61, 111–12, 212–14, 218, 274n111; on Mexico, 182–84; religious background, 14–15; vision of William Blake, 126–27, 158
———, works of: "America," 35–37, 107, 217–18; "Bop Lyrics," 95; "Death to Van Gogh's Ear," 35, 175, 251; "Footnote to Howl," 216; "The Green Automobile," 213; "Howl," 16, 38, 111, 150, 169–70, 188–89, 210, 213–17, 223, 272n86; *Howl and Other Poems*, 6, 19, 31, 177, 179, 210–11, 218, 250; "Laughing Gas," 249; "Love Poem on Theme by Whitman," 210; "Lysergic Acid," 251; "Many Loves," 210; "Metaphysics," 65; "Paterson," 92–93, 172; "Pull My Daisy," 145, 223; "Refrain," 95; "Siesta in Xbalba," 182–84; "Song," 154–55; "Sunflower Sutra," 211; "Supermarket in California," 210–11; "The Terms in Which I Think of Reality," 105, 149; "Two Sonnets," 27; *Yage Letters*, 182
Ginsberg, Louis, 60
Ginsberg, Naomi, 60
Goddard, Dwight, 242, 245–47, 292n49
Goethe, Johann Wolfgang von, 45–46, 66, 264n7
Golding, Alan, 278n30

Goodman, Benny, 259n10
The Gospel of Buddha (Carus), 242
Graham, Billy, 21, 27, 53–54, 55, 58, 242
Guattari, Felix, 264n78
Gysin, Brion, 224, 233, 291n17

Hagedorn, Hermann, 24–25
Hammet, Dashiell, 122
Hawthorne, Nathaniel, 161
Hearst, William Randolph, 53
Hebdige, Dick, 189
Hegel, Georg Wilhelm Friedrich, 39, 44, 66
Heisenberg, Werner, 57, 199
Herberg, Will, 21–22, 55, 58, 266n49
Herder, Johann Gottfried von, 42, 46, 264n11
heroin, 161–62
The Hero with a Thousand Faces (Campbell), 38
Hiss, Alger, 83
Holmes, John Clellon, 15–16, 119, 148, 224, 259n4, 279n56
Hooker, Samuel, 28
Hook, Sydney, 55
House Un-American Activities (HUAC), 51, 83, 191
Howe, Irving, 38, 55
Hubbard, L. Ron, 229, 233, 234–36
Huncke, Herbert, 29, 87–88, 120–22, 125, 134, 179, 207, 256, 275n137, 276n141
Hutchison, Anne, 83
Huxley, Aldous, 250

The Irony of American History (Niebuhr), 57
"It," 109–10, 126, 277n161

James, William, 31, 98, 170
jeremiad, 27–28, 36–37, 39, 40, 51, 52–59, 63, 76–77, 147, 177, 184–85, 214, 238, 252–53
Jesus, 99, 151, 172, 195, 207–9, 214–15, 245, 283n145
Joans, Ted, 259n4
Johnson, Joyce, 259n4
Jones, Hettie, 259n4
Jones, James T., 239, 260n25, 292n38

Kafka, Franz, 86
Kammerer, David, 90–92
Kazin, Alfred, 47
Kennan, George, 48, 67
Kerouac, Jack: and Buddhism, 75, 151, 231–32, 239–48, 292n49, 293nn61,65; and Ca-

tholicism, 14–15, 61–62, 73–74, 151, 231–32, 239, 240, 243–44, 248, 271n47, 288n131; evangelical poetics, 165, 170; family background, 14, 61–63; friendship with Burroughs and Ginsberg, 4–5, 37–38, 59, 85–92, 134–36; and homosexuality, 111, 274n113; on Mexico, 98, 184–87, 246; similarities to C. Wright Mills, 56, 266n53
————, works of: *Desolation Angels*, 292n38; *The Dharma Bums*, 239–40; *Doctor Sax: Faust Part Three*, 106, 146, 184, 241, 244; "Essentials of Spontaneous Prose," 245; *Mexico City Blues*, 239, 245; *On the Road*, 19, 30, 31, 95, 106, 108, 109, 110, 113, 119, 124–26, 139–40, 146, 151, 160, 165, 177, 179, 185, 188, 201–10, 213, 218, 223, 241, 248; "The Origins of the Beat Generation," 120; "Pull My Daisy," 145; *Some of the Dharma*, 243, 245–48; *The Subterraneans*, 9, 272n66; *The Town and the City*, 6, 42, 71, 72–76, 104, 108, 129, 134, 146, 175, 184; *Tristessa*, 184; *Visions of Cody*, 31, 56, 63, 108, 111, 125, 141–42, 144–45, 151, 166, 177, 179, 184, 185–87, 188, 201–10, 218, 240, 279n64
Kierkegaard, Soren, 116, 119
Korzybski, Alfred, 10, 13, 15, 68, 82, 86, 93–94, 102, 138–39, 143, 147, 160–61, 164, 190, 236, 255, 279n67, 283n144

Lears, Jackson, 286n60
Leary, Timothy, 251
Leaves of Grass (Whitman), 109, 289n142
Lerner, Max, 265n36
Lewis, R. W. B., 212
Lewis, Wyndham, 47
Lhamon, W. T., Jr., 145, 206
Life magazine, 18, 19
The Life and Times of Allen Ginsberg (Aronson), 256
Literary Kicks (Web-site), 254
The Lonely Crowd (Riesman et al.), 55–56
Long, Charles H., 6–7, 9
Lowell, Robert, 251
Luce, Henry, 50, 51, 53, 54, 266n40, 286n57
Luther, Martin, 39
Lydenberg, Robin, 237, 238
lysergic acid (LSD-25), 31, 249–53

MacDonald, Dwight, 55
Mailer, Norman, 18, 210, 226, 276n140
Mann, Thomas, 43, 44

Marcus, Greil, 20, 256, 261n49
Marcuse, Herbert, 56, 176
marijuana, 6, 19, 98, 100, 123, 134, 180, 249
Marx, Karl, 37, 193–96
Mather, Increase, 28
Mayan civilization, 85, 86, 88, 180–81, 182–84
May, Elaine Tyler, 268n93
McCarthy, Mary, 176
McClure, Michael, 14, 224
McLoughlin, William, 21
McLuhan, Marshall, 145, 286n57
Melville, Herman, 10, 72, 267n60
Merton, Thomas, 22
Merz, George, 58
mescaline, 249
Metropolis (Lang), 197, 214
Miller, Alan, 240
Miller, Glen, 259n10
Miller, Perry, 28, 161, 263n71
Mills, C. Wright, 55–56, 58, 176, 266n53
Moby-Dick (Melville), 267n60
Moeller-Bruck, Arthur, 43
Monk, Thelonius, 251, 259n10
Montrose, Louis, 284n1
Moral Man and Immoral Society (Niebuhr), 56
morphine, 123, 249
Mottram, Eric, 181
Mumford, Lewis, 27
Murphy, Timothy S., 163, 193

Naked Angels: The Lives and Literature of the Beat Generation (Tytell), 13–14
Naked Lunch (Cronenberg), 256
National Security Agency (NSA), 51
Nature (Emerson), 12, 163
The Nature and Destiny of Man (Niebuhr), 56
neo-orthodoxy, 56–58, 116
Neurotica, 145
New Criticism, 134, 140–43
The New Criticism (Ransom), 140
new physics, 82, 86, 105, 199
new vision, 5, 82, 85–92, 96–98, 118, 126, 129, 130, 133–38, 154, 166, 220, 229
Nicosia, Gerald, 114, 245, 289n139
Niebuhr, Reinhold, 27, 56–57, 58
Nietzsche, Friedrich, 44, 45, 81, 82, 245

Ockenga, Harold, 50
Olson, Charles, 163, 251
The Organization Man (Whyte), 38

Orlovsky, Peter, 210, 225–27, 250

Panwitz, Rudolph, 44
Parker, Charlie, 7, 10, 13, 19, 61, 88, 108, 157, 259n10
Parker, Edie, 128
Parker, Theodore, 18
Parsons, Jack, 234
Partisan Review, 18, 38, 55, 58
Patchen, Kenneth, 145
Peale, Norman Vincent, 21, 99–100, 272n57
peyote, 98, 249
Playboy, 17
Podhoretz, Norman, 18
Pollack, Jackson, 176
The Power of Positive Thinking (Peale), 99
Pound, Ezra, 47, 143, 169, 206, 264n7
Presley, Elvis, 32
Protestant, Catholic, Jew: An Essay in American Religious Sociology (Herberg), 22–23, 55
Prothero, Stephen, 15, 21, 239
Pull My Daisy (Frank), 224–27
Puritanism, 27–28, 36–37, 39, 52, 57, 161, 188, 206, 253

Ransom, John Crowe, 138, 141, 143, 165
Rebel without a Cause, 18
Reich, Wilhelm, 10, 13, 15, 68, 82, 101–5, 108–10, 146, 155, 156, 164, 237, 255, 272n66, 278n54, 280n68
religion: definition of, 5–10; postwar climate, 38–39, 48–59, 230
religious imagination, 7–8, 9–10, 13–15, 17, 31, 81–85, 136–38, 227–28, 230–31
Rexroth, Kenneth, 18, 224
Rieff, Philip, 145
Riesman, David, 55, 58, 96, 266n51
Rimbaud, Arthur, 10, 13, 82, 85, 86, 91–92, 133, 153, 156, 172, 267n60,
Rivers, Larry, 225
Robinson, Douglas, 24
The Rolling Stone Book of The Beats (ed. George-Warren), 254
Roosevelt, Theodore, 59
Rosenberg, Julius and Ethel, 52
Ross, Andrew, 67
Rumaker, Michael, 15

Une Saison en Enfer (Rimbaud), 85, 91
Sampas, Sebastian, 72–73, 74, 125
San Francisco Chronicle, 18

Savran, David, 189, 196
Science and Sanity (Korzybski), 93–94, 138
Scientology, 31, 229, 231, 232, 233–238
Shearing, George, 108
Sheen, Msgr. Fulton J., 21, 54
Shields, Karena, 182
Shotwell, James T., 49
Sinatra, Frank, 54
Sinclair, Upton, 190
Sisk, John P., 17
Skerl, Jennie, 282n125
Slotkin, Richard, 90, 122
Smart, Christopher, 210
Smart, Ninian, 24
Snyder, Gary, 124, 224, 228–29, 239, 292n40
Solomon, Carl, 134, 216
Sorrel, Richard, 62, 239
The Source (Workman), 256
Spengler, Oswald; *see The Decline of the West*
St. John of the Cross, 126
Students for a Democratic Society (SDS), 252
A Study of History (Toynbee), 47
Sunday, Billy, 27
Suso, Heinrich, 44
Swedenborg, Emanuel, 12
Swift, Jonathan, 10

Tate, Allen, 141
Taussig, Michael, 9, 206
"This Is the Beat Generation" (Holmes), 15–16
Thoreau, Henry David, 10, 15–18, 68, 99, 118, 163, 164, 171, 212, 241, 252, 271n54, 289n139
the Three Stooges, 206, 207
Time magazine, 107
Time and Western Man (Lewis), 47
Toynbee, Arnold, 47
Transcendentalism, 17–18, 84, 99, 118, 137, 161, 249, 271n54, 289n139
Trilling, Lionel, 55, 61, 140, 141, 149, 179
Truman, Harry, 3, 26
Turner, Victor, 28–29, 259n7, 287n102
Twain, Mark, 10
Tytell, John, 13–14
Tzara, Tristan, 233

Understanding Poetry (Brooks and Warren), 141

van der Leeuw, Gerardus, 262n60

Van Doren, Mark, 140–41, 142
van Gennep, Arnold, 29
Verlaine, Paul, 91–92
"A Vision" (Yeats), 85–86

Wagner, Richard, 42
Walden (Thoreau), 99, 241, 289n139
Wallace, Mike, 248
Wang, Richard, 259n10
Warren, Robert Penn, 141
The Waste Land (Eliot), 47
Wayne, John, 37, 211
White Collar (Mills), 56
White, Hayden, 31
Whitman, Walt, 17, 61, 68, 111, 115, 143, 157, 184, 200, 210–12, 219, 252, 274n108, 289nn139,142

Whyte, William, 38, 96
Wigglesworth, Michael, 27
Will, George F., 20
Williams, Peter W., 129, 285n48
Williams, William Carlos, 67, 71, 82, 143, 210, 278n40
Wimsatt, W. K., 141
Winthrop, John, 39, 52, 54, 188
Wittgenstein, Ludwig, 43
Wolfe, Thomas, 62, 72, 114, 115, 275n121
World's Parliament of Religions (1893), 242

"yage," 100, 182, 187
Yeats, William Butler, 47, 82, 85–86, 91, 126, 156, 264n7, 270n12,
Young, Lester, 10, 61, 87–88, 108, 156

John Lardas is a Ph.D. candidate in religious studies at the University of California, Santa Barbara. He is a contributing writer for *Speak* magazine and is working on a secret history of *Moby-Dick*.

Typeset in 10.5/13 Minion
with Avant Garde display
Designed by Paula Newcomb
and Elizabeth Kleine
Composed by Jim Proefrock
at the University of Illinois Press
Manufactured by Thomson-Shore, Inc.

University of Illinois Press
1325 South Oak Street
Champaign, IL 61820-6903
www.press.uillinois.edu